ELECTRI_CITY

THE DÜSSELDORF SCHOOL OF ELECTRONIC MUSIC

RUDI_ESCH

Es lebe unsre Welt.
Die Liebe und das Leben.
Long live our world.
Terra nostra – Viva!

La Düsseldorf, VIVA Düsseldorf, 1978

ELECTRI_CITY
THE DÜSSELDORF SCHOOL OF ELECTRONIC MUSIC

RUDI_ESCH

OMNIBUS PRESS

London / New York / Paris / Sydney / Copenhagen / Berlin / Madrid / Tokyo

Dedicated to the dead.

The music companion, Klaus Dinger and my beloved dad, Walter Esch.

As well as to those who turn Graceland every day into a place of Peace, Love and Understanding. Anschi and Cosi, Leon and Lia.

Contents

Contents

Contents

PREFACE

ELECTRI_CITY – the electronic town. That is Düsseldorf.

It's a great global legend, spanning from Detroit to Tokyo, from London to Madrid, that always refers to Düsseldorf as the origin of electronic music. That is where it all started, on the banks of the tiny river Düssel. Here is the birthplace of electronic music. In the same way that the petite Düssel flows into the mighty river Rhine, it only took a very few inspired sources to create such important and enormous new waves of modern music.

The first electronic sounds created by us were analogous to the etymological origin of the name Düssel, with its meaning of 'roaring, rushing or thundering'. The huge roar that followed when we decided to market our musical ideas in a purely electronic form, together with cover designs that were so clean they could almost be described as austere, was tremendous. We released *Autobahn* in 1974 – that is nineteen hundred and seventy four; half a lifetime ago.

The magical river Rhine, with its heavily populated and industrialised banks, both attracts and incites people at the same time. It seems to harness huge creative powers. The river bed constantly broadens until it flows into the North Sea; similarly the new trends that fuel the said legend broaden and become mainstream: industrial, synth-pop, EBM, techno, house, electronica, ambient, drum 'n' bass, trip-hop, jungle, drone and dubstep. All these styles discard conventional song structures without taking away from their danceability. Based on our music, which concentrated on technology and the then-not-so-widely used computer, musicians and technocrats were able to become artists and pop stars.

Even to me – and I was a part of it – it sounds almost beyond belief, like some modern day fairy tale. In our rehearsal room, studio and shared flat, a sound was created that would travel the world.

It was a fantastic time. Everything seemed possible. The first synthesisers were instruments that cried out for a new musical path. One didn't have to have a music education to use them. Musical virtuosity would be replaced by a boffin-like hunger for knowledge. Suddenly everyone was able to make music. On the one hand, this had a big influence on our self-image and our music; on the other, it gave us a reputation as nothing more than 'knob-turners'.

That said, you have to admit that there were some brilliant musicians, even in our own group. Did we know what we were putting into motion at the time? I don't think so. Fact is, there was a small group of people, totally independent of each other but with the same background and coincidentally from the same town, who tried to create something entirely new. We consciously broke with the musical tradition of the Allies and were looking for a European identity. We wanted to oppose the superiority of Anglo-American music with something frightfully German, and people loved us precisely for that reason. That was a strange feeling.

It was the days of krautrock, cosmic music and prog rock; of electronic pioneers in Munich, Berlin and Düsseldorf. It was the time of an extra-parliamentary opposition, the Summer Olympics in Munich, and burning warehouses. It was a period of long hair, psychedelic drugs and the pill. An era of student revolutions and rebellion. Back with Uschi Obermaier, Amon Düül, Benno Ohnesorg and Cluster or Can, the Baader-Meinhof Group, David Bowie, Böll, Fassbinder and Visconti – exciting times, somewhere between Mogadishu, Mao and the Mahavishnu Orchestra… and amongst all of that Ralf, Florian, Karl and I were getting our hair cut shorter and shorter and were growing more and more self-confident. Finally we did the unthinkable: we bought suits and wore ties.

That is how we managed to leave the largest possible impression during our tour of the UK and the US in 75. Naturally the audience was a little disturbed by our stage show, which was so far removed from the prevalent rock clichés of the day. But all in all we were pleasantly surprised by how well us four krauts were received abroad. In the same way the Americans had earlier introduced rock'n'roll, swing and blues, thus infecting a whole youthful generation, we had infected a whole generation of English musicians with our sound: Ultravox, OMD, Joy Division, Human League, Heaven 17, Depeche Mode, Visage, Gary Numan. Even David Bowie claimed to have been inspired by bands like Kraftwerk, Neu! and La Düsseldorf.

This book is a first. It doesn't just tell the story of Kraftwerk as the electronic Messiah. It tells the story of Düsseldorf as the cradle of electronic music. As a former member of the electronic quartet, I am flattered by the shortened formula, of course – the one that always equates electronic music with Kraftwerk. Naturally Kraftwerk were central and important, but there was a time before and after, people for and against, not to mention the whole surrounding fuss! Musicians like Klaus Dinger, Michael Rother, Eberhard Kranemann, Wolfgang Riechmann and Bodo Staiger were in Düsseldorf; bands like Rheingold, Liaisons Dangereuses and Propaganda had their home here – and one can't forget Conny Plank, who discovered a lot of them and produced almost all of them. That is why tracks and traces lead us not only to the Kling Klang Studio, but also to Wolperath, into the Weser Hills and to Wuppertal; to the Ratinger Hof and the big wide world. This book deals with the mindset of a city, an electronic way of life; and the next generation of bands who confidently pointed their sequencers at us, and made music so powerful that they were soon on everyone's lips: DAF, Der Plan and Die Krupps.

Rüdiger Esch comprehensively follows all of these complex and sometimes intricate trails for the first time. He documents the history of electronic music from the early days in 1970 to the end of the analogue phase in 1986. He doesn't just tell the story of individual bands; rather he stages the story of a town as a multi-voiced canon. It is only right that he lets those who made and experienced this history tell it in their own words. We meet some of the obvious and not so obvious protagonists, the visionaries and doers, sophisticates, libertines, loudmouths and rockers. The pioneers, boffins, dandies, fans and holy lunatics – stirred together into a colourful mix, sometimes evident even in one person.

Great myths are invariably a mix of fact and fiction, of genuine portrayal and hyperbole. Esch dissects carefully. Some Düsseldorf bands at the height of their career seemed powerful and superior when viewed from afar; but when examined closely under the magnifying glass they all get cut down to size. He deals with some of the smaller stories that in the presence of the mythological would easily have faded into the ether. It is possible that the people of Düsseldorf are as much in love with grand gestures as they are mawkishly attached to their native town. There are bands who treat their place of origin as a gift; so much so that they feel obliged to carry the reference to their town in their name: La Düsseldorf. Besides all that is grand, it's the village-like feel, and not the provincial, that makes living in my hometown so attractive.

The town and the omnipresence of the Art Academy, combined with the cultural activity of artists with names to be savoured – Beuys and Richter, Lüpertz and Immendorff – offered the backdrop for many bands who became internationally successful. One feels the modernistic objectivity and thoroughness, which are appreciated abroad and usually identified as typically German, come easy in Düsseldorf.

We don't just experience the modernism, futurism, industrialism, style and glamour that defines the Electri_city, but also the social reality underpinning it. We get to know Düsseldorf as both a cosmopolitan city and a village; as a place for art, fashion and the typical Rhenish laissez-faire. You sometimes wonder what others see in this town, especially as someone who lives here. Lots of amazing things are supposed to have happened here. It will be more fascinating now to discover the truth behind the myth; to lift the shroud of compliments in order to determine their truthfulness.

Esch delivered the questions, and the players provide lively and enthusiastic answers. It is only a few who choose to stay silent, in order to glow with more brilliance from afar. Others like Riechmann,

Plank and Dinger are sadly no longer with us, but these conversations bring them back to life. The electronic capital eventually comes into clear focus: global successes and blueprints, not to mention flops and crashes, but also break-ups and discord; the reader discovers it all. During times of musical transition, from kraut to punk for example, constants like Plank or Dinger provide continuity; they are the real protagonists leading us through the 16 years.

Düsseldorf-born Esch was predestined to write this book. Not only is he himself part of the music scene, but because of his age he also has enough distance from the subject to be interested without being a fan. He has captured many international voices for his book so as to balance the conversations from the Dorf with views from the outside. He interviewed the British bands who were initially preoccupied with music from the Dorf and became infected by the 'virus electronicus'. Rudi Esch has drawn upon these exclusive interviews and only used a few external sources. Here the main characters from the Seventies and Eighties talk about their experiences and tell us their personal stories. The collected material has been put together into a well-informed volume dealing with the first and second generation of electronic music. Of course there were influential music pioneers in other towns and cities as well, but this is Electri_city. Today's music scene in Düsseldorf is still unique and very productive. Very many young bands leave their impression on the electronic sound of the place. That is something I'm very proud of.

The book at hand is a fascinating document of the 16 years that not only changed analogue electronic music, but also changed my life. It is the direct speech of those that were there, attesting to a time that won't come back. A time without computers, without internet. A time that tried to be futuristic, but worked with the tools of a silent movie. I am sure that everything told and revealed in between the front and back cover constitutes the truth, the whole truth and nothing but the truth.

Düsseldorf, August 10, 2016   *– Wolfgang Flür –*

PROLOGUE

BERND CAILLOUX_At the end of the Sixties the Old Town in Düsseldorf was something very special; a bit like the Saint Germain District of Paris: full of students, most bohemian, very arty. It was all about modernism, jazz and literature, the transitional stage from existentialism and beatnik influences to pop and early psychedelia. This bubble of a few hundred individuals, all messing around there later produced these 10, maybe 12, real world stars.

EBERHARD KRANEMANN_For me, Düsseldorf in 1967 was a place for the jet-setter; a fashion town. It was too hip for the likes of me and the other students, which is why we organised all of these anti-things, dumping dirt on the jet-setter, the in-crowd attitude and on the ever-so-clean Königsallee. We hated that.

BERND CAILLOUX_The rather liberal atmosphere was certainly responsible for the instant and almost atomic explosion of innovations that happened *on orders from above*, as Sigmar Polke frequently used to say. The group ZERO formed; Wolf Vostell, who was the first to use a TV set in a piece of art; Beuys and all of those German artists that are now the most expensive in the world, like Richter and Polke. Then Kraftwerk and the whole entourage, finally punk; even the first German free jazz combo was formed in Düsseldorf, by Gunter Hampel. Somehow these people found each other here, and behind the first 10 are 10 more in the shadows; eventually there are several hundred. As a young guy you think: "That's where I wanna be. This place seems to be amazing!"

EBERHARD KRANEMANN_My first project was called Piss Off. That was in 1967. I was looking for like-minded people and found them at the Art Academy in Düsseldorf, where we were studying at the time. I was studying painting with Professor Rupprecht Geiger. The

13

other members were in Joseph Beuys' sculpture class. We rehearsed at the Academy, if you want to call it rehearsing. Beuys heard us play. He was one of the professors at the Art Academy and liked what he heard, so he asked us to perform together with him. We did exactly that in 1967 at Creamcheese. Creamcheese was a bar for people in the know, a very hot joint in the Old Town party district, a real drug den – everything went down there.

BERND CAILLOUX_Peculiar to Düsseldorf was that art could be felt as part of the everyday life, not as an isolated event, but always present. That was fantastic, exciting and stimulating; an absolute joy. By contrast the art scene in Hamburg was no more than a sectarian group. They weren't integrated into the town to the same extent. There were enough bastard ad men everywhere of course, but no real symbiosis. Serious art and subculture were at best smiled at by the old patricians of Hamburg, whereas the Düsseldorf bourgeoisie appeared more broad-minded. They came to Galerie Schmela to watch Beuys busying himself with his coyotes. Some even made it into Creamcheese.

EBERHARD KRANEMANN_I came to Düsseldorf as early as 1965 to study at the Art Academy. I had saved the money from playing in the orchestra at the Theatre Düsseldorfer Schauspielhaus under Karl-Heinz Stroux. I spent countless nights in various jazz clubs, with the Holger Clausen Trio amongst others. Sometime around 1966/67 I started to experiment with other instruments, with sounds, noises and repetitions. The sounds were weird, not really heard anywhere else in music. I was fascinated by it. Experimenting with sound. I wasn't the only one in Düsseldorf at the time as far as these experiments were concerned.

BERND CAILLOUX_Beuys was the boldest of them all. He just said, "We can do anything! And we'll take everything as well! We'll take over the whole academy and the rest, bugger it. Who is gonna stop us?" Later he coined the slogan 'every human is an artist'!

WOLFGANG SEIDEL_Beuys had experimented a lot with music during his performances, sometimes with Conrad Schnitzler, another electronic pioneer with roots in Düsseldorf. From the inside of Beuys' masterclass in sculpture it wasn't a big step for him to say, "Even as a non-musician I can make music! Sculpture and performances of sound." The same as Peter Brötzmann, who was assistant to Nam June Paik, before he started playing saxophone without paying attention to traditional rules. In this aspect the Fluxus approach was very productive, because the gigger's constraint of being able to play never came into it.

BERND CAILLOUX_There was this Rhenish laissez-faire, a fundamental liberality possibly going back as far as Heine; also a certain open-mindedness towards the insane that for the first time appeared in the extravagant, more or less chic, fashion on the Kö, Düsseldorf's fashion street. Nobody got angry. There was very little trouble with the petty bourgeoisie whatever crazy outfit one was sporting. Unlike in Berlin, where even years later you got accosted for your long hair or beaten up in the street if you weren't quick enough by self-appointed block wardens. I never experienced this kind of trouble in Düsseldorf.

EBERHARD KRANEMANN_Piss Off was the ultimate anti-music. It was the revolution then, after all, in the famous year of 68 where student revolution was the flavour of the month. 'Street Fighting Man' and the like. The others went onto the streets throwing stones. We manifested our stance against society differently: by making music. At that time a young guy was skulking around in dark corners peeking and listening to what we were doing. He seemed quite interested. His name was Florian Schneider-Esleben, was still going to school and played the flute.

BERND CAILLOUX_Our 'Beuys Boys', Stefan Runge and Christof Kohlhöfer, went on to create Piss Off – I seem to remember they only played three times or so, because they had no skill whatsoever. Stupidly we had booked them for the opening party of our studio in Hamburg. What a disaster! It was loud all right, speakers screaming, and there was some decent shouting as well – unfortunately the audience was also well pissed off.

EBERHARD KRANEMANN_Beuys himself had learned to play the cello and also piano. Even as a student he went to the Bach Society and turned pages for the cellist. He always did exactly what no one expected him to do. He sported a princely attitude, talked of sculptor's pride, and he enjoyed drinking plain tap water from crystal glasses.

WOLFGANG SEIDEL_Back then in the underground it was important it not be called subculture. We preferred anti-culture, which is not the same thing at all.

BERND CAILLOUX_At that time Florian Schneider-Esleben and Ralf Hütter were definitely part of it, but they hadn't come to the fore and weren't particularly freaky. Hütter did have long hair, but was also wearing cheap horn-rimmed glasses. Florian Schneider looked the same as always: the archetypal amicably nice son. Nothing at all like a robot. There were excellent parties with beat bands and everything at his architect-parents' villa when they weren't around.

EBERHARD KRANEMANN_Man! We smoked joints together, or sat nude in Florian's father's swimming pool. Joints, LSD, we did it all and then drank his father's champagne cellar dry – it was brilliant! They were really nice parties!

WOLFGANG SEIDEL_If you analyse what developed musically in the different regions in post-war Germany, you quickly see the influences of the different occupied zones. One could draw a map of early krautrock showing exactly which band grew up in which occupied zone socialised by what radio station. I know of no band from a region where you didn't have either AFN or BFBS. AFN started off by playing swing and then moved on to modern jazz. BFBS, available in the Rhineland, later became the platform for the British Invasion. The French never broadcast rock music, only chanson and Franz-Josef Degenhardt.

EBERHARD KRANEMANN_Paul Schneider-Esleben was a famous architect. He had designed the Mannesmann building on the Rhine promenade, and he had received the contract to extend the Cologne/ Bonn airport. He was one of the leading architects in Germany, his business was good. The Schneider-Eslebens were a real upper-class family.

BERND CAILLOUX_Joseph Beuys and Charles Wilp are basically antipodes that define the spectrum and area of controversy within culture in Düsseldorf, even if they supposedly had been sniffing around each other at some point. Art on one hand, commerce on the other – art was always more important to us underground freaks. Of course there were always these broad tendencies towards cretinism as well. In-crowd behaviour is to this day present everywhere in Düsseldorf.

BODO STAIGER_I sometimes wonder how many things are supposed to have originated from Düsseldorf. Düsseldorf was somewhat provincial in the early Sixties when it came to rock and pop. There was nothing independent, just a cover band scene. My colleagues and I often went to Holland to listen to the originals. On the way back we felt cut down to size and thought, "Boy are we bad."

WOLFGANG SEIDEL_Besides the regional differences between the occupied zones, the year of birth plays an important role when it comes to the protagonists of krautrock. There is a clear defining line between those who consciously experienced the war and the time immediately after it. Ralf Hütter, Florian Schneider, Wolfgang Flür of Kraftwerk, Klaus and Thomas Dinger of Neu!, respectively La Düsseldorf, or Michael Rother were all born after the war to my knowledge. They, unlike me, never experienced what it was like not to know when you were going to get your next meal.

BODO STAIGER_The Beatles and the Stones were the first musical idols for me and many others of my generation, as well as Tamla Motown and everything else that came our way in 66/67: The Who, The Small Faces, The Yardbirds. We were glued to the radio for hours listening to that stuff. Beat was the first really cool time for music. We were lucky to grow up exactly at that time! It was a cultural revolution. In the past your boss would say, 'You there, your hair is growing over your collar! Time for a visit to the barber!' All of a sudden everyone was wearing extremely long hair.

WOLFGANG SEIDEL_Even the WDR studio for electronic music wouldn't have been possible without the influence of the occupying forces. They built the radio station following the blueprint of the BBC, recruiting people without a past like Herbert Eimert, who fostered new music on behalf of the broadcaster against the resistance of the still 'Brownshirted' personnel at the music academies. When men like Stockhausen and Bernd Alois Zimmermann were appointed professors the effect could be felt even in rock music. Stockhausen wanted nothing to do with popular music; never mind that nowadays he is heavily used in pop. Pop gets a very angry dressing-down as neo-primitivism. He had to restrain himself not to call it the new Hitler Youth.

BODO STAIGER_I started to play the guitar in about 1960 when I was 10. Over the years there has always been a very nice club culture here where bands were able to play. I started off at scouts accompanying songs by the campfire. Later little Bodo went to the Liverpool Club with his fake student ID. Every week a different English band was playing there. I watched with big eyes and copied everything I could. They were good times. In the morning 'Paint It Black' was playing on the radio and in the evening you could go and see a cover band play it live in a club.

WOLFGANG FLÜR_It became our 4 p.m. Saturday ritual to listen to the UK Top 20 on Radio Luxembourg, 1604 AM, our top favourite radio station.

EBERHARD KRANEMANN_I was born on March 7, 1945, in Wismar, raised in Dortmund and did my A-levels there. I learned to play the traditional double bass at the academy of music. I played classical music by Telemann, Bach, Mozart and Handel, but I also played in a number of jazz ensembles.

HANS LAMPE_I am from Hamburg, maybe that is why The Beatles are one of my earliest influences. I always ran to the record shop to devour any new single by The Beatles. One didn't have any money to buy it at the time; so you just listened to it 10 times in the record store and learned it by heart.

WOLFGANG FLÜR_When I came to Düsseldorf, I was lucky to have had an English teacher who played records by The Beatles in class. She played their first record, 'Love Me Do', on a turntable, and we had to write down what we could understand. We found the whole thing silly, because we only understood 'love me, love me, do it' [sic], but we just loved the music.

HANS LAMPE_Conny Plank was from Palatine [Pfalz], where GIs were stationed for quite a while after the war. That is why you got American radio there, and that way Conny discovered black music. He told me this story once: he used to hitch-hike a lot, and on one occasion a GI gave him a lift in a huge black Mercedes. That is where he heard Ray Charles' 'What'd I Say' for the first time. It must have been playing on the car stereo. He was hooked straight away. It was a really important impulse for him. From that moment on he collected everything he could find from blues to soul.

WOLFGANG FLÜR_A classmate and I had a lil' skiffle band with washboard, harmonica, rumba balls and a guitar. We called ourselves The Bellos. We thought the name was catchy. We knew The Beatles started off as a skiffle band as well.

HANS LAMPE_Nothing could stand up against The Beatles, especially *Sgt. Pepper's*. You listened to The Kinks or the Stones from time to time, but that was nothing compared to The Beatles; they were saints.

BERND CAILLOUX_Music turned in the mid-Sixties from early rock and beat to psychedelic rock, more Pink Floyd than The Beatles. The lack of political interest compared to other places, possibly as a result of relative affluence and Rhenish slackness, furthered the relatively easy departure to psychedelic in Düsseldorf. One didn't have to tow the SDS-orthodox line, that is to say the Socialist German Student Union-line, as much as in Frankfurt, Hamburg or Berlin. In Düsseldorf you had very few dogmatists constantly explaining how world revolution had to function, or what was counter-revolutionary behaviour.

HANS LAMPE_Klaus Dinger listened to The Beatles and The Who, The Doors and Bob Dylan, but first and foremost he loved The Velvet Underground. He loved 'Sister Ray'. In 67, 68, 69, right at the beginning when everyone had to be a revolutionary. I also liked Vanilla Fudge and the first Deep Purple album, as well as Cream,

Zappa and Hendrix – musical taste had changed somewhat. The Fab Four weren't so fab any more.

BERND CAILLOUX_There were three happening beat bands in town: The Beathovens, The Spirits Of Sound and a little later Harakiri Whoom! The last band became famous because of its eccentric singer, Marius Müller-Westernhagen. Incidentally, Bodo Staiger used to play the guitar in that outfit, whilst the crazy Englishman Allan Warren played the drums.

WOLFGANG FLÜR_We got fed up with the beautiful singing of The Beatles at some point. I had done enough of that with The Beathovens, my first band. The music we were making became weirder, more psychedelic, progressive.

Creamcheese

BERND CAILLOUX_Getting practically forced to open Creamcheese was a real stroke of luck for Hans-Joachim Reinert. It was all happening there right from the start, full house every night. The artists had more or less pushed him and his wife Bim into opening a boozer. He had never been a landlord before. He was an agent for a photo company, Agfa or Kodak or something like that, and had been dabbling in the art scene. Maybe that is why the artists told him, "Listen, you are going to open a place for us." They found a location in a small alley near the Kommödchen, Kay and Lore Lorentz's famous cabaret, and the Galerie Schmela, who represented Beuys. The artistry stayed true to their word and played the place every day, even printed programmes. It became a permanent-action gallery: concept art, performance art, op-art, pop art, all of this had just started in Germany.

EBERHARD KRANEMANN_Yes, true. Those were the buzzwords of the day: action, agitation, agit-pop, décollage and happening. Anti-art, total art, Fluxus, Refluxus and everything else was happening at Creamcheese.

WOLFGANG FLÜR_ Creamcheese was right across from the Ratinger Hof, just around the corner. Today it is a gallery. When you came in you had to climb down some stairs into a big basement. We went there to dance and to have a look at the girls.

BERND CAILLOUX_ Creamcheese, this long tube-like room, opened in 1967 on Neubrückstraße 12 opposite the regional court. Ferdinand Kriwet, the filmmaker Lutz Mommartz, Guenther Uecker, Sigmar Polke were constantly there, also this mirror artist, Heinz Mack, from group ZERO. He did the bar. The foyer and entrance were designed by Uecker. He had installed 24 or 48 televisions and nailed them shut. There was a room for all the technical stuff in the back, from where music, light and projections could be cast into the main room, which opened right out. That was handy if you wanted the space for all the action and dancing. There was a stage there as well. The walls were painted white, so you could project onto them. Kriwet used them a lot for his mixed media shows with constantly rotating numbers and letters.

EBERHARD KRANEMANN_ It was a long tube with a dance room to the left at the back. They had built a stage for us in the back room. It was packed, an elitist circle. I think everyone important in Germany and Europe was there. For all intents and purposes, Creamcheese should have only held 100 people, but 300 or 400 had come. They were packed in like sardines, and everyone was smoking. It was hot and smelly! The TV installations were all flickering. The performance went like this: we put the speakers onstage, turned them to max and started without arrangement, without rules, without key, without defined rhythm, everyone playing as loudly and for as long as they could.

BERND CAILLOUX_ In December 68 Beuys and his pupil Anatol Herzfeld chained themselves to a table for hours as one of his Creamcheese activities: an apt parody of regulars in a bar.

EBERHARD KRANEMANN_ We played only one piece. It lasted for about three hours, ranting and raving against norms, conformance and convention. Joseph Beuys stood in the corner at the back on a plinth for the whole of the performance. It was so hot in there. He stood three metres in the air, barely moving throughout, still wrapped up warm in his fur coat and hat. From time to time his hands moved in front of his face. It was called 'hand-action'. Beuys was very calm, concentrating intently on these minimal movements. Us by contrast: sound – music – noise – terror. Three hours of the apocalypse. Loud! Noise! Chaos! Pain barrier!

ROEDELIUS_Düsseldorf had many sources of beer in the Old Town, a designer scene, a scene revolving around Kraftwerk, Neu! and the rest. We didn't mix with them much. Our lives and actions had a different context: our point of reference was Beuys.

EBERHARD KRANEMANN_Back in the day there were infamous carnival parties in the vaulted cellar of the Art Academy. Three nights without break. Everything happened there, the possible and the impossible. I played there in 1967 with Piss Off. Three hot nights. Absolute combat. Music, tones, sounds, noise to the bitter end. The audience raved and danced like mad. I told Florian to come along with his flute. He came, sat down on the edge of the stage without attracting attention and tried to play his flute against the deafening riot.

WOLFGANG FLÜR_The Sixties were a good time, because everything was new and extremely experimental. The Ratinger Hof was still an underground joint for hippies. That's were all the artists went. Immendorff started saloon fights there every evening. It was quite an aggressive way before punk. Crystal ashtrays came flying through the air; often ambulances had to be called. Those artists from the academy couldn't hold their liquor and became extremely aggressive. They were cretins, especially Immendorff. He was a rocker, a real rowdy one. His stupidity frightened me. Some just referred to him as Jörg Immerdoof, meaning blockhead, as 'immer doof' means 'always stupid'.

EBERHARD KRANEMANN_Beuys preferred fine clothes. He was the best dressed man at the Academy. His shirts, shoes, the hat – only the best would do. In the beginning he wore flannel suits and shirts and used a tiny rabbit's jaw as a tie pin.

ROEDELIUS_We moved to Düsseldorf towards the end of 1969. Only Conrad had a real connection to Joseph, who was called Beuys by everyone, even his children. One would meet him from time to time, not only in Düsseldorf, but also later in Berlin.

BERND CAILLOUX_The group ZERO was a group of artists like Kurt Link, Heinz Mack, Otto Piene; in the beginning Charles Wilp also and later Guenther Uecker were extremely important for Creamcheese and for the Ratinger Hof in the early days, and indirectly also for Kraftwerk probably, because they used to work with a lot of abstraction, light and movement, formally resorting to the pre-war avant-garde, but with a new and optimistic post-war and space-age spirit.

EBERHARD KRANEMANN_We had a guitarist who wasn't really a guitarist; but he had a guitar. He was a sculptor in the Beuys class. Like everyone else he used to take drugs, totally loved ether. He had brought an ether mask to the gig, put a little bottle with ether, the mask and cotton wool behind his speakers. We started to play like always, full blast, dog eat dog, when he reached down to take his bottle of ether and fill his mask. He must have taken too much, because he keeled over backwards, totally inebriated, bashed his head against the speakers and landed on the floor with his guitar. He lay there like a corpse, but the guitar was still on, turned to 10, maybe 11 – massive feedback. The guitar was screaming. That said, we weren't bothered, meaning we didn't notice, because we were also stoned to the hilt. It just continued. We made noise and Beuys rested peacefully on his plinth as if nothing was the matter.

ROEDELIUS_There was turmoil in Berlin as well, for example, at a Human Being concert at the Academy of Arts. The audience stopped the show with a noisy protest and considerable damage to our audio equipment.

BERND CAILLOUX_The emergence of drugs was par for the course in Düsseldorf, same as everywhere else. Sweti, a 19-year-old ad man genius and star of the local scene, had parked his Opel Admiral in front of Creamcheese, and you could see the clouds of smoke billow out of the car windows.

Origins

KLAUS DINGER_It's always coming down to the individuals and their socialisation. You can't just pin it on a town. In my case it happened like this: I lived in Düsseldorf-Unterrath, quite a poor area. From there I suddenly went to school on the posh Königsallee, a totally different social structure, very close to the Old Town. That was quite a difficult shift.

MICHAEL ROTHER_Klaus Dinger went to a different grammar school, on Königsallee I think. Florian Schneider-Esleben – he was still called that then – went to the same school as me. He was a couple of years above me, but I had already noticed him, because he was somewhat grumpy and had a silly walk.

EBERHARD KRANEMANN_From the age of 14 I had set myself this one goal: to become a professional artist. I didn't want to become a musician, that was just some fun on the side. I wanted to be an artist. It was mainly because we had an unbelievably good art teacher at school. He was really great. The other teachers were wearing black suits, white shirts and tie. Stiff, real assholes. And there was this one oddball with his colourful Hawaiian shirt and beard. I thought it was brilliant that there was one totally different to the others.

WOLFGANG FLÜR_As I said, with us it was this English teacher, she fostered the process. Shortly afterwards I saw a drum kit for the first time. I was able to sit down on it and was in awe immediately. It was a positive shock, the initial spark. I wanted to play the drums. I had always been drumming on everything I could find. I would beat sticks together when we were out walking, or bashed the railing with them. My father was always rattled by this and said, "Stop it now son!" And when I asked him why, he just replied, "Because I said so." He was very strict, but in an unnecessarily dictatorial fashion.

MICHAEL ROTHER_I was born in Hamburg. We went via England to Pakistan. We came to Düsseldorf in 1963. It was just supposed to be a stopover, but my father died two years later so my mother and

I stayed. We had a flat in Achenbach Street and I went to Rethel-Gymnasium, the local grammar school. It wasn't easy for me in the beginning, as my German wasn't too good. I had to have private lessons to catch up. The teachers were a problem as well. They had a strange concept of motivation for my taste.

WOLFGANG FLÜR_Düsseldorf is important for me, because all the components came together here: I failed at the Max-Planck Gymnasium, the school for the high achievers, and had to instead repeat a year at a different school where things were a bit more easy going. Suddenly my marks improved, and I managed to relax as well. Maybe it was because I had finally moved away from my twin brother, who only produced straight As and always came first at everything. We were referred to as Flür I and Flür II when we got back our course work. I was always number two. How horrible for a child.

BODO STAIGER_I met Wolfgang Flür for the first time in 1967. He was playing with The Beathovens, and I was playing in a band with Marius Müller-Westernhagen. We were in a movie called *Harakiri Whoom*, and because the drums were nicely painted with the logo we thought, "OK, cool name, we're going to stick with that." That was where I met Klaus Dinger; he also starred in the movie, a 45-minute TV drama with Marius in the lead role. It was a story about the singer of a rock band who had been called up to join the Bundeswehr, compulsory national service, and had to think of a way to get around it. Klaus even played a drummer in the film. I had completely forgotten he was in it. I had seen him in the Old Town, he went to the Görres grammar school and was already playing the drums. His band at the time was called The No. When I recently saw the film again I realised just how long I had actually known Klaus: from 1967 to his death.

WOLFGANG FLÜR_Harakiri Whoom, Bodo Staiger's and Marius Müller-Westernhagen's band, were our big adversaries. We did a gig with them once at the Max-Planck Gymnasium. Marius admired Steve Marriott and Rod Stewart a lot, and as an actor was able to imitate them convincingly.

KLAUS DINGER_The first band I played in, still an amateur, was a cover band. We played dance music and such, and we were called Swingkombo. We played 'Satisfaction' and the like at school fêtes, Malkasten and Rheinhalle. Then I borrowed some money, bought myself a drum kit and locked myself away in the old baths in Oberkassel for half a year. Next I landed a job with a somewhat professional group, The Smash, with their guitarist Houschäng Nejadepour and a singer everyone just called The Rat.

MICHAEL ROTHER_I played guitar in a school band, Spirits Of Sound; later Wolfgang Flür and Wolfgang Riechmann joined as well. We played cover versions of Beatles and Kinks songs, and I discovered my penchant for melody. We played a few gigs and even earned some money.

WOLFGANG FLÜR_The Sprits Of Sound weren't as successful as The Beathovens, so I was always a bit hard up. With The Beathovens we played a lot, as we fitted into every school fête. We also played at the Liverpool Club and at Club 55. At that time we were rehearsing in a garage in Stockum that belonged to someone the singer knew, a rich banker and patron of the arts. His son was always there, did the set-up for us. We were almost a part of the family, helped ourselves to stuff from the fridge and always got a cold drink. The father parked his Porsche in the street so we could rehearse. That was nice.

MICHAEL ROTHER_Rich people were always involved with music at the time, a kind of early patronage. We were allowed to rehearse at this villa in the north of Düsseldorf. During the wild Sixties everyone who wasn't bourgeois wanted to be progressive. That's what they called it. They gave wild parties, hot and steamy, and one couldn't help but notice the new flair that was entering even into the world of the adults.

WOLFGANG FLÜR_Our biggest achievement was a gig with The Lords at the Rheinhalle. Together we were supporting The Who. The Beathovens could typically play Beatles tunes quite well. The Lords came after us and then The Who. You could clearly see when they kicked over the drums at the end and smashed their guitars, although they only used papier mâché dummies. It was anti-establishment, and we liked this revolt a lot.

MICHAEL ROTHER_Wolfgang joined us in the late Sixties. We had become more experimental and weren't a pure cover band any more. He had a refined style, played in a minimalist fashion with a good beat, and was way better at backing vocals than his predecessor.

HANS LAMPE_Even before coming to Düsseldorf, when I was still in Hamburg, I played a lot of percussion in various outfits. There was always a session one could join in one of the many clubs: Große Freiheit, in small bars, hot spots like Gibi at Pferdemarkt, where various people just met and played. Ritchie Blackmore's girlfriend came from Hamburg and he was in town for Christmas. We were sitting in Gibi when he walked in all of a sudden and asked, "Can I have the guitar?" That is how we came to jam with Ritchie Blackmore.

MICHAEL ROTHER_As a guitarist I have always tried to stay away from the Anglo-American stuff, but Hendrix, Clapton and Jeff Beck are without a shadow of a doubt masters of the guitar. I even went to see Jimi Hendrix live at Robert-Schumann-Saal in Düsseldorf. That was awesome. Not only what he was playing, but also the kind of signals he was pushing through various effects. Especially in studio productions we have always paid close attention to the effects of reverse playback and band echo. It was always a kind of free, intuitive handling of music and the instrument. I took my girlfriend to the gig, which seated about 500 to 600 people.

HEINO RIECHMANN_My brother Wolfgang's very first band – he played with them from 1966 to 69 – was called Why. He left them to join The Spirits Of Sound. He became their singer and Michael Rother played the guitar – lead guitar to be precise, because Uwe Fritsch played rhythm guitar. Wolfgang Flür played the drums and Ralf Ermisch bass. They practised at the house of the Kaminskys at Mörikestraße, a banker family, and in this formation they played gigs at school fêtes, and once at the Teenage Fair in Düsseldorf.

BODO STAIGER_We played our last show as Harakiri at the Teenage Fair in the summer of 69. That was a fair for young people in the town hall on Fischer Street. Everyone great and famous played there, it was massive and, at the same time, our last gig.

GÜNTER KÖRBER _Progressive music really started at the beginning of 1970, when the Sixties slowly became the Seventies. I was working as A&R for Metronome in Hamburg. We were distributing Rolf-Ulrich Kaiser's stuff, the music journalist and promoter, who had founded the Ohr label. Kaiser, who had already helped organise the international Essener Songtage in 1968, was able to draw on his experiences and the artist contacts he made at the Burg Waldeck festival, and released in quick succession a series of outstanding records starting in the latter part of 1969: Embryo, Guru Guru, but first and foremost the new electronic scene in Berlin revolving around the Zodiac Club: Tangerine Dream and Ash Ra Tempel.

BODO STAIGER_I met Karl Bartos in 1970. We started the band Sinus, a jazz-rock affair influenced by Zappa. Karl played the drums.

BERND CAILLOUX_Our company was called The Leisure Society. Tag line: 'Experiments in Art and Technology'. That is exactly what we did with our strobe and other lighting effects. Doing something yourself was positively encouraged by the zeitgeist, because under conventional circumstances or by today's standards the idea to change the world with flashing strobe lights and psychedelic light shows was pure lunacy and totally removed from reality. As such, it is perhaps no coincidence that the primeval soup of electronic pop was simmering precisely in Düsseldorf at that time.

KLAUS DINGER

++ **JAN 70** The Kraftwerk forerunner Organisation releases their first album, *Tone Float*, on RCA Victor in the UK, with producer Konrad Plank ++ **MAR 70** Ralf Hütter and Florian Schneider leave Organisation and start Kraftwerk ++ **APR 70** Paul McCartney announces the split of The Beatles ++ **JUL/AUG 70** Conny Plank records the first Kraftwerk album at Rhenus Studios in Cologne ++ **AUG 70** Klaus Dinger plays the drums on track B2, 'Vom Himmel Hoch' ++ **DEC 70** The newly founded Philips label releases Kraftwerk's debut album in a gatefold cover showing an orange-striped traffic cone ++ Ralf Hütter leaves Kraftwerk for a few months ++ Kraftwerk give a concert on Boxing Day at Creamcheese in Düsseldorf with the line-up of Schneider/Kranemann/Weiss ++

Early Stages

KLAUS DINGER_Only from time to time, every now and then, a few mad men come along who have just what it takes. They appear out of the nowhere. I think all the outside influences aren't as important as the boys themselves and what they made of it. These were magic moments; you can't explain that. It's made of madness. That's why we have music. You don't have to explain it. Just listen to it. Listen.

WOLFGANG SEIDEL_The beginnings of Düsseldorf krautrock at the end of the Sixties weren't really felt in Berlin at all. What was keenly observed, and heavily influenced aesthetics, were the fine arts, the psychedelia, Beuys and Creamcheese, Uecker, Polke, that whole scene. Dusseldorf bands were little known back then, including Kraftwerk's precursor Organisation.

ROEDELIUS_We jammed with Organisation once. I thought they were nice guys but I didn't much care for their music; although I did quite fancy Florian Schneider's sister Claudia.

EBERHARD KRANEMANN_The official opening of the Düsseldorf Schauspielhaus in January 1970 was accompanied by angry protests. I was there as a bassist. When we started looking for a flautist I didn't hesitate in inviting Florian along with me to the next recording session. It all worked out pretty well and the new Schauspielhaus was opened to our music.

MICHAEL ROTHER_In my mind, the early stages of our development in Düsseldorf are mainly linked to people and to places. We played at a lot of school fêtes, the dance and youth clubs, such as the one on Lacomblet Street, as well as at carnival parties. It was this Düsseldorf which was for me the most defining.

WOLFGANG SEIDEL_Conrad Schnitzler, who later founded Kluster and was one of the true pioneers of electronic music, was also born in Düsseldorf and had a lower middle class background.

ROEDELIUS_Beuys was our link to Düsseldorf, and with his first student, Conrad Schnitzler, we founded Kluster. We travelled the world of fine arts; mainly museums, art galleries and rarely at festivals or in pubs.

EBERHARD KRANEMANN_Florian Schneider-Esleben and I played together a bit; sometimes at my apartment, other times at his parents' house, and always with different musicians and various line-ups. Basil Hammoudi was there on conga, also Cap on trumpet, as well as a classical guitarist. One day Florian brought along a Hammond organ player with him from Krefeld and we rehearsed together. It went pretty well. His name was Ralf Hütter and he was studying architecture. Together we formed a quartet and even got a couple of gigs. The line-up was Florian Schneider-Esleben: flute; Ralf Hütter: Hammond organ; Eberhard Kranemann: bass; Thomas Lohmann: drums.

ROEDELIUS_Florian was a little peculiar; somewhat introverted and not the best communicator. Ralf was open and friendly and we were on cordial terms.

EBERHARD KRANEMANN_ The work with Florian and Ralf was moving forward. We had a rehearsal room in a courtyard between a brothel and the train station, where we could make as much noise as we wanted without any hassle. Back then there was a lot of experimenting going on with different sounds and various musicians.

BODO STAIGER_ Ralf and Florian were in this case like everybody else: always going along to different jam sessions. That was the time of the youth centres; like the stage at Kolpinghaus hostel on Bilker Street or the youth centre on Lacomblet Street. Back then there were quite a few little joints and bars where bands could perform.

EBERHARD KRANEMANN_ In the beginning not a soul was interested. It was experimental music, way off target. People ran away from it. There were only a few insiders who couldn't get enough of it and it was they who came to every gig.

ROEDELIUS_ What they were doing musically didn't really interest me at all. Because of my friendship with Florian's sister I was often in and out of his parents' place.

EBERHARD KRANEMANN_ At that time Florian was working primarily with his electronically amplified flute that he modified with all kinds of filters to create new and different sounds. He had every kind of flute: piccolo, C-flute, alto and bass flute, the latter of which is particularly rare and difficult to play. Florian hooked up echo machines with different echo rates between the electronic module on the flute and the amplifier, creating waves and waves of overlapping flute sounds with various times and rhythms. I liked the sound he had on the alto flute best. It was cool, calm and full of depth.

WOLFGANG FLÜR_ Florian had spent a few months studying at a music conservatory, a jazz academy in Remscheid-Küppelstein. He was really good at tinkering with experimental stuff.

EBERHARD KRANEMANN_ Florian had electronically modified his flute. It was a type of transitional step for him: an acoustic instrument yet an electronic result. This they eventually developed further and further to the point where they could put aside the instruments altogether and just make purely electronic music.

WOLFGANG SEIDEL_ Kraftwerk as well as early Kluster were more electroacoustic than electronic. That is to say, they really only had a few amplifiers and taped contact mics onto everything that would go 'ratatat' and 'dengdeng'. Their favourite toy was the famous Dynacord Echocord Mini, an ingenious machine with a sliding tape head. You could really make some noise with that. But synthesisers were still nowhere to be seen.

EBERHARD KRANEMANN_ At this early stage Florian was experimenting with an electronic violin that he played on his lap whilst seated. He would play around with these Arabic scales which back then sounded quite unfamiliar. Ralf tried to extract unusual sounds from his Hammond organ, but avoided any velocity and vibrato effects. The blue notes and syncopation of American jazz, soul and rhythm and blues were all thrown out. The result was a neutral sound impression; something you would more likely hear in modern classical music by the likes of György Ligeti, for example.

WOLFGANG SEIDEL_ In the early days of Kluster almost all the instruments were self-made; only some were bought and out of them, it was the Farfisa organ that became the most important one. You could really get that thing to squeal; you could tape down keys or, like Conrad Schnitzler, who was a trained toolmaker, hold down several keys with self-made metal fingers. This created the wildest harmonic constellations – Kluster as it were. Wah-wah pedals came a short time later; they too were good for making loads of noise. Then along came Klaus Freudigmann with his machines that were originally intended for radio engineering and testing; that was electronic music in its truest sense.

EBERHARD KRANEMANN_I played a four-string electric bass guitar and an electric cello that I had built myself, and a Hawaiian guitar. The bass was, to me, both a rhythmic and a harmonic instrument. On the one hand, it outlined the chords and, on the other, it was modified with wah-wah and fuzz pedals. The resulting sounds were strange and otherworldly, best used for solos.

WOLFGANG SEIDEL_Klaus Freudigmann was the key technician, who not only played in Kluster but was responsible for their recordings. He had studied sound engineering and was the first to introduce the sound generator into the group, long before anybody else knew what it was. He also built his own ring modulator and this went on to characterise the sound of Kluster's string instruments: a board with two strings strung across it, not only guitar strings but anything and everything, including piano strings. They were fixed on one side, and ran over a roller mechanism on the other in the same way as a vibrato arm on a guitar, except that there were individual ones for each string and it had an unbelievably wide range. With that you were able to make the most absurd sounds.

EBERHARD KRANEMANN_With my electronic cello I was able to elicit both arco and pizzicato sounds, ranging from soft, harmonic and sweet, to aggressive, distorted, loud, scratchy and screechy. I would retune my Hawaiian guitar so as to play with a piece of iron across the strings, somewhat like a slidebar, which at that time was unconventional and new. Charly Weiss was a free jazz drummer who joined us from Berlin, and his job in Kraftwerk was to take care of the rhythm section, but, in addition, he provided free, percussive sound elements as well.

WOLFGANG SEIDEL_The first two Kluster records, released on the label for christian music, Koch-Schwann, with the portentous recitations over harsh industrial and electronic noise, were Schnitzler, Roedelius and Dieter Moebius together. Shortly afterwards they split and from then on Kluster was only Roedelius and Moebius.

EBERHARD KRANEMANN_Around 1970/71 Ralf bid farewell to Kraftwerk; I guess he felt like he needed to finish his architecture studies first. We continued working as a trio: Florian, Charly and I. It was a tough way to make a crust. Practising every day from 5 p.m. to midnight. No job. No money. Little success to reassure ourselves of the work we were doing.

WOLFGANG SEIDEL_Roedelius and Moebius were soon to become Cluster. They saw the West German art gallery scene as their chance, whilst Conrad, who had initiated all those contacts in the first place, could never get out of Berlin for lengthy periods because of his family commitments. The two of them sort of took the Rolodex and the concept and absconded to the West, to the Weser Uplands – which led to bad blood for many years after. And, as a compromise, they had to at least change one letter in the band's name to do that, and so called the band Cluster instead of Kluster.

EBERHARD KRANEMANN_Kraftwerk had a few gigs towards the end of the year. For example, there was the Kraftwerk performance in Creamcheese on Boxing day 1970, from 4 p.m. to 10 p.m., with Florian Schneider-Esleben, flute; Eberhard Kranemann, bass, cello, Hawaiian guitar; and Charly Weiss on drums.

WOLFGANG SEIDEL Charly Weiss showed up later in Berlin, at Klaus Freudigmann's studio. He was the first one to show me that you actually can tune your drum kit.

WOLFGANG FLÜR_Ralf was a natural. When I met him he had already been playing Hammond organ in a jazz band for ages. He really knew his stuff. I haven't got any idea as to what made him want to go and study architecture in Aachen.

EBERHARD KRANEMANN_Ralf was kind of banned from music; I don't know whether he imposed it on himself or if it came from his father, who was seemingly worried about his education.

KLAUS DINGER_We, by contrast to Florian, had no musical foundation whatsoever. I believe Ralf also had a solid musical education. I, on the other hand, am more or less illiterate when it comes to music. In school I always thought music class was absolute bollocks and I had to first recover from that. It was terrible. Although I was a Mozart fan when I was a kid, I was a self-taught musician with no musical background – typical rock'n'roll. No real musical foundation, only a strong will to succeed. "Come on, let's get this done. Somehow, but on our terms."

EBERHARD KRANEMANN_The most famous Hammond organ player in the world was, and is, Jimmy Smith, an Afro-American. Back then Jimmy Smith gave a concert in the Tonhalle in Düsseldorf. Afterwards the whole band went to the Dum Dum jazz club in

Düsseldorf's historic town centre, where we were really firing things up: Ralf on his Hammond M-100, Florian with the flute, I was playing bass, and the drummer was making sparks fly. Blue notes and syncopated sounds were flying all over the joint.

WOLFGANG SEIDEL_Lots of important krautrockers started out as jazz musicians – and often remained so in their heart of hearts. If you ask Lothar Meid from Amon Düül II what his greatest musical experiences were, he'll tell you: one was when he played with Coltrane's drummer, Elvin Jones; the second was when he had a blues jam with the then-unknown Jimi Hendrix.

EBERHARD KRANEMANN_The vibe in the Dum Dum club was great, the joint was full to the gills – all hell was breaking loose! In jazz clubs it's common for guest musicians who are in town to join in; that is to play with other bands just for kicks. It was expected that Jimmy Smith would do that, too. But he looked at Ralf's organ and said: "Mickey Mouse organ," and he took off again. He only ever played the Hammond B-3 and Ralf's smaller model, the M-100, was too tiny for him. Kenny Burrell, however, his guitarist, stayed around, unpacked his guitar and amp and joined us. It turned into a fantastic session that night.

I Knew Conny for Ages

KLAUS DINGER_At some point Ralf from Kraftwerk called me. That same day I drove to the studio in Cologne. I saw Conny Plank for the first time that day and cut a few drum tracks for the guys from Kraftwerk. 'Vom Himmel Hoch' was the name of the tune, but I didn't learn that until later. I didn't really realise just what was going on then.

BODO STAIGER_I had known Conny for ages. He was originally from Hütchenhausen, near Kaiserslautern. He worked for Saarländischer Rundfunk at the radio station SR1 Europawelle Saar and was a trained sound engineer. From there, he went to Cologne-Rodenkirchen, Godorf to be exact. Today there's an IKEA where Rhenus recording studio once was. He was the chief sound engineer there, a friendly Viking of a guy. Very normal, very polite and obliging.

EBERHARD KRANEMANN_From 1967 Conny worked at Rhenus Studios, which belonged to German schlager musician Margot Eskens' husband. They recorded German schlager, an easy listening kind of pop music, there during the day, and at night Conny Plank used the empty studio to record musicians he was friends with.

BODO STAIGER_The first time I recorded with Conny had to be in 1970. The band was a real hodgepodge, made up of Marius Müller-Westernhagen, Karl Bartos on drums, me on guitar and the bass player from Lilac Angels.

EBERHARD KRANEMANN_I met Conny at a very early stage, back in the 1960s. I was with him at the same studio as a session musician making crappy advertising videos with me on electric bass for Maggi stock cubes or VW. A decent session musician could earn 300 marks per session. That was good money back then. And Konrad – who had yet to become the famous Conny Plank – needed money too, and was doing the same rubbish. Sometimes you'd record with a big orchestra, but you also did advertising jingles – whatever. That's how I met him. I was there to play bass and we just kind of hit it off.

BODO STAIGER_It was a huge studio. At that time studios were still gigantic, and that WDR orchestra studio was as big as a sports hall. Back then the mixing desk and recording equipment were in separate rooms. Additionally you had rooms for recording vocals, drums or percussion. You could easily get lost in there.

EBERHARD KRANEMANN_Conny was looking for inspiration from studio musicians or others. Thanks to his good communication skills, he was able to approach things that were new to him without prejudice and always with an inquiring and questioning mind.

ROEDELIUS_We were introduced to Conny, or rather to the studio he was working at in Godorf, by a music lecturer and producer of new church music in Düsseldorf, Oskar Gottlieb Blarr. From then on, things kept moving forward with Conny as our record producer, as our sound engineer and as a fellow musician at live performances.

MICHAEL ROTHER_When chance suddenly carried me into the Kraftwerk studio, a whole new chapter began. I was doing my alternative civilian service in Neuss at the time in the psychiatric ward of St Alexius hospital and a colleague of mine told me that a band in Düsseldorf was looking for a guitarist and asked if I wanted to go to a jam session with him. That day we went to some demonstration near the elevated road, the Tausendfüßler, and then we went to see Ralf and Florian on Mintrop Street. The place had a generously laid out room with some equipment in it, but it was nothing compared to the famous Kling Klang Studio, which came later. Florian Schneider and Klaus Dinger were sitting on the couch, just listening. First, I grabbed a bass that was standing around and started jamming with Ralf Hütter. It was a life-changing experience; I had rarely come upon anyone who had such similar harmonic and melodic ideas. I immediately got the feeling that I had found a special counterpart in that Hammond organ player. We played and understood each other fantastically on a musical level; he, too, followed distinctly European harmonic and melodic contours. Everyone in the room noticed it could work, including Klaus and Florian, who still sat on the couch. We exchanged phone numbers and everything ran its course.

MICHAEL ROTHER

71

++ **FEB 71** Kraftwerk play live with Eberhard Kranemann in art school Werkkunstschule Krefeld and at the Forum in Leverkusen ++ **MAY 71** The trio Schneider/Dinger/Rother play as Kraftwerk in their first live performance on German TV ++ Radio Bremen TV show *Beat-Club* broadcasts 'Rückstoss Gondoliere' on May 22, 71 ++ Krafterk perform on WDR TV show *Okidoki* ++ **JUN/JUL 71** Concerts in Berlin, Cologne, Düsseldorf, Bremen and Karlsruhe ++ Problems occur during preparations for the second Kraftwerk album ++ Dinger and Rother separate from Schneider and work with Plank on a new project called Neu! ++ **SEP 71** The album *Kraftwerk 2* is recorded in seven days by Hütter/Schneider/Plank at Ralf Arnie's music studio Star in Hamburg ++ Kubrick's film adaptation of Anthony Burgess' *A Clockwork Orange* is released with a soundtrack by Walter Carlos, the first famous performer of electronic music ++ **NOV 71** Release of the album *Kraftwerk 2* ++ **DEC 71** The debut album by Neu! is recorded at Windrose-Dumont Studio Hamburg and mixed at the Star Studio by Conny Plank ++

Social Background

WOLFGANG SEIDEL_Another criterion that is important, yet often overlooked, is the socioeconomic background of the krautrockers themselves. How often is it said: 'Kraftwerk – the soundtrack of the Ruhr valley! The sound of industry!' But it does make quite a difference whether you are the factory's owner or if you rummage in there as a blue-collared grafter in the dirt.

HANS LAMPE_Kraftwerk, and in particular Ralf and Florian, were always very interested in technology and, most importantly, had the required financial resources to deliberately fund their interest.

It is most likely they were the first in Düsseldorf to own a Moog as they could have easily bought one with just their pocket money.

WOLFGANG SEIDEL_The first real and genuine synths began to appear in the underground scene courtesy of the English company EMS. They were themselves part of an avant-garde music scene and had their own musical ambitions regarding prog rock. It was around this time that London became 'Swinging London' and one could go to EMS, have a talk about synthesisers, both with or without keyboards, and share a joint. Pink Floyd used an EMS synthesiser, as they were featured prominently in the music of the avant-garde; so too Tangerine Dream – but naturally it was only the true die-hards who went minus keyboard. Why use keys?

EBERHARD KRANEMANN_It needs to be said: Florian and Ralf both had very rich parents; they came from affluent households and had no financial concerns. Ralf's father was a textile merchant and Florian's a highly regarded architect. They came from millionaire households with money coming out of their ears. I, on the other hand, had no money. Florian had a very generous monthly allowance with which he could buy the best and most expensive instruments in the world. He had electronic equipment at a time when most people didn't even know what 'electronic' meant. Same for Ralf.

KLAUS DINGER_Yeah, of course, first of all it's about the social background. I had a more working-class upbringing with a Polish great-aunt that couldn't even write; so I was always at odds with Florian and Ralf. There were things that they never experienced, as they were both well established from the very beginning and never really had to work. Michael's life was like mine, not necessarily a bed of roses.

WOLFGANG SEIDEL_If one retrospectively wonders why there is so little direct interaction between the academic avant-garde and the pop music of the time, you have to remember that these were two distinctly different scenes that evolved separately from one another, yet relatively simultaneously. The Düsseldorf bands seem to have been more influenced by everything else than the nearby Cologne Studio for Electronic Music and Karlheinz Stockhausen. On the one hand, the prohibitively expensive and very rare electronic equipment functioned as an insurmountable obstacle; and on the other hand, the academics who were in charge of these valuable devices were intent on holding on to them so as to not lose their privileged status. Their struggle for recognition as *real musicians* was forcing them into an excessive academicism. Düsseldorf, in contrast, would rather promote someone like Beuys, with his more anti-academic approach.

KLAUS DINGER_I come from a real suburb of Düsseldorf: Unterrath, and as the name suggests this was pretty much right at the bottom of the totem pole. In the early Sixties it was all just dirt roads and huts. I was a good student in elementary school and as such was accepted into the best secondary school, which happened to be on Königsallee, our equivalent to Champs-Élysées. That was some radical change, but at the age of 10 you don't realise this in full. Right next to the Königsallee is the Old Town, the party district where you definitely end up a few years later. That's where everyone goes, it's a melting pot. At a glance it appears as if it would not be important for the school whether you have money or not; but as you follow the students' routes back you'll end up in very different households.

WOLFGANG SEIDEL_A similar significant case for whom money was no object was Florian Fricke of Popol Vuh in Munich. As a result, he had, shortly after Eberhard Schoener, one of the first big Moog synthesisers in Germany. Munich did indeed have an experimental electronic scene, although it is remembered today for its sequencer-driven disco scene; the Munich Sound led by Giorgio Moroder.

HANS LAMPE_On the back cover of the *Ralf & Florian* album you will see an early Minimoog inside the Kling Klang Studio. Around this time the Moog was not so easily available; although Giorgio Moroder also had one this early.

WOLFGANG SEIDEL_One of the earliest and most innovative German electronic musicians was Wolfgang Dauner – one of the first to use the big EMS Synthi 100. There was a clear dividing line between the ruthless avant-garde plumping for the EMS, as they did not want to play 'Ring Around the Rosie' on their keyboard, and those who preferred melody, such as Kraftwerk or Klaus Doldinger; they chose the Moog, particularly the Minimoog.

BERND CAILLOUX_ As The Leisure Society was situated on York Street in the city's north, I remember that one day Kraftwerk came by with this monster of a synthesiser that they had just imported from England, but which supposedly didn't seem to work. Our electrician Becker had a large working space, his electronic laboratory, and as they didn't know how to operate the thing they had hoped Becker would enlighten them. They took it into his work room and played around with it. There was an English instruction manual only and it was pretty complicated to figure out. The only question was: 'What now can be done with this?' Becker immediately felt for the new piece and offered a crash course on the subject to Ralf and Florian. Not that they would have come up with any music that day, but for a short period of time we were afraid of losing Becker to these Gilbert and George lookalikes. If they had offered him a job as their technical director he might have accepted and we would have been left looking stupid. Thank God that at the time he was still completely on this laser-light trip, so no immediate danger for us. I only remember this scene because it was touching in a way to see these gentlemen with no clue of how to run the system at all. Later on when they were famous and so confidently standing behind their music racks, I wondered who was working in the background as their new 'Becker'.

GÜNTER KÖRBER_ For the Metronome label, which belonged to a Swedish parent company, this new musical direction was a great opportunity to position themselves within the German music scene, later known as krautrock. Other major record companies had already established sub-labels to put out these new innovative sounds. EMI owned Harvest Records and Philips had Vertigo, with whom Kraftwerk signed for their earlier records.

EBERHARD KRANEMANN_ For me, Kraftwerk was not about the money, it was all about the music. But somehow I had to live off something. To finance my studies I started working as a musician at a theatre in Düsseldorf, the Schauspielhaus. I said to Florian:

"Right now I can't play too many gigs, I need to earn some money." So we decided that I would take a short break away from the band, while he continued making music with a new team. He asked Klaus Dinger and Michael Rother if they would carry on with him instead.

HEINO RIECHMANN_Once the Spirits performed at the same venue as Kraftwerk, but in a different room. It was like a huge party. Florian Schneider had with him his audio effects and tape echo, with which he distorted his flute. Shortly after this Rother split with The Spirits Of Sound to join Kraftwerk, and that ultimately signalled the end of the Spirits.

WOLFGANG FLÜR_At the end, just before disbanding the Spirits, we had a show where we accompanied a stage play held at a theatre in the neighbouring city of Neuss. We had just started to write our own songs, our own lyrics, and were performing them as part of this play. That was only days before Michael Rother departed to join Kraftwerk.

KLAUS DINGER_I went with Florian to some club, I think it was in Krefeld, and Michael was playing there with his band. They put on quite standard rock'n'roll tunes, you know, pretty much what most people were playing at the time. Nevertheless, the guy had something special, some kind of his own touch. A special style that he was to expand upon later.

WOLFGANG FLÜR_There is a word for that: Talent. The guy had talent. And unlike the rest of us he already had a kind of cosmopolitan approach. He just had to be a musician.

MICHAEL ROTHER_I had thrown all my musical idols overboard and wanted to create something new, something different. It was during that session with Ralf Hütter that I had this feeling that we had a similar musical mindset. It was effortless; we clicked harmonically and melodically, and that was something I had not experienced before. At first Eberhard Kranemann was also in the picture, contributing some exceptional dissonances, and Klaus Dinger sat in as the drummer; as such a real event. I have never seen a drummer who has attacked his drums with such power, determination and ferocity. That was overwhelming and quite an experience.

EBERHARD KRANEMANN_ It was around this time that I used to play a simple, very cheap bass guitar; all I remember is that it was red... and not a Fender. I'd bought it second hand for a few hundred Deutschmarks, but at the same time Ralf Hütter had already got his real Fender – a Fender Precision Bass. He and Florian later released *Kraftwerk 2* on which Ralf played bass, and he played it very well, I have to admit.

MICHAEL ROTHER_ My first guitar was an Ibanez, a pre-lawsuit Stratocaster copy, and it did sound pretty good. That is why I still have it. The now legendary Les Paul Goldtop is the one I played in the early performances of Kraftwerk at the *Beat-Club* and *Okidoki* TV shows. It originally belonged to a colleague of mine who had been given it by his father and I'd borrowed it from him, before I bought it off him later.

KLAUS DINGER_ Ralf Hütter was for some significant time not present in the Kraftwerk line up; he may have had some mental issues along the lines of: "I can't play any more, I have to get out of here." With his departure Rother took over and prominently provided the melody parts.

EBERHARD KRANEMANN_ No, no, Ralf stopped playing with Kraftwerk because he wanted to focus on completing his architectural studies at Aachen University. While he was away the rest of us continued to play as a trio creating this dirt-like anti-music.

KLAUS DINGER_ Well, I had joined Kraftwerk at a time when we had very varying line-ups; Ralf got lost on the way and Michael joined eventually. All this within a period of half a year. Mainly as a trio with Michael Rother, Florian Schneider and me performing some great live shows together.

Ruckzuck

MICHAEL ROTHER_ To me the music of Kraftwerk, and pieces like 'Ruckzuck', came from completely far away, from somewhere out of nowhere. It was non-established, untraditional and brand new; yet minimalistic and modern. A perfect music with no role model.

KLAUS DINGER_We played a lot of shows under the band name Kraftwerk at that time; as we had to promote the early album. Actually things were working out much better with Michael than they did with Ralf. A solid guitar is money in the bank and with Rother you had a great, great guitarist. That was very different to the Hütter Hammond organ; nothing against Ralf, sorry, but this Hammond thing was one thing most of all: extremely heavy!

GÜNTER KÖRBER_Unfortunately Kraftwerk had already signed with Philips and so there was no need for us to even think about getting them on our roster. From the start the album was a solid success and the opening track, 'Ruckzuck', was not only played in every discotheque, but was picked as the theme tune for the political show *Kennzeichen D* on ZDF TV.

WOLFGANG FLÜR_In the summer of 71 Kraftwerk's 'Ruckzuck', an instrumental track, was being heavily promoted on WDR radio, and naturally this left us a little jealous. Remember, they had poached our guitarist, which led to the eventual demise of The Spirits Of Sound. In the end he was irreplaceable and we didn't want anybody else. We loved the guy.

GÜNTER KÖRBER_From September 71 'Ruckzuck' was played during the opening and closing credits of the political television show *Kennzeichen D*. Florian's hypnotic flute riff proved to be hauntingly modern; now it was combined with pictures of the industrial production of Germany's number plates, the meaning of 'Kennzeichen D'. Later, 'Ruckzuck' was replaced as theme music by the Santana song 'Waiting'. In this tradition the other big German TV channel ARD has been using 'Lucifer' by The Alan Parsons Project since 1990 for their political programme *Monitor*.

HANS LAMPE_Klaus once said it was Florian's greatest strength to be able to produce very noble and sophisticated musical dirt. He meant that in the most positive of ways. Where Michael produced the beautifully harmonious melodies, Florian came up with the distorted flute and cut the air sharply; a lot of which did not particularly impress Michael. He was not amused and according to Klaus this was one of the reasons why this trio did not last long. Rother and Kranemann were, at the bare minimum, just as explosive a mixture; that's why it all went downhill trio-wise.

MICHAEL ROTHER_The music we were creating as Kraftwerk in 70/71 was pretty harsh and rough; particularly in comparison to the electro pop they are known for nowadays. It was more progressive and had a lot more drive and pressure. It was pure expression.

KLAUS DINGER_With this line-up of Schneider Rother Dinger we played five concerts in June alone, including Berlin, Düsseldorf, Bremen and Cologne for the Photokina fair. We also did a show at the Kunsthalle with some Swedish laser artist and his amazing light show – Carl Fredrik Reuterswärd. A bunch of people basically freaked out as they were all jam-packed inside to see our show and the stunning laser show. We had to play twice that night, due to popular demand, and the square in front of the hall was overcrowded. Additionally, The Small Faces – although by then they would have been The Faces – had played at the Philipshalle earlier that evening, so all in all it was a busy night in the city.

MICHAEL ROTHER_We played concerts and basically a whole tour to promote the album. Some evenings were better than others; people were euphoric. All in all, it was quite an incredible experience for all of us. We did have one scary experience too though: we had a show lined up with Cluster in Hamburg, at the Auditorium Maximum, on April 8, 71. Kraftwerk was seen as the main act as we were the more popular band; but we felt that we were all of equal importance and so got together with the guys from Cluster and asked them whether they would prefer to go on first or second. "Oh, you can play first, we'll go on after you," is what they said and so we went on and rocked the house, or in this case the auditorium. The audience wanted us to go on and on, and at some point we had to say, now we have to stop, because there is one more band that now wants to play as well. The people were outraged, they were out of their minds and stormed the stage in protest. They turned off the PA for Cluster and threatened them. For a while we were really anxious that they would get beaten up. It was frightening to see the enthusiasm and excitement for our music turn into pure aggression.

HEINO RIECHMANN_ Through the use of all their electronic sound manipulation techniques Kraftwerk, to me, no longer sounded 'home-made' at all. If you need to take a tape machine onto the stage, that's clearly not home-made. Rother, in contrast, would just turn on his amplifier and create a nice, nice handmade tone. He just went for it, making it all by himself. Not waiting for the next tone to come around randomly from a soulless machine.

MICHAEL ROTHER_ In this one case, when we were concerned about Cluster's well-being, it all probably corresponded to the rough and experimental sounds that had stimulated the audience. Live we came with some very, very harsh sounds. No comparison to what we recorded for the TV show *Beat-Club* later on. On *Beat-Club* we played in front of five technicians, but the particular quality of our performance obviously only became apparent in an actual live situation. It didn't work in the TV studio; not even in our own studio. That's why we cancelled the recording of the second Kraftwerk album after 20 minutes. We knew that the magic of our performances could not be repeated in the vacuum of a sterile studio. We were very dependent on the interaction with the people. It's like they say in the touring business: 'If there's no audience, there is no show'.

KLAUS DINGER_ From the very beginning, we were kind of successful; especially live, landing slots at some festivals. I remember seeing Lou Reed crying once at a gig in Walsrode, Lüneburg Heath. I didn't understand all the reactions we were causing. What the hell was going on?

MICHAEL ROTHER_ It became apparent that young people had an ear for this new kind of music. For example, at our concert on February 15, 1971 in the small hall at Leverkusen Forum, 1000 people showed up. Occasionally the legendary Houschäng Najedepour, the son of a Persian rug dealer and, in my opinion, the best Jimi Hendrix impersonator the city had to offer, would perform with us and all the girls would be all over him. You see, we performed often with different line-ups and it is not easy to remember who performed with whom and when or sometimes why. Around this time a lot was happening; particularly around the art scene. When we performed as part of the laser show, we knew this was a time of transition. It was a period of change; also in terms of aesthetics.

HANS LAMPE_The fact that it didn't work out between Klaus and the other members of Kraftwerk was due solely to personal quarrels and a clash of personalities. Ralf and Florian had their names written in blue neon lighting; Klaus wanted the same, but in red. It was clear from this moment on that he wouldn't remain a member of the band; that was his ultimate fail, Klaus told me. After Klaus asked for the same sign in red, Ralf replied: "Come on, you're only the drummer!?! Why should you get red lettering?" Ralf probably saw this as an inappropriate sign of dominance and with an eye to the future didn't allow this. At this time Klaus already had his regular drum set at their rehearsal room on Mintrop Street, where they played together, hung out and everything; but now this was over because of wounded vanities. In the aftermath of this unhappy event they simply lacked the will to resolve conflicts. Klaus was not amused. On one rainy night he went to the rehearsal room to pick up his things.

MICHAEL ROTHER_It was during this exciting chapter that there was also a lot of push and shove going on between Klaus and Florian. The main problem, of course, was the stubborn-headedness of the two parties involved – neither one was willing to back down. In between, there was me, the peace-loving hippie caught in the crossfire.

KLAUS DINGER_Oh yeah, it was all done in a minute; everything went pretty quick. The first call from Ralf, the first recordings we made as Kraftwerk in November, December 70; Hütter then left in February and between February and July 71 we played a bunch of shows. Then it was over. Done.

HANS LAMPE_In retrospect the *Beat-Club* TV show is quite well known, because it is one of the few recorded and broadcasted shows. That digs deep into the collective consciousness. Deeper than only the live shows. The previous formation with Ralf was successful too, but is not that well documented.

MICHAEL ROTHER_The concerts went off with a sensation because the first Kraftwerk album including 'Ruckzuck' was doing really well. Klaus and Florian decided it was best to reduce the group and so the three of us were touring until summer. Unfortunately as the tour went on things got bad. It all became far too stressful. We had no roadies, and musically it was no fun any more. Finally the two extreme characters, Klaus and Florian, began to quarrel. It was a short, yet intensive period of perhaps four or five months. We had great times; but in the coming autumn Klaus and I decided to continue making music as a duo, as Neu!.

EBERHARD KRANEMANN_This is often misinterpreted by the press; neither of them had much to do with it. Klaus Dinger drummed on only one track of their debut album. And? Nothing more. This is nowadays way too overstated. All they needed was someone to play a basic beat, as they did not have any rhythm machines yet. And there was no form of electronic drums they could play themselves; so they simply asked Klaus Dinger. Big deal. He didn't even get any money for that. When asked what he wanted for payment he said, "Oh, just give me 10 records, that will do," so they went to the studio where Conny Plank already waited with his tape machine and Klaus went *bang, bang, bang*. It was all over in 10 minutes. Finished! Done! It's oh so completely exaggerated, like he was a member of Kraftwerk. He wasn't. At most he was a hired hand that filled in as a temporary drummer.

MICHAEL ROTHER_We simply made music for at least half a year. We played wild and exciting shows that stick in my memory. I wasn't really thinking too much of the future; it was the moment that mattered.

EBERHARD KRANEMANN_It was a quarter of a year at most; and the line-up wasn't working for Florian. He was unhappy. That led to an eventual dispute between him and Klaus Dinger. They must have really yelled at each other, attacking each other verbally. I don't know, I wasn't there, but why invite Klaus to join in the first place? Anyway, he was completely dissatisfied and that was why he threw them out after two or three months. Thankfully, it was around this time that Ralf Hütter returned.

MICHAEL ROTHER_ It was a highly explosive mix, this trio, with its very own ideas; it got quite violent at times. Typical good times, bad times; some was really exciting, some not. In the end we had an endless battle of quite different characters. We failed during the recordings for the second Kraftwerk album in Hamburg. At the Star Studio, even under the direction of Conny Plank, our very own intuitive music couldn't be reproduced, it simply did not develop. The atmosphere suddenly felt cold and sterile, we just didn't feel the excitement that we felt live. In addition, there were again tensions between Klaus and Florian, which got almost apocalyptic. The aggression that was going back and forth between them – and I won't go too much into detail – all this made me very sad at the time. However much I liked the music and however exciting it may have been, the atmosphere between these two very extreme people was something I wouldn't stand any longer. With the failure of the recordings for *Kraftwerk 2* it was clear that we needed to close this file. Klaus and I already had a common vision of how we would go on as a duo. We were somehow closer, as we had a strong feeling of a musical partnership. After we left Florian Schneider, he again teamed up with Ralf Hütter, a fact which is often left out in all the official Kraftwerk biographies.

++ **JAN 72** *Kraftwerk 2* is released by Philips in a gatefold cover bearing a green-striped traffic cone ++ The first track on the second album is titled 'Kling Klang' ++ **MAR 72** *NEU!* released through Brain ++ **MAY 72** The trio Dinger/Rother/Kranemann play a non-public Neu! live gig in the church community St Mary Under The Cross in Düsseldorf-Unterrath, recorded on compact cassette ++ **JUN 72** The trio Dinger/Rother/Kranemann play the Fabrik in Hamburg and at the audimax of the university in Freiburg ++ **JULY 72** Roxy Music record 'Virginia Plain' from July 10 to 12 at the Command Studios, London; Brian Eno plays a solo on his EMS VCS 3 synthesiser in the middle part ++ **AUG/SEP 72** The Summer Olympics take place in Munich ++ **SEP 72** Synthesiser hit 'Popcorn' by Hot Butter is number one in the German charts ++ **OCT 72** Neu! issue a seven-inch single featuring 'Super' and 'Neuschnee' ++ **NOV 72** Early elections for the Bundestag, Germany's lower house of parliament, with the slogan 'Vote for Willy!' ++

NEU!

MICHAEL ROTHER_An automatism had thrown us back to this two-man line-up; somehow subconsciously we were driven into a duo after our Kraftwerk experience. In this confusing and exciting time, Klaus and I developed and then realised our common musical vision: we simply wanted to play and strive forward, align ourselves to the horizon; so we called ourselves Neu!. We didn't look at what was left or right; nothing was going to slow us down. We wanted to push through walls. Spring over barriers. Fly.

KLAUS DINGER_At heart it's one hell of a long way from having the idea, the wish, the dream to make your own music, to actually creating something that no one else has done before and to put that into action.

MICHAEL ROTHER_I can imagine it was the same for the audience as it was for the musicians: this new breeding ground had people moving away from the long-established traditions and ways of thinking; things were changing both politically and artistically. This led people to search for new, innovative sounds; and in this case Neu! were at the right place at the right time.

KLAUS DINGER_We didn't play typical rock standards, with common song structures and so on; but rather our own stuff, something like 'Hallogallo', our very first piece.

MICHAEL ROTHER_Neu! had no frontman, no individual leader; we were both in charge of the music. Klaus and I were a team and together we came up with our vision of sound and structure. It was this vision that proved incredibly important, particularly given that we were trying to assert ourselves against all opposition. Had we only created the music to make a quick buck or find instant success, then we never would have attained these hugely satisfying results.

KLAUS DINGER_Take 'Hallogallo', for example, something like that just can't be replicated. Everything was played by hand; we'd think it out in our heads and then just shit it out. That was our way of doing things; the complete opposite to Kraftwerk.

MICHAEL ROTHER_'Hallogallo' really captures the essence of what Neu! was all about. Klaus and I never spoke openly about music, but it was clear to both of us that we were going to make this long, fast forward-flowing tune in E major. How it was going to sound, though, was actually left to chance, or rather to the magic of the moment. We began to build the song up note by note. And in the end you can only surprise yourself.

KLAUS DINGER_We sounded more natural than Kraftwerk, freer and less structured. For me it was a great escape; songs like 'Sonderangebot' were totally far out, like a musical outburst.

MICHAEL ROTHER_We never really discussed the theory aspects of our music. Klaus provided the driving beat and dynamic structure, and I provided the right timbres, layers and melody. That was my job as a guitarist. I was inspired by the music of Pakistan, which longs for eternity and is based on repetition.

KLAUS DINGER_The direction had to be clear: forward, always only forward. My own German motto was 'immer geradeaus' which basically meant exactly that, 'straight forward'. And this referred not only to my drumming style but to the direction of the band as well, to our vision.

MICHAEL ROTHER_We never sat down and said: "Let's make something totally new." It all came from the magic of the moment, from pure coincidence. To worship the moment as a constant continuity.

KLAUS DINGER_As a duo Michael and I were way more focused; we both had to assume frontman duties. We were no longer just the accompanists; now we were centre stage.

MICHAEL ROTHER_And you can hear this! If you compare the first Neu! album with the second Kraftwerk album, you will understand why the split from Florian was inevitable.

KLAUS DINGER_Florian decided to reunite with Ralf after Michael and I left. We called ourselves Neu! and we were exactly that – brand New!

MICHAEL ROTHER_Musically speaking, Klaus and I together was the perfect match. That said, due to major differences in temperament and character it was hard for us to get along. In fact, I would go as far as saying: we were not even friends.

KLAUS DINGER_But we had something in common, something very unique: a mutual understanding of where we wanted our music to go.

MICHAEL ROTHER_To me it was always the differences rather than the similarities that you had with someone that was more important. I'm sure that's the same for most other artists too; you prefer to define yourself as an individual more than a member of a group.

KLAUS DINGER_As soon as someone was able to get the two of us in a studio at the same time, incredible things could happen. Many others have to spend their whole lives looking for magical moments like this.

MICHAEL ROTHER_The equipment we used was still pretty basic and simple: I played my guitar through a wah-wah pedal and distortion and Klaus played his regular drum kit. But with a different approach we were able to achieve very different results. We made new and innovative music with the same old traditional instruments we always had.

KLAUS DINGER_Hütter, on the other hand, was fascinated with his Farfisa organ, which had an inbuilt rhythm accompaniment. I can still remember how excited he got when he played it; he would exclaim: "Here, listen, the fastest drummer in the world."

MICHAEL ROTHER_The techniques, the templates, through which I had learned to play guitar, were what I now wanted to overcome. I concentrated on finding new forms of expression – no more scales, no more chord progressions. This meant quite a minimalistic approach; everything was notably reduced down to individual tones, individual strings, and so only gradually it became a framework for new forms of expression. The first change of harmony, for example, was always well thought out; I had to weigh things up and consider whether a change was even necessary. We focused further on repetition to create this feeling of endlessness. That was what we wanted, to develop a musical form, a wave, if you like, that always went on and on with no additional energy supply, so beautiful, so powerful that it would run off towards the horizon.

BODO STAIGER_At first I knew Klaus only as the drummer and it wasn't until much later that I discovered just how good a guitarist he actually was as well. Although Michael was the more technically and harmonically proficient of the two, it was Klaus who provided the pulsating rhythmic elements also on guitar with the earlier Neu! recordings.

MICHAEL ROTHER_Initially on 'Hallogallo' Klaus played both, drums and guitar. He contributed the rhythmical elements and some wah-wah effects. It wasn't until much later, though, that he properly learned how to play guitar.

BODO STAIGER_Most people assumed that it was Michael who played those rhythms, but it was actually Klaus. Within the group it was he who was the more daring of the two, experimenting with different ideas; some of which paid off and some of which did not.

Conny

MICHAEL ROTHER_The unofficial member of Neu! was undoubtedly Conny Plank, whom we'd first met during our studio time with Kraftwerk. He was the third man.

KLAUS DINGER_Conny played an incredibly important role as he was really open-minded and could recognise quality when he heard it. He definitely wasn't in it for the money.

BODO STAIGER_Back in those days the title 'producer' meant something slightly different than it does today. Conny was using the spare studio time to work and record younger bands. He had a great feel for new vibes and original artists.

MICHAEL ROTHER_We always split the royalties three ways. We financed the record out of our own pocket, produced it during night sessions in the Windrose Studio in Hamburg, and then offered the finished product to various record labels.

EBERHARD KRANEMANN_I'd also produced with him, and everything was done by handshake. A handshake sealed the contract. When it sold all profits were split equally. He contributed just as much with his genius and the studio so naturally he deserved half. It was the same agreement with Klaus and Michael and probably also Ralf and Florian – three people means a three-way split. There were never any written contracts.

KLAUS DINGER_At least with Neu! I can honestly say we started every work unbiased and without any inhibitions. If we only had four days to get it done, we did it in four days. Easy. Conny was supporting us all the time. I thought that was really great.

MICHAEL ROTHER_The three of us worked extremely well together as a team, so it was easy for one of us to ask: "So, what's not working? How can we fix it? What needs to be done?" Conny was a team player and his secret was that he never tried to be at the centre, he wasn't drawing attention or building up his own image. As Klaus and I had no idea about studio technology, we couldn't have asked for a better teacher than Conny.

CONNY PLANK

ROEDELIUS_ Conny was a true friend and helper. He was the third part in Cluster with a great creative input.

MICHAEL ROTHER_ Conny was a real hippie and a huge bear of a man. He approached his creative work with great energy and passion.

BODO STAIGER_ Conny Plank would get things started; and he would know how to show directions. Most of all he was a perfect sound engineer, who redefined that role for us. He wasn't the old-school tech nerd telling others what to do or how to sound. He had an impeccable ear for talent and knew how to convey the skills of the musicians he was working with. Like they say: all you need is ears.

ROEDELIUS_ Conny was a crafty devil with a big heart. He was really tuned in and had his fingers on the pulse of time and music.

EBERHARD KRANEMANN_ Conny was the quiet one, but certainly not shy. He was calm but confident. He knew exactly who he was and what to do. For some he came across a little grumpy, but to me he was always an incredible, open and friendly guy. Just the perfect sidekick.

MICHAEL ROTHER_ Conny Plank played a very important role in all of our productions; partly it was his mixing skills, partly because of his great personality. He was a great character and a good buffer between Klaus and I. The three of us together worked much better than only Klaus and I did; trios are more flexible than duos, I guess. And his skills at the mixing desk were unquestionable.

BODO STAIGER_ It is only the top producers that are able to create an atmosphere that fosters creativity and enables the artist to reach the top. Conny was one of those.

ROEDELIUS_ He would greatly immerse himself in the music of each group; he wanted to understand every idea so as to lift the quality to the next level.

MICHAEL ROTHER_ Suddenly I had this really shrill feedback coming from the amp and it was creating a sustain-like effect on every note. Conny recorded this and then played the tapes to us backwards; creating an analogue reverse effect. That was genius. He did it very casual, just to see how it sounded, yet it turned out to be an incredibly innovative act.

ROEDELIUS_Pure chance was a big part of our work. The first take was often the best take, the most genuine; so we didn't have to polish it up much. We focused on the work that came after; post-production, cutting, editing. Conny even cut 24-track tapes himself, which was relatively uncommon yet quite special. We would tinker around a bit on the mixing desk afterwards, so perfection during the recording wasn't our priority.

BODO STAIGER_Conny got the best out of everyone, without being a perfectionist. There are producers that work their prescribed office hours, counting every hour until tea break, and then quickly head home at the end of their shift. With Conny it was different. He wasn't satisfied until he had got the best out of the situation and his musicians. Near enough was not good enough for him.

MICHAEL ROTHER_We had little time – but lots of luck. With Conny we were happy to be working with someone who allowed creativity to flourish. He played an important part.

BODO STAIGER_Conny and I used to spend some time together privately. Occasionally, when we had dropped some acid, we would walk to a nearby airfield to clear our minds and to really take off. Sometime Klaus would join us, but he was mostly tipsy from cognac or liquorice schnapps.

GÜNTER KÖRBER_I first met Conny when he was working at Star Studio, owned by the German pop composer Ralf Arnie. It was situated in a semi-detached house in Wrangel Street, in the posh district of Hamburg-Eppendorf. The musicians Conny was working with were welcome to stay overnight and as such there was always a bit of commotion, always something going on. And I don't think Mr Arnie was all too amused.

BODO STAIGER_We were all smoking pot like chimneys back then; it was the time of Humphrey Bogart and the Marlboro Man. If you didn't smoke you were not part of the cool scene. That's it. That's why we smoked, and not just tobacco but weed as well. Now that would be something I would recommend to today's politicians – to have a drag on a spliff – it might ease them up and make them look at the planet in a different light.

EBERHARD KRANEMANN_It was the Age of Aquarius, the high time of the hippie. People were smoking dope, experimenting with sounds and substances. Conny was working his day job recording with an orchestra and at night the studio was his for private use. That's when he would invite stoners and other no-goods, drug freaks, hippies like me, or as the German word of the time was: gammler.

GÜNTER KÖRBER_In 1972 Metronome decided to set up their own label for this new German music, and called it Brain – to accommodate the new style. Before that we were only distributing records for the independent label Ohr, but now we signed a lot of seminal bands that proved to be happening: Neu!, Cluster, Harmonia, Guru Guru, Tangerine Dream and Klaus Schulze, along with Amon Düül, Popol Vuh and Birth Control. Up until 1975 I was responsible for these signings as Brain's A&R manager, before I left to start my own business. Aside from the experimental output we had, there were the debut albums by Accept and The Scorpions, which, funnily enough, were our first releases.

EBERHARD KRANEMANN_A typical day at Conny's? Hmm. It would have included a long, long stroll through the woods with a break for a major spliff at the nearby lakeside so as to clear your mind of the drab monotony of everyday life. You'd spend your day stoned and worked all night at the studio.

GÜNTER KÖRBER_For sure Brain intended to be more commercial than the alternative noise labels such as Ohr, Pilz, Calig and others, who would usually attract musicians like Schnitzler and other progressive underground bands.

BODO STAIGER_When Marius Müller-Westernhagen left Düsseldorf to move to Hamburg in the early Seventies, he resided in the legendary Rondell Villa, home to many famous artists and musicians, including Udo Lindenberg and Conny Plank. It was during this time that Conny founded Kraut, his own music publishing company, from which krautrock got its name.

GÜNTER KÖRBER_Plank worked as a freelancer for a number of different recording studios and was living in a flat share community in an apartment house in Hamburg, home also to Udo Lindenberg and Otto Waalkes. It was whilst in Hamburg that he first recorded Neu! and Kraftwerk, working tirelessly throughout the nights.

HANS LAMPE_The first Neu! album was pretty wicked stuff. Unbelievably awesome music! That said, it wasn't just about what Michael and Klaus delivered, but also how well it was captured, transformed and transported to the listener by Conny.

GÜNTER KÖRBER_As a head of A&R I was often guided by Conny. He would bring us recordings on behalf of the bands he had been working with and we knew that if he had been involved in a production then it was most likely something we would like to put out immediately. Around that time there were only two producers within the successful progressive niche: Dieter Dierks and Conny Plank.

BODO STAIGER_Conny actively promoted progressive music and indie bands that were too off-the-road for the commercial mainstream. He wanted to escape the clutches of German pop and discover something new, something that experimental German musicians could proudly identify themselves with internationally. It was a constant theme for him, this absence of recognition for modern German music, and their lack of musical identity. It irked him a lot that everybody was too tuned into the English or American markets.

EBERHARD KRANEMANN_I could see Conny had other things in mind than to be a hired gun for different labels. He was more interested in working with young, alternative bands and so he began to work with such groups during the night, when the studio was available.

HANS LAMPE_Conny was extremely passionate about his art. He was the untiring sound engineer that always enjoyed tinkering around with tones, experimenting with different effects a lot. Reverse echo, reverb, phaser, every possible effect had to be tried out; but that was the same with everyone infected with the 'electronic virus'. Guided by curiosity, their guitars, basses and acoustic drum kits were temporarily cast aside to be replaced by modern technology.

GÜNTER KÖRBER_Hans Lampe was working as Conny's sound assistant, back when he had a full head of hair. In fact, both were presenting the then-pre-fashionable long hair look for men.

HANS LAMPE_Conny was constantly looking for this experimental touch; he liked to experiment. He liked unorthodox things and was quite alternative; also in his political views. He remained socially and politically critical; left, or left-wing liberal. He stood for progress.

GÜNTER KÖRBER_Hans Lampe is the last surviving member of La Düsseldorf. I knew him as he was connected to the Hamburg scene. He's a trained retail salesman and spent his evenings gigging at the Star-Club, the interim home of The Beatles. He played drums and collaborated with Hamburg celebrity Achim Reichel. It was only thanks to his work with Neu! and Conny that he later came to Düsseldorf.

MICHAEL ROTHER_The first Neu! album was a decent local success. You could hear 'Hallogallo' and 'Negativland' in almost every discotheque in Düsseldorf's city centre. The record sleeve was visible in the windows of the record shops; though we didn't play live a lot.

HANS LAMPE_The heavy phasing, flanging sound you hear throughout 'Negativland' was created using a Japanese banjo, the koto, a traditional Japanese string instrument, together with lots of tape loop. This was a mammoth task; nowadays it can be done with the push of two buttons. Back then you needed two tape players running parallel and you would have to run your finger along the side of one tape so as to gradually slow it down. Only then could you create these cool tone pulsations.

NEU! live

MICHAEL ROTHER_Our first gig was at some festival in Essen. I had prepared various backing audio tapes in the studio with the intention of using it to accompany some of our songs. In a way, I guess, it was an early form of sampling. Anyway, unfortunately it didn't really work out and the crowd wasn't particularly thrilled.

EBERHARD KRANEMANN

KLAUS DINGER_ It's always difficult in the beginning. There are only a few people who are looking for new ways. The majority is lame; it will always take time for them to follow.

EBERHARD KRANEMANN_ Eventually things got started. I'd been experimenting with harsher sounds and played them to Klaus Dinger and Michael Rother. This is what convinced them and got me into the band Neu!.

MICHAEL ROTHER_ We had just recorded the first album and were trying to play some gigs; but that didn't come easy and, on top of that I was feeling quite lonely with my sole guitar.

EBERHARD KRANEMANN_ For the forthcoming live performances of Neu!, Klaus and Michael asked me to join them, so I played bass and Hawaiian guitar. We had to rehearse an awful lot, 'cause they never stuck to the formula of the songs on record. Every time we played a song it came out different; we would just jam, just improvise.

HANS LAMPE_ The songs were not static. When they played, let's say, 'Negativland' or 'Hallogallo', they only had a basic framework to start from; they never tried to recreate the album versions.

MICHAEL ROTHER_ We jammed with a number of guys, although none really fit what we were looking for. For example, Uli Trepte, bassist of Guru Guru, was a really likeable person but his different feel for the beat didn't allow him to join us.

HANS LAMPE_ To satisfy live requirements a duo wasn't the way to go. A trio was way more effective. That was the favourite live line-up for both Kraftwerk and Neu!. Three is a magic number. As such Eberhard Kranemann joined them onstage for a short time, as a live session musician, although it didn't last too long as it quickly showed he wasn't only living in his own world, but he also had his very own ideas about music.

EBERHARD KRANEMANN_ At first we would just sit down and look at each other; Klaus would be rolling a joint and then he and I would share this while Michael would enjoy an apple or a cheese sandwich. For one or two hours we would just sit around and meditate, just hang. Sometime later we'd crank the amps to 11. It was pure and spontaneous, much like free jazz. We'd be improvising, playing what we were feeling. It was the same onstage – no form, no rules, just whatever came into our minds.

MICHAEL ROTHER_ Eberhard Kranemann would use his heavily distorted Hawaiian guitar to try and overpower all my melodic ideas. That was his whole approach. He called it 'de-construction'. Fine. Personally we got along well, but musically this wasn't the perfect match I was looking for. I was already quite motivated and perhaps a little too demanding when it came to the sounds and structures, so unfortunately we had to go our separate way to Eberhard.

EBERHARD KRANEMANN_ We played six or seven concerts together in a bunch of different cities; one in Freiburg, another at the university in Münster – or perhaps it was Osnabrück, I forget, we played a lot of universities – and a particularly famous one in some factory in Hamburg. They were always packed and well received, despite the fact that we completely freely improvised and would play without a break for hours until we were physically done. We weren't too respectful towards our audiences though – for example, if the show was advertised to start at 8 p.m., we wouldn't arrive any earlier than that. In fact, sometimes we would arrive a full hour late, which meant we didn't go onstage until 10 p.m. The crowd would just have to wait, all 500 to a thousand of them. And even when we had arrived and finally set up all drums and guitars, Klaus and I would first relax and smoke a joint together onstage, and everybody would be sitting waiting, wondering what was happening. Michael didn't complain, he seemed to be fine with it and didn't criticise us; although he would sit a little further away eating his apple or a cheese sandwich.

MICHAEL ROTHER_ It wasn't about friendship. It was the artistic potential that led us to each other. No social aspect. Klaus and I, we were never friends. Not in all the years.

WOLFGANG FLÜR_ Klaus Dinger was a very difficult character to get along with. So naturally I was quite surprised when I found out he was now playing with Michael Rother, who has the complete opposite personality. Although they may not have clicked personally, they did have a similar musical vision that proved to be more important and became highly successful.

EBERHARD KRANEMANN_Klaus and I, we were buddies. We were both punks before there was punk. We just got along fine. Michael Rother, however, was the perfect aesthete; a gentle guy, very sensitive, no drugs, no alcohol. In contrast, Klaus and me: whoop – dropped some acid, shared the odd joint before hitting LSD, combined it with more weed, you name it: everything, whatever we could get our hands on. I guess that shone through in our music – amps cranked, distortion full. Pure noise! And, in between, Michael, the thoughtful guy, with his guitar always too soft and delicate. Klaus would smash away like some madman on his huge Ludwig drums with these specially made metal drumsticks. Man, that was crazy fun!

WOLFGANG FLÜR_With Klaus you never knew whether he was going to give you a headbutt or an invitation to dinner. He was unpredictable as hell and heavy on drugs. He had a split personality and was quite an unpleasant character. All in all, I didn't like him. I couldn't hang with him or have him around.

EBERHARD KRANEMANN_Looking at it in hindsight I really have to say: it was a little unfair, the way Klaus and I were acting towards Michael. He went through all this and never made a big fuss out of it; but nowadays when we meet I sense a certain animosity directed towards me. I didn't notice it at the time, but now I can feel that he hasn't forgotten. I guess Klaus had maybe tried to get me in the band to play me off, in a way, against Michael.

GÜNTER KÖRBER_We knew how good Neu! were, that's why I instantly signed them through Brain. We'd first heard of them from Conny, and so when the offer came through, naturally we snapped them up right away.

ROEDELIUS_Neither Kraftwerk nor Neu! would be amongst my list of favourite artists. My music was made more by gut feeling than anything else, and I certainly didn't take much notice of their concept music. I had enough to do with finding an original, authentic form of music without being aware of it. Through subconsciousness.

HANS LAMPE_Krautrock, the term, was not used at the time of Neu!. I think the British music press came up with this; we just called it 'cosmic music'. Bands performing this new style of German progressive rock included Ash Ra Tempel, Popol Vuh and Tangerine Dream with their exquisite, ethereal soundscapes – all this was signed by Brain Records.

GÜNTER KÖRBER_Most of my business with Neu! was done through Conny, although it is worth noting that all three were equal partners. So I had worked with Michael from early on, as he was to become particularly important to me some years later when I formed my own independent label, Sky Records.

MICHAEL ROTHER_I always had a pretty clear idea of how I wanted my music to sound, and under which name and label I would want it to be distributed. Our final show with Neu! was in November 1972 at the Düsseldorf Trade Fair at a political event for the young social democrats of the SPD, a party led by Willy Brandt.

DIRK FLADER_Klaus and I were a bit like cousins, maybe second cousins or something – our mothers were definitely cousins at least. Anyway, I'd first got in contact with Klaus through my older brother, who'd helped them at a couple of concerts, including at the 'Vote for Willy' election campaign at the Trade Fair. There Klaus drummed like a maniac. He'd popped so many pills that my brother had to hold him in place just to stop him from falling off his drum stool.

MICHAEL ROTHER_I really admired Willy Brandt, he was a figure I really looked up to and Neu! once played for him at a local political rally. He stood for the reconciliation of Germany with the Eastern countries, kneeling down in Warsaw, asking for forgiveness in the name of Germany. That was something that really appealed to my thinking. I liked his way and his attitude, as everyone else was just trying to leave German history behind; swept under the carpet. The Nazi times still left their mark on society, although a new start – the 'Stunde Null' – was proclaimed, which basically meant the 'zero hour'. I felt the same way about music – I wanted to start afresh with something new.

IGGY POP_Oh boy...! To put Neu! into words: the drummer was playing in a way that when you listened to it allowed your thoughts to flow; allowed emotions to come from within and occupy the active parts of your mind, I thought. It allowed beauty. To get there the guy had somehow found a way to free himself from the tyranny of stupid blues, rock, of all conventions that I'd ever heard. This is some sort of a pastoral pyschedelicism.

++ **JAN 73** Rother and Dinger record their second LP as Neu! at the Windrose Dumont Studios, Hamburg ++ **FEB 73** Conny Plank and sound engineer Hans Lampe are responsible for mixing *NEU! 2* ++ The small budget of the record company Brain causes problems ++ Neu! are forced to use the songs from the 'Neuschnee' seven-inch single as album fillers ++ **MAR 73** Roxy Music release their second album *For Your Pleasure* ++ It is the last one with synthesiser specialist Brian Eno ++ **MAY 73** Roxy Music play together with Eno at the Rheinhalle ++ **MAY/JUL 73** The album *Ralf & Florian* is recorded at Kraftwerk's studio, Düsseldorf, and in the Cornet and Rhenus studios, Cologne, with Conny Plank ++ **OCT 73** *Ralf & Florian* marks the third studio album by Kraftwerk and the first one with synthesiser sounds, although strictly speaking, it's not released under the Kraftwerk moniker ++ **OCT 73** The 'repatriation of Joseph Beuys' in a canoe on the River Rhine takes place one year after his dismissal ++ **OCT 73** Flür plays with Kraftwerk on the ZDF TV show *Aspekte*, the debut of the world's first electronic drum kit ++

NEU! 2 the Second Album

HANS LAMPE_The only reason 'Neuschnee' existed was because Michael and Klaus were set on releasing a single. Back then singles were really 'in' – everybody had to have one, and so too Neu!. Conny said: "Let's try something different. Giorgio Moroder has opened a new studio in Munich's Arabella-Building. It's in the deep basement, with a killer mixing desk. Why not go to Munich?" Moroder had one of those legendary Neve mixing desks; naturally Conny was pretty intrigued by that and keen to play around with it. So we all headed on down to the Musicland Studios – Conny, Michael, Klaus and I.

GÜNTER KÖRBER_Both Dinger and Rother were obsessed with the idea of releasing a single. Maybe they thought it was cool... or maybe they didn't have enough material for a complete album.

HANS LAMPE_On our journey south to Munich we were full of excitement; on our return journey home full of frustration. It had turned out that the studio was just a muddle of stuffy, unventilated rooms in the basement of some modern skyscraper in Bogenhausen. The whole atmosphere was kind of gloomy and as such it was quite an intense experience for all of us. It was perhaps more difficult, in these foreign surroundings, to come up with something good rather than in our studio that we pretty much knew inside out.

GÜNTER KÖRBER_Musicland was a studio in Munich that had just been founded by Giorgio Moroder. It was there that he recorded with Donna Summer and came up with all his early big hits.

HANS LAMPE_Neu! had signed a record deal with Körber committing to three LPs with the Metronome label. Their debut album was well received, garnering many positive reviews, and tracks such as 'Hallogallo' and 'Negativland' were highly acclaimed. Then came the idea of the 'Neuschnee' single. Unfortunately this was less successful and proved to be expensive to produce. With their high hopes quickly dissipating they had no option but to quickly move on and start work on the second album. Once again with Conny, once again at the Windrose Studio in Hamburg.

MICHAEL ROTHER_It was during these recording sessions that we began to encounter difficulties. As a result I started to play around with the 16-track tape recorder, wanting to see how many layers of guitar I could superimpose over each other; one backwards guitar after another, and so on.

HANS LAMPE_Back then reverse tape effects were becoming popular. Neu!'s first two albums featured extensive use of backwards guitar. Rother would record something, we'd turn the tape around and then he'd play again over the top. This is how we created the forward-flowing guitar sound of 'Hallogallo'. We'd combine forward and backward guitar and the result is a beautiful polyphony which sounds as if you are simply soaring through time.

KLAUS IMMIG_As a drummer I was promptly fascinated and hypnotised by 'Hallogallo'. I heard it and thought: "That is simply incredible. Absolutely brilliant. This is energetic and mesmerising." Klaus' style does not compare to that of Keith Moon or John Bonham though. Moon the Loon was crazy, and played the drums like a solo instrument. Bonham was simply The Beast – heavy and powerful. In contrast Klaus played tight, confident and passionate, at the same time extremely monotonously. His rhythm flowed continuously without pause and I was just fascinated by it; it was great. That was something that always stood out to me about Neu! – their non-stop, drastic repetitive beat that created a specific cosmic and spacious atmosphere.

GÜNTER KÖRBER_Klaus had a great sense of beat. In fact he was a time-keeping machine; he ran like clockwork, only better.

EBERHARD KRANEMANN_You can't beat the Dinger-Beat. It's simple and repetitive; a very minimalistic way of drumming. It's so rudimentary yet genius. This is a great example and the essence of the Düsseldorf School.

KLAUS IMMIG_The rhythm was relentlessly repetitive; linear but evolving. Klaus was a great drummer in a minimalist, limited, autodidactic way. I found it fascinating. This was brand Neu!. So the name was a good fit. It was something completely different to the backbeat style of The Beatles or anything by Creedence Clearwater Revival.

EBERHARD KRANEMANN_When I was playing festivals with Kraftwerk or Neu! we would often appear alongside Cologne-based group Can. Now they were a tight band and their drummer, Jäki Liebezeit, was great, although I still prefer Klaus Dinger. Jäki played too dry and too cold. I needed something with more soul, something more brutal. Jäki Liebezeit is more like what Klaus Dinger was accused of being: too mechanical. It wasn't until much later, though, that I too realised that Klaus wasn't all that mechanical, in fact he was quite human. Jäki is the metronome, Klaus was not.

KLAUS IMMIG_Jäki also liked to play these repetitive patterns, but a little jazzier; more groovy.

MICHAEL ROTHER_With 'Für Immer' we were trying to build on our earlier success, we wanted to create a sequel to 'Hallogallo'. Unfortunately this wasn't to be and we seemed to lose any sense of creative direction.

HANS LAMPE_They were finding it difficult to come up with new material and were faced with the dilemma of not having enough songs for the second half of the album.

MICHAEL ROTHER_We were desperate; it was done out of desperation. With our 16-track tape recorder we could potentially record double the number of tracks; but we didn't have double the number of ideas. We had too little material and only one more night left at the studio.

HANS LAMPE_Seeing that the 'Neuschnee' single was basically ignored by their record company they came up with the idea of filling the second half of the album with variations of it.

MICHAEL ROTHER_So Klaus and I decided to include the two songs from our single on the album, but even then there was not enough for one whole album side.

HANS LAMPE_The other reason for this decision stemmed purely from a lack of money and time. And that's how these variations of the 'Neuschnee' single came to be on the album.

MICHAEL ROTHER_And so it began. Klaus, who was much more impulsive and audacious than I, began to play the 'Neuschnee' single on the turntable whilst at the same time playing along over the top. My initial feeling was that this was something way too radical for release.

HANS LAMPE_It was only a very pragmatic solution. Later it was often cited as the birth of the remix and an early sample technique. Oh boy, what to say? I don't know if I agree with that.

MICHAEL ROTHER_It was during one of our wild night-time sessions that we came up with the idea to play our single at varied speeds, and I had this wobbly old cassette player that I introduced into the game. I'd always been interested in tape effects, having previously experimented with voice recordings taken from the shortwave radio. And that's how we came up with this idea, which today is considered revolutionary. But I was sceptical as to how well this practice would be received by the critics, and unfortunately my doubts proved correct and our press reviews were quite scathing. Nowadays our actions are considered visionary and we are heralded as the true exponents of the avant-garde; but I know of no radio station that would have played us at the time. Despite the negative press the album sold well and I realised one thing: you should never be influenced by either criticism or appraisal.

GÜNTER KÖRBER_From the perspective of the record label, we were, to say the least, a little confused by the second half of the album where previously released tracks were simply played backwards or at different speeds, suggesting they couldn't come up with any new material. To us this came across as quite discourteous and shameless. Come on – you can't get away with something like that.

KLAUS DINGER_With the second half of the album we played around with the speeds of the single, using our hand to slow them down or speed them up. I mean, we were overtime, our money was gone; so we had to do something, and do it quick. Conny just went with it. He never seemed to argue or question it. That was great.

GÜNTER KÖRBER_At the time the fans of ambient and minimal music were impressed – and remained impressed – by the strict style and unconventional output. Even today tracks such as 'Neuschnee' or 'Lieber Honig' remain fan favourites.

MICHAEL ROTHER_Tarantino later included it in *Kill Bill 1*. The story goes: back in the Seventies our music was used in a Chinese kung-fu movie without our consent; it was simply taken and nobody seemed to know about it. The movie is called *The Master Of The Flying Guillotine* and every time the antagonist, this evil assassin, appears in the film he is accompanied by the metallic sounds of 'Super 16', as well as during the slow motion scenes where he used our slower versions of 'Neuschnee'. Tarantino knew the movie because he was an admirer of these Chinese directors and as such he also wanted to use the music.

KLAUS DINGER_Michael and I were an explosive combination. Ralf and Florian also had their problems, but were able to overcome them. At some point they realised: 'We have to work together, going against each other will get us nowhere.' For Michael and me, however, we just couldn't get past that and always remained at loggerheads.

MICHAEL ROTHER_In all honesty, I was fairly unhappy with the second album. Klaus and I always had differing opinions though. Let me put it like this: when it came to music he had no principles. 'Für Immer' is one of our great tracks but to him it lacked the magic of 'Hallogallo'. We couldn't agree on much during our recording sessions. With our 16-track device we had double the channels, and double the recording possibilities but couldn't come up with any ideas. We were caught in a trap.

KLAUS DINGER_We were always at each other's throats, so it was very difficult to create a comfortable and constructive working situation for us.

Ralf & Florian & Wolfgang

EBERHARD KRANEMANN_It was around this time that Ralf and Florian decided to bring some others into the mix – firstly Wolfgang Flür, followed by Klaus Roeder, who was later replaced by Karl Bartos. For many, this line-up proved to be the most productive and important, and that's why they remained together for the next 15 years or so.

BODO STAIGER_Wolfgang was well known for having drummed previously for both The Beathovens and the local supergroup The Spirits Of Sound. It was around that time that Wolfgang had put his drumsticks down so as to concentrate on his new job in a Düsseldorf architects office.

WOLFGANG FLÜR_Unfortunately I'd just sold my drum kit to Klaus Dinger. It was a fantastic Pearl kit with a Rogers snare. The larger drums were all from Pearl and the cymbals from Zildjian and Paiste. The bass drum actually displayed a Ludwig logo, like Ringo's, even when it wasn't a Ludwig at all. Klaus never did find that out though. If only I had kept my drums! Here stood Ralf and

BODO STAIGER

Florian in my office on the Fürstenwall road offering me the chance to be the drummer for Kraftwerk.

BODO STAIGER_Wolfgang was invited to join Kraftwerk, firstly because he was a good drummer, and secondly because he looked the part. He played a simple yet steady beat without being too flamboyant.

WOLFGANG FLÜR_I couldn't do a lot, but what I could do was exactly what they were looking for. At that time, they'd already started down the road of minimalism, and this simple beat that I'd learnt from The Beatles opened the door to Kraftwerk for me. They weren't at all interested in either a trained super jazz drummer, no Klaus Dinger, or anybody else who was only interested in his own fame. I never bothered with paradiddles or other drumming rudiments, but this suited them just fine as anything more would have been too much.

BODO STAIGER_Wolfgang is a lovely chap, what can I say; and he was a good fit for the band.

WOLFGANG FLÜR_When Ralf and Florian first approached me, they did so in quite a complacent, nonchalant manner. They both seemed stiff and upright, but also quite funny. We always had fun, and after a while we even had our own language. They were the good times; we laughed a lot.

BODO STAIGER_My God, were those guys awkward! And I've heard that from others too; mutual friends, as well as some pretty girls who also hung out with them. They were real odd types, pretty boring and stiff in a way. Wolfgang was the exception though. He has always been the ladies man.

WOLFGANG FLÜR_Soon I was to be invited into the Kling Klang Studio, which is where I saw my first ever synthesiser. It was a Minimoog, and while I was not too impressed by its appearance, as it looked like the typical electronic organ, I was blown away by the sounds that it produced. Wow, now that was something. They had it connected to these huge speakers and the powerful sound that emanated from them was just enormous, enough to excite anybody. It was the real deal. A perfect thrill.

EBERHARD KRANEMANN_By the time Wolfgang was invited into the studio the *Ralf & Florian* album was just finished. At this point they were not yet purely electronic but they were certainly moving in that direction, away from acoustic instruments. In fact the first track from their album, 'Electric Roulette', featured only Minimoog.

WOLFGANG FLÜR_At that time Kraftwerk became more and more attracted to modern sounds, but most of their synthesisers had this beautiful, old-fashioned walnut-coloured wood finish in the style of a typical Wurlitzer organ. Florian also had an ARP Odyssey, which had a much more modern appearance with its metallic exterior, the rubber-headed slide and button controllers alongside the keyboard. That was particularly eye-catching.

WOLFGANG SEIDEL_With their attention to technical and musical accuracy Kraftwerk stood apart from other German krautrock bands such as Tangerine Dream, who although they consisted of talented electronic musicians, focused more on melodic improvisations, and tended to neglect any rhythmical aspects.

WOLFGANG FLÜR_Ralf and Florian had this children's drum kit in the studio, and expected me to play on this, but I wasn't having it. I gave it a fair attempt and spent one evening trying to play on it but it was simply impossible and embarrassing, and I told them. Having sold mine to Klaus Dinger I hoped that they would buy a new one.

BODO STAIGER_Electronic is a bold word considering most of us were still using guitars and other conventional instruments.

WOLFGANG FLÜR_Nevertheless, having no proper drum kit to play on, the idea arose to create an electronic one. We had this small beat box that we had extracted from a Wurlitzer or Bontempi organ, and from that we generated the different drum tones. We mounted it on a board so I could play the individual sounds of the bass drum, snare and hi-hat by pressing a number of different buttons with my fingers. At some point I said to Florian: "We should use a decent speaker to amplify this." Florian is also quite the tinkerer, but at first he found this idea quite silly because they'd already done this on their *Ralf & Florian* album and were now looking to move away from using these predetermined rhythmic patterns. Then the idea came to connect each of the individual tones to its own metal plate where the sound was created via contact with a metal drumstick. We came up with that idea pretty quickly.

WOLFGANG SEIDEL_Kraftwerk were actively collecting a variety of electronic equipment: mixing consoles, stereo amplifiers, tape bands, contact microphones, electric percussion and other 'new instruments'. With all of that they produced the tones that sounded as if they had been created in some sound laboratory: the monotonous, pulsating rhythms; the musique concrète noise collages; everything from machine gun sounds to explosions.

WOLFGANG FLÜR_I spent the next four or five days fiddling around with this thing until it was finished, and although it looked positively primitive with all its cables hanging out the back, it actually worked. Not only that, but I could actually control the volume of it using a guitar pedal that I'd installed as part of it. Thankfully I was always quite good with my hands – I guess that was something else that drew me into the band.

WOLFGANG SEIDEL_The early rhythm boxes were not programmable so you could only use pre-set rhythms such as tango or foxtrot. When you pressed both options down, like Conrad Schnitzler had done, you could create an interesting musical chaos. Conversely, Kraftwerk were less daring and used these inbuilt playback rhythms only to decorate their music.

WOLFGANG FLÜR_Having wired everything up we were now at the point where we no longer had to rely on the pre-set rhythms but could play the individual sounds separately. This was revolutionary. Florian added a little twist of delay from an Echolette or Dynacord unit; with that device he could further embellish the sounds of the percussion.

WOLFGANG SEIDEL_Much of what we considered electronic avant-garde was probably just a result of not being fully informed as to how to use a synthesiser.

WOLFGANG FLÜR_Before our appearance on the *Aspekte* TV show we had performed two, no three, warm up shows at different venues around Düsseldorf: firstly in the Boutique, some underground bar in Mönchengladbach; next at Röhre, a jazz club in Krefeld; and finally at the University of Leverkusen. At each of these gigs I remember being truly shocked at how poorly our performance was received – at the Boutique we were actually booed, the atmosphere was so negative. The music was too different for the audience, they didn't know how to take it and with my electronic drum board I must have looked quite strange. People were used to seeing the drummer sweat. They expected the physical drumming of John Bonham, who played like a man possessed, with such speed and power. I, on the other hand, looked too elegant with my electronic board and 'knitting needle' sticks. I didn't sweat at all and couldn't work the audience into that frenzy. Though I had to concentrate a lot, more so than the average drummer, as the dynamics could not be controlled with the actual strikes.

WOLFGANG SEIDEL_The benefit of instrumental electronic music was that you didn't need any English words, which in Germany always sounded a little too much like school English. The sexy charisma was also unnecessary. We were able to do as we pleased; there was nothing to be compared to. It was completely uncharted territory.

Aspekte TV show

WOLFGANG FLÜR_Our long-awaited TV appearance finally took place in October 73, on the cultural TV show *Aspekte*. While I was not yet completely taken by this type of electronic music, I for sure wanted to be on TV. There was also a 300 Deutschmark reward to sweeten the pot. All this was incentive enough to stick with it. Deal.

WOLFGANG SEIDEL_While the proletarian youth of the Fifties was embracing rock'n'roll, the older generation, as well as the upper class, were still at home listening to Bach and Wagner, complaining about the destruction, or Americanisation, of German culture. For the German youth, American culture promised freedom from

Germany's recent past, and distance from the beliefs of their parents.

WOLFGANG FLÜR_For our TV appearance we had to fly to Berlin, which in itself was an exciting experience. At that time propeller planes were still flying to the walled city. It was my first ever flight and we were all excited. As Lufthansa wasn't allowed to fly to Berlin we flew with British Airways instead; the only other two options available would have been Pan Am and Air France. Only the allies were allowed to fly this air corridor. We planned to play three pieces: 'Tanzmusik', 'Morgenspaziergang' and 'Kometenmelodie'. Due to time reasons we were only able to play one song, and so we immediately decided upon 'Tanzmusik'; a clear, serene composition. The album version of this was underlaid with the pre-set shuffle beat from the Wurlitzer organ by Florian. This time live, though, I was going to put my skills on my electronic 'ironing board' to the test. This was to be something completely new. As such, it wasn't for musical reasons alone that the Allies' warning sign came to mind: 'You are leaving the American Sector'.

WOLFGANG SEIDEL_It's a well known Ralf Hütter quote: "After the war, the German people were robbed of their culture, putting an American head on." So why, then, didn't he sign with the GDR label Amiga? Somehow it was first and foremost the East German people who always criticised the Americanisation of the West.

WOLFGANG FLÜR_Our electronic drum kit was only thrown together at the last minute, because I was too embarrassed to play the little kid toy one that they had back at the studio; not good enough to be presented on TV. Seeing as it was so different to anything that had come before, the cameramen at *Aspekte* continually zoomed in on me. When you look at it today, though, you can't help but think: 'What's so special about that?' But back then they'd never seen anything like it before. All the technicians came rushing up to me afterwards, wanting to know how I could play such a thing. They weren't at all interested in either the organ or the synthesiser; no, they only wanted to know what this funny type of tray was. It turned out that this was actually the real highlight of the show, which made me a proud man. Up until then I'd thought it was too over the top and cramped, but this was a turning point for me. From then on, I too was switched on.

WOLFGANG SEIDEL_It wasn't until we heard Señor Coconut's Kraftwerk covers that we realised how close their music was to that of the feel-good tunes of the Fifties Wirtschaftswunder period – had they been played on traditional instruments, that is.

WOLFGANG FLÜR_I was caught in two minds. At this time we were still a trio – my ally Karl did not join until a year later – and I was not yet fully immersed in the music we were playing. Ralf and Florian were keen to know if I was to remain the drummer of Kraftwerk, but I was noncommittal, putting off my answer over and over again and eventually I stopped attending rehearsals. I was a pop musician at heart and had not yet adjusted to the experimental scene; it was all too intellectual for me.

++ **MAY 74** First production in Plank's own studio in Wolperath ++ **MAY 74** Rise and fall of Dingerland Musik company ++ Lilac Angels' album *I'm Not Afraid To Say Yes* is the only release before insolvency ++ Planned releases for Fritz Müller Rock (Eberhard Kranemann) and Achim Duchow fail ++ **SEP 74** Label presentation with free concert featuring Lilac Angels, Fritz Müller Rock and Neu! at Open Air Theatre Blue Lake in Ratingen, near Düsseldorf ++ **OCT 74** Nico, John Cale and Brian Eno play Nationalgalerie, Berlin ++ **NOV 74** Release of Kraftwerk's *Autobahn* album ++ **DEC 74** *NEU! 75* album recorded in Conny's studio ++

Conny's Studio

HANS LAMPE_I had completed my apprenticeship in Hamburg but was not too sure of what I wanted to do next. Through my part time job at the Star-Club I met some musicians, and to me every aspect of the music industry seemed to be very interesting; not only making music, but also the technical side and the studio work. And it was only the eggheads, those old-school technicians working at the Windrose Studio that sometimes put me off. But, thank God, the really exciting projects weren't run by them, because they didn't have the practical experience. So therefore I now opted for an additional apprenticeship with Conny; although unfortunately this was at a time just prior to him pulling up stakes in Hamburg.

EBERHARD KRANEMANN_ At first he wanted me to join him in Hamburg, but later he was thinking of going back to the Rhineland. He didn't want to serve the pop industry any longer; at least that's what he said. They did want to keep him. They wanted to buy him, but he ran off.

HANS LAMPE_Together with his actress girlfriend Christa Fast, who at that time was working in Krefeld, northwest of Düsseldorf, Conny wanted to escape the city life and settle down amidst the peace and quiet of the countryside. Having searched for somewhere in North Rhine-Westphalia they eventually found this farm in Seelscheid which really appealed to them both, with a farmhouse, a stable and a pigsty. Therefore much had to be renovated: the house remained a residential home but the stable and pigsty were converted into a production room and studio respectively.

EBERHARD KRANEMANN_"Hamburg is asleep, the scene is dead," Conny said. "It's all kicking off in the Rhine valley now!"

HANS LAMPE_Having told me of his plans to relocate to the Rhineland he asked me if I wanted to come along. What did I have to lose? So I accompanied him on his adventure.

EBERHARD KRANEMANN_Ultimately he just wanted to do his own thing with us Düsseldorfers. This seemed to be good for his soul. We were a good fit.

HANS LAMPE_It was whilst in Hamburg that Conny produced both *Kraftwerk 1* and *2*, the *Ralf & Florian* LP and the two Neu! albums, amongst many others; and it was from his equal share in all of these productions that he started to bring in some cash. He never lived in a particularly grand style, always preferring to save his money. By the time he moved to the Rhineland his reputation as a producer was growing, and with the support of Philips and Metronome he experienced no difficulty taking out a property loan – neither Philips nor Metronome were interested in losing him as a producer or supplier; even if he was sitting on some farm! They knew that products that went through his hands were destined for success.

GÜNTER KÖRBER_Knowing that Conny was not only a good talent scout but also always provided us with great quality productions, we granted him an advance on his future work. That is why all the early Brain productions were made by him, including the early Scorpions.

HANS LAMPE_The construction of the studio almost demands a chapter in itself. In front of us lay a mammoth task, and so I invited a carpenter acquaintance of mine along to help out. Then, together with Rüdiger Barth, an electronic engineer from the Weser Uplands, we built the mixing desk ourselves. With him we were in the best of hands – he had previously fitted out both the Star Studio and the Peter von Zahn-owned Windrose Studio in Hamburg, as well as the Cornet, Rhenus and EMI Studios in Cologne.

GÜNTER KÖRBER_With our advance Conny was able to fulfil his dream in Wolperath.

HANS LAMPE_Everything, from the foundation walls to the roof, had to be completely renovated and all within a short period of time, before the funds ran out. In the production room alone, or rather the stables, all walls had to be covered and everything removed, including these huge standing stones, to make way for new floorboards.

GÜNTER KÖRBER_I visited them several times and observed how a production room evolved from a stable; how a farm became a studio.

HANS LAMPE_Naturally it was quite a big step for Conny to strike tent in Hamburg and to build his own studio in the middle of nowhere, but he was convinced it would all come out great in the end. We had to work through the winter to get the studio ready in time for the first Metronome bookings, which put us under a lot of pressure. That said, it was actually a positive thing: the sooner we finished, the sooner the money would start coming in.

EBERHARD KRANEMANN_Conny didn't want his studio straight in Düsseldorf; he found it too fancy a place, a real jet-setter's city. He was certainly a down-to-earth guy and city life was the exact opposite of what he was looking for. Living on a rented farm – which he would later go on to buy – fitted his image perfectly... as did building his studio in a pigsty.

HANS LAMPE_Such a studio was an expensive undertaking; the costs of the equipment alone – the 16-track two-inch tape recorders, the self made mixer, as well as everything else – all nice products, but pricey. When short of finances Conny would drive to Cologne, where he still had some honourable contacts at the respectable Cornet Studio, and procured the necessary funds. At least the money was sufficient enough to finish the studio, get on with production and make some money. The daily rate for the studio was between 800 to 1500 Deutschmarks, depending on the band and how complicated the recordings were.

EBERHARD KRANEMANN_I was there at the beginning, when things were still in a state of disarray. There were all these typical technical problems. For example their two 24-track recorders, which were supposed to run in time with each other, were constantly going out of sync, and every time that happened the guy who had sold them to Conny would have to drive down from Hamburg to reset them. They were also having some initial problems with their monitor speakers, where the bass created this annoying buzz.

Autobahn

HANS LAMPE_ By now Conny already had the full mobile studio equipment – complete with mixers and multitrack recorders – which he would pack into the back of his VW van. With this we had a lot of bookings. Who else offered such a service, with portable multitrack recorders inside of flight cases? That got us a lot of jobs, especially making live recordings: Van Morrison in Amsterdam, Juliette Gréco, Kraan, Guru Guru and many others. We would pack the van and drive anywhere, including soon to Mintrop Street. It was there at their Kling Klang Studio that we made the initial *Autobahn* recordings using our mobile equipment. For the mixing, though, which took place at a later date, Ralf and Florian would come to Conny's studio.

BODO STAIGER_ For Ralf and Florian, as well as for most of their fans, the true Kraftwerk era begins with *Autobahn*.

HANS LAMPE_ When Conny was making the *Autobahn* recordings I helped him assemble his mobile equipment. During this period he'd overnight at Florian's villa, although on weekends he'd always return to Seelscheid; the festive villa lifestyle was not really his style. Conny was a worker; when he started something he didn't like to stop until it was done. He liked to use the mornings to get set up and would then work tirelessly for the rest of the day. First get the job done, and get drunk afterwards, that was his motto.

BODO STAIGER_For me 'Autobahn' is the classic Kraftwerk track, and it is thanks primarily to Konrad in his role as producer or engineer that they were able to achieve this revolutionary sound.

EBERHARD KRANEMANN_In my view it was Conny who first taught them how to use this electronic stuff. It was he who developed the song 'Autobahn' so that it would be commercially successful.

BODO STAIGER_*Autobahn* was the first purely electronic record from these gentlemen. Later Florian referred to the earlier albums as nothing more than 'dummies'.

EBERHARD KRANEMANN_Conny produced the first three Kraftwerk albums, and did so again here with *Autobahn*; but he was only listed as the sound engineer and that upset him. In my opinion, the music was made by Ralf and Florian but the sound came from Conny.

HANS LAMPE_Conny really felt sore and disappointed that Kraftwerk no longer credited him as a producer on their record. They'd forgotten where they'd come from, denied their roots with him – up until this point Conny had always been loyal and supportive. I don't know where Kraftwerk would be today if it wasn't for Conny.

WOLFGANG FLÜR_With our Minimoog we tried to recreate the sound of engines and the airflow. They sounded pretty good in the end, but it took us a while. All this was recorded on multitrack with the help of 'Head-sound-master' Conny Plank and his mobile equipment. Later we did the final mix at Plank's brand new studio.

HANS LAMPE_Meanwhile during the mixing I thought, "Okay, this is a consistent concept, a cool idea, hats off to that!" Both the lyrics and the music made perfect sense: "Wir fahr'n, fahr'n, fahr'n auf der Autobahn," meaning "We drive, drive, drive on the motorway." The sounds were matching the lyrics – I liked it. But there was never a feeling of: "Whoa, this is a historical moment; what we are mixing here will go on to be a milestone in music."

WOLFGANG FLÜR_What's the story behind 'Autobahn'? It's basically the musical description of a car journey from Düsseldorf to Hamburg. If you know the route you'll recognise the sounds. The mechanical sounds represent the industrial Ruhr valley, the conveyor belts of the mining towns of Bottrop and Castrop-Rauxel. Then you have the long stretch through the rural Münsterland, where the countryside is symbolised by the flute and the song is completely different in feel. In short: VW and Daimler, Thyssen and Krupp, beautiful landscapes, and in between the long and winding Autobahn – a late classical German story.

HANS LAMPE_It takes a lot of courage to create something new and to say: 'Yes, that is exactly as we envisaged it.' There was something curious about *Autobahn*, with its entirely electronic sounds and the electronic beat manually provided by Wolfgang. When you start something new you can never tell how people will react to it. In this case Ralf and Florian knew exactly what they were doing. They wanted it just as it came out. Precisely like that, and no other way.

RAINER ZICKE_The synthesiser finally gave you the opportunity to work with electronically generated sounds, rather than simply acoustic tones that have been electronically modified. Additionally it offered the long-awaited possibility to create something new, original, from scratch, different from all the clichés of an Anglo-American rock'n'roll.

HANS LAMPE_'Autobahn' – that provided the initial spark; even abroad! From an artistic point of view I thought the cover of the German edition was fantastic, very atmospheric; it really captured the essence of the track. From a marketing perspective, however, the English version, with its iconic motorway logo cover, was much more effective.

EBERHARD KRANEMANN_Unfortunately what happened next was a real shame. Having recorded 'Autobahn', a 20-minute long piece corresponding to the entire side of an LP, Conny then got a call from Ira Blacker, from New York. Blacker was representing the American label Capitol Records. "I like this song but it is too long," he said. "Instead of it lasting 20 minutes I'll turn it into a three-minute track and then sell it in America." Conny replied: "Yeah, we can do that, but I don't yet know if the guys agree to have their piece cut up like that." Blacker then arranged to meet Conny in Hamburg to discuss a deal, but on the day of the appointment Conny was regrettably held up and sent along Ralf and Florian in his place. In the aftermath of this unlikely event Florian proudly told me what had happened. The two of them had driven up to Hamburg to meet Blacker in his hotel room. Blacker was sweating, having just arrived, and had removed his jacket, under which he had a holstered a Smith & Wesson, or some pistol of the like. He had with him a plastic bag full of cash, like in a mafia movie. To cut a long story short; in the end he got the song, they got the money, and then they all drove or flew back home again. Up until now everything is fine, but here comes the worst part, which I still have not forgiven Ralf or Florian for. When they arrived back home they gave Conny 5000 Deutschmarks and said: "Here, this is for you, now you are paid." Unfortunately he took the money; something he shouldn't have done, because from then on they no longer credited him as their producer. From then on Ralf and Florian were the only rulers in the Kraftwerk Cosmos.

MICHAEL ROTHER_Conny was in need of some serious cash for his studio and I think they simply offered him the sum he required, essentially buying him out of 'Autobahn' before it became a success. For every deal there needs to be two parties in agreement, and whether that was a good or bad decision was irrelevant at that point and impossible to foresee. Five thousand Deutschmarks was a whole lot of money.

HANS LAMPE_Conny was a recognised authority, although he was never authoritarian. People always felt very at ease with him. In such an atmosphere things can happen, develop, people were inspiring each other. He would push creativity to the limit, and songs such as 'Autobahn' can be the result; although from then on Konrad Plank was never to work with Kraftwerk again, the mood was irreversibly disrupted. What I still don't understand, and here is my question: How did they shift from their experimental free music to their uniform, strictly structured music that they make today? That I can't figure out. The first three Kraftwerk albums are completely different from what followed; they do not seem to fit together at all. Why is that? Many of my musical friends think the first three LPs are brilliant, but they just can't relate to the later stuff.

MICHAEL ROTHER_I think it's a shame that the first three Kraftwerk albums are only available as bootlegs and have never been officially rereleased, as there is a lot of beautiful and innovative material on them. They are more authentically improvisatory and they sound less strictly structured.

HANS LAMPE_*Kraftwerk 1* and *2* have never been officially released on CD. Perhaps this is done to protect their reputation; that said, releasing them wouldn't destroy their reputation either – it's simply the stuff they did before they became the major electronic pioneers.

Oskar Sala

RAINER ZICKE_In the mid-Seventies I had nothing to do with Kraftwerk. What really interested me were the synthesisers and all the subsequent new opportunities. Historically speaking, electronic music is a German product, a classic German product. One of the first functioning synthesisers, the Trautonium, was built in 1930 by the legendary Oskar Sala, together with engineer Friedrich Trautwein – from whom it got its name.

WOLFGANG SEIDEL_In Berlin, during the Zodiac times, we were kinda aware of Oskar Sala, although he indeed wasn't integrated in either the academic avant-garde or the underground scene.

RAINER ZICKE_Florian Schneider was a huge fan of Oskar Sala. He would repeatedly say: "Kraftwerk are not the pioneers, it is the people like Sala." That was how he used to perceive it; to him it was Sala who had laid the foundation. Sala was quite a controversial figure though.

WOLFGANG SEIDEL_Within the avant-garde scene he was seen as a suspicious character, known for having played his Trautonium not only in films and advertisements, but as well for Goebbels' propaganda movies and the soundtracks of Veit Harlan films. Within the underground scene he was simply unknown.

RAINER ZICKE_Once I attended a lecture given by Sala in Karlsruhe which had been organised by Florian. Someone had reconstructed a Trautonium and Sala spoke about the history of the instrument; as well as about Trautwein and Hindemith – Hindemith actually composed specifically for the Trautonium.

WOLFGANG SEIDEL_Sala was, without a doubt, the city's first electronic musician. He had his Trautonium and cutting table adjacent to each other, so that he could fit his effects directly to each movie frame. In his soundtracks for *Stahlnetz*, and naturally also for Hitchcock's *The Birds*, the border between music and noise was radically fluent.

RAINER ZICKE_And then he said: "An ounce of experience is worth a ton of theory. Let's make some noise!" He turned the knobs to 10 and there came a full-blown Trautonium – it really blew me away. Maximum volume, great presence and a sharp sound that smacked you right in the face. Brilliant.

WOLFGANG FLÜR_Compared with the age of a stringed instrument, the synthesiser is only a baby. We owe a great debt of gratitude to the genius of people such as Lew Thermen, Professor Friedrich Trautwein, Oskar Sala and Robert Moog, who took the first steps towards a new era of electronic sound generation.

NEU! 75

HANS LAMPE_It was in 1974 that Klaus asked me if I wanted to play with Neu! on a regular basis. As such I left Conny's yard and relocated to Düsseldorf. Klaus said. "First you'll join us for *NEU! 75*, after which we'll start our new project."

MICHAEL ROTHER_Musically speaking, Klaus and I complemented each other well. After the second album, however, I was becoming less and less happy and began to look for an ally to join us. We were invited by an English record company to do a tour of England, but as a duo it was clear to both of us that we were unable to truly perform our music; so we began the search for musical collaborators.

HANS LAMPE_When I joined Neu! it was a time of many changes – Thomas Dinger, Klaus' brother had just joined and Klaus was wanting to play more guitar. Michael was not at all convinced that the band was heading in the right direction, especially considering that the actual drummer no longer wanted to play drums and had replaced himself with two new drummers. All in all, the music was becoming too loud, wacky and offbeat for him, until he finally said 'No' to Neu!.

DIRK FLADER_The contact with Hans came through Conny Plank, and Thomas came aboard simply because he was Klaus' younger brother and had nothing better to do.

KLAUS DINGER_My brother had lost his job as a result of several pretty stupid circumstances and had remained jobless since. I'd always been told to 'take care of your brother', so I did. I showed him how it worked and what he had to do.

ROEDELIUS_Thomas was a lovable guy, whereas Klaus was far too self-centred and sure of himself. With Hans, I don't know, I never really got to know him.

KLAUS DINGER_Now I'm going to leave the drums, I'm going to stand out the front. I won't go back there again. That's it for me. And so I taught them both to play, and now watch me, here comes the next step.

HANS LAMPE_Klaus was surely the undisputed leader, the frontman of the band; and that's why he needed to perform at the front of the stage. You capture the audience with harmonies, the melodies and the words, whereas the rhythm is more subtle. If you want to convey something, a message, then you have to have great lyrics and to be the singer, or even better: sing and play guitar. Somehow this all belonged together. And Klaus wanted that.

MICHAEL ROTHER_I had just recently made contact with Hans-Joachim Roedelius and Dieter Moebius of Cluster, both of whom seemed the perfect choice to join our Neu! line-up. Their records were likewise produced by Conny Plank and the song 'Im Süden' from *Cluster II* was comparable to our music: it was based on four notes and the harmonic foundation was similar.

ROEDELIUS_We became friends with Rother very easily, but the first major challenge to our friendship was the album *Musik Von Harmonia*; this was still mainly dominated by our Cluster work process.

HANS LAMPE_Prior to the *NEU! 75* recordings, a conflict arose within the group. Michael was not particularly enthusiastic about making the record with Thomas and me, as the traditional line-up had always been only himself and Klaus. Despite his initial reservations, he moved on pretty quickly and soon enjoyed playing the multitrack recorder live with us.

MICHAEL ROTHER_I had visited the two members of Cluster during Easter 1973 at this 16th century house in Forst, in the Weser Valley, where I still live today. I immediately fell in love with the landscape as well as their music.

Hero

HANS LAMPE_Eventually we came up with a compromise, even if it sounds a little silly by today's standards: the first side of the album would feature only Klaus and Michael, whereas on the second side Thomas and I would join in.

MICHAEL ROTHER_The second side is more a reflection of Klaus' view of the world more than anything else; it is his anger that he is trying to express, and that is a feeling that I do not share with him. That said, it would be too simple to say that the first side is Rother, the second side is Dinger; because it's not so easy to divide the two of us either.

HANS LAMPE_This separation worked perfectly for getting the songs on tape; the credits then again would be shared in typical Neu! style: 'dinger/rother'. Same with the production credits: 'neu/c. plank'.

MICHAEL ROTHER_Klaus had a precise appreciation for melodies and softer sounds, but at the same time I additionally liked his dynamic and up-beat songs. Truth is, the desperate and frantic screams on 'Hero' and his nihilistic words pretty much reflect his own view on life, and not mine.

DIRK FLADER_Klaus had sung and played guitar with Neu! before, and if I may say so: it really wasn't bad. That fantastic, driving, fully distorted guitar that you can hear on 'Hero' – that is Klaus with his beloved Hagström guitar.

MICHAEL ROTHER_When Julian Cope said that with 'Hero' we had invented punk rock, even before the Sex Pistols, it's of course nice to hear but not quite right. We didn't invent anything, and certainly not punk; we simply made music.

ROEDELIUS_Michael was always very sure of how to put things and how to express his own artistic view. He was the introverted and self-confident guy and nowadays you can see how successful he's been with that.

MICHAEL ROTHER_Nevertheless, 'Hero' is one of my favourite Neu! tunes and I'm glad that it worked out that way. Later, punk came along; perhaps the Sex Pistols and other bands from their scene had been listening to our music. We had already been released in England by United Artists; after Germany it was our second most important market – that's where we sold most of our records.

DIRK FLADER_I found *NEU! 75* quite innovative and modern, because of its instrumental pieces and also because of the brutal manner in which Klaus delivered the vocals. 'Hero' is my favourite song. Here he is singing about his lost love Anita Heedman, who went to Norway and no longer wanted to be with him. She holds an important place in the Dinger-mythology. He even went to Norway with his huge motorbike to get her back. No such luck.

MICHAEL ROTHER_The first take often has something magical about it. When Klaus was recording the vocals for 'Hero' I sat with Conny in his control room. Klaus let out all his rage and despair with his singing and Conny and I instantly looked at each other and thought: "Wow, that's it," but Klaus said: "No no, I have to do it again, it still needs to be better."

KLAUS IMMIG_To me it was more about the sounds and rhythm; the singing was just an accessory. It was an instrument-like decoration; not at the forefront but rather used as an instrument.

MICHAEL ROTHER_The second take was accepted as the 'right one' in the sense of the more structured one; but it certainly wasn't that strong or as powerful as the emotional first take, which still grips me. Even today.

DIRK FLADER_Yeah, the voice was used like an instrument in this Klaus Dinger elegy. This song is somewhere in between, let's say, Hawkwind's 'Silver Machine' and Iggy Pop's 'Passenger'.

MICHAEL ROTHER_What you can hear on *NEU! 75* is not a protest, not a call to the new youth movement to show the finger to the world; but rather the expressions of one individual with a real punk personality – Klaus fuckin' Dinger.

HANS LAMPE_'Hero', the song which we're best known for, was developed by Klaus, Thomas and I. Utterly important within the song were Klaus' direct vocals: this roughness, this steam and this energy! Michael wasn't too sure about it and mentally he was already on his way to the Weser Uplands.

Harmonia

ROEDELIUS_There was already a long-existing feud between Dinger and Rother which led to his extended stay in Forst, and after this his break from Dinger and Neu! became inevitable.

MICHAEL ROTHER_Klaus and I had already started to split musically, but despite that we released this third album as Neu!, partly to fulfil the contract with Brain. I was having more and more difficulties with Klaus' unpleasant personality, if I can put it like that; and the joy that I found with Harmonia – that is Roedelius, Moebius and I – really led me away from Klaus. In the beginning I had hoped he could join us and we could be a four-piece band, but he had plans of his own. Fair enough. Me too. Plans with a greater musical substance.

ROEDELIUS_For Cluster, Harmonia was an attempt to make something that would be financially successful, but we tried too hard and for that reason it had to fail.

MICHAEL ROTHER_It was peaceful, friendly, abstract; and at the same time completely experimental. A major difference to the music I made with Klaus was that I could improvise good quality music onstage with Roedelius and Moebius. Roedelius played electric piano, Moebius had his so-called 'warbler-machine' with all sorts of tone-modifiers, and I played guitar, organ and electric drums. During these good times we created fascinating music that put me right under the spell; as did our beautiful home and the surroundings on the River Weser.

ROEDELIUS_It was our decision: to slow down and lead an easy life on a marginal, rudimentary basis.

MICHAEL ROTHER_Sadly Harmonia never received as much attention as Neu!. We failed on the economical side of the venture.

ROEDELIUS_Rother was one of the two already-successful Neu! guys and so I thought he would know exactly what to do; but in the case of Harmonia we failed – at least financially – all three of us.

HANS LAMPE_Somehow we managed to get our brand new album *NEU! 75* packaged and released but after that we didn't know what to do. What was to come next?

MICHAEL ROTHER_Harmonia came to be a real shelf warmer. The music was made with the same love, the same conviction, but absolutely no one listened to it. At the concerts people either fell asleep, left, or didn't turn up in the first place! Once we toured North Germany, to play in a discotheque. The contract said we had to organise and promote it ourselves and, as such, we didn't have a guaranteed fee. In the evening only three people showed up. That was symptomatic with Harmonia and not a good sign.

JOCHEN RAUSCH_As a young reporter I would often speak with the bands and, financially speaking, the guys were usually pretty broke. They were hippies, living in shared flats and driving their second-hand hearses to the concerts, where they overnighted in back rooms; never in a Nightliner coach or hotel.

MICHAEL ROTHER_My colleagues from Cluster didn't have too much money, which is why we were happy to receive advances for Harmonia. We'd been playing concerts but these certainly didn't bring in enough dough to live off. I was lucky that the record sales from Neu! yielded just enough to get us through the financial loss that was Harmonia.

ROEDELIUS_Neu! were successful during their own lifetime, as proven by the many statements of famous contemporaries such as Bowie, Eno and the like.

JOCHEN RAUSCH_During the Seventies there were no German bands with 'star status'; instead these groups played in small shops, cultural centres, at universities or festivals. Their music was basically ignored by all German radio stations, except special interest programmes such as *Rock In* presented by Winfrid Trenkler on WDR. Often they didn't even apply to have their music played on the radio; even the song 'Autobahn' was designed as an album track, not to be played on the radio.

HANS LAMPE_So, now there were no more contractual obligations to Metronome. We had an arse full of debt, or Klaus had to be more precise, and we'd lost Michael to the Weserbergland. Man overboard!

Dingerland

HANS LAMPE_A lot happened in 1974. Klaus tried to establish his Dingerland label by signing Lilac Angels, Fritz Müller Rock and Neu!. As Michael and Metronome didn't approve this for Neu!, he could only get the other two.

KLAUS DINGER_ In 1974 I founded the Dingerland Musik Ltd with the aim of pressing and distributing records. My pilot project was the Lilac Angels, a rock'n'roll band I saw perform at the carnival celebrations in Malkasten, a typical Düsseldorf venue. I'd liked what I'd heard and seeing as nobody else seemed to be playing that type of music at the time I decided to produce their first record. Conny came aboard, we got some expensive sleeve covers, everything seemed to be going really well, but it didn't last. Instead it all went belly up and I was left 50,000 in debt. On top of it all we had a long, cold winter, and at the end of all this we had: La Düsseldorf.

HANS LAMPE_ The Dingerland label was founded by Klaus to first produce records and then sell the finished product to the bigger companies; like a subsidiary label, which should have been financially lucrative. Great idea, but it failed in the making. He already had all the 5000 Lilac Angels albums printed but was overdoing the business side of things. Nobody wanted to buy the record at Klaus' asking price; still he was having to pay the pressing plant immediately. Three or four Deutschmarks per unit, plus the design for the cover and so on. Check out the cover photo! This was done by a famous artist: Peter Lindbergh! He did the whole visual concept; and the photo shoot took place at his studio in some courtyard on Acker street. That's where he was working back then. Jesus, if Klaus hadn't been so strict and inflexible, it could have worked out really well, but you know how he was.

BODO STAIGER_ As the Lilacs we released two albums; the first to launch Klaus' label in 1974 and the second one recorded with me in 1977, then released through EMI Electrola in 1978, before our split in 1979.

HANS LAMPE_ Fritz Müller Rock represented the extreme left wing of the Dingerland Empire. Klaus said it was a bit like in parliament, where Eberhard expressed his political views through the lyrics he wrote. Lilac Angels were rather the traditional rock band; with their conservative glam rock appeal, they were supposed to be more successful. And La Düsseldorf were seen to be at the epicentre of it all. Then everything took a totally different direction.

BODO STAIGER_The Lilac Angels were like a springboard for me. We were a glam rock band who often played live. I was studying guitar and was in my training. I simply wanted to play. Although the Lilacs were not a great love, at that time they were just right for me. We played the pieces of Joe Stick; he was the singer, songwriter and band leader.

HANS LAMPE_Fritz Müller Rock was very interesting. The record tells the story of the average worker, or more precisely the daily routine of the average worker. It's a very simple story and was meant more as a criticism of society: "I get up in the morning, go to the bathroom, wash myself, brush my teeth, eat breakfast, and then go to work" – all about this automated daily routine. The singer then goes on: he comes home in the evening, drinks a bottle of beer, lies in front of the TV and goes back to bed again.

EBERHARD KRANEMANN_Fritz Müller was my stage name; I became Fritz Müller. I'm actually an intellectual guy but I wanted to make music for the average person – German rock music, with simple, down-to-earth German words. So I thought to myself: "Well, I need a German name," and the most primitive, cheapest was, of course, Fritz Müller, a real cliché name. I wanted to make cliché music, to distance myself from Kraftwerk and Neu!, and so I came up with this – but it was misunderstood. These were intellectual, ironic texts, but the irony went unnoticed. It just didn't take off.

HANS LAMPE_That was a sign of the times, typical German reality. Klaus joked: "I get up in the morning, go to the bathroom, have a bottle of beer, and then go back to bed." That was the quintessential Fritz Müller to him: bad, dirty, harsh sounds played with wah-wah pedals and distortion.

EBERHARD KRANEMANN_Real hard, angry rock guitar with distortion, and I screamed into the microphone in German. It certainly wasn't singing, but rather bellowing, like an animal. I aimed to counteract the softer shit that everybody else was doing. I was the anti-role-model. That was at a time before punk. A few years later punk arrived – and then they all started doing it like this.

HANS LAMPE_ The label foundation party took place at Haus KöBlick, on Königsallee, Düsseldorf's fanciest street. Klaus wanted to be a big shot now, he was tired of the suburban surroundings of our Neu! studio Im Grund 3b. Instead he now wanted to be on the 'Kö'. We held on to the Im Grund location anyway though, as it didn't cost that much. After all, it nowadays holds cult status as the best-known Neu! and La D address.

EBERHARD KRANEMANN_I visited Conny with a brand new concept: the ironic twist on the commercialisation of music. He liked that too. We had a lot of fun taking the piss out of the music industry, working out all the clichés in the music business.

HANS LAMPE_ When spin-offs like Haus KöBlick didn't work out, we always had the Im Grund studio location as a secret hideaway. Like Klaus used to say, and I think that's a Leonard Cohen quote: "If you can't get off the ground, stay on the ground."

EBERHARD KRANEMANN_ At first Dinger absolutely wanted to do it – he'd brought in Conny Plank, everything was mixed and finalised, but then his money ran out. For four years I was busy working on my recordings at Conny's studio, and finally my Fritz Müller Rock album was released in 1977 by the Roth-Händle label, a cigarette company-owned label.

Ratingen, Blauer See

HANS LAMPE_ Neu! rarely performed live. Two of our concerts were in Ratingen – the first on July 20, 1974, at a private label presentation on Jochen Nolden's estate, and then another one on September 14, at the open air theatre Blauer See, meaning 'blue lake'. Both shows were with Michael and both shows were no more than just okay.

KLAUS IMMIG_ The setting was well chosen. The stage was appropriately lit and in front of us we had this blue lake. That was quite something. Even the way to the location, which actually took some time getting there, went along a magical forest path.

HANS LAMPE_We wouldn't really rehearse a great deal, we would just play. It was so typical of Klaus to just say: "How about this one? Come on, let's play, let's do it," and then we would. It's no wonder the world wasn't particularly blown away by it.

KLAUS IMMIG_When Klaus Dinger performed he naturally had to be at the forefront. It had to be a big event, with him and his guitar in the spotlight. He presented himself really well onstage, with his white overalls, and perfectly shit-faced. Rother, on the other hand, was ever a little shy, standing apart from the others with his guitar and quietly operating his tape recorders. Both drummers, Thomas and Hans, came across as a real blend of glam, kraut and hippie. That was very cool; totally the spirit of the Neu! times.

HANS LAMPE_Well, yeah, a lot of money went down the drain and not much came back in. We'd planned everything ourselves, without an organiser... in fact I don't remember if there was even an entry fee charged! Anyway, there wasn't much left afterwards because the costs were all too high – we even had to pay for the stage and lights ourselves. It was a beautiful location though, and there was a large turnout... although they weren't all that amazed by us.

EBERHARD KRANEMANN_Klaus was extremely extroverted and responsible for the band's innovations, whereas Michael took charge of the melodies. Thomas, with his white platform boots, was a real rhythm king. They were hip and had street cred, no question. Live they were simply brilliant, and the whole thing gave me the opportunity to present my Fritz Müller Rock project.

HANS LAMPE_With Fritz Müller Rock the people couldn't really get into it. Lilac Angels, on the other hand, were well received I believe, and for us, we had our first decent result, although without any great 'wow' effect. What the people really wanted was to finally see Neu! perform; although we weren't as good as we could have been.

JOCHEN RAUSCH_You could consider German krautrock as one component of the progressive music movement. In England you had prog rock bands like Pink Floyd, King Crimson, Genesis, Gentle Giant, Van Der Graaf Generator etc etc. They were the album bands, you wouldn't hear them on the radio or on TV. The discotheques were playing both black music and dance music, and so the new art form for the progressive bands became whole concept albums. No seven-inches! For them the album had to be the centre of attention.

ROEDELIUS_It was Cluster that left Harmonia and not Rother. To have continued performing these pieces live in their truest form we would have had to have practised day after day, over and over again, and we simply weren't willing to do that. That was the real reason for the split. Despite this there was never any animosity between us and Rother.

KLAUS DINGER_My brother and I stayed in England longer than expected. Our plan was to stay a week – that quickly became six. We were trying to organise a Neu! tour but nobody was interested. At that time Neu! weren't successful enough to go on tour, but that encouraged us to push on with our Düsseldorf thing instead. There was no other chance, the only logical conclusion: Let's do only Düsseldorf. We'll stay here, in beautiful La Düsseldorf.

WOLFGANG FLÜR

++ **JAN 75** *NEU! 75* mixed in Conny Plank's studio ++ **FEB 75** Karl Bartos joins Kraftwerk as an additional percussionist ++ **APR/MAY 75** Kraftwerk play their first major US tour with their classic line-up of Hütter/Schneider/Bartos/Flür ++ **JUL 75** Hütter/Schneider submit their patent for an electronic drum kit in the USA ++ **SEP 75** La Düsseldorf start recording their first album in Düsseldorf and Wolperath ++ **SEP 75** Kraftwerk tour the UK, performing 17 shows across England ++ **NOV 75** Kraftwerk's fifth studio album, *Radio-Activity*, is released ++

Tour de USA

WOLFGANG FLÜR_ One day Ralf and Florian rang us up and invited Karl and me to a café out of town to discuss things. They were very secretive and didn't want to give any reasons on the phone. And so we drove out to the country in Ralf's grey VW. At that time I had my fire-engine red Opel Kadett sedan with a 55 PS motor. In the spring of 1975 the weather was already quite warm and so we sat outside. Ralf cleared his throat in his familiar way and said, "What do you think of America, you guys?" We had no idea what he meant by this. He continued: "Our single is in the charts in the USA and is moving up fast. It's just reached number five so we've been given a great offer to tour all over the States." We were flabbergasted. Madness! Crazy! Us in America? It was unbelievable. What had we done? How could this have happened so quickly? Elated, we considered how we should present ourselves in that huge country, the birthplace of sweaty guitar rock. The tour was scheduled to start in April and according to our American manager, Ira Blacker, an initial schedule of 21 concerts had been planned... in reality it turned out to be a lot more.

MICHAEL ROTHER_It was in 1975 that I got a call from Kraftwerk asking me to go to America with them on their *Autobahn* tour. I was too busy with Harmonia, though, and politely declined.

WOLFGANG FLÜR_We wanted to be visually different from anything coming out of England or America, so we wore our hair short, had grey suits and elegant footwear specially made for us. Never again were we to be seen wearing blue jeans. We saw ourselves as both engineers and musicians; fully aware of our German identity. We were the proud sons of Wernher von Braun and Werner von Siemens.

WOLFGANG SEIDEL_The reaction to German pop music abroad differed greatly depending on the time and place and cannot be thought of in general terms; although some trends did exist. Everyone either loved or feared the German stereotypes; the comb-overs, Autobahn, the machines. The way Kraftwerk bundled it all together though was very clever.

Bartos

WOLFGANG FLÜR_We commissioned new autograph cards from an old portrait photographer in Blumen Street. On these cards the image of Kraftwerk – which would remain unchanged for the next 16 years, also the most creative period of the band – was seen for the first time. At the beginning of the Seventies, Ralf still had shoulder-length hair. That may have been appropriate during their musical experimentation with Organisation and the *Kraftwerk 1* and *2* albums, but I clearly remember that, at the time of *Autobahn*, we adopted the 'German' image at Florian's suggestion, based on his love of the fashions of the Fifties. Classy. Conservative. The Discreet Charm of the Bourgeoisie. I think I liked that. I still reminisce about having our hair cut and buying suits in town. Ralf and Florian bought theirs from a Düsseldorf bespoke tailor. For Karl and me they purchased something ready-made. In our case these off-the-peg suits were seen as work clothing, and could therefore be reclaimed on tax.

WOLFGANG SEIDEL_Within Kraftwerk, Schneider and Hütter represented the upper middle class while Bartos and Flür were the working class boys. The 'mateship' model of a classic rock band didn't exist here.

WOLFGANG FLÜR_We were not to be compared with the typical American rock stereotypes, those who indulged in mind-altering drugs to become guitar gods or egomaniacal frontmen.

WOLFGANG SEIDEL_With Kraftwerk everything was about de-individualisation: the identity of the group grew more important than the identity of its individual members. Therefore Kraftwerk always portrayed themselves as a strict working unit and so the group image strengthened; it seemed to be more than just the sum of its parts.

WOLFGANG FLÜR_Prior to our American tour, Rother turned down the offer and Karl Bartos was invited into the group. Florian knew a professor of music from his time at the conservatory and he put him in contact with this extremely talented musician who was studying drums, piano and vibraphone and was close to graduating from the Düsseldorf Robert Schumann Institute.

MICHAEL MERTENS_Seeing as Karl Bartos was almost finished with his studies he was invited to audition with the Berlin Philharmonic Orchestra, a world class orchestra in the same league as Cleveland, Chicago or the Vienna Philharmonics. He received the offer through his teacher. Karl was a very good percussionist; he was young, perhaps in his mid-20s, and was encouraged to apply for the Herbert von Karajan Scholarship. He could easily have had this scholarship in his pocket and would have gone on to become an orchestral percussionist; playing snare drum, bass drum, cymbals, triangle, xylophone, glockenspiel, vibraphone and bells – the entire percussion section, sometimes even the whip or air pistol. He had the offer, but at the same time he got the call to join Kraftwerk. When his teacher learned of his decision for Kraftwerk he almost had a heart attack!

WOLFGANG FLÜR_ When Florian brought our new colleague Karl to the studio he still looked very much like the typical student, with his brown duffle coat, white trainers, blue jeans and a dark red velour sweatshirt which he never failed to wear every day. He was several years younger than us and I noticed right away that he was a confident and self-assertive individual, which left me quite envious. At first he played his conventional vibraphone, which was his favourite instrument back then. We even lugged it around America on our first tour, costing us a fortune, but first and foremost he was hired as an additional drummer. He was a trained concert percussionist and could play rhythms that I was simply unable to. For this reason alone he was a colossal acquisition for us; though I expected competition.

MICHAEL MERTENS_ In regards to the compositions, Karl was to become an integral member of Kraftwerk. In the course of their career, more and more of the melodies and harmonies were created by him.

BODO STAIGER_ Later on it was him who wrote and played many of the beautiful and catchy melodies. After Ralf and Florian he's most important to Kraftwerk. Nowadays he's only referred to as one of the 'other two', and sometimes even then it's more Wolfgang who's mentioned.

WOLFGANG FLÜR_ Karl was already a great guitarist and drummer, and as a result of his studies he was definitely able to make our songs more interesting rhythmically.

BODO STAIGER_ It was actually Karl who was responsible for writing many of Kraftwerk's big hits, and the way he was treated following his departure was a real disgrace.

WOLFGANG FLÜR_ He was by far no visionary, but more a great 'Kraftsman', always coming up with the right tones. A natural-born musician.

BODO STAIGER_ He is without doubt one of the best musicians I know. He can play it all, from guitar to vibraphone. It was thanks to him that I was accepted into the conservatorium and I owe him a lot for that.

MICHAEL MERTENS_ We were classmates at the conservatory; both of us were drummers, percussionists. We are only one year apart, Karl and I, and it was there that I got to know him well; it had nothing to do with electronic music or any band connection. At one point I was just sitting in the hallway practising when along came this guy and said: "Hi, I'm Karl. Karl Bartos. What are you up to?"

WOLFGANG FLÜR_I later built an electronic percussion set for Karl out of another rhythm box and a smaller percussion pad I had. The principle was just the same although the sounds were different. These could be played as rhythm patterns or individually. All the sounds were triggered with our metal 'knitting needles'.

MICHAEL MERTENS_ Karl understood that to make popular music you had to retain some degree of naivety; something many qualified musicians forget. He wasn't always thinking about what he had learned, but instead would just simply immerse himself in a given situation.

WOLFGANG FLÜR_ We travelled to the United States with our tourist visas; it was only later that we received working permissions from the American Consulate. We were greeted in the hall of Kennedy Airport by our fat manager Ira Blacker, who took us into town in a big, black limousine with his big, black chauffeur. Karl and I had been booked into the Gorham Hotel on 55th Street while Ralf and Florian were staying nearby in the more upmarket Mayflower Hotel on Central Park West. A nice social separation. Just the way we liked it.

WOLFGANG SEIDEL_ By this point no one in America could continue to ignore German electronic bands; even the conventional German rock bands such as Novalis, Birth Control, Triumvirat, Atlantis, Jane or Nektar had started touring America all of a sudden! Ears were open to krautrock... and *Newsweek* began to refer to it as the 'German Invasion'.

MICHAEL MERTENS_ For those hits that he co-wrote, Karl of course received his PPL shares, but always at a reduced royalty rate since he had only joined the band after their first big success. The other two simply said: "Well, we had *Autobahn* before we had you."

Broadway

WOLFGANG FLÜR_One of our first US shows took place on April 3, 1975 in Rochester Town, upstate New York. It proceeded in an entirely unspectacular way and went unnoticed by the press. This was part of the plan, because we first had to warm up, and didn't want to make any mistake in front of the cameras or the greedy reporters. The venue in Rochester was a rather uncomfortable, cold hall and the audience really didn't know how to take us. I would be inclined to think that they hadn't heard our music on the radio before.

WOLFGANG SEIDEL_In the Seventies there was varied reaction to the use of synthesisers and other devices used to reproduce the tones of traditional instruments. Generally speaking, it was considered somewhat fake if people couldn't actually play real instruments; there was a fear that musicians were to be replaced by machines.

WOLFGANG FLÜR_In the US as well as in Germany we were obviously light years ahead with our music. When Ralf panned the thunderous sounds from left to right and back again over the whole stereo width of the stage during 'Autobahn', all I could see were open mouths and bewildered faces with wide-open eyes. That song was our battering ram... and we loved it.

WOLFGANG SEIDEL_With all the technical equipment onstage the musicians were forced into this type of static immobility. The antics of the typical rock musician – jumping around or windmilling the microphone – were redundant here. Besides, it reflected the mood and mentality of a German musician quite well.

WOLFGANG FLÜR_They'd never seen or heard anything like us before. The heavy, deep synthesisers were completely alien to the audience. Although synthesisers had been discovered and were manufactured in America they had only played a subordinate role in pop music; up until that point, they were primarily used to add effects or play a riff line. Our complex and exclusive use of electronic instrumentation was completely new to the Americans.

WOLFGANG SEIDEL_Over this once purely instrumental music they added a remarkable German text; all in their distinctive 'sing-speak'. That suited their music well.

WOLFGANG FLÜR_We stayed in New York for the next few days, spending our time window-shopping and rehearsing in the afternoons. Ralf had brought a special device with him, the Vako Orchestron, a further development of the Mellotron, which was relatively new on the market. With this gadget it was possible to reproduce samples of instruments and choirs by means of thin cellophane discs on which optical sound lines were printed. The wafer-thin transparent discs were as big as seven-inch singles, and like them had a hole in the middle. However, optical sound lines don't run in a spiral from the outside to the inside like records do; instead they form individual, enclosed rings. On the Orchestron each ring created an individual voice or tone pitch. It was possible to play them polyphonically, by means of a normal keyboard, because all of the rings were simultaneously touched by a row of photoelectric cells. The sound was fantastic. The device worked well, and it was really a great find. During this tour Ralf started using the Orchestron in our songs. The choir and string voices were the most fascinating, their droning and melancholy quality caused by the unstable drive across rubber bands resulting in variations in synchronism. On the contrary, the slight wobble was a particular characteristic of the instrument, which was housed in a huge, heavy wooden box. "Jetzt schalten wir das Radio an. Aus dem lautsprecher klingt es dann: 'Wir fahr'n, fahr'n, fahr'n auf der Autobahn'."

WOLFGANG SEIDEL_These were the words that were understood by the Americans – even when sung in German. On the one hand, these words have a meaning, on the other hand, one gets to think they're only used for phonetic reasons.

WOLFGANG FLÜR_We were scheduled to play at the Beacon Theatre on Broadway, and when we left our hotel and walked to the venue in the afternoon we were pleasantly surprised. The Beacon was a well-maintained, elegant art deco theatre and we learned that it had been under a preservation order for many years. With several rows of balconies it must have had about 2000 seats. All of the ornamentation was gold coloured and the seats had been upholstered in purple velvet. To a certain extent it reminded me of the Olympia in Paris, where we had already made a minor appearance the previous year and which was also reddish and plush. Here, however, everything was larger and more luxurious. This was, after all, America, where everything was bigger and more expensive. On the artistically designed façade outside, an enormous neon light with our names and those of our two support acts, Greenslade and Michael Quatro, attracted the attention of the public to the evening's unusual musical event.

WOLFGANG SEIDEL_ Quickly this led to one of the most amusing yet absurd misunderstandings in America. The Americans understood "fun, fun, fun on the Autobahn" and were reminded of the The Beach Boys song with the same name.

WOLFGANG FLÜR_ On one afternoon we were photographed by Maurice Seymour, the famous New York celebrity photographer. Three years later this black-and-white shot became the cover photo for the German release of *Trans Europa Express*.

MICHAEL MERTENS_'Autobahn' defo hit the spot for the many car-crazy Americans. Additionally they thought it was some type of tribute to 'Fun, Fun, Fun' by The Beach Boys and drew a parallel between the fun of surfing in California to the joy of speed-limit-free driving on German motorways.

WOLFGANG FLÜR_ One evening Ralf and Florian – who were always attending business appointments without us in the daytime – came to our hotel. They proudly showed us the new wristwatches that their music publishers had bought for them that afternoon in an expensive jeweller's shop as a bonus for sales of the record, which had so far sold 450,000 units. Ralf happily told us that they'd been able to choose the watches themselves. His was an elegant watch, manufactured completely from gold, which told the wearer what the time was anywhere in the world. The dial represented the globe and was divided into time zones by vertical lines, and the continents were picked out in different shades of gold. A small aeroplane formed the tip of the large second hand, which ticked regularly around the Earth. It was a quite beautiful and certainly very expensive work of art. In contrast, Florian had decided on a heavy Rolex watch, a showy piece of techno platinum with a heavy winder and large buttons, with which it could be used as a stopwatch. Ralf and Florian were as different in their taste as they were in their musical talent; and I felt deeply hurt that they were separating themselves from us and showing their valuable gifts to us like this.

Beach Boys

WOLFGANG SEIDEL_One unfortunate advertising slogan referred to them as 'The Beach Boys from Germany'! It is unlikely Kraftwerk have ever been more misunderstood than at that moment. Similarly, 20 years later, Die Krupps toured America and were promoted as 'Die Krupps – more than just a coffee maker'; another painful misunderstanding.

WOLFGANG FLÜR_The great evening drew nearer and all of the 2000 seats in the theatre had been completely sold out. Our hit 'Autobahn' was the best advertisement for the concert. When we began our minimalistic show the room was as quiet as a mouse. The people were fascinated, probably even shocked by our meticulous appearance; all suits and ties to underline our merciless formality. The exotic, electronic sounds really knocked them out.

WOLFGANG SEIDEL_They were the noise-makers whose sounds could not be trusted. Who produced the tones? Who was in control and who dominated who? These so-called musicians with no traditional instruments were only plugging cables or turning knobs. It was a mystery to the audience, comparable to the awakening of the home computer, somewhat the work of a devil with no soul.

WOLFGANG FLÜR_When performing live our equipment could be set up quickly. We didn't have much anyway, only two synthesisers, a Farfisa organ, both our electronic drum kits, Karl's vibraphone and Florian's electronic flute, as well as our new Vako Orchestron. The blue neon signs that spelled out our first names, which I had built in the previous year, were placed directly onstage in front of us. Since we didn't have many songs, we had to play the few we had, very, very extended. We played pieces from the albums *Ralf & Florian* and *Autobahn* twice as long as on the recordings. Songs such as 'Tongebirge', 'Mitternacht', 'Tanzmusik' and 'Kometenmelodie' we expanded too. Karl and I beat our electronic percussion boards stoically like madmen. So we managed to achieve a respectable length for our show. We quickly recognised that even the protracted tuning and recalibration of the synthesisers between the songs was so interesting to the audience that our mini-repertoire wasn't a problem.

WOLFGANG SEIDEL_The Moog was very expensive, clunky and difficult to operate; it was not truly suitable for travel. Unfortunately it was prone to fluctuations in temperature, which made the reproduction of certain pieces quite difficult. So musicians were confronted with a completely new challenge: the dark side of the Moog-tuning.

WOLFGANG FLÜR_We wanted to create a very Germanised style of modern pop music that drew on our romantic roots and folk traditions. The music was created by Ralf and Florian, but together with Karl and me they developed this intellectual and entertaining musical style. All this in strong interaction with technological themes; modern instruments and our distinctive, self-conscious attitude. That was our creed. Slowly I began to understand what we were going for, what we could achieve; and from that point on, I was more than pleased to be a humble part of it.

Outside View UK

ANDY MCCLUSKEY_I saw Kraftwerk in September 1975 at the Liverpool Empire. I was sat in Row Q, Seat 36; this is all burned into my head. I said it before and I'll say it again: This was the first day of the rest of my life.

RUSTY EGAN_All we ever knew of German music was the 'oom-pah' from Munich's October Festival; the music of the lederhosen-clad men in beer cellars. German music was either Hitler's ghastly marching music or Wagner; obviously all the stuff that you don't wanna talk about here.

ANDY MCCLUSKEY_I'd already heard of Tangerine Dream, who were also from Germany. I'd seen them play around the same time at the Liverpool Cathedral. That was quite a hippie fest. They all sat cross-legged on the floor wearing Afghan coats and smoking dope. People were running around with flares and long hair; longer than the hair, though, were the drum and guitar solos.

RUSTY EGAN_To me the Germans made cars and rockets. Mercedes and Messerschmitt were the names I knew before Kraftwerk.

ANDY MCCLUSKEY_Then along came these guys with their short, slick haircuts, and their neat suits and ties. The two in the middle played on some sort of tray with weird and wired 'knitting needles'. They used video projectors and had their names illuminated in neon. I'd never seen anything like it before. It was as if I was watching the moon landing; the whole presentation was so radically different and new, as if it was from another planet.

WOLFGANG SEIDEL_Inscrutable things, especially when new, can scare the hell out of people. Though later they will idolise you and praise you as the new messiah.

ANDY MCCLUSKEY_The concert wasn't sold out, not even a third full, but to me, a fresh-faced 16-year-old, it was just transformational. Something totally different. It was like: cancel history, this is day one of the new dawn.

CHRIS CROSS_As I was born in the UK, European music before the Seventies was seen as very, very uncool. American music dominated the airwaves. British radio didn't play any foreign language records except 'Je T'aime' by Serge Gainsbourg. Then all of a sudden it was actually exciting to hear German and French records; the mystery of a music from another land.

ANDY MCCLUSKEY_Each week I would go to Liverpool just to buy new records. I'd rummage through the import section in particular.

I'd discovered Kraftwerk and was now curious to see what else there was on offer – and that's how I found Neu!.

CHRIS CROSS_I'd already heard of Tangerine Dream, Amon Düül II, Can and various others. I'd go to the Roundhouse in London on the weekends where I would hear all of those bands. It was terrific. Most of all I liked Neu!, who instantly proclaimed the dawning of a new age. As Ultravox! we were immensely inspired by the art-school aspect of glam rock. Musically speaking, Ultravox! were the sons of Roxy Music, New York Dolls, David Bowie and later of Kraftwerk too; but the exclamation mark in our early band name was a direct reference to Neu!

PAUL HUMPHREYS_We liked The Velvet Underground, David Bowie, T. Rex, Roxy Music and Brian Eno. To us the sophisticated art school approach was really appealing, while our older brothers were still listening to either prog rock acts such as Genesis or Pink Floyd, or hard rock bands such as Deep Purple, Led Zeppelin and Black Sabbath.

CHRIS CROSS_The almost 'industrial work' system of Kraftwerk, with their fearless acceptance of simplicity, left a strong impression on us; we were totally inspired and full on.

GLENN GREGORY_We were into Roxy Music and David Bowie; we always listened again and again to Can and stuff like Atomic Rooster and Gong. We were young and easily led. Once, when I was 14, we went to see Gong live at Sheffield City Hall. We sat around and smoked dope; the fucking band were ambling around onstage, playing just a little bit and then walking away, but it was great and I used to love it. After that I was more drawn into glam rock. Roxy Music with 'Pyjamarama' did it for me, I really liked the song. Suddenly Brian Eno got a synth, and I was going, "Whoah – I am liking that; I am seeing that." So, to me, it kind of all started there.

WOLFGANG SEIDEL_Faust had already moved to England as early as 1973 and had signed a record deal there. Their album *The Faust Tapes* was a complete flop though, and this wasn't helped by the fact that the emerging Virgin label sold the entire album for the price of a single, at 48 pence. Despite this, quite soon afterwards Tangerine Dream and Klaus Schulze also signed with Virgin. Earlier that year Virgin boss Richard Branson had landed a tremendous coup in signing Mike Oldfield – the British version of the electronic maverick. For that reason the international potential of the German electronic musicians became recognised. Soon the tag 'Electronics made in Germany' became some sort of an unofficial quality control.

GLENN GREGORY_Listening to Faust was great. You put it on and mum and dad would freak out – which made it even more fun. Yes, finally I'd found something that they really hated. Faust or Neu! played loud was great. I'd think to myself: "Oh yah, I'm listening to music that my parents don't like!"

MARTYN WARE_Faust were a big influence for us. They once played in Sheffield, where they had onstage with them a pinball machine, a pneumatic drill and a piece of concrete, as well as a couple of mannequins and musical instruments... just a lot of weird stuff. Onstage they produced only noise and their singer shouted into the microphone. After about 15 minutes the audience had had enough; it was nothing like what was on their album. One guy broke up the concrete block with the pneumatic drill and then made the mistake of throwing a piece of it into the audience. He was totally spaced out. Finally the audience had enough. It was sad. The record was good, but their live performance was too different.

GLENN GREGORY_I remember that I almost got beaten up once because of 'Autobahn'. I went to a youth club, and there was this wannabe Hell's Angel; Big Mick was his name, who was playing 'Born To Be Wild' by Steppenwolf. I went over and replaced his record with 'Autobahn'... he then came along, took mine down and put his own back in place. I was just a skinny little kid, he was a real huge bloke, but despite that I went over and again replaced his record with mine. He said to me: "If you do that again, I'll smack you one in the face," so I went back over to the turntable, took away his record, accidentally scratched it – loud enough that you could hear the 'scraaaatch' through the speakers and then launched 'Autobahn' again, before running off. He probably knew he would not catch up with me, and as a result I made a huge impact on the music scene in my hometown of Sheffield.

DANIEL MILLER_I had heard of Kraftwerk before *Autobahn*, but their earlier material was not really my thing. What I actually liked most was the cover art; from their first albums too. The picture of the Kling Klang Studio was a great inspiration to me, as you could almost envisage what was coming. It was really only after *Autobahn* that I truly noticed them though.

MARTYN WARE_I had all the albums from Kraftwerk and Neu!, everything, including the early stuff. *Autobahn* was a huge hit in England, although at that time I was not one hundred percent sure about how to take it; I had not been completely grabbed yet. But *Radio-Activity* I liked very much; that convinced me.

ANDY MCCLUSKEY_*Autobahn* was a key moment; all teenagers are looking for something new that they could make their own. I was absolutely hooked.

DANIEL MILLER_I first came across the English cover of *Autobahn*. I liked that a lot. It looked so simple and so very iconic. In the end it was just a picture of the German motorway street sign. Although when I found out that the band had not actually wanted this cover – as in Germany they actually had an entirely different cover on the same album – I was truly shocked.

RUSTY EGAN_I first heard the *Ralf & Florian* album and I particularly liked the cover art, especially the back cover with its neon-lighted text. You could see the two of them sitting opposite each other in their studio. I got to know their set-up back to front: egg cartons on the ceiling, cabling everywhere and the guy on the right playing his flute. There was also a Minimoog and a Fifties-style lamp. It was such a perfect scene, with its staged ambience, you could tell it was some type of cryptic counter-proposal to the rock world.

MARTYN WARE_I listened to a lot of krautrock: Amon Düül, Can, Neu!, the usual suspects. I found it really interesting, although still quite hippie. For me the visual presentation of Kraftwerk was just as important as their music. Looking back I know that it was *Autobahn* that was like the birth certificate of electronic music.

DANIEL MILLER_Before hearing *Autobahn* I was actually really into drone music, especially that of Klaus Schulze and Cluster. It was *Autobahn* that showed me the potential of electronic music, with its humorous yet atmospheric approach. Despite what many think, Kraftwerk's music is full of emotion; emotion and also tradition. It's the perfect blend of romanticism with a look into the future.

COLIN NEWMAN_I'd already heard Kraftwerk by the time we'd started making music as Wire. In fact I'd heard a lot of German electronic music. The term 'krautrock' was naturally created by the media and was quite offensive towards the Germans, although it was useful.

MICHAEL ROTHER_I don't particularly like the term 'krautrock'. Nowadays it is no longer used in a derogatory fashion, but at the beginning there was certainly some ambiguity – sauerkrauts, Nazi Germany and so on. Thankfully this connection is less obvious these days, but the word itself used to be confusing and misleading back then.

COLIN NEWMAN_What did it mean to be labelled 'krautrock'? For me, it was a term for all those early German, electronic hippie bands; those guys with their synthesisers and long hair. Not really my cup of tea.

RUSTY EGAN_It was the driving rhythms that truly characterised krautrock; this forward-flowing beat that distinguished it from everything else. This inspired a lot of different people.

MICHAEL ROTHER_I have always been interested in creating this forward-striving sound; a fast-flowing, driving music that represents a dynamic movement.

COLIN NEWMAN_The only exception amongst the hippie bands was Can. Everyone liked Can, and similar to Neu! they used these repetitive beats too. Neu! was less well known though. When people heard them for the first time, they were always well-received because of their driving rhythms, I guess.

MICHAEL ROTHER_It was always my desire to be different; and then to be put in a drawer labelled 'krautrock' meant that I was being compared with others. I am a human being though, of course, and have many things in common with others; I'm not an alien, but as an artist I've always preferred to show off my differences.

COLIN NEWMAN_In the Seventies Kraftwerk were my favourite band. Their music was the soundtrack of my youth.

RUSTY EGAN_I was a drummer; I'd always wanted to play drums. I listened to all kinds of things, including Billy Cobham and the whole jazz-rock stuff. Everything! I played my paradiddles, triple paradiddles, racing back and forth across the whole kit. That was my style. And then along came a bunch of guys who would play a straight beat like *bum-cha-bum-bum-cha* with a pair of knitting needles and more importantly were singing in German. Now that was unheard of!

DANIEL MILLER_I was a fan of Neu!, even before Kraftwerk. I had cassettes of *NEU!* and *NEU! 2*. I really liked that repetitive rhythmic thing. Kraftwerk reinvented this in an electronic way.

RUSTY EGAN_I like German music, I like the European and especially the German approach. Kraftwerk looked German and this was quite provocative with their pure blue cover for *Autobahn* and their communistic red shirts and black ties. I mean, what the fuck? But that's exactly what I liked.

NIGEL HOUSE_For me Kraftwerk and Düsseldorf always went hand in hand. That much was clear. It was different for other groups though: I saw no obvious connections between Neu! and Düsseldorf for example.

RUSTY EGAN_I am from my innermost against the Third Reich and everything it stood for; that said I am an artist and look for creative inspiration in all things. Florian Schneider once explained to me that his father was an architect, and that led to a conversation about Albert Speer. I find Speer's architecture damn impressive, and as an artist that's okay to say. I like the creativity of Albert Speer, of Leni Riefenstahl, but of course I don't like people dying. What I'm trying to say is, that I am fully aware of German history, but that there are many things that came from Germany that were simply fantastic. Fritz Lang's film *Metropolis* for example – very German and very good. I've always had a keen interest in all things

German; whether that be Baader Meinhof, Rudolf Hess or Rainer Werner Fassbinder. I think just because Albert Speer's client was a little coo-coo, doesn't mean he wasn't a great architect.

Radio-Activity

DANIEL MILLER_From then on I always bought every Kraftwerk album as soon as it came out. I can still remember hearing *Radio-Activity* on the Alan Freeman show on Radio 1 before it was officially released. At first I had no idea who or what it was, but suddenly I realised, it was the new album. This is Kraftwerk.

ANDY MCCLUSKEY_Looking back it seems ironic to me that I first heard *Radio-Activity* on the radio, seeing as that was what the concept behind the album was: a certain radio activity. With this album, Kraftwerk wanted to thank all the college radio stations for promoting *Autobahn* in America.

PAUL HUMPHREYS_I'm sure that Andy would agree that although it was *Autobahn* that opened the door for us, it was actually *Radio-Activity* that was the most important record for us. I still listen to it today and I know every single note. I play it over and over and over again.

DANIEL MILLER_In my opinion *Radio-Activity* was conceptually more complete than *Autobahn*. It is arguably the most strictly themed Kraftwerk album.

ANDY MCCLUSKEY_*Radio-Activity* was inspired by both radio technology and nuclear power; it is about radio waves, antennas and transistors, as well as uranium, radioactivity and Geiger counters. To the listener it seemed as if the album had a double meaning – even the name of the title song seems quite ambiguous, referring to both the activity of radios as well as to the discoveries of Madame Curie.

PAUL HUMPHREYS_Andy and I both come from working class families with little money. Electronics had always been a hobby of mine since childhood; I was always tinkering with something or

123

other. Eventually we decided we wanted to be like Kraftwerk. We were kids. We heard Kraftwerk and thought that they were the future. Like Wolfgang I even built my own electronic drum kit. Had our band not have changed our life, I would for sure have become an engineer. It was through *Radio-Activity* that we were inspired to make electronic, futuristic music. We listened to that one album every day.

IGGY POP_I would fall asleep at night to the sound of 'Geiger Counter'.

ANDY MCCLUSKEY_We were naive enough to write songs called 'Electricity', 'Telegraph' and 'Messages'. We were the personification of, and the punky, simple, young answer to, *Radio-Activity*. We were everything we could be, with our trashy equipment, our personalities and our limited abilities.

RUSTY EGAN_All the English bands wanting to make electronic music too were strongly influenced by the German groups. All of them! Whether it be Soft Cell, OMD, The Human League, Heaven 17, Depeche Mode, Yazoo, Eurythmics or Visage; we were all fans of German music, especially Kraftwerk, but also La Düsseldorf, Michael Rother and Wolfgang Riechmann.

PAUL HUMPHREYS_Our song '4-Neu' was written as homage to Neu!. We wanted to highlight their considerable influence on us. It was released as the B-side to 'Genetic Engineering', which in turn was a tribute to Kraftwerk, with its repetitive vocoder voice.

ANDY MCCLUSKEY_Looking back Kraftwerk's impact is perhaps best evident with their *Radio-Activity* album, which was a huge success in France at the time and received gold status. There was nothing that sounded as beautifully futuristic and other-worldly as *Radio-Activity*. Nowadays it sounds so nostalgic, handmade, fragile and melancholic. In a strange way the reception of the same song can vary so much over time, and many times.

PAUL HUMPHREYS_At the risk of sounding quite old-fashioned: I truly loved the LP as an art form. There were some albums that you would hear as only one long track, you couldn't pick out the individual songs. Sometimes the songs that didn't grab you at first became your favourites. This could happen with Kraftwerk and also Bowie. Would you download the entire *Low* or *Heroes* album onto your iPod, or only the song 'Heroes'? It's the same with *Radio-Activity*.

ANDY MCCLUSKEY_Well, yeah, at some point John Peel played 'Silver Cloud' by La Düsseldorf, and I thought to myself: if that's from Düsseldorf it has to be interesting. That was another album we were totally in to.

PAUL HUMPHREYS_Despite our enthusiasm for Düsseldorf bands, it never occurred to us to copy their sound. OMD never sounded like Kraftwerk; we adopted only their approach as technicians, as engineers, as the independent anti-rock stars that they were.

ANDY MCCLUSKEY_I had little idea about the background or history, but I began to develop a serious interest in German music. Düsseldorf was the Mecca of electronic music; the Holy Grail. We bow down to Düsseldorf. We salute you.

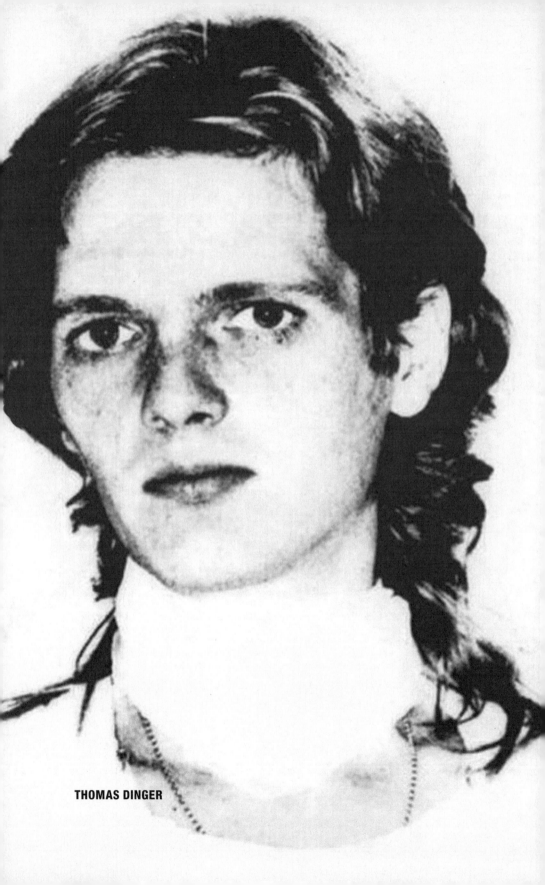

THOMAS DINGER

++ **JAN 76** Bowie releases *Station To Station* ++ **FEB 76** Kraftwerk release 'Radioactivity' single ++ La Düsseldorf release self-titled debut ++ **APR 76** Bowie appears live in the Düsseldorf Philipshalle ++ **JULY 76** The Ramones perform live at London's Roundhouse ++ **JUN–SEP 76** Michael Rother records *Flammende Herzen* with Conny Plank ++ **OCT 76** Kraftwerk perform live at London's Roundhouse ++ **NOV–DEC 76** Kraftwerk start work on *Trans Europa Express* album in their Kling Klang Studio ++

Bowie

RALF DÖRPER_ When Bowie was touring *Station To Station* he had one complete side of *Radio-Activity* played over the PA at full volume as a kind of support act, before taking the stage. Bowie was very impressed by the Düsseldorf quartet although they weren't at all interested in being his opening act on the European tour. Nevertheless, Bowie played the songs of Kraftwerk as loud as possible over the speakers. His worship of Kraftwerk proved to be an enormous career boost for them.

JÜRGEN ENGLER_ At my first Bowie concert in April 76 he had Kraftwerk played over the speakers before the show; at the same time he screened *Un Chien Andalou*, a silent surrealist short film by Luis Buñuel and Salvador Dalí, featuring a scene in which a woman has her eye slit open with a razor.

RALF DÖRPER_ When Bowie had *Radio-Activity* played at his concerts thousands of people heard the sounds of their Düsseldorf home town: Kraftwerk. At that time though, Kraftwerk, as electronic music missionaries in their own country, played only the smaller venues that didn't sell out.

JÜRGEN ENGLER_Back then it was rare for a concert to sell out, and that goes for Bowie too. For The Who or Kiss no problem, the room would be packed, but not for Bowie.

RALF DÖRPER_Sure, in October 75 The Who sold out both their shows. In the Seventies Düsseldorf was a regular fixture for many of the touring international top acts; alternatively there was the Grugahalle in Essen. As such, we got the chance to see many concerts from the likes of Bowie, Lou Reed and early Roxy Music. For all of us it was the analogue sounds triggered live by The Who on their Moog in 'Baba O'Riley' or 'Won't Get Fooled Again', or by Keith Emerson, who would stab his Minimoog with his stiletto; that really got our attention – they were our prehistoric inspirations. It was incredible to experience the sheer power of these synthesiser sounds live in concert, from bands who showed off their volume.

JÄKI ELDORADO_In 76 the punk rock scene started and at the beginning everything was totally weird and completely silly. That was a good thing! That was what it was all about! At first people in Berlin were only listening to Iggy Pop and David Bowie. That was the soundtrack to Berlin's Bahnhof Zoo, particularly Bowie's *Station To Station*.

WOLFGANG FLÜR_It was Bowie's dream to tour with us as his supporting act. Ralf and Florian refused though; they said we were too independent to do that.

JÄKI ELDORADO_One could, for example, go to the Sound discotheque where Christiane F. usually hung out and listen to the hard, neurotic funk of Bowie's new album *Station To Station*; the first single 'Golden Years', for example. Unfortunately I never got to see Bowie perform live, but I saw him at night at the disco, when he was fully switched on and alive.

WOLFGANG FLÜR_We wanted to see one of Bowie's concerts and decided on his show in Frankfurt. We drove down to the Frankfurt Festhalle in Florian's black Mercedes 600, taking it in turns behind the wheel – at least Ralf, Florian and I did; Karl didn't particularly like driving and nor was he particularly good at it. Florian had purchased a used Mercedes 600 Pullman – the same model was used by the Pope – while Ralf was still stuck with his grey VW Beetle. Ralf was always a cautious, graceful driver while Florian was much more reckless.

JÄKI ELDORADO_That was exactly the way the Thin White Duke preferred travelling from town to town: in his black Mercedes 600 limousine. During the longer car trips he would listen to the sounds of *Autobahn*. He'd become way too paranoid for air travel; and as well as his paranoia he couldn't go for too long without his staple diet of cocaine, milk and cigarettes.

WOLFGANG FLÜR_He was the Thin White Duke and it was his White Light tour that we saw. His band wore black suits and white shirts. Bowie himself also appeared in an elegant black and white outfit, with white shirt, black suit pants and a matching vest, complete with his slicked back hair. The stage set-up was particularly eye-catching, and as the tour name suggested, featured only white light – there was not a single coloured spotlight to be seen.

JÄKI ELDORADO_After the deep crisis of a failed marriage, a bummed-out Bowie arrived in Berlin Schöneberg in the late summer of 76. His plan was to kick his cocaine habit by relocating; little did he know, though, that at that time Berlin was the cocaine capital. Together with Iggy he lived at Hauptstraße 155. At night they would get high and go to parties; during the day they had to go down to the studio, to work with Visconti, Fripp and Eno at Hansa by the Wall.

WOLFGANG FLÜR_Bowie came to Düsseldorf twice, to meet with Ralf and Florian. Although unfortunately a collaboration never happened.

IGGY POP_When I was with David in Düsseldorf we wanted to meet up with Kraftwerk; David desperately needed some sleep though, so he sent me along alone instead. I met Florian who suggested we go to the Carlsplatz market, as it was asparagus season. So I went asparagus shopping with Florian Schneider-Esleben. How great is that? We had a nice time.

WOLFGANG FLÜR_Before deciding on the Hansa Studio, Eno visited the Plank Studios together with David Bowie. He had several projects in mind when he had visited Plank. Christa, Conny's wife, told me that Brian Eno was a really down-to-earth type of guy. During his productions he lived with them, helping out in the kitchen in his apron, peeling potatoes and whatnot. As soon as a journalist appeared, though, he would flip the 'professionalism switch', replacing his apron with a cosmopolitan façade, and off to a side room he would go to give his interviews. As soon as the journalists were gone, the apron would reappear and he would continue peeling his vegetables.

HANS LAMPE_Brian Eno came over to check out the whole set-up, but he didn't even make it through the door at La Düsseldorf and Neu!. Nor did he make it to Kraftwerk; only Harmonia allowed him to join them in the Weser Uplands. He obviously drew a lot of inspiration from those guys, as evident in the music he made after his visit. We thought he'd incorporated much of what he'd heard in the Weserbergland into his own music, stuff which actually came from Moebius, Roedelius and Rother. Eno had had a good look at what they were doing and made some of it his own.

EBERHARD KRANEMANN_I preferred Brian Eno over Bowie, and back then he was often to be found in Conny's studio. He was a modest, reserved individual. When not recording he would often cycle around Conny's farmyard on a small children's bike, dressed carelessly in his far too narrow and worn out Adidas sweatpants.

ROEDELIUS_We met Eno in 1974 after a Harmonia concert in Hamburg where he jammed with us spontaneously. We knew him from his time with Roxy Music and were impressed with his early solo work, so we invited him to visit us in Forst. Two years later he took us up on our invitation, and we made the *Harmonia & Eno* album together.

EBERHARD KRANEMANN_Looking back I view the visits by those two to Conny's studio in a much different light. In my opinion it was a form of industrial espionage. Sounds and methods that they had learnt from Conny were later incorporated into their records and transformed into money.

ROEDELIUS_Brian Eno was only a temporary guest of ours, when he joined us for the production work. He'd also stayed with Conny for a week while we recorded both our albums, *Cluster & Eno* and

After The Heat. He came to Forst only once; well before he became as famous as he is today. Whilst with us he shared his expertise, enthusiasm and his views of his ideal world. He showed himself to be a sympathetic and caring individual.

MICHAEL ROTHER_In the autumn of 1976 Brian Eno visited Harmonia in the Weser Uplands. From there he travelled further to Berlin where he teamed up with David Bowie to record *Heroes*. The next day the phone rang: an employee of Bowie asking if I would be interested in working on his new album. I agreed, but as a favour asked if Bowie could give me a call personally. The next morning I actually got a call from him. We got along well and I accepted his invitation. Later, however, I got a call from Bowie's management who told me he had supposedly changed his mind and there would be no collaboration.

ROEDELIUS_I think what fascinated Bowie most was the independence, the authentic approach, and above all the fact that it didn't have any Anglo-American flavour.

MICHAEL ROTHER_There was a fear that sales would slump, that my contribution to Bowie's sound might be too experimental and thus unsellable. An employee of Bowie's told me he'd cancelled the meeting; Bowie was told I had.

ROEDELIUS_The only one of us ever invited to be a guest performer was Michael. For some reason, though, he was too shy I think, and as such he missed out on his big chance.

HANS LAMPE_Rother's role in *Heroes* was assumed by Robert Fripp of King Crimson. Fripp was such a nutty intellectual guy; he was dubbed the 'Mr Spock of Rock' by the music press. When you know, though, that it was actually Michael who was initially invited to the recordings of *Heroes* you will immediately recognise the similarities between his style and the guitar work of Fripp: the same long, drawn-out atmospheric sound. I was always pleased that Bowie never made a secret of the fact that the inspiration for his album title came from our song 'Hero'.

WOLFGANG FLUR_The track 'V2 Schneider' was a direct allusion to us, to Kraftwerk, and more specifically to Florian, with whom he got along best. The V2 was a rocket developed by Wernher von Braun during the war which was launched against London. That's what this piece is naturally about – German history and Florian Schneider, whose name Bowie sings very detached through a vocoder: "Vee-Too-Shnye-Dah…"

Role Models

RALF DÖRPER_As a teenager Kraftwerk were of little interest to me; I was more into Alice Cooper and David Bowie. Instead of 'Morgenspaziergang' or 'Kometenmelodie' I preferred listening to 'School's Out', 'I'm Eighteen' and 'No More Mr Nice Guy'.

JÄKI ELDORADO_It was the same for me; glam rock was the most appealing style. I remember eighth or ninth grade, being on school exchange to England, hearing David Bowie's 'Life On Mars' from *Space Oddity*, with loose-fitting velvet trousers and so on. This was quite distressing for my father who was forced to buy me high-heeled shoes; although in this case he then ordered only the cheapest ones.

JÜRGEN ENGLER_I first started listening to Bowie and Roxy Music. My theory is: everyone born before 1960 grew up totally hippie and Woodstock-inspired. Everybody had a background in Hendrix or other guitar gods and wore their hair from head to toe. For us it was easier to hear these new sounds, as we didn't have to give up a former musical identity.

JÄKI ELDORADO_I never had long hair, for that my hippie period was too short. After buying the first Roxy Music album, all I listened to was either glam rock or electronic stuff. I had records of Kraftwerk, Schulze, Tangerine Dream, and Eno's earlier albums, such as *Taking Tiger Mountain* and *No Pussyfooting*. Oh yeah, and I was a member of the Sparks Fan Club. So, yes, if it had to be glam, then please, at least something a little more witty.

WOLFGANG SEIDEL_Glam was the glitzy farewell to the Sixties and heralded the arrival of the fun culture of the Seventies; it was the transition from hippie to punk.

GABI DELGADO_When I was 15, young people defined themselves through music. Some bought the new Pink Floyd album, others Deep Purple – it all depended on the social group you belonged to. It was a statement; a statement about yourself. For me, I was more interested in film and literature, even as a child. I knew who Luis Buñuel was, well before I had ever heard of Tangerine Dream or ELP.

JÄKI ELDORADO_Emerson, Lake & Palmer – what a terrible band! I actually saw them live at the Berlin Philharmie. My parents said: "If that's the way to get young people listening to classical music – well go ahead then."

GABI DELGADO_Many of the rebellious guys at school tagged their Latin books with emblems of the local football clubs such as BVB and 1. FC Köln, as well as T. Rex or the RAF logo; and that would be Red Army Faction not Royal Air Force. At 14, 15, we thought it was pretty cool.

ROBERT GÖRL_I was into Cream and Zappa, Hendrix, The Who – I kind of liked these bands. I was a big fan of Ginger Baker. That was during my rock phase; I was a real rocker. We covered a lot of their songs, rehearsing in a Second World War bunker in Munich where I used to drum day and night. 'White Room' by Cream, all of that stuff. We were 14 years old.

KURT DAHLKE_Wolla Spelmans was listening to Taj Mahal, I to Brian Eno, Michael Kemner... who knows, most likely a crude mixture of everything; and Frank had his beloved jazz records.

FRANK FENSTERMACHER_Well, for me it all started with the blues, the British blues like John Mayall; that was the first record I had. From that I quickly discovered jazz, the Afro-jazz of the Sixties. Heavyweight saxophonists such as Keith Fergus, Pharoah Sanders, John Coltrane, Archie Shepp – I for sure still have all my Impulse records.

BERNWARD MALAKA_I started listening to records around the time 'Autobahn' was released. I bought the seven-inch. That was the only German hit that was not played on the Schlagerhitparade, the German pop charts. Typically pop music was always too loud for my grandparents: "Turn that music down", they would say. That said, 'Autobahn' was fantastic; perhaps because of the German lyrics, which they could obviously understand and relate to.

RALF DÖRPER_I can still remember the context in which I first heard 'Ruckzuck'. At the time we did not have a record player, but we did have a Grundig or Telefunken tape recorder. With that I would record songs off the radio. One radio show worth listening to was the more progressive *Radiothek* on WDR, because it avoided the annoying habit of fading songs out. I remember presenter Winfrid Trenkler playing three songs in a row and only then giving their names. That was fantastic. The piece that really appealed most to me was Kraftwerk's 'Ruckzuck'. I was electrified. Those names fitted perfectly together: Ruckzuck and Kraftwerk.

GABI DELGADO_At that time it was common practice, recording good records onto compact cassette. You would lie in wait for something cool and then record it directly off of the John Peel sessions. There, little has changed, music has always been copied. Nowadays it's easier yet no different from before. I'm no big fan of copyrights, I'm more in favour of a copyleft!

MEIKEL CLAUSS_It's Kraftwerk that has proved the most influential on today's music, and not rhythm and blues or anything else; but we didn't know that then. We were wary of the other groups as well: Amon Düül, Can and Neu!; but we thought long hair looked terrible. For us krautrock was always a dirty word. What we didn't understand, though, was the position krautrock held worldwide. It was basically Germany's 'birth of cool', but still no one gets this.

JÜRGEN ENGLER_I've got nothing to say against long hair in general, although there are different ways of wearing it. I would never compare Novalis with Guru Guru for example, Can with Flaming Bess and nor Jane with Neu!; although all had long hair.

MEIKEL CLAUSS_At that time Kraftwerk had not achieved the status they hold today. In comparison Can had always been cooler. With 'Spoon' they had written a Durbridge thriller theme song that became a hit. Their hypnotic hippie stuff was becoming more and more popular. Kraftwerk had to undergo several transformations before they slowly became what they are today: Kraftwerk.

JÜRGEN ENGLER_Cluster and early Popol Vuh – those are the true electronic bands. For me Cluster are one of the most important electronic bands that ever existed. The first three LPs, *Cluster 71*, *Cluster II* and *Zuckerzeit* are incredible; they were certainly a massive leap forward.

MEIKEL CLAUSS_I've always said that it was probably Cluster who had the greatest worldwide influence, through their work with Eno and all the others that heavily borrowed from them. Everybody was thinking, okay, here is this small band from Germany that has created something, that if copied, will have people worshipping us, kissing our feet. And all because they were so unknown back then.

BERNWARD MALAKA_For me it was the German words more than the electronic instrumentation that I thought was special about 'Autobahn'. There were other German songs of course: schlager songs, but all those had ridiculous, corny lyrics. Kraftwerk were the complete opposite.

JÜRGEN ENGLER_Talking of schlager, Kurt once told me, that for him it was 'Der Computer Nr. 3' by France Gall that was his earliest contact with electronic music.

KURT DAHLKE_The first single I ever bought myself, back in 1968 at the tender age of 10, was 'Computer Nr. 3' by France Gall. This song had come third in the German schlager song contest and I just couldn't get it out of my head. "The Computer No. 3 is looking for the right boy for me" were the words of the chorus, and this line was answered by some computer animated voice giving the details for a potential rendezvous. It sounded futuristic and came six years before 'Autobahn'... but please don't tell me it was of any influence on Hütter.

JÜRGEN ENGLER_I also had a similar close encounter of the third kind, but with Daisy Door and her song 'Du Lebst In Deiner Welt'. The chorus was underlaid with some fantastic Moog synth; I found that simply electrifying. It was a recording done by the Peter

Thomas Sound Orchestra who had also done the theme tune for *Space Patrol – The Fantastic Adventures Of The Spaceship Orion.*

KURT DAHLKE_To me it was logical: music and computers, that's my kind of thing. Oh yeah, and singer Dorthe had just achieved second place in the German schlager song contest with 'Wärst Du Doch In Düsseldorf Geblieben'.

RALF DÖRPER_Television and science fiction films played an important role in the development of electronic music; in fact that was where the first electronic sounds were actually used. Paul Humphreys and Martyn Ware have both spoken of the influence of the legendary Delia Derbyshire on them and her sounds created for the English sci-fi TV series *Doctor Who.* In the Sixties it was via such media that a wider audience was exposed to these avant-garde sound creations. The German movie *Space Patrol Orion* featured the spacey-sounding jazz of Peter Thomas, which although sounding futuristic, was actually played on conventional instrumentation.

MARTYN WARE_In England it was via the BBC and their tradition of radio plays that mainstream audiences were exposed to a wider range of electronically generated sounds. Even back then in the nerdy electronic music history there were some influential women musicians: Daphne Oram, Delia Derbyshire, Ruth White, Eliane Radigue, Teresa Rampazzi, Bebe Barron and Pauline Oliveros. As a rule of thumb, the further away from pop music you went, the more likely it was you'd find women in the driving seat. In fact it was because of the war that there were many women in positions of authority that would have otherwise been unavailable to them.

BERNWARD MALAKA_To make the most significant impact with electronic music you had to combine it in some way with classical music. Walter Carlos, for example, performed Bach on a giant Moog Modular System. Bach was much loved, probably because he had something mechanical, mathematical about him. In that regard he was a good fit.

RAINER ZICKE_*Switched-On Bach* was the name of this record, but these days I would describe it more as an experiment or showcase of electronic instrumentation more than anything else. Walter Carlos was a sound engineer and had his own huge modular system made especially for him by Dr Robert Moog. Professional sound engineers from the Fifties and Sixties had to have a classical foundation in music, which is why Carlos was such a good performer and not simply just a good technician. Seeing as Bach himself had such a technical approach to music it seemed to make sense to reproduce his work using modern, electronic sounds and technologies. As I say, it's more of an experiment and doesn't aim to devalue Bach at all; it's a presentation of a new product and provides audible evidence that these 'monsters' could be used for music and not just artistic sounds. Using Bach was a good way of appealing to a larger audience. Recorded in 1968 by Carlos, *Switched-On Bach* is genuinely one of the earlier electronic records.

JÄKI ELDORADO_On my way home from school I would pass a library. There I would go to borrow records, mostly odd stuff like Walter Carlos' *Brandenburg Concertos* or Gong. They also had the soundtrack to *A Clockwork Orange*, which featured these cool, early analogue synth sounds. Within the movie, lead character Alex-boy is in seventeenth heaven when listening to the sound of Beethoven and Wendy Carlos. My God, how often have I seen this movie?

MARTYN WARE_This soundtrack changed my life. Wendy Carlos created a completely electronic score for this magnificent Stanley Kubrick film. The Moog-driven beauty of the arrangements still mesmerises me to this day

BERNWARD MALAKA_The *Clockwork Orange* soundtrack featured only classical and electronic music and it is only now that I fully appreciate the true influence of cinema. People were encouraged to head along to the independent cinemas; alongside the records that you had to have there were also the movies that you had to have seen. The better ones every single week.

RALF DÖRPER_Before Carpenter or Lynch there was of course Kubrick and his *A Clockwork Orange*, with its great and influential soundtrack provided by Walter, and then later Wendy Carlos, before his sex change he was known as Walter.

La Düsseldorf

KLAUS DINGER_La Düsseldorf was the continuation of Neu!. This time, though, we were no longer purely instrumental but instead had our own text, a clearer statement, our own tonality and, all in all, a more unique sound. The structure of the music was much more structured and composed, with very little left to chance, even if that can be both positive and negative.

HANS LAMPE_The difference between Neu! and La Düsseldorf was that the latter was much more rocky, more concise and catchier. The music was much more structured and included lyrics.

KLAUS DINGER_Naturally the first album is always the most difficult. Maybe we weren't coming from nowhere – I mean we'd been playing as Neu! for some time – but from close to nowhere. And if you try too hard to create something completely new it can be doubly as hard to establish yourself. Ultimately one should just judge the music. Side A of our debut album is made of two tracks: the first, which is particularly long, is called 'Düsseldorf'; the second one is 'La Düsseldorf'.

HANS LAMPE_The reference to the city of Düsseldorf in our band name was definitely Klaus' idea. From our very first song we made it clear what we were about: "Düsseldorf, you are our home, our home on the River Rhine. Düsseldorf, Du bist unsere Heimat, unsere Heimat am Rhein." That was our idea: Who are we? Where do we come from? We're Düsseldorf guys. So why not make a record about it and call the group exactly that?

KLAUS DINGER_Initially I wanted the project to be simply called 'Düsseldorf' but we couldn't trademark that. And 'La' was somehow a symbol of that blend of art, advertising and fashion that existed in Düsseldorf. It actually makes a lot of sense that we came up with the 'La'. The 'La' comes from our attitude towards life. The 'La' makes Düsseldorf even more beautiful than it already is.

HANS LAMPE_Well, Klaus' initial idea was to name the band 1a Düsseldorf, 'cause 1A in German is the same as A+ in English; but if you type '1a' onto an old typewriter it looks like 'la' and so our name read as 'La Düsseldorf'. And there it was: 'La Düsseldorf'. But why should we go with 'La Düsseldorf'? A few people read it aloud, which got us thinking about it. Why not 'La Düsseldorf'? '1a' would somehow have been so typically German sounding, like '1a Liver Wurst' or '1a Mercedes'. This 'La', on the other hand, was something more feminine. So we stuck with it.

DIRK FLADER_ The 'La' came partly from 'voilà' and was thought to suggest something more French.

HANS LAMPE_ We thought about what was characteristic of Düsseldorf at this time: art, advertising, trade fairs, fashion and then later the music scene. Düsseldorf had the largest fashion trade fair in the world as well as many pretty women: models, just like in the song by Kraftwerk. Düsseldorf has always been described as a 'Little Paris'. In this respect we were very happy with La Düsseldorf as our name. '1a Düsseldorf' would have been too exact, too angular, too Kraftwerk-like, and not rounded enough – and La Düsseldorf should be rounded at the edges.

DIRK FLADER_Düsseldorf was the silver lining on the Ruhr district; with the Königsallee and Hofgarten it left quite a noble and polished impression.

HANS LAMPE_ That's why 'Spiegelglas und Edelstahl', meaning 'mirror glass and stainless steel', summed it up really well. Düsseldorf had only few of the darker corners that are commonly found in the cities of the Ruhr district, like in Essen, Bottrop or Gelsenkirchen. You just wouldn't find these places in Düsseldorf. From the way the bridges cross the Rhine to the Rhine Stadium, all these places are referenced in our song: "Ah Düsseldorf, La Düsseldorf/Gold'ne Brücke, stolze Schwäne/Gold'ne Brücke, stolze Schwäne/Düsseldorf am Rhein" (Ah Düsseldorf, La Düsseldorf/Golden bridges, proud swans/Golden bridges, proud swans/Düsseldorf on the Rhine"). All of which is still prevalent today: Spiegelglas und Edelstahl represent the Mannesmann and Rheinmetall corporations. Okay, so Mannesmann is nowadays Vodafone, but Rheinmetall still exists, right? It was important for

HANS LAMPE

us that these references were made on our debut album, or more precisely it was important for Klaus. This reference to home was important.

KLAUS DINGER_The good thing about Düsseldorf is that it doesn't take long at all for you to get to the greenery. In three minutes you can go from the airport to the River Rhine; to the beautiful Lower Rhine Valley where you will see nothing of the industrial surroundings.

HANS LAMPE_The Thyssen skyscraper, referred to locally as the Dreischeibenhaus, the house of three layers, was deliberately chosen and immortalised on the back cover of our first album, as it perfectly symbolised Düsseldorf's modernism. And that together with the airport on the front side! The Düsseldorf airport was very different to Cologne-Bonn, which was more of a provincial airport; the entire air traffic of NRW went through Düsseldorf. As such this created a jet-setter, metropolitan atmosphere. Our aim was to take this and transfer it into words and music.

JÄKI ELDORADO_Düsseldorf was a great town back then and when you look at the correlation between the jet-setters and all the possibilities on offer thanks to its new elegance, then you can understand how it was. Jet set was just a phrase to get out of the narrow-mindedness of this stuffy post-war Germany. To dress chic and to deny WW2 depressions was a defining moment that, to give you a perfect example, you could find vividly in Düsseldorf.

HANS LAMPE_The album cover photo of the airport was taken by Heinz Dinger, the father of the two brothers. Klaus told him to "take a photo of the airport" and so it was that he set off in the late evening with his camera stand and whatever else he had and took the picture. I think that's brilliant, that division of labour within the family, where the father is sent to shoot the album cover. Brilliant cover; respectable and not too pushy. Thirty years later and it's still a nice cover. It fits together so well. The text font, for example, was originally developed by Achim Duchow and Thomas then revised it. After that it was then simplified by Tina Schneider-Esleben. Initially Klaus did not like the way it came out because there was a minor printing error on it. It had a small misprinted triangle fudged between the La Düsseldorf logo as well as the 'o' in La Düsseldorf being printed as a dot. I said, "But Klaus, this is exactly what we want to have! This is unique, the un-imitable!" And so we decided to release it like that. Which is why it's on the cover now.

Klaus and Thomas

DIRK FLADER_La Düsseldorf were the two Dinger brothers together with Hans; with Klaus as their managing director. It was like Thomas used to say: "I can't talk right now, Mr Director is on his way."

KLAUS IMMIG_Klaus felt fully entitled to be the CEO of the La Düsseldorf company and this division of labour worked well. He assigned different tasks to the others: Hans was the driver, Thomas was in charge of visuals and Klaus was simply the boss.

DIRK FLADER_Klaus was not born in Düsseldorf, his parents had moved here for work when he was still young. Previously they had lived in Scherfede, a small town in Westfalia. Thomas, though, was born in Düsseldorf in 1952 and Hans is from Hamburg. Because of his formal and correct manners they used to call him 'the accountant'.

HANS LAMPE_Every one of us signed the record contracts so it was sealed and official: Thomas, Hans and Klaus were La Düsseldorf. Full stop. End. It was the three of us together, and we each had our own role to play. Yes we had guest musicians and a little help from others, namely Conny, but in the end it really was just the three of us.

KLAUS DINGER_We didn't have the usual type of a record deal, we didn't have a fixed due date for every album; we just had a contract for three albums with no defined time frame. Everything we did we did ourselves. We had no management, no roadies and we talked to the record company only when urgently necessary.

DIRK FLADER_ Thomas was a very visual person, and the physical appearance that became a defining characteristic of La Düsseldorf, that was all Thomas' doing. He was a trained window dresser.

HANS LAMPE_ That was the great thing about us as a group: we each had our complementary strengths. Thanks to my technical training and my experience with Conny, the recording side of things was taken care of. Thomas looked after everything visual – from the artistic design to our outfits. And Klaus, well he was in charge of everything. He adopted the pseudonym Nikolaus van Rhein and as such he became our phantom keyboardist. He always had a very complex or split personality and he thought he could play different roles on the same album, which was fine with me.

MÂRI PAAS_ Amongst the La Düsseldorf guys Thomas was easily the most flamboyant. He'd worked as an apprentice window dresser as well as a model-builder in an architects office. He enjoyed that in particular and was very good at it – crafting and decorating that is. He decorated his garden and studio, his house as well as himself. He was well known in the scene, and was often out and about in the town – more so than Klaus and Hans ever were – and because of that, he contributed a lot to La Düsseldorf's public image. Thomas always dressed very extravagantly, although more punk than hippie. Or perhaps somewhere inbetween, with a lot of white, a lot of pink and a lot of silk. He even went around in his grandmother's blouses and furs; other than that the majority of his clothes came from flea markets. He had freckles and dyed blond or red, long hair; I actually don't know his natural colour.

JÄKI ELDORADO_ And then suddenly there was pre-punk, only we didn't know that. During this transitional period we were all about the clothing, about trying things out, about expressing ourselves in different ways and searching for new things. Berlin wasn't for the rockers; in fact it was more gay than rocky. Yeah, that's it: Berlin was always about the flamboyance and decadence. Düsseldorf was more interested in fashion, about looking chic. Both scenes were great though, and both were Bowie-esque. Along the Haupstraße in Berlin you had the gay cafés, the Café Anderes Ufer, where we used to hang out. Bowie would go there too; he lived only two doors down. And then punk kicked off.

MEIKEL CLAUSS_Absolutely. Berlin was the total opposite. It was the home of the drifters and the freaks. Leftist slogans covered the walls, and poorly dressed guys hung out in the dreary pubs – it was desolate, decadent and gloomy.

JÄKI ELDORADO_When you think about Düsseldorf quite a few clichés quickly spring to mind: the Rhine, the Old Town, Carnival, Krupp and Thyssen, Japanese culture, fashion, advertising, money. Elegance and sophistication, industry and villas in beautiful suburbs. Above all though: it had to be très chic.

MEIKEL CLAUSS_While some were snorting coke or smoking joints, others were drinking champagne. Everything was very exclusive, very decadent and a bit porn-style, in the direction of The Velvet Underground. Charles Wilp sometimes referred to Düsseldorf as 'Dazzledorf' because that's exactly what it was like, dazzling. People were taking drugs, then there was the glamour scene; it was all very cool. People were dressed up in white overalls; everything was either silver or white. Because of the airport and the fashion shows Düsseldorf had the by far coolest scene. 'Dazzledorf' would also have been a great name for La Düsseldorf, as it was this 'dazzling' mood that they tried to convey through their music.

KLAUS IMMIG_To me La Düsseldorf was always a bit too kitsch, especially considering how much I loved the cool Neu! stuff. La Düsseldorf sounded too cheesy and sometimes too poppy; I found Neu! much more innovative.

DIRK FLADER_During their entire career La Düsseldorf did not appear live at all. They were purely a studio project; apart from Blauer See, which was more an introduction for them than anything else, they never played live. Basically La Düsseldorf were Neu! 75 minus Michael Rother. Who knows what Klaus was thinking.

KLAUS DINGER_I am proud of every La Düsseldorf record. Even from a lyrical point of view they are much more concrete than what came before. Above all, though, they sounded good. What didn't work was playing live, but that had never been a problem before. We didn't want to perform with guest musicians; we didn't like that too much, it would have felt like renting a bassist and guitarist. For me, music making was a very personal thing, an intimate experience. Further, I think the understanding that the three of us had for one another provided a perfect musical basis for us. Much more intensive than working with hired hands.

MÂRI PAAS_Klaus was not really a great team player. It all depended on the people he worked with, and on his mood. I could tell you stories about his moods; we were a couple for nearly 20 years.

KLAUS DINGER_Had we done this in a more Hollywood kind of way then we would have handled everything much more professionally. But back then it wasn't that easy and La Düsseldorf was a controversial concept from the start. Without performing live you couldn't make it big; that's what everybody thought anyway. But I proved them wrong.

MÂRI PAAS_Klaus was an artist through and through. To him expression was everything, even if there wasn't a positive reception. He would send mixed messages though. On the one hand, he didn't care what you thought of him; his opinion was: "They can all kiss my ass, they're all stupid." On the other, he liked to be surrounded by people who idolised him and he would occupy them for hours and hours with endless monologues. He looked like some sort of guru, and felt like the reincarnation of Vito Corleone from *The Godfather*, his favourite book.

GERHARD MICHEL_To Klaus Dinger art was a combination of blood and sweat. According to Klaus it was these two things that defined an artist. 'Art through pain' was the credo; he was like the Joseph Beuys of music. One had to pass through a valley of tears to reach success. That was what Klaus believed. Blood, sweat and tears were the terms and pictures that he preached, mumbling over and over again his mantra: "There's gonna to be tears and teeth-grinding!"

KLAUS IMMIG_ "Mr Dictator is coming" – that's what we always said jokingly; from time to time Klaus' martial behaviour could really get on your nerves. But, hey, I don't know, perhaps that's okay, I guess.

GERHARD MICHEL_ It was the younger brother who got away with everything. As the first born, Klaus was ridden hard by his parents while his brother Thomas was more pampered. That was probably why the two brothers didn't see eye to eye later on; Klaus stood for austerity, Thomas was more laissez-faire. Maybe it was because Klaus wanted to get back at Thomas, who had always gotten away with much more at home. Klaus didn't become who he was because of the day he was born – he was Aries – but because his parents wanted to make a real Dinger out of him. He was disciplined hard.

MÂRI PAAS_ Thomas was the more calm and level-headed of the two; a little androgynous, very creative of course, but also very vain. Both of them were incredibly narcissistic – Thomas would always say he was the most handsome boy in town and he actually meant it that way.

DIRK FLADER_ Thomas was always more likeable than Klaus, more likeable and more drunk.

GERHARD MICHEL_ Klaus often told me that as a young boy he used to be locked up in the basement; that was something he never forgot. He was brought up by his mother; his father was working six days a week and was rarely at home. He held a position as some managing director at a larger company in Düsseldorf. From the outside his parents seemed very friendly, you could get along well with them really well; maybe a little simple. Mrs Renate Dinger was always particularly interested in culture though. What do I mean by 'was'? She survived them all – her husband, her sons. And even today she is living in an old people's home in Düsseldorf-Derendorf.

KLAUS DINGER_ Anyway, when you shoot yourself in the foot things start to fall apart; yeah, that's one of our hard-learned truths. Suddenly successful, suddenly money is coming in, unbelievable. But to keep both feet on the ground when you're on this path is not so easy.

Silver Cloud

HANS LAMPE_When I returned to Düsseldorf in May or June 1976, there were suddenly two drum kits standing there; he'd been practising with Thomas. The foundation for the song 'Düsseldorf' came from the fact that he wanted a longer piece in which he was able to play the guitar while at the same time experiment with some different structures. He never just sat down and said: 'Okay, I will play these three chords'. Instead he thought in blocks of bars: four blocks, eight blocks, eight by eight, four by four. The piece ended up being 13 minutes long. Thomas provided the rhythm and together we came up with the text.

GERHARD MICHEL_Previously Klaus had always had Conny Plank; now he was working with Hans Lampe. Hans was a sound engineer Klaus had recruited from Conny. Although Klaus is listed as the official producer of their records, Hans was actually the one who could operate all of the production equipment. It was as Klaus said: "With Hans Lampe, naturally I thought I had the perfect Conny substitute in the studio." According to Klaus it was a very deliberate step towards making La Düsseldorf more commercially successful, which is exactly what they wanted as the instrumental music of Neu! never made much money.

HANS LAMPE_At this time we still maintained our regular jobs, or at the very least I did. I worked at Barth corporation in Hamburg, which meant I earned enough to stay afloat whilst still having enough for new equipment, such as our Revox A-77 tape recorder. While I was doing that, Klaus was taking music and guitar lessons at the community college and Thomas was working at the architect offices of Pfeiffer & Voss on Augusta Street.

GERHARD MICHEL_I would be one of the few who actually saw Dinger playing drums. Later on he refused to even get behind the kit, despite it being his drumming that made him famous. He taught his younger brother Thomas how to play drums and brought in Hans Lampe, just so he didn't have to play them any more. He wanted to move away from being a drummer and become a bandleader.

HANS LAMPE_At that time I shared a flat with Klaus and we would often work together on our lyrics. For example, the line "Multi Klamotti Internationali in the Boutiquie of Düsseldorf City" – that's something we came up with whilst sitting together; that was our poetry teamwork.

GERHARD MICHEL_I once saw him behind the drums in the studio. That was incredible. That was the best I have ever seen drums played. There was one piece Klaus wanted to play drums on and I wished I'd recorded it. Klaus learned drums in the late Sixties from listening to guys like Ringo or Moon, but no one played in that style any more.

HANS LAMPE_For the song 'La Düsseldorf' we recorded the team choir of the DEG Düsseldorf Ice Hockey Club. Back then we figured the ice hockey club represented Düsseldorf better than the football club Fortuna. I made the recordings over a half hour period on a Sunday afternoon at the hockey stadium with a Neumann Dummy Head microphone which I'd borrowed from Conny.

GERHARD MICHEL_Back in those Beatles times there were no microphones for projecting the drums to the back of the hall. As such the drummer had to really smash away so that those up in the back row could hear the bass drum. Nowadays that just isn't an issue at all. Keith Moon was one of Klaus' greatest heroes, second only to Ringo Starr. In Klaus' eyes, Ringo was at the pinnacle of drumming. It was Ringo who had established the beat; he was the start of everything.

HANS LAMPE_None of us were ice hockey fans, but what came across was this great atmosphere that was in a class of its own in Germany. In fact none of us liked any sports; but if you listen to the intro of the song you'll hear the festive mood of the chanting fans: "Heja, Heja, D-E-G."

GERHARD MICHEL_I was standing in some 10 by 10 square metre room directly in front of Klaus. When he started to play I couldn't hold on to the mixing desk; I was literally blown away. I will never forget how he drummed: with such an energy and precision that everything around us exploded.

HANS LAMPE_Towards the end of 75 Conny came by for the first time with his mobile equipment to Grund 3b and we played our songs over and over. The long version of 'Düsseldorf' was done in no time at all. But we soon realised that we couldn't go on with our work because we hadn't enough material prepared. The song 'Zeit', for example, existed already in a simpler form, but the bridge wasn't there yet. 'Silver Cloud' was nonexistent. There were other songs of course, but all in all it was all too problematic. And so we ended the recordings and said: "Conny, leave it for now, we'll do the rest at yours in autumn."

GERHARD MICHEL_On drums Klaus gave his all. He was a devoted guitarist and really lived for the moment, but on drums you really had to worry about his health. His extreme concentration and output led to a near-collapse. That was his whole approach though. The ritual was as follows: he sat behind the drums, threw his medium-length hair behind his ears, took a deep breath, brushed his hair to left and right and looked really crazy. Then he began to play, without any convention. He'd beat anything that was around: stands, rims, as well as the drums.

HANS LAMPE_It was only much later that we thought: "Okay, now we're ready"; so we went into the studio, to Conny, with our material. And by then it was really good. Conny admitted that we had worked properly on it. We recorded for one week, played in the overdubs and mixed it two weeks later. Then the album was finished. Nothing else was altered. They were the good times.

DIRK FLADER_In 1976 'La Düsseldorf' was spray-painted out the front of every school in Düsseldorf. The brothers and Hans along with some other volunteers had spent one night going around with their spray cans and a huge stencil, which still exists today, spraying their name everywhere. On the Königsallee as well, which was the best promotion of all.

MÂRI PAAS_I liked *La Düsseldorf* as soon as I heard it, because within the record there was so much of Klaus' personality. I still remember one night spent listening to 'Silver Cloud' without interruption. At first Klaus had wanted to call it 'Rheingold', but I didn't think it sounded golden, so instead he named it 'Silver Cloud', like the famous Rolls-Royce model.

HANS LAMPE_It was only after finishing the entire record that we decided on 'Silver Cloud' being the single. It was probably the most commercially appealing; the melody was very catchy and somehow we thought it appropriate for the times. The record company reacted quickly, and from our seven- or eight-minute original they cut a three-and-a-half-minute single.

RALF DÖRPER_Winfrid Trenkler had a radio show on WDR which dealt only with electronic music. Trenkler and John Peel on BFBS had long been the only ambassadors for the electronic scene. Unlike Peel though, Trenkler played predominantly cosmic electronica, and a lot of what he played would become a hit in Germany. He had a deep passion for La Düsseldorf and Michael Rother, playing them over and over again, and as such they penetrated the sales charts.

HANS LAMPE_Finding a suitable label was not the easiest thing. Klaus had once again pissed everybody off: Phonogram, Metronome, WEA, nobody wanted the record. Klaus was asking far too much. Nobody had considered Teldec and so the tapes were simply sitting on our desk. One day I went up to Hamburg, something that's still lodged in my mind. It was a very cold day in January but the sun was shining, and with my last penny I gave Teldec a call from a telephone booth. The woman who answered suggested that I send a demo tape but I snapped back: "No, no, this is different, this is something Conny Plank produced, who famously worked with Kraftwerk and Neu! You've heard of them, right? So just sending a demo wouldn't work for us. I think it's better that we meet face to face." Then she to put me through to Uwe Tessnow. And that was with my last penny from the booth in Sternschanze train station, my old turf. Tessnow was immediately interested, so I straight away went to his office and played him our stuff on his Revox tape machine. Tessnow listened to it from start to finish, seriously tuned in to the music, and we didn't speak much. At the end he said: "Yeah, I like that." He said that in a low and quiet voice. "I'm a little spaced out, and really high on that. It's great. So let's see where we go

DÜSSELDORF

Dortmund

KARL BARTOS AND WOLFGANG FLÜR

from here." He wanted to have it and was able and willing to pay a little more than the usual. As I stepped out of his office, I instantly gave Klaus a call to pass on the great news. He flipped out. Conny too was very excited. Later he visited Uwe Tessnow himself to talk about the plan and the contractual modalities. Then all three of us went to Hamburg to sign the contract and Conny received his cheque via mail.

77

++ **JAN 77** Bowie releases *Low*, part one of his Berlin trilogy ++ **FEB 77** Michael Rother releases *Flammende Herzen* ++ **MAR 77** *Trans Europa Express* is released ++ **APR 77** Studio 54 opens in NY ++ **MAY 77** *Star Wars* premiere ++ **JUL 77** 'I Feel Love' by Giorgio Moroder and Donna Summer captures the atmosphere of the summer ++ **AUG 77** Presumed death of Elvis Presley ++ **SEP 77** Kidnapping of business executive Hanns Martin Schleyer by Red Army Faction ++ German autumn ++ **SEP 77** Jäki Eldorado licks Iggy Pop's leg ++ **OCT 77** Sex Pistols release *Never Mind The Bollocks* ++ **OCT 77** Bowie releases *Heroes*, part two of his Berlin trilogy ++ **NOV 77** Wire release their debut album *Pink Flag* ++ **SEP–NOV 77** Michael Rother records *Sterntaler* at Plank's studio ++ **DEC 77** *Saturday Night Fever* starring John Travolta hits the screen ++

Mata Hari Shopping Mall

JÄKI ELDORADO_Being 'left wing' was the order of the day; but in such an intense way that it became a real pain in the ass. The student movement of 68 was so much stronger here than in any other European country, because it was in direct response to Germany's Nazi past. Depression and paranoia ruled the political and financial worlds; the daily papers were first and foremost reporting on Baader-Meinhof, economic downturn, and the oil crisis. Following the decadent time of glam in the early Seventies, and prior to the new messiah, disco, there was a period of fluctuation; it was a time of 'everything goes', there was no dominating musical style. This led to a standstill, and a supreme tasteless mix of all.

RALF DÖRPER_There existed this sort of a Bowie art scene, where people would meet up in various boutiques, clubs and bistros around the city. In Düsseldorf's Mata Hari Passage there was The Cabaret, a café turned nightclub, where you could find all the hippies dressed in their loose-fitting Ibiza-style clothing. Nightclubs such as Malesh were completely Arabic in design; they were wonderful, decadent yet sophisticated.

JÄKI ELDORADO_That said, people wanted to establish themselves once again on the international scene, but the question was 'how'? For some it was to associate with early electronica, whilst others either idled around on their rural communes or fled to the discotheques. That was before the likes of Praunheim, Fassbinder and Claudia Skoda paved the way for New Wave.

RALF DÖRPER_It was absolutely not my scene, and even if I would have been interested in it, it was impossible to get into. I was too young and they had a strict closed-door policy. If you did make it through the door though, then you ended up listening to either Bowie's 'Golden Years' or 'Young Americans', as well as stuff by Moroder, Space or even Kraftwerk.

MEIKEL CLAUSS_Kraftwerk had such an intoxicating coolness to them; they were completely un-rocky yet somehow danceable. Nowadays that is difficult to imagine but back then we all danced to it, myself included. It didn't matter if it was 'Ruckzuck' or 'Autobahn', the dance floor was full. It was the same for 'Gamma Ray' by Birth Control or 'Kashmir' from Led Zeppelin, which was an amazing piece. And even with 'Whole Lotta Love' and 'In-A-Gadda-Da-Vida' by Iron Butterfly; everyone danced to those. Unbelievably catchy rhythms! The pieces had to be long enough, though, to encourage those orgasmic solo dances; couple dances didn't fit so well. Wow, that really generated some ruckus.

JÄKI ELDORADO_Bowie's post-Ziggy image had the same elegance as, say, Kraftwerk or Fassbinder, but not Golden Earring or Led Zeppelin. I call it elegance; to me it had a subtle and aesthetic feel to it. Everybody else was still listening to Uriah Heep, Led Zeppelin, Black Sabbath or Deep Purple. Even when you had the humour and were willing to try out the discos down at the Catholic youth centre in Moabit, you still wouldn't find any good reason to be part of it.

RALF DÖRPER_I'm not referring to the Creamcheese, where you could hear the deafening sounds of 'Ruckzuck' or 'Elektrolurch' by Guru Guru, but more to the special clubs on the Konigsalle and in the Altstadt, those that catered for the rich and famous, such as Malesh, Sheila, Cabaret. Here the Kraftwerkers could listen to things other than repetitive funk; songs like 'Magic Fly' and 'From Here To Eternity'.

MEIKEL CLAUSS_The Mata Hari Passage was a little similar to Carnaby Street, only a scaled down version, and people would go there to meet during the day. Kraftwerk first met Wolfgang Flür there, before inviting him to the Kling Klang Studio. I also saw the two Dinger brothers there for the first time. Down the back of the passage there was a discotheque which was very cool; that was where the crazy, drugged up people would hang out.

JÄKI ELDORADO_Bowie in women's clothes, Reed in his gay leather outfit and Marc Bolan dressed as a glittered space angel with stardust in his hair: behind us lay a time of moral decadence, narcissistic self-centredness and exaggerated aesthetics. The divide between art, fashion, music and even sexuality became increasingly more blurred. In front of us was an avant-garde future... and so – eventually – we cut our hair.

MEIKEL CLAUSS_That was the beginning of the jet-setter era, the hippies and the fashion scene, with everyone dressed in their tiger fur, leather and glitter balls. Thanks to drugs the hippie and glam rock scenes were totally mixed up and suddenly all these rich hippies were either on a supernova glam rock high, or on heroin. And Bowie provided the perfect soundtrack: 'Golden Years'.

WOLFGANG FLÜR_Yes, that's true: in 1973 I sat with my neat d'Artagnan moustache and shoulder-length hair in the Mata Hari Passage and awaited the arrival of Ralf Hütter and Florian Schneider. When finally Ralf appeared he was clad in a pair of black leather trousers in the style of Jim Morrison. I had on my golden chains and platform shoes which I'd sprayed a metallic green colour, and I guess I looked somewhat feminine in appearance. But, hey, that was my style before Kraftwerk.

New German Style

JÄKI ELDORADO_Praunheim, Fassbinder, and especially Visconti with his move away from neorealism; they were the big names in Germany at that time, as it was they who encouraged the return to the cool elegance that had at first been banned post-war. In particular, Visconti's elegant style re-established the identity of the European cinema that stood in strong opposition to the domination of Hollywood and the American Dream. In Germany we had influential art house directors such as Wim Wenders, Werner Herzog and Hark Bohm, but they, as the Seventies progressed, became more and more intellectual and modest in their approach. In stark contrast, the others went ahead with opulent and colourful cinematography, a decorative and artificial stylisation, that paved the way for the neon Eighties. An early movie like *The Damned*, for example, explores the evil-doings of the Krupp-Halbach munitions family, although in the movie it's a great depiction of the fictitious German industrial dynasty of the Essenbecks. It was the main inspiration for Ralf and Jürgen to name the band Die Krupps.

WOLFGANG SEIDEL_If you were sympathetic to either Die Krupps or Kraftwerk then you could interpret their Visconti-Germanic front in the ironic and critical way it was meant. That said, it was less obvious with the latter though, which is why shutting up about their motives and beliefs was probably the best thing for them to do.

JÄKI ELDORADO_There was a high degree of mutual respect between Fassbinder and Kraftwerk; Fassbinder loved Kraftwerk because of their independence and their strong German identity. On set, his team of actors would at times be forced to listen to either 'Autobahn' or 'Radioactivity', setting the mood for the various film scenes, until they could endure it no longer.

WOLFGANG FLÜR_Actor Kurt Raab once told me that cult director Rainer Werner Fassbinder was one of our greatest admirers. In addition to his large stock of sausages, brandy and cocaine that he always had on set with him, he also had a record player with which he would play our songs. Kraftwerk were a kind of drug to him it seems. He would have liked for us to compose specifically for one of his films and had this come about I'm sure it would have been an ideal artistic collaboration, as we were just as equally fans of his work.

RUSTY EGAN_I was interested in all things German, from Baader-Meinhof to Rudolf Hess to Fassbinder. I've seen all the movies from Germany, including *Cabaret*, which was set in Berlin just prior to the Nazis' seizure of power. I was intrigued by the decadent, burlesque Berlin of the late Weimar Republic. That is why I wanted to go to Berlin, firstly because of the war, secondly to look at the wall, and finally because of David Bowie's song 'Heroes', which I'd first heard in German and which has been stuck in my head ever since: "Ich bin dann König, und Du Königin. Obwohl sie unschlagbar scheinen, werden wir helden für einen tag." Meaning, "I, I will be king and you, you will be queen. Though nothing will drive them away. We will be heroes. Just for one day." Does it get any better than that? I absolutely fucking loved it. That is what we were – heroes for one day.

JÜRGEN ENGLER_'Heroes' was recorded in the summer of 77 at the Meistersaal in the Hansa Studio. This was exactly around the time of Jäki's legendary pop history act where he's seen biting Iggy's leg. The photo was published by *Stern* and became a symbol for the starting point for punk in Germany. My little punk band Male was one of the first punk acts in Germany and Iggy and Bowie attended our show at Berlin's SO36 club. At the time Jäki had been labelled the 'erster Punk Deutschlands' – Germany's first ever punk.

JÄKI ELDORADO_I decided to trademark my name – Jäki Eldorado – although I actually wanted to be remembered as Punk Rocker No. 5. To be labelled the first ever punk was a little bit too much; I mean, the first in Germany, c'mon. But then the story in *Stern* newspaper happened and, from then on, I was promoted like that.

RUSTY EGAN_I've been to Alexanderplatz and crossed the border at Checkpoint Charlie together with Romy Haag. I've seen all the films set in Twenties and Thirties Berlin. I went everywhere. When I did Visage, I got Helmut Newton to do the album cover, I had women dressed as men and Steve Strange dressed in a military outfit, they called it Nazi-Chic in the papers. We did a song called 'The Anvil' and did it in German too, 'Der Amboss'. Right, you covered it with your band Die Krupps later on.

JÄKI ELDORADO_Hindsight is a great thing. Take for example this unique situation in Berlin. Why did it attract guys like Iggy? And all the other hangers-on? In Berlin back then everything was allowed. But that Berlin we'll never see again. This island of castaways. Looking back you start to see the importance of a band like Ton Steine Scherben. At the time, though, we thought to ourselves: What the hell is that? What are they trying to prove?

WOLFGANG SEIDEL_The fascination the English had towards krautrock and Kraftwerk is very complex and differentiated. Sure, there still existed this obsession with the Nazis – for some it was partly ironic and for others not – in the course of British pop it could easily provoke, even without any substance. Take Sid Vicious, for example, with his swastikas, or Siouxsie Sioux.

JÜRGEN ENGLER_Johnny Rotten, lead singer of England's first ever punk band, Sex Pistols, and as such in the eye of the hurricane of the new movement, was a devoted Hawkwind and krautrock fan. Faust, in particular, were always well known in England, and it remains that way today.

JÄKI ELDORADO_Some also credit this to Bowie because of his fascination with the Nazis and his collection of their memorabilia. He stoked the rumours himself by saying in an interview that Hitler would have been one of the first ever rock stars, just as good as Jagger. He added fuel to the flames with his arrival in London in an open top Mercedes, greeting his fans with a Hitler salute. There is video evidence of this and the *New Musical Express* went on to coin this as the 'Victoria Station incident'.

RALF DÖRPER_As a teenager I travelled to England to improve my language skills. Besides becoming acquainted with the locals I also came in contact for the first time with the British music press. One of the weekly newspapers had Kraftwerk as their lead story and so I bought the paper. Inside there was the famous interview with Lester Bangs where he was particularly scathing of Kraftwerk. The cover of the magazine was decorated with images of toy Wehrmacht soldiers, deliberately Nazifying the content.

JÄKI ELDORADO_Close to the Philharmonie you'll find the Nationalgalerie, where the Meta Music Festival was held. Eno, Nico and John Cale all played there on October 5, 1974, although it wasn't exactly the best of concerts. Halfway through the show Eno and Nico suddenly began to sing Germany's national anthem, and included the banned verse "Deutschland, Deutschland über alles" [Germany, Germany, over everything]. The audience was totally outraged and the concert had to be stopped.

WOLFGANG FLÜR_Since mid-76 we'd been working on a new album – *Trans-Europe Express*. This album contributed much to our exaggerated German image because of its European themes, the over-the-top portrait pictures on the front cover as well as the deliberately kitschy interior poster.

JÄKI ELDORADO_All of Kraftwerk's themes were deliberately Germanised. Take an idea like Autobahn, for example, Hitler's so-called legacy to Germany. Too often this is used by anybody right-wing as a desperate attempt to cite at least one thing positive about the Nazis. The same thing with the Volksempfängers, Goebbels' present to each household, another idea utilised by Kraftwerk. In Berlin, if you'd combined these themes with the way these four guys looked, you'd have been beaten up.

WOLFGANG FLÜR_We were often described as doll-like, emotionless, cold, or even robotic by the English press. This gave us the idea to adopt this image that directly reflected the way the public saw us, as emotionless mannequins, showroom dummies. That was our first step on the road towards the man-machine image, but for now we were just showroom dummies. This was an image we liked; in fact, it had been floating around in Ralf's head since our American tour. It fitted our rigid image perfectly.

Trans-Europe Express

MARTYN WARE_During the mid-Seventies I started hanging out with Cabaret Voltaire in Sheffield, they were friends of ours. We met regularly and often went to parties together. One day I went to a garden party at one of their houses, they were big fans of dub music, reggae, and had hired a powerful sound system, a rig. I have no idea what the neighbours were thinking. The first thing they played on it was the brand new Kraftwerk record; they were very keen that I would listen to it and they played it on this big PA. That was: *Trans Eu-roh-pa Exx-press*. So that was the first time I ever listened to it, on this big, powerful sound system, it was a real lightbulb moment. This is what I had been waiting for. This is actually what made me want to do it myself.

ANDY MCCLUSKEY_Some Kraftwerk sounded almost classical in style. When you hear *Trans-Europe Express* you can hear some similarities to Mahler. There was nothing there that had been digitally produced: no Sync, MIDI, Cubase or Logic, nothing. It was like a small chamber orchestra. The sounds emanated from the first generation of analogue synthesisers, were recorded with a tape machine and then sung along with over the top. The drums were played by hand, and there exists this calm yet tense atmosphere as heard in chamber music. Although Kraftwerk wanted to look all cool and technical, everything still had to be played by hand.

WOLFGANG FLÜR_With our black suits and ties we looked like some string quartet. Karl appears in his bow tie and comes across almost like a bank manager. To Ralf it was always important that we resembled a classical ensemble; we even had a piece dedicated to Franz Schubert, and with 'Europe Endless' an opening track that sounded typically classical. We wanted it to sound as stiff and as different as it still does today. That was our goal. In much more than only a figurative sense, what we were actually doing at our Kling Klang Studio was creating an electronic form of chamber music.

MARTYN WARE_The song 'Trans-Europe Express' begins with a series of noises, creating a soundscape representative of an approaching train, and which was as atmospheric as that heard on the start of 'Station To Station'. It paints an impressionistic journey for the listener, in the same way 'Autobahn' does, with its assured, ornate, mechanical monotony. A brilliant work of musical art.

ANDY MCCLUSKEY_My favourite piece is 'Europe Endless'. It has this romantic feel to it that reflects the German soul, and in the best sense. With 'Europe Endless' they'd obviously spent some serious time searching for the appropriate sounds. At the time it seemed radically stripped and electronic. But now that you are used to computer quantise, I can hear the missed beats, I can hear the flams where the snare and the bass drum are not hit at the same time. They are playing it by hand, and it is not exactly on the beat. That is what I like most about it, this irresistible human touch.

MARTYN WARE_This album is by far my favourite, which resonated with me when I was young particularly because of our connection to industrial 'found sound' and the expressionistic use of synthesisers to create powerful atmospheres underpinned by massive electronic beats. The dons of pure elegant electronic pop: Hütter, Schneider, Bartos, Flür.

WOLFGANG FLÜR_'Trans-Europe Express', 'Europe Endless' and 'Metal On Metal' are still my favourite pieces today. They contain such romantic melodies and those metallic strikes of the hammer sound like something from the production line of the Krupp steelworks.

ANDY MCCLUSKEY_Wolfgang never sounded better than he did on *Trans-Europe Express*. His playing was purely minimal and mechanical, without any embellishment, truly stunning and provocative simple sounds.

MARTYN WARE_*Trans-Europe Express* had everything: it was retro yet futuristic, melancholic yet timeless, technical, modern and forward-looking yet also traditional. You name it, it had it all.

GLENN GREGORY_In England it is rare to hear music sung in another language. And then when you do hear something that unique but not sung in English, it is very interesting, almost exotic. I only ever listened to Kraftwerk in German as you always feel closer to the original versions. *Trans-Europe Express* in German sounds so much more romantic; why, I have no idea, it just feels so much better.

MARTYN WARE_The German versions sounded so much more serious; on the English versions one can hear the slight twinkle in Ralf's eye as he plays with the material and the pronunciation. That was an obvious difference. He speaks with a slightly German accent, which made it sound sexy somehow. It was similar with ABBA; they too did not sing in their native language. Real diehard Kraftwerk fans always prefer the German versions.

DANIEL MILLER_*Trans-Europe Express* always reminds me of my summer holidays spent in Europe with my parents; in a sense it is the European soundtrack of my childhood. I remember lying awake in the night train looking out of the window, and having the metallic sounds of the tracks below in my ears.

JÄKI ELDORADO_There was this film called *Rheingold* by some local German filmmakers. The story was set in a train, like the Trans-Europe Express, that ran between Arnhem and Basel via Düsseldorf and along the River Rhine.

WOLFGANG FLÜR_Paris, Vienna, Düsseldorf, these stations were all referenced by name in the verses. Each verse corresponds to a different station. Iggy Pop and David Bowie, alongside Schubert, are the only real musicians ever referenced in a Kraftwerk song.

JÄKI ELDORADO_"From station to station, back to Düsseldorf city" is a direct reference to Bowie's album of the previous year. It's somehow funny how a myth could be created that Bowie in this case was inspired by Kraftwerk, when actually, chronologically, he came first. "Meet Iggy Pop and David Bowie" – a line like that was unheard of from Kraftwerk. It was so not their style. Why did they meet with Iggy and Bowie in the first place? That always left me wondering. It's like Captain Kirk would meet the Cartwrights.

WOLFGANG FLÜR_We never wanted to merge different musical cultures. We always wanted to remain independent and as self-referential as possible. That is why we rejected Bowie's offer to tour with him; although now we were name-dropping him in our song.

MARTYN WARE_Since *Radio-Activity*, not only have the Kraftwerk albums differed in language versions, but also in the album cover motifs. Take *Trans-Europe Express*, for example, where they made good use of photorealism, which was unusual for any band. With this they made the cover look like a movie poster, or a commercial ad. That had a big impact on us. We were so inspired by that, that we as Human League and Heaven 17 decided to dispense of photos entirely.

WOLFGANG FLÜR_The cover was a gentle colour reproduction of the four of us created from a skilful photo-collage made by the celebrated Paris photographer J. Stara. We were thrilled with his montage technique and soft hand-colouring. Stara was well known for his large-format photographs of monarchs, heads of states, kings, first ladies and famous show and film stars. He photographed each one of us individually in a separate corner of his studio in front of a black molleton cloth. If we'd all been photographed together we would have ended up looking at each other and it certainly wouldn't have been the strong projection of our personalities that can be seen on the album cover. Stara took shots in all perspectives, in both colour and black and white, later developing the best negatives and mounting them into a dynamic grouping; making sure that the one in the back hadn't a smaller face than anyone in the front. Everyone had to have the same significance in the picture. For reasons of perspective, Florian's head appeared blown-up, like a big head. He was placed behind us, but his head was the same size. That looked funny. We always took the piss out of him.

GLENN GREGORY_With Heaven 17 we wanted to avoid band photos completely and therefore preferred graphical solutions. The artwork of *Penthouse And Pavement* is not that dissimilar to that of *Trans-Europe Express*. Coloured drawings only, no photos: to portray ourselves as businessmen and composers. All in a pastel collage. That was our attempt to make the album look more German. We wanted it to appear Kraftwerkian.

DANIEL MILLER_One must not forget that the novel impression we had of the German stuff first came across through the artwork. This was exactly the case with Neu!; the graphics were a real eye-catcher. The simpler, the more iconic, the better.

WOLFGANG FLÜR_Stara realised that we weren't a band in the classical sense but were instead a group of four individual personalities, a work unit or, in this case, we looked like the cast of a movie. After he had finished taking the photographs he coloured it in with a special spotting technique that he had also developed, which he executed with a brush less than a millimetre thick. The fee for his laborious work was horrifying, but the outstanding result was worth every penny.

DANIEL MILLER_With *Trans-Europe Express* Kraftwerk quickly became a significant part of the international music culture. In America the album had a huge impact on black music, thanks largely to the famous process whereby Afrika Bambaataa drew upon the sounds of 'Trans-Europe Express'. With Bambaataa's maxi single 'Planet Rock', he had raised the profile of Kraftwerk in America and had made them more accessible to a black audience. He thus contributed to the popularity of Kraftwerk, although he did not have their permission to use the sounds in his track. That was one of the first examples of sampling.

WOLFGANG FLÜR_A large poster, folded up and included in the album, shows a comfortable group sitting at a table with a red-and-white-checked cloth in a coffee house under an oak tree on the Rhine, a romantic setting. This work was also a montage, from a photograph and an oil painting created by Emil Schult. The poster later became a cult item because it was only included in a limited number of records. It was pure irony, and a counterpoint to the tousled image of the punk scene that was then emerging.

EBERHARD KRANEMANN_'Trans-Europe Express' is a great track. This simple text together with some elegiacal music seemed to transcend everything. When I listen to this album I genuinely get goosebumps. It floats effortlessly above the clouds, completely separate to everything down below. Way up high, floating free.

Completely detached. How they managed to create this massive achievement... They were real artists.

Flammende Herzen

MICHAEL ROTHER_Each Harmonia member also had his solo projects. Moebius and Roedelius worked as Cluster together with Plank and Eno. I sat at home and experimented with my 4-track recording device. I took my pieces to Jäki Liebezeit, the drummer of Can, and asked him if he wanted to join me. When we recorded *Flammende Herzen* in 1977 I played all other instruments, bar the drums. All done at my own expense.

GÜNTER KÖRBER_By 1976 I just had founded my own record label, Sky Records, and looking back Wolfgang Riechmann and Michael Rother were the two most important artists signed to me. Rother was my salvation and my star. He came from Harmonia and had with him his solo product, which he called *Flammende Herzen.*

MICHAEL ROTHER_In the Seventies I retreated from everything and focused only on my own music. For sure I knew Can; I'd always found their music great and we'd even appeared alongside them on one occasion as Kraftwerk. I love their piece 'Yoo Doo Right'. And Jäki Liebezeit, well, he is one of the greatest drummers I know.

GÜNTER KÖRBER_Nobody was interested. Michael was out and about peddling his wares – he always had a copy of the finished product with him – but no such luck, the record companies just weren't interested. Such music offered no commercial success. When he offered it to me, though, I grasped it with both hands.

MICHAEL ROTHER_I released my record through a one-man company in Hamburg, Günter Körber's. He'd previously worked for Brain, and he knew my music and appreciated it very much. He grabbed on to it, he had a good nose for the business. The other record companies had rejected it, they hadn't believed it would go on to be such a success.

GÜNTER KÖRBER_The success of *Flammende Herzen* must have really frustrated Metronome, not just because I used to work there but now I ended up working with their artists. After the deal went south with Dinger and Rother two years earlier, Metronome wanted nothing more to do with them under any circumstances.

MICHAEL ROTHER_The three LPs *Flammende Herzen*, *Sterntaler* and *Katzenmusik* were made in quick succession. In the space of five years we'd sold more than 250,000 records, and that was when the major labels started to prick their ears up.

GÜNTER KÖRBER_At that time Kraftwerk were on tour in America in support of their surprise success *Autobahn*, and Capitol was wanting to take on more krautrock bands. And so they made Metronome an extremely generous, six-figure offer for Mr Dinger and Mr Rother together, but that was rejected simply because they were already going their separate ways. That, Metronome neither forgot, nor forgave.

JÄKI ELDORADO_The five tracks on the album, which were all instrumental, were used as the soundtrack for Walter Bockmayer's movie of the same name. Its use here helped promote sales of the record.

KLAUS IMMIG_I was a little disappointed by La Düsseldorf's debut album; the hypnotic element of Neu! had been lost. I felt the same about Michael Rother, someone had let all the air out. That positive tension between Dinger and Rother was missing – and that was telling.

MICHAEL ROTHER_The title song 'Flammende Herzen' is a very emotional piece. The title was inspired by a silhouette portrait that had been left behind by a previous resident of our house in Forst. At some point I looked at this silhouette and thought: "Right, that is it, I'll make something from that."

KLAUS IMMIG_Later on Michael Rother snared Jäki Liebezeit; he needed someone who could replace Klaus. Liebezeit played on all four of Rother's successful solo albums, and although they complemented each other very well, gone was that excitement of Dinger/Rother.

MICHAEL ROTHER_I was allowed to present my album via Trenkler's radio show. Afterwards the phones did not stop ringing and Winfrid said that was a clear sign of things to come. In the years that followed, he would often play our music and, as such, he performed quite an important role in shaping Germany's musical landscape, comparable to John Peel's dominant role for the alternative scene in England. Back then his show was still called *Radiothek*, although later on in the Eighties its name changed to *Schwingungen*, meaning 'Vibrations'. It was Winfrid Trenkler who ensured that all attention was directed towards Germany's burgeoning instrumental music scene and for that I am eternally grateful to him.

KLAUS IMMIG_ Many songs were typical of Michael and were particularly beautiful, although they were often 'shot up' by the drums. Liebezeit is a genuinely creative drummer but his work on this album didn't grab me. To my ears it sounded like 'Liebezeit plays Dinger'. Probably he was told to play in the tradition of Neu! – and if so, he can't be blamed for that.

EBERHARD KRANEMANN_ Michael's LPs from the period after Neu! were all too sweet for me, and all played too smoothly. Take for example the title track, 'Flammende Herzen'. I mean, that's just not on – 'Blazing Hearts', that's just so absolutely kitsch! The music was too cheesy – too soft and too tender. That was Michael though. With Dinger it was different because they were opponents; they had differing opinions which together worked well. That was where the energy came from.

MEIKEL CLAUSS_ Rother is a pivotal figure in all of this. He developed his own sound that was later widely referenced. Both nationally as well as internationally there are musicians who cite him as an influence. Rother is a very big number. His sound was really sophisticated and elegant, without being too flashy. It was just really cool; I wanted to have that type of guitar as well. He produced such long, drawn-out, beautiful tones, and the melodies he conjured from his Gibson seemed to float like a magic carpet, creating a beautiful dreamy atmosphere.

MICHAEL ROTHER_ The Ruhr valley, with its industrial landscapes, was an inspiration to some but never to me. Even though I now live on the River Weser, which gives me a great feeling, I never try to convey landscapes through my music. I look for inspiration elsewhere.

MEIKEL CLAUSS_ Even La Düsseldorf themselves, with their slower numbers, such as those on *Viva*, had a touch of Rother about them. That can't be denied. Even though he wasn't involved at all, you can certainly hear his influence in their melodies, particularly in 'Rheinita'. And so too Bodo Staiger; he was enormously inspired by Rother, which is clearly audible in his music.

JOCHEN RAUSCH_ People always associate bands with their origins; you always want to know where each band is coming from. Theoretically speaking, there exists a link between the music of every band and their place of origin, and a change in location is somehow a statement. Take Bowie's move to Berlin, for example. Exactly the same.

GÜNTER KÖRBER_I have always had a good rapport with Michael, even today. Unfortunately his contract with me ran out after five years and he then moved on to Polydor, which had the resources to offer much more than I.

MICHAEL ROTHER_ The major labels reacted very late and, as such, ended up having to offer me a lot of money. I then made a couple of records for Polydor before starting my own label in the early Nineties.

MEIKEL CLAUSS_I know a few Japanese krautrock fans who certainly know what they're talking about; they've read everything about Neu!, Dinger and Rother and have all the records. Including *Flammende Herzen*. And although I was around during those times I don't know half as much as these guys, who seem to know every Harmonia album back to front.

RYUICHI SAKAMOTO_ From the outside Düsseldorf is seen as the capital of electronic music. That is the predominant image. For us Japanese it also stands at the centre of the European economy. It is home to the one of the largest Japanese communities in Europe. The first two Kraftwerk albums, those with the coloured traffic cones on the front, I've had since the early Seventies. Around the same time I also discovered Cluster, Can and Neu!, and I loved all of them equally. It's impossible to cite only one. My favourite album is *Radio-Activity* and my most utilised synthie would be the Prophet 5, which I still have and use to this day.

WOLFGANG FLÜR_ It was a very hot summer, and an even hotter autumn, because it went on to become known as the 'German Autumn'. It was a time of terrorism and manhunts in Germany, and in Düsseldorf too. Everywhere you went there were wanted posters identifying the different RAF activists. And the typical German philistine liked to think there was a terror suspect behind every long-haired guy.

JÄKI ELDORADO_ The saying 'German Autumn' reflected the atmosphere in Germany, and above all Berlin – or should I say West Berlin. Back then you always had to refer to it as West Berlin and West Germany. There was no Germany so to speak, in fact you could even say there were two.

WOLFGANG FLÜR_ On one occasion I had actually had the police come to my flat and arrest me. Someone had seen me driving over Düsseldorf's south bridge, had mistaken me for Christian Klar and had thus followed me home. There was quite a lot of RAF hysteria at the time, especially seeing as RAF sympathiser Willy Peter Stoll had been shot and killed in a Chinese restaurant in Düsseldorf in 1978. I knew the restaurant well as it was close to my apartment in Derendorf, a part of Düsseldorf where I've lived most of my life. There was a lot of RAF activity in my area. Unbelievable today. I got a real fright, and those guys that looked even freakier than us Kraftwerkers would always have to keep their eyes open, particularly on the bridges into town, so as not to be pulled over and dragged out of their cars by the police.

RALF DÖRPER_ Now I could hang my wanted posters with all the terrorists on them directly over my bed, alongside my Alice Cooper posters. I still have them and most recently lent them out to a museum. Back then you had to be careful; even taking a poster would have been enough to land you in trouble, what with the way people were behaving.

GABI DELGADO_At my young age I was quite naive to all of this RAF thing. They were real heroes to me, like pop stars, and it was only later that I realised what they were actually about. I routinely only watched *The Avengers* on TV, and news about the RAF and their struggle against the system. As a kid, you are more innocent to everything. They were the heroes of my youth, alongside the likes of Bruce Lee or football player Wolfgang Overath.

JÄKI ELDORADO_Thanks to the RAF there developed this political hysteria whereby any dissenters were denounced as sympathisers or communists and told to 'go on over to the other side', meaning East Germany.

GABI DELGADO_Ulrike Meinhof was a real superstar, up there with Emma Peel and Raquel Welch. A real team of superheroes would have been Overath, Cassius Clay, Che Guevara, Bruce Lee and Andreas Baader.

Moroder Munich Sound

GIORGIO MORODER_Around the time that we reached number three in the German charts with 'I Feel Love', Eno and Bowie started working together in Berlin. I was told by Bowie later on, when he and I were working on the soundtrack to *Cat People*, that one day Eno came rushing into the studio and told him: "David, we can stop looking for the music of the future now, I have found it, it's already here." I would like to believe this is true, and he didn't just tell me to be polite.

JÜRGEN ENGLER_I thought Donna Summer's 'I Feel Love' was absolutely awesome. It has this great sequence that runs throughout the whole song – in fact this sequence was the song; it always remained the same, with its continuous pattern, occasionally changing pitch.

RALF DÖRPER_For me it was the arrival of the sequencer that really made electronic music particularly interesting. Previously the synthesiser was really only used to create the weird sounds, but with the sequencer you could have the instrument play itself – and play things that you perhaps weren't able to play by hand. Things that only the machines could play.

JÜRGEN ENGLER_That was something we tried out later ourselves, with 'Wahre Arbeit – Wahrer Lohn' for example, which featured a sequence playing octaves on only A and G.

GIORGIO MORODER_I used the Moog Modular System, the one that looked like an entire wall unit. I had to rent the system on a daily basis because back then I couldn't afford such a thing. Anyway, it worked the same back then as it does today: you'd play a code on the tape with which you could control the rhythm of the synthesiser and the sequencer. Everything you hear is generated electronically; even the percussion and drums were triggered by the Moog. Everything, that is, apart from the bass drum, which I simply added with my foot. Everything else was sequenced and electronic.

RAINER ZICKE_Working with Moog meant you had two things. Firstly, the killer bass sounds that you could get out of this wooden box. Secondly, the drum beats, which were generated using the oscillators and filters.

GIORGIO MORODER_Before 'I Feel Love' there had never been a song triggered by one single synthesiser. Sure, Vangelis had triggered a number of different sequences, but not a whole song, and definitely not to this extent.

JÜRGEN ENGLER_Moroder's addition of delay during the final mix really strengthened the overall effect of this eternally spiralling sequence.

GIORGIO MORODER_I triggered every single instrument myself: the snare, hi-hat, all the percussion in fact, as well as the bass figure which sounds doubly as fast because of the delay we added. This doubling effect was completely unheard of, and it formed the basic DNA of the song. There was no way to create this line manually; you needed this modern equipment. I was always aware of the Moog technology and this dawning of a synthesiser age. Even before 77 came along I was already on my way to America. Thankfully, I had Reinhold Mack as my engineer back at the Musicland Studios in

Munich, and it was thanks to his expertise that we were able to come through with everything; he knew the Moog inside out.

RAINER ZICKE_With Moog it was all about self-experimentation; and you had to have a vision of what it was you wanted to achieve with these strange synthetic sounds. Prior to the development of the portable Minimoog, Moog was a brand for only those with money, time and space. Such as Kraftwerk.

GIORGIO MORODER_Machine music reflects its teutonic origins: Berlin, Munich, Düsseldorf. The difference is that Kraftwerk used the synthesiser like a computer; for me it was more of an instrument.

MARTYN WARE_The undisputed master of electronic dance pop is Giorgio Moroder. His work with Donna Summer as an example of hypnotic disco dance is unsurpassed. The quality and innovation of his production has set the bar for me.

RUSTY EGAN_I had a photo of Giorgio Moroder hanging in my studio. Him with Hans Zimmer. They are standing in front of a Roland MC-4 MicroComposer. I would see this picture every day. For me the Munich sound was a blend of Kraftwerk and Moroder. There is only Kraftwerk and Moroder, and that will never change.

GIORGIO MORODER_Back then it was up to me to play everything. I played guitar and piano, although neither particularly well, so instead I focused on the MicroComposer. That could do what I couldn't.

RUSTY EGAN_Vince Clarke is such a big fan of the MC-4, so much so that even in the time of MIDI he has remained faithful to it. He has continued to use it on his recent albums, and, what is perhaps more incredible, he has actually appeared with it onstage. That is a real risky business because that equipment is incredibly vulnerable.

GIORGIO MORODER_For the special recordings I always had to hire good musicians; for the simpler things such as 'I Feel Love', I would let the sequencer take care of it. I did everything with the sequencer apart from one or two things. You didn't have to be a good musician.

GABI DELGADO_Sure it's great when you are an accomplished piano player, but alternatively you could also just get a sequencer to do the job for you. You don't actually need to be able to play at all. It may be spiritually fulfilling to devote 10 to 15 years practising piano, to become a supreme virtuoso. Like the long road of Buddhism. But that is one hell of a mistake as you miss out on 10 or 15 years practising sex, drugs, partying and many other things.

GIORGIO MORODER_I went to nightclubs only for one reason: I've always worked with rhythmic music and occasionally I'd head along with my demo tapes to the Eastside Club in Munich where I knew the DJ. There I would watch whether people would dance to my music or leave the dance floor. That way I got an idea whether the songs were on track or not.

GABI DELGADO_As a 15-year-old disco dancer I was very impressed: 'I Feel Love'. It was purely electronic; almost exclusively only used sequencers and Donna Summer's groans. Sex and electronics – in my head that seemed to be the most divine connection.

GIORGIO MORODER_'I Feel Love' offered something new, which was then picked up and imitated by many. When I listen to music these days I can still recognise my walking bassline. That's how things always evolve.

GABI DELGADO_That was the DNA of DAF: sex and electronics. That's the whole story behind us. Sex and electronics. Sequencers and Moroder. That was more important for electronic music than the entire legacy of Kraftwerk, Neu! and La Düsseldorf.

WOLFGANG RIECHMANN

++ **APR 78** Kraftwerk release *The Man-Machine* ++ **APR 78** Pere Ubu release *The Modern Dance* ++ **APR 78** Anti-Nazi League Rally in London's Victoria Park featuring The Clash ++ **MAY 78** Ultravox record *Systems Of Romance* at Plank's studio ++ **JUN 78** The Art Attack gallery opens ++ **JUL 78** Brian Eno produces Devo's debut album *Q: Are We Not Men? A: We Are Devo!*, recorded at Conny's studio ++ **AUG 78** Wolfgang Riechmann is stabbed in Düsseldorf shortly before the release of *Wunderbar* ++ **SEP 78** Kraftwerk release 'Neon Lights' as a maxi single in England ++ La Düsseldorf release *Viva* ++ **OCT 78** Daniel Miller releases his first single, 'Warm Leatherette', on his own Mute label ++ **NOV 78** Wire play Ratinger Hof ++ **DEC 78** Pere Ubu play Ratinger Hof ++

The Man-Machine

WOLFGANG FLÜR_The automation of our own musical production at the Kling Klang Studio led directly towards the robot theme. Ralf and Florian maybe unconsciously still had the poster from the US tour on their minds – 'Kraftwerk – The Man Machine' – a phrase so strong and rich with associations that it simply had to be developed into the title for our next album.

GERHARD MICHEL_When Kraftwerk went completely electronic the critic in Klaus came out. His own band La Düsseldorf, who also made use of electronics, had a very different approach. His definition of soulless music was anything that had been synchronised with sequencers. He liked synthesiser and Farfisa organ, as long as everything was played by hand; the moment the instrument was no longer operated by man, but rather a machine, when it ran via synchronised processes alone, it was over for Klaus.

KLAUS DINGER_It may well be that I was one of the first involved with electronic music. Basically, I make no distinctions between music whatsoever. There's music I like and there is music I don't like; whether it is electronic or not is beside the point. What I genuinely dislike, though, is music made purely with the assistance of technology; I don't find that inspiring at all. That is something I am trying to fight against.

WOLFGANG FLÜR_Melodies and rhythms would run automatically for days and days with only minimal changes to test their effects. Ralf would play variations on the synths and would then transfer them to the sequencer, which gave him a free hand to play another keyboard, to add accompaniments or anything else that he wanted in the composition. It was a never-ending cycle of trying out, setting new devices or resetting our electronic slaves.

RAINER ZICKE_When Ralf and Florian completed a piece of music, they listened back to it for hours and hours, to determine whether or not it would stand the test of time. It was very important to them that whatever they created was something that could be listened to years later.

WOLFGANG FLÜR_The music of Kraftwerk didn't actually emerge from emotions or spontaneous group sessions, like with a normal band; instead it tended to be created via a process one would find in a research laboratory or on a musical research programme; as if an academic professor and his tutors were developing a new musical format for the needy in the world.

RAINER ZICKE_It wasn't like they said: 'That sounds good, all okay,' and that was that; the two of them really proved the long term suitability of all their material. And when you hear their pieces today the sound and technology is indeed still very interesting. *The Man-Machine* continues to sound unbelievably good to this day. In fact perhaps it sounds the best of all – yeah, for me it's *The Man-Machine*.

RUSTY EGAN_I like their scientific approach towards their music, where they go to work, they program their music, they delegate – this is all very German. I like that. I like them being German. We are the robots. Brilliant. Can it be any clearer now? I like everything about it.

MARTYN WARE_They clearly lived up to the earlier uniform and electronic appearance of *Autobahn*. The tinkering of *Radio-Activity* and the romanticism of *Trans-Europe Express* were gone and gave way to a clearer general electronic impression. *The Man-Machine* was stone-cold urban and design-led. I have always been obsessed with graphic design and photography and to me this was the soundtrack of the cities. It was like a manifesto that wrapped up graphic design, photography and music, all in the same bag. Brilliant.

ANDY MCCLUSKEY_With *The Man-Machine* suddenly they were sounding really tight. The drums were either triggered or completely replaced by sounds from the Minimoog. This was the moment when Kraftwerk became completely static – they appeared as if they were programmed; and that was exactly the image they were going for. On their previous albums you could hear a slight touch of melancholia; originally, they had a real romance to them. Their music began to lose what I liked most about it: its humanity.

WOLFGANG FLÜR_We had a song called 'Metropolis'; that was a reference to a film by Fritz Lang. The whole concept behind the album was drawn from him. This track came out sounding beautiful; really dramatic and is one of the best on the album in my opinion. Karl is a romantic at heart, and here he had the chance to incorporate his musical studies into Kraftwerk's music. Many of the classically-tinged melodies were written and played by him; he was very important for *The Man-Machine*. In fact, he contributed to all of the six songs on the album and as such is listed as a co-composer. That was his songwriting debut; it was the first time they'd shared credits with him. It was only now that he started to get involved with the creative side of things; I think it was just because the other two were getting kind of lazy. They had already adopted the man-machine principle and were acting like the company executives of 'Kraftwerk Ltd'. They instructed Karl, Emil and me to create the album. "Ja twoj sluga, ja twoj rabotnik."

ANDY MCCLUSKEY_I'm a fan of the Russian constructivist El Lissitzky, as well as Mondrian. Both of those guys obviously inspired Kraftwerk. I liked what they were trying to express through their work: the trans-human myth; but you could easily recognise the human elements within their works as well. It is extremely difficult to imitate something mechanical by hand – but that was the overarching theme behind *The Man-Machine*. Just have a look at the way the title is written on the album. In 78 the font looked real technical; today it looks more like arts and craft-work.

WOLFGANG FLÜR_Nowadays Günter Fröhling probably has the most famous staircase; because it was there that we took the photos for the album cover, in the hallway of his film studio. By a stroke of luck, Günter brought the dynamic course of the red handrail into the picture. Our stepped presentation and our austere eastward gaze, combined with the static design of the cover, betrayed our constructivist stance and our love of the movement.

JÄKI ELDORADO_The record looked like a communist manifesto, but also played on the Nazi-associated red, white and black colours. For this reason it was a brilliant juxtaposition of politically-motivated imagery.

WOLFGANG FLÜR_We were ready to finalise the whole robot theme after deciding that we really wanted to have doppelgängers made of us who looked deceptively similar to us four. We asked the leading fashion houses in the city if they could tell us who were the best manufacturers of showroom dummies, and the name of the Obermayer company in Munich was mentioned again and again. It was said that the models in their shop windows had the most realistic faces.

JÄKI ELDORADO_Have a look at their complex appearance: these clean-shaven, ultra-German geezers, with their Bauhaus traditions and Braun aesthetics – if you look close enough you start to doubt whether there is any irony in it at all. Braun's industrial designer Dieter Rams would have been proud to have designed these man-machines. It may be their deliberate ambiguity that makes this a kind of ironic statement, but I don't really know.

WOLFGANG FLÜR_ After several telephone calls Florian arranged for us to meet the manufacturers. We drove to Munich in his Mercedes 600 over the course of some consecutive weekends, where we stayed at the classy Bayerischer Hof. In the daytime we each had a session with Mr Obermayer which would last for several hours and then somehow the idea slowly formed to send only the robots on tour to promote our music. Ralf explained this idea repeatedly in interviews and it sounded fine in theory; from Ralf's intellectual perspective it was almost genius. I thought to myself, though, that it would be close to impossible to equip the puppets with the complicated technology needed to enable them to perform our show fully automated.

FRANK Z._ Kraftwerk were always seen as some kind of art project, a group of artists more than a band. To have robotic dolls performing a show would have been simply sensational, regardless of the music actually played. Unfortunately this idea was not realised; man, they could have completed the whole German leg of a tour within one day.

WOLFGANG FLÜR_ In Düsseldorf we found some standard clothes for our 'Robbies', which had wooden ball-and-socket joints at their shoulders, elbows and knees to allow them to be bent into position. Wooden pegs rose from the top of the models' torsos, and our finished dolls' heads were set on these. Now all we had to do was buy red shirts, black trousers and shoes for them. Our technician, Peter Bollig, welded small plates covered with rows of red LEDs behind the mannequins' black ties, which stuck out from tiny holes that he cut in the material, and these blinked in a rapid rhythmical succession from top to bottom, powered by very small-scale electronics and a hidden nine-volt battery.

RALF DÖRPER_ Shortly before *The Man-Machine*, Kraftwerk had a sort of early pop star period, living the corresponding lifestyle. They would often be seen out and about in the city with their outfits on. I'd regularly see their Mercedes 600, somewhat like a German stretch limo, pull up in the parking lot in my street, and out would get a flock of black-clad party people. I was at an impressionable age and the elegant cars, attractive robo-maids, and these men in their tight pants and futuristic jackets – taken from the collection of French designer Serge Kruger – really left an impression on me. 'Kor-rekt' – that's what stylish pop stars should look like. They'd then disappear into the nearby clubs: the TV, which later became Peppermint, on the corner of Jahn and Herzog Street. This club would go on to become famous within the Eighties gay community as initially Rockin Eagles and then Relax.

MEIKEL CLAUSS_There was Mora's Lovers Club in the Schneider Wibbel Alleyway in Düsseldorf's Old Town, behind the photo shop and up the stairs. The Kraftwerkers were often to be seen there, and their song 'The Model' reflects the scene: people coming from all over the world; ultra-jet-setters with a distinctive degree of decadence. Mora's had a waiter who typically greeted every new guest with the same words: "Welcome! Glass of champagne? Corrrect!" You had no chance to reply; he'd already answered for you. For the song 'The Model', Kraftwerk actually invited this waiter – I think his name was Sasha – in to the studio, where he delivered his catchphrase directly into the microphone. Too often Ralf, Florian and Wolfgang heard him say this; to them it really summed up the trendy vibe of Düsseldorf. This guy now has his tag line featured in Kraftwerk's best-known song.

RUSTY EGAN_Naturally you're an expert on your own story; for this reason Ralf would be the best to retell his story and for me, I'd prefer to hear it straight from the horse's mouth. When I asked Kraftwerk about the story behind 'The Model', they said, "Look around you – she is a model, she is a model, and she is model… and they are all looking good!" These were the beautiful daughters of the Düsseldorf industrialists; there were beautiful girls in Mora's and Malesh Club – I can tell you right now that they were all looking good and I would have gladly taken them home with me, I guess that's understood.

GABI DELGADO_I personally never got into Kraftwerk; in fact I hugely disliked their lyrics. Take for example: "She's a model and she's looking good". That is so terrible! It sounds so undecided and lacks confidence, at least in my opinion. I mean, it's so bloody obvious, what are you actually supposed to do with that? It's like saying: 'If you watch the Premier League, then you can see some football'. That is such trite, a true Hütter platitude. "I'd like to take her home, that's understood" – that is what I call the Kraftwerk-conditional, where they only comment from afar yet don't have the courage to score.

JÜRGEN ENGLER_After the release of their hit single 'The Robots' Kraftwerk were really starting to become well known internationally, although in Germany, and in particular in Düsseldorf, well, you know how it was – nobody really cared for them. If this would have happened in the States, Kraftwerk would probably have had a monument dedicated to them straight after the release of *Autobahn*; not so in Germany.

WOLFGANG FLÜR_Our robots looked great, and we presented them for the first time, along with the song 'The Robots', in our spot in the ZDF TV show *Szene 78* hosted by Thomas Gottschalk on March 29, 1978. We were already building in little tricks by now, such as installing an electronic counter on the foreheads of the robots and moveable mouths which spoke portions of the text: "Ja twoj sluga, ja twoj rabotnik" – I am your servant, I am your worker.

FRANK FENSTERMACHER_I thought the whole man-machine concept was very logical and futuristic. It summed them up perfectly. I would go as far as saying that following the album *The Man-Machine*, they came up with nothing else of any interest. Not for me anyway.

WOLFGANG FLÜR_To my regret we didn't go on tour to promote *The Man-Machine*, although our robot-puppets would have certainly caused a sensation. We even had the idea of simultaneous shows in Germany, to play the whole tour in one day, where in each and every city our Robbies would have snapped into action at the same time. They would have represented us and summed up the whole concept behind *The Man-Machine* all too perfectly. I always loved touring a lot because I enjoyed travelling and presenting our music live, but as my colleagues grew older they lost the desire to travel. I heard Ralf and Florian often questioning the sense of such exhausting undertakings, without even discussing that with Karl and me. This worried me because the planning of everything to do with Kraftwerk was only in their hands; they didn't even pass the business administrations over to a professional manager.

RUSTY EGAN_The secret is: Ralf and Florian together are Kraftwerk. That's all there is.

Riechmann

HEINO RIECHMANN_After he stopped singing with the Spirits and Streetmark, Wölfi, as my brother used to be called, focused on his solo album. To this day it is considered a gem of the German electronic scene and he is greatly respected within this specialist circle. For some people *Wunderbar* is artistically on the same level as *The Man-Machine*, which was released at the same time.

WOLFGANG FLÜR_Wölfi Riechmann had been a good friend of mine since our days with The Spirits Of Sound. We always hung out together and had a lot in common, even after the band broke up. On one occasion we went with my azure blue Mercedes 220 b, all complete with its sharp characteristic tail fins, to a flea market in Amsterdam. With our girlfriends, who sat in the back, giggling as we took it in turns to drive. There was always a lot of laughter when Wölfi was around; he had a great sense of humour. It was a wonderful day and he was a wonderful person.

HEINO RIECHMANN_He was a year older than me and would always be playing at home, whether it be on his guitar, bass, electric piano or his ARP 2600 or ARP Odyssey. It was here that preparations for his solo album took place. I sometimes gave him a hand, as I also play guitar. In the summer of 1977 Streetmark released their album *Eileen* on Sky Records. All songs are written by him, together with Thomas Schreiber, and he can be heard playing guitar, synthesiser and contributing vocals.

GÜNTER KÖRBER_Wolfgang Riechmann recorded his solo album, his legacy, for Sky in Hamburg's Star Studio. With this record he was able to walk the line between both the Berlin and Düsseldorf electronic scenes. He combined the atmospheric sounds of the Berlin

School, with the likes of Tangerine Dream and Klaus Schulze, with the minimalism of his colleagues in Düsseldorf, namely Kraftwerk and Neu!.

RUSTY EGAN_Eventually we arrived at a point where there was only the Berlin or Düsseldorf School – nothing else mattered. I had everything, and especially anything that was released on Sky. The label was very attractive to me. I played Riechmann's *Wunderbar* daily in my Blitz Club. It always hit the spot immediately. That's exactly how we projected the Eighties – cool and synthetic. If you listen to 'Fade To Grey' today, you'll hear more Riechmann in it than Kraftwerk.

HEINO RIECHMANN_There was never any contact or relationship between Kraftwerk and my brother; it just didn't turn out that way... only the two Wolfgangs knew each other well, from a time before Kraftwerk; being in a band is like family or being in the same fraternity.

GÜNTER KÖRBER_With *Wunderbar* we had a unique album that not only anticipated the look of Gary Numan, but also had its very own personal style. *Wunderbar* was pure modern, pure electronic pop.

RUSTY EGAN_I then ran around Düsseldorf, I went to every record shop I could find and bought everything I could get my hands on: Neu!, La Düsseldorf, Riechmann, Rother, everything. Then I would check the credits on the back cover, and bought everything else that had been on Sky Records. I especially loved *Wunderbar* by Riechmann, as well as *Flammende Herzen* by Michael Rother. Back in London I would play all this ambient music in my club and when I was asked if I had anything to dance to, I'd say: "I don't want you to dance; just listen and enjoy this wonderful music."

GÜNTER KÖRBER_At around midnight, Riechmann, together with his girlfriend, went for a casual stroll around the block. It was then that he was fatally and senselessly stabbed. It was the Sunday night of August 21, 1978. There had been some trouble in a local bar, and the two troublemakers decided to attack the next person they came across; it just so happened to be the 31-year-old Wolfgang Riechmann. The whole of the city was completely stunned by this senseless act. Fortunately they caught the two perpetrators and sentenced them to life imprisonment.

HEINO RIECHMANN_It happened on the Mittelstraße, where those two bronze statues are standing now, close to the Hinkel bakery. Wölfi was on his way to Carlsplatz. It wasn't like he was dressed flashy or he acted provocatively in any way. He didn't look at all like he does on his album cover, he was dressed in a corduroy jacket and jeans. It was awful. He fought for three days in the intensive care unit at the Marienhospital – but sadly didn't make it because those bastards had hurt his lungs and heart too badly.

RUSTY EGAN_I recently posted a picture of Wolfgang Riechmann on Facebook, and his influence is still enormous. He was murdered in the street, like Jaco Pastorius, the bassist from Weather Report. Just terrible! *Wunderbar* is a wonderful and unique album, and it helped found the New Romantic scene in London. Riechmann is dead – long live Riechmann.

HEINO RIECHMANN_The way Wölfi looked on the cover of *Wunderbar*, that really hit us hard. The record was released shortly after his death and the cover photo showed him with this deathly pale make-up. That was not easy for me to see, and especially not for our mother. The photo had been taken by Ann Weitz, a Düsseldorf-based photographer and the then-girlfriend of Michael Rother. My brother, posing in front of a frozen, crystalline backdrop, with lipstick and blue hair. Our mother was horrified with all of this. In the end, it was her who ensured that his gravestone read Wolfgang 'Wölfi' Riechmann, with his nickname. For the international electronic music scene, though, the only thing that mattered was the last name: Riechmann.

Viva

HANS LAMPE_Eventually it got to a point where I had no choice but to get a job – I had to earn a living. And so it happened that I started working in construction. At some point, Thomas asked if there was any way I could get him in the door too, and then Klaus. So there we were, a united La Düsseldorf working together on a construction site. That was how we were able to cover our running costs. Working in the regular, blue-collar industry was a very interesting and formative experience and it was at this time that we came up with *Viva*; even the title owes itself to this experience.

KLAUS DINGER_This whole experience really brought us together. That was our foundation, and it proved to be very stable and successful in the years to come. It provided us with the opportunity to buy our own studio, together with the help of the record company and our friends. At Conny's studio the schedule was getting tight so it made a lot of sense to us to get our own private studio. Thanks to the success of our first album we were able to take a loan of 200,000 marks from two different banks, so as to help fund *Viva*.

HANS LAMPE_It worked as follows: prior to us going ahead with the studio, the tech company Barth had given us their financial quote of what they expected it to cost. This we presented to our record company, who agreed to foot the bill of all equipment in exchange for our next record; this would be in place of a cash advance that we would have normally got. Instead this cash was now paid to Barth who then sent us their equipment. Two banks were also involved, as well as a private investor, Brigitte Bühler; Thomas had recently separated from Tina Schneider-Esleben, the sister of Florian Schneider, and was now with Brigitte. She had a pretty good job at Team BBDO, an advertising agency, and as such was financially solid. She was eager to help us out and offered to provide a financial guarantee for us. This reassured the record company as it meant that their money was not being wasted but, in fact, invested. And seeing as the record company was in agreement, so too was the bank. What with all these different parties involved, we were feeling the heat and things could have easily fallen apart, which would have meant personal bankruptcy for us. But it was precisely because of our time spent on the construction site that we had this feeling of: 'We can do anything! We can make it anywhere! So we were all up for it. VIVA!

KLAUS DINGER_First our time on the construction site, then the construction of our own studio – that was a very, very good time, when we really got along well. The inner energy that we created was probably the secret to our success. You can hear this energy overflowing with vitality on *Viva*.

RALF DÖRPER_The perfect complement to Kraftwerk was, at least in terms of their style, La Düsseldorf. Here we had the glam and glitter hippies who would hang around at local boozers such as Einhorn on Ratinger Street in their white overalls and matching ankle boots.

KLAUS DINGER_Those we wore for years. These are very good trousers, very cheap and very convenient, and came from our days working in construction. Here in Düsseldorf, though, something like that is always interpreted as a fashion statement. Maybe we shouldn't have credited ourselves as stylists on our albums.

JÜRGEN ENGLER_With La Düsseldorf it was weird; nobody seemed to actually like them or indeed have heard anything by them. It is most likely they became well known because of their white uniforms – that and their stencilled tag, which had been graffitied all over the streets. You would see it on every pavement, it was absolutely everywhere. At first we didn't even associate it with music.

KLAUS DINGER_That all came with the new experience from the time of the construction work. White overalls were becoming our band outfit and the song 'White Overalls', for example, captured the way we felt working in this uniform. We were "Sons of the city, sons of the future. White overalls, white overalls."

HANS LAMPE_The studio was simply called La Düsseldorf studio and was set up in the street Im Grund 3b. From the Hamburg-based company Barth we had delivered a MCI JH-400 mixing desk and a Sony MCI, 2-inch, 24-track tape machine. That was very, very classy studio equipment back then. To install all this took between two and three weeks. By the start of 78 we were finally finished and ready to start producing.

KLAUS DINGER_To assume full responsibility for the studio and the loan left us feeling a whole lot of pressure. We tried to channel this pressure into our music though, even writing a song about money: 'Geld'. All the songs on *Viva* are very true-to-life.

HANS LAMPE_So, after recording the A-side of the album, the pressure slowly kicked in and with that grew the tensions within the group. You really had to have a lot of self-discipline to stay focused and on task for the entire day. Every day.

KLAUS DINGER_A lot was going on at the time. We were having to deal a lot with different companies and banks, and this was creating personnel conflicts within the band. Accordingly, we had a nice variety of themes for our songs.

HANS LAMPE_Additionally, we invited other musicians to join. Harald Konietzko had previously played on our debut as a bassist on 'Silver Cloud'. The vibe with him was very positive so he once again played bass for us, this time on 'Cha Cha 2000'. Now all we needed was someone to play keys. Thomas had met Andreas Schell and had at some point brought him along with him. We all hit it off immediately. Andreas was a pianist, and with our advance from the bank we were able to buy him a nice Grotrian-Steinweg piano. Then we all got together in Düsseldorf-Lohausen – Klaus, Thomas and I together with Harald and Andreas – and rehearsed. Even when the rehearsals were going well it became more and more clear to us that if we weren't successful we were pretty much screwed. For Thomas the pressure was too much, so one day he just took off. In the middle of the production, he just left; he'd packed his bags and headed to the south of France. Well, yeah, so there stood Klaus and I, alone. What could we do now, with Thomas gone? We had to tear along and go on, we had no other chance. Andreas Schell played a very, very big part in getting the record finished. The bridge-part of 'Cha Cha 2000' had this quiet piano section which he came up with. We rehearsed this piece over and over again for a couple of weeks until we were happy with it. Then we recorded it in one take. We played, played and played – and Andreas sat directly next to the tape machine. When we were through he stood up, pressed stop, looked at the timer, and what was there? 20.01. One thing was clear: that was the take! It was somehow mystical; that was real magic.

KLAUS DINGER_And the lyrics were magical too: "Dance to the future with me, Cha Cha 2000, watch out that no one destroys the dream, Cha Cha 2000." To me that's magic. 'Cha Cha' encapsulates all that is La Düsseldorf; anything we had to say is in this one song. I am completely satisfied with every version we did; though I'm still dreaming of the 'Super-Nova-Cha Cha 2000'. Maybe one day...

GERHARD MICHEL_I liked La Düsseldorf's second album, *Viva*, the best. To me *Viva* really hits the spot. I like 'Cha Cha 2000', 'White Overalls', 'Geld' ['Money'], Vögel ['Birds'] and also the title track; as well as their single 'Rheinita', which was a play on words: combining Klaus' beloved Rheinland with his then-muse Anita Heedman. Anita had left Klaus to move to Scandinavia, and for a long time he couldn't get over that. He even went with his massive motorbike to Norway to win her back, but ultimately he didn't succeed.

HANS LAMPE_The story with 'Rheinita' was as follows: we bought a Yamaha organ – again with the help of Brigitte Bühler, who gave us an additional loan – and were now trying to explore every possible sound that we could get out of this thing. We created the harmonies on the piano, but the recognisable sound of 'Rheinita' is actually what's done by the organ.

BODO STAIGER_'Rheinita' was a great song and was chosen to be performed on TV. There were video recordings made by Harald Tucht when the four of them travelled down to Munich to Thomas Gottschalk's TV show. That was quite a historical TV moment, when the two Dinger brothers suddenly decided to stand up halfway through the song having spent the first half lying on the ground, took each other by the hand and danced the ring-a-ring-a-rosie, choosing not to mime along with the playback. That looked somehow spaced-out; it was closer to performance art than music. Hans stood behind his two toms and drummed stoically throughout the song, while Thomas and Klaus got more and more carried away. The Munich team was quite perplexed: "What the hell are they doing? What's wrong with them? First they don't want to play live; now they decide to mess up their playback."

GERHARD MICHEL_And apart from that we had the famous Colgate story that Klaus always liked to recite. The Palmolive corporation had offered a large sum to use the middle part of 'Rheinita', the piano part, in a Colgate 'super white' toothpaste advert. Klaus felt quite flattered, because he had always had a great interest in advertising, but again he refused to be bought, and categorically declined – another thing he was very proud of.

HANS LAMPE_The WDR radio station was all over 'Rheinita'. I remember when we were aired on the Schlagerrallye, as it was known back then; we were heavily competing with 'Go Your Own Way' by Fleetwood Mac and Abba's 'Take A Chance On Me'.

KLAUS DINGER_Three hundred thousand copies of our second album were sold in Germany alone. We were also selling well in Britain, America and Japan, as well as in France and Italy. With *Viva* La Düsseldorf was becoming a well-known name... if it wasn't already!

HANS LAMPE_Recordings were in the bag and the question arose: What are we doing for cover art? We were under a lot of pressure time-wise and hadn't had the chance to think about the cover beforehand. All we had was the name, *Viva*, that was our whole concept. But the artwork? Okay, so we'd always had this affinity towards spray cans so again we turned to them: Viva. During the mastering process in Hamburg we were given different vinyl masters as proofs and they came in white, neutral covers. They didn't stay white for that long though – they'd been lying around too long in the studio – in fact they actually looked a little worn out and vintage-like. So we decided to spray 'Viva' on to one of these generic, white covers. We liked it, left it to dry in the studio and then went home. When we got back the next day we still liked how it looked so asked Achim Duchow to stamp it with the now iconic La Düsseldorf lettering, leave the leftover scotch tape in place, and take it as it was. What more did we need? That said it all. It was in a similar vein to the purist Neu! covers and really captured the essence of what we were about; everything else was too frilly. And on the back is a photo of Thomas taken by Klaus in front of our studio. Right opposite was a field, home to horses and in this case donkeys. Thomas was good with animals, which is why Klaus took this snapshot of him kidding around with this donkey, and exactly when the donkey stuck out its tongue, Klaus pulled the trigger.

BODO STAIGER_Back then there was a Düsseldorf journalist by the name of Konrad Schalensick who was a critic for the *Neue Ruhr Zeitung*. He absolutely savaged one of La Düsseldorf's albums, I think it was *Viva*. One fine evening he came along to Ratinger Hof; Klaus saw him, stood up, walked straight up to him, shouting "Konrad" and bang, his nose was broken. That was Klaus. You had to be careful around him. He took no prisoners.

New Wave

PETER HEIN_We'd heard about Pere Ubu only because of the first *Max's Kansas City* sampler, which featured them alongside Suicide. This was a compilation of all the NYC bands that were part of the early days before punk after The Velvet Underground had set the stage for all forms of non-traditional-based music from punk to industrial. Max's Kansas City was the name of a club in New York, where the Warhol entourage hung out. A bar for burgers and live shows.

KURT DAHLKE_My perfect role model was Allen Ravenstine, the synthesiser player for Pere Ubu. He had the cheek to enter the stage with a VCS 3; an EMS instrument not particularly suitable for stage action. With this thing and all its pins and joystick, though no keyboard, Ravenstine was making all theses incredible noises. Only noise was coming out of this little box. Just noise! He was my shinning idol.

PETER HEIN_And now they were to play at Ratinger Hof? We all had to go. The awkward keyboardist of Pere Ubu made all those noisy sounds. They'd left their theremin at home I think, but they still played well with their guitar, bass and drums.

FRANK FENSTERMACHER_Chrome from San Francisco and Cabaret Voltaire from Sheffield also used guitars and sounded already really experimental, but now here came Pere Ubu sounding so perfectly industrial.

PETER HEIN_Associations to this mega-harsh industrial sounds immediately came to mind; there was always this one noise as if a bottle was spun on the empty concrete floor. Railroad cars that passed, doors rattling like large roller shutters. How he did that, I don't know. The atmosphere was certainly clumsy, felt like a night spent in an empty factory hall with freight trains passing outside – that was the sound. In some way that was an early precursor to *Stahlwerksinfonie*.

RALF DÖRPER_If you thought Brian Eno's approach was avant-garde then Pere Ubu was one hell of an ear-opener. Their debut record *The Modern Dance*, and even more so their concert at Ratinger Hof, wow! They had perfected their synthy-noisy-sounds – and all that came from the rock environment of Cleveland. Something like this would be expected from Britain, where you had bands like Cabaret Voltaire or Throbbing Gristle. Noise in its purest of forms could now be experienced live at the Ratinger Hof.

PETER HEIN_Pere Ubu were frickin' awesome, but then Wire came along and played the Hof as well, so we all had to go again. Those two shows in November 78 were massively influential. Düsseldorf became Wire_city. With their sophisticated arty punk they were very well received here. Pere Ubu and Wire were the best ever shows at the Hof, probably the best concerts of all time. You can ask anyone you want.

KURT DAHLKE_My other great idol was an English guy, David Cunningham. He had just released a record called *Grey Scale*, upon which he played radically reduced synth music; completely minimal, reclusive and grim. That wasn't too common at that point. When you listen to the Berlin School, for example, everything sounds so opulent; and he did the exact opposite. I thought that was very, very cool.

FRANK FENSTERMACHER_By the late Seventies, I began to lose interest in my beloved jazz records. From the first moment I heard Wire or Suicide, jazz was quickly forgotten. Actually I was already developing a passion for punk after Muscha had visited us with the first Ramones album on tape. That was my first encounter with punk. I was living like a hippie, I was 23 and was kind of a hippie latecomer, but this seemed to be a revelation. To me, at first it was kind of hard stuff to hear, but for Muscha the Ramones were the real deal. It was around that time that he shot his first movie, 'Blitzkrieg Bop', which he filmed at Ratinger Hof. Muscha was always a little ahead of his time as well as everybody else's, but now I too was beginning to share the same feeling: something new is about to start.

KURT DAHLKE_At some point we realised: something beautiful and exciting is happening to music, especially in Düsseldorf. Things were changing. To us it was clear: we had to evolve in this more exciting and experimental direction. That was our first radical step away from our jazz-rock band You, along a noisier, more progressive path. Robert Görl and Chrislo Haas had both studied jazz in Graz and were ready to start afresh. Michael Kemner played bass and I the synthesiser. With this line-up we performed avant-garde instrumental music; the next challenge was to find a singer. Along came Gabriel Delgado-López, a Spanish immigrant who'd landed in Wuppertal. Gabi was ex-Mittagspause, the art-punk band formed by Peter Hein and Markus Oehlen. He was the self-proclaimed dancer within the group, while Franz Bielmeier played a great stoic guitar. No bass.

FRANK FENSTERMACHER_Moritz Reichelt and me had just opened the art gallery Art Attack in Wuppertal. We exhibited things by Muscha and it was there that we got to know the jazz-rock group You, who we'd printed posters for. They lived up the hill in Gevelsberg, Silschede, in some eco-alternative-hippie-hideaway, The Green-In, where they recorded their first record. The team was: Kurt Dahlke, Wolfgang Spelmans, Michael Kemner, Robert Görl. They had no singer at that point and this was pre-Chrislo Haas. They played their first show at the Ratinger Hof, where Gabi saw them and immediately joined.

GABI DELGADO_Mittagspause, meaning 'lunchbreak', was the name of the band that got me started as a performer, though I wasn't a hundred percent seriously involved. I just wanted to be part of it, as I always had a great, great time with Franz Bielmeier, a.k.a. Monroe. His alias came from his time with his first band, Charley's Girls, where each member adopted a girl's name: Mary Lou Monroe. Peter Hein did the same thing, calling himself Janie J. Jones. In this feminine context Muscha got his name, which was derived from his surname Muschalek – and I was known as Gabi, already a girl's name and the short form of Gabriel.

KURT DAHLKE_Mittagspause was a great revelation for me. I was previously surrounded by real musicians – people who could play their instruments or at the very least tried to play them technically correct. Mittagspause, on the other hand, was the exact opposite. Markus Oehlen on drums only ever played one single beat: *Oom-pa-pa-Oom-pa-pa*. That combined with this sassy guitar and sassy vocals was a real eye-opener. I was a massive fan.

ROBERT GÖRL_I have always been interested in music; I played the trumpet by the age of 12 and later studied percussion and piano. I loved music from the day I was born, and I always had a weak spot for minimalism, especially the unspoilt energy of the 'Geniale Dilettanten', which would translate to 'ingenious amateurs', if you want to take it straight from the German meaning. On top of that, they always misspelled their band name on purpose, which again confused everyone.

GABI DELGADO_We all had this Lou Reed thing going, everything that was different in a way was interesting to us. We soon had a whole plethora of things that we were interested in: from Kurt Schwitters to The Velvet Underground, from El Lissitzky to Iggy Pop. All of that was our world. What we didn't know, we had to look up. Monroe had the much broader perspective, he read studies on Dada and Constructivism; and in the public library we had our art books and studied the Russian production art, almost like at a private university, only for the both of us. We felt connected to this art world. We took a lot of LSD and inhaled the books on Dada, we even wrote our own Dada lyrics. They were the times. Dadaism was the way to go. As cool as the Pistols.

RALF DÖRPER_On closer inspection, the Düsseldorf electro bands that defined the Ratinger Hof scene all came from the surrounding countryside. DAF came out of the woods, from nearby Gevelsberg, Der Plan came from Wuppertal, and S.Y.P.H. were from Solingen. Ultimately though, Düsseldorf was the catalyst. It's said that Liaisons Dangereuses also came from Düsseldorf, but not one of them is actually from this city.

MORITZ REICHELT_The punk movement had ensured that different records were coming to the shops now; sometimes some very obscure things. The music that would later be called industrial, was new wave, so I liked everything new wave. One song, 'Warm Leatherette' by The Normal, really captivated me. The Normal was the stage name of Daniel Miller and the song was about a car crash. It was made completely with synthesisers and had all these harsh industrial sounds. This is one of the legendary seven-inches for me. This record did it for me, beside The Residents and especially Devo from Akron, Ohio. That was my music.

JÜRGEN ENGLER_Between November 77 and August 78 all the very important albums were released, one after another. The really good ones, the most important ones that influenced us and formed our taste, are the ones that I would take to a desert island with me: the debut albums from Wire, Pere Ubu, Suicide, Devo and the Buzzcocks. Everything besides is nice, but not essential.

KURT DAHLKE

++ **FEB 79** DAF play their first show ever at Ratinger Hof ++ **MAY 79** Bowie releases *Lodger*, the last part of his Berlin trilogy ++ **MAY 79** Margaret Thatcher becomes UK prime minister for the first time ++ Beginning of the neo-liberal era ++ **JUN 79** Joy Division release *Unknown Pleasures* ++ **JUN 79** DAF's album *Produkt Der Deutsch-Amerikanischen Freundschaft* released on Warning ++ DAF play the second In Die Zukunft festival at Hamburg Markthalle ++ **MAR–JUL 79** Michael Rother records *Katzenmusik* in Forst and at Conny Plank's studio ++ **SEP 79** DAF go to England and record at Cargo Studios in Rochdale ++ **NOV 79** DAF tour with The Fall in England ++

Ratinger Hof

GABI DELGADO_Every movement needs a location. That is something I'm convinced of. There are always these places from where things emerge. Take Dada at the Cabaret Voltaire in Zurich, a place where magic seemed to exist, where people were starting something, striking the first spark. It was the same here in Düsseldorf. Everybody at the Ratinger Hof was in some way creative. It was amazing, such an incredible energy.

TINA SCHNEKENBURGER_Ratinger Hof was the place to be. I was such a lucky bastard to be at the right time at the right place. Punk rock changed my life; it totally saved me, allowing me to leave the alcohol and drugs behind. I was 21 and had just come from Spain to Düsseldorf when I had this moment of truth, where I woke up one morning, looked in the mirror and knew: If I don't give up, one year from now I'll be on a park bench, in rehab, or worse, dead.

PETER GLASER_It was indeed the decisive factor – the proximity of the Ratinger Hof to the Art Academy. It was there that art and punk came together. It played a massive role in not only the formation of the second Düsseldorf electronic music generation, but also in defining its character. At the epicentre of this new scene was Kurt Dahlke, who seemed to know, have and use everything before anybody else.

KURT DAHLKE_Our time was clearly connected to the Academy of Arts. A lot of what was happening had something to do with the nearby Art Academy. Had Imi Knoebel not decided to transform the entire punk club into a living, breathing work of art; had his wife Carmen Knoebel not been such a good manager; had the whole Academy, from Immendorff to Peter Bömmels to Walter Dahn, not frequented it, then this melting pot of art and music would not have existed.

MICHAEL KEMNER_There was a strong connection. Each one influenced the other – the musicians the artists, and the artists the musicians. It was from there that Junge Wilde emerged.

GABI DELGADO_For days, if not weeks, we kept ourselves busy with all kinds of things; not just music but art as well. On the one hand, you had the 15 to 20 young punks who were the original Hof crowd; on the other hand, you had the Art Academy people – the Oehlens, Walter Dahn and so on – frequenting the Uel, the neighbouring pub. On top of that you had the performance art people such as Minus Delta T as well as members of the AAO, the Aktions Analytischen Organisation founded by Otto Muehl. All of them in such a small area created a particularly special blend of artist and punk. Beuys-trained artists from the academy, Viennese Actionists, the DIY punks, the performance artists: together that created one hell of a strange, highly explosive mixture.

KURT DAHLKE_It was a busy time back then, we were exchanging a lot of ideas with a bunch of different people; Holger Hiller came for a visit from Hamburg, so too S.Y.P.H., who came from Solingen to make music with us. The same goes for Der Plan, who had built up a lot of contacts through Frank and Mortiz's Art Attack gallery. It was just one big network and for the weekends we'd head along to Ratinger Hof to check out the latest crazy bands on offer.

MORITZ REICHELT_The Old Town was our internet. It was there that you networked, even without Facebook. We had our address printed on our debut record, which meant we built up contacts all around the world. We were connected internationally.

DANIEL MILLER_I still remember the Fad Gadget show at the Ratinger Hof. We spent the day with Moritz, Frank and Kurt at Ata Tak; and the nights too. We knew the early scene there – what Der Plan, Die Krupps, DAF or Minus Delta T came to represent was something we were already familiar with.

MARTYN WARE_In fact, it's unfortunate but thanks to punk a lot was simply thrown overboard; not with us, but for many others though. Suddenly it all just seemed so old-fashioned. Take Kraftwerk, for example. They where yesterday's news, at least in their hometown, as soon as the second generation of electronic musicians came up.

JÜRGEN ENGLER_Vice versa there was a lot of momentum coming out of England. OMD were well received from early on. They came from the Factory world and really struck a nerve with their first single. 'Electricity' was played over and over again at the Hof, becoming a huge hit there.

TINA SCHNEKENBURGER_I lived in Düsseldorf; Gabi was still with his family in Wuppertal. Where all the others lived I can't recall, but in the end it was the same for all of us: the Ratinger Hof was our home. Seriously. I spent every goddamn day at the Ratinger Hof; there and nowhere else.

JÄKI ELDORADO_When in Düsseldorf, you thought even the punk scene seemed somehow more chic than elsewhere. The Hof, with its mirrors, neon lights and stainless steel dance floor didn't look at all punk, that we knew. Conversely, Berlin was gloomy and lacking any humour, while in Hamburg everything was left in the hands of the leftist squatters. Düsseldorf had a different vibe to it, with its advertising industry and the fashion and art scenes. It had a sense of pride. It stood tall.

PETER GLASER_Having come from Graz, to me Düsseldorf was the gateway to the world. In my eyes the Rheinknie Bridge was almost like the Golden Gate Bridge. It was only after I started to travel and see other cities that I realised Düsseldorf actually wasn't a big city at all, despite its large centre. It is nice, friendly and clean though. And when you had no money for the tram, you could, if you had to, go home by foot, which is obviously completely different to New York or Berlin. It is exactly this combination of clarity with its metropolitan flair that made many things possible here.

GABI DELGADO_When you wanted something to do, then you had to go to Düsseldorf. That's where you could really experience culture, in its artists and galleries scene. The first punk fans were the artists, Beuys' students, and the gallery owners. Back then polit-magazine *Der Spiegel* described punk as the new fashion of the ghettos. Suddenly everybody understood: 'Aha, they are punks. That's what they look like.' Instantly there was a huge influx of people and the Ratinger Hof was packed. Many of them, though, were simply onlookers who just wanted to see the punks. And the bourgeois people crowded into the Hof – on the dance floor, there was 20 to 30 people tops who danced and represented the punks; around them were 300 spectators.

TINA SCHNEKENBURGER_I was part of the Ratinger Hof scene for a good year-and-a-half, from the start of 78. Towards mid-79, though, the whole punk thing started to dry out and by the time we went to London I knew that punk rock was already over. That was something that made me sad. They were the best times of my life, that's something I stand by. It's not that I haven't had other good times, it's just that they were easily the best.

DIY

JÄKI ELDORADO_The order of the day was: do it yourself. That was the challenge, and slogan, of punk and new wave. DIY. A new way of thinking was evolving and we naively assumed that anything

JÄKI ELDORADO

was possible as long as you tried passionately and really wanted it. To this day our generation is characterised not only by the strong belief that we can invent ourselves, but moreover are forced to do so.

MORITZ REICHELT_The catalyst was the documentary *Punk In London* by Wolfgang Büld. I first saw that in 1977 in a cinema in Wuppertal. A week later I had my own leather jacket, bought from a secondhand shop, complete with safety pins.

TINA SCHNEKENBURGER_There was absolutely nothing prefabricated. There were no shops where you could go and buy punk clothing, you had to add the cuts in your clothes, sew in the zippers yourself. Along with all the other shit. Everything was DIY. When you had no money to go shopping in London like me, then you had to tinker around with whatever you could find.

GABI DELGADO_I liked the punk attitude, the whole approach, the DIY and the business strategies. Like you'd say today: I don't need to have studied music to be able to make it. If you can't find a label then do it yourself. Everything about that attitude I liked very, very much.

KURT DAHLKE_We needed a record and as quickly as possible. We recorded something at Studio 56 in Mühlheim but it turned out to be utter crap and we didn't want to release it. We knew we couldn't get that released, we needed something new. That's how we came up with the idea to do the whole thing ourselves. So I bought a tape machine with two mics, we set up all of our equipment in Wolfgang Spelmans' bedroom and there we recorded our experimental music for the next two to three weeks. We met with so many labels and told them what we had in mind. Nobody was interested. Again, we thought to ourselves, we can do this alone, so we went to the Pallas Record Press and started pressing them ourselves. I went to see my bank in Wuppertal, Landessparkasse, to get a loan and told them that I was producing a record and needed the money. They asked for a guarantee, so I offered them my car and that was accepted. We then used this money to produce our record. As soon as they were printed, they were basically ripped out of our hands. That was the very first DAF album, the yellow *Produkt Der*

Deutsch-Amerikanischen Freundschaft, and on the back sleeve it read: 'Aufgenommen von Februar bis April 1979 allein'. 'Recorded February to April 1979, by us alone'.

GABI DELGADO_We had absolutely no money, but were helped by technological advancements: parallel to the founding of DAF in 1978 arrived the first cheap Japanese synths from Korg for a thousand marks, and with those we could realise our vision. Music equipment manufacturers such as Yamaha or Korg were offering us a challenge, and whoever was brave enough to accept, to have a go and say that it is art, the way it comes out of the machines, was the winner. In my opinion, the inventor of the sequencer was almost more important to DAF than Robert or me. No joke! DAF was a zeitgeist gimmick, it was a style that fitted perfectly, like a neon triangle. The perfect sign of the times. People said that it just was some beeping, but our reply was: 'No, my friend. That just was the music.'

JÄKI ELDORADO_The idea to do something that at first sounds weird, but in the next moment opens the door to a huge new world of unknown sounds; that's what art should do. One autonomous artist should follow his own path, and not any widely accepted ones. That meant: variety was widespread. It was stimulating, yet electrifying. That's what 78 to 82 was all about. A new era.

GABI DELGADO_New music needed new instrumentation. It was time for a second generation. To me Kraftwerk were sounding too boring; too beautiful, too sedate and too sterile. And why should a new style use the instruments of their fathers: guitar, bass 'n' drums? That was old school. We wanted to develop in a more electronic direction, using machines to make our music. So we quickly separated from our fellow musicians. Now we were able to express ourselves the way we wanted. With us, as well, the machines would sweat.

ROBERT GÖRL_I had always been a trained musician and that made me a bit of an outsider. Many of the others were amateurs and didn't really have any skill at all, but they had great ideas. They were dilettantes but within this scene that certainly wasn't a bad thing to be. First you had to get your poster on the wall, then you would decide on your instrument. That was somehow cool though. It was all about doing stuff. On your own, and in contrast to what had been done before. Usually trained musicians wouldn't have been able to come up with something like this; they wouldn't have had the balls.

MORITZ REICHELT_Musically speaking we wanted to do something nobody else had done before. We wanted to make something that would otherwise not have been heard. Our name was in reference to a book about environmental problems by Gordon Rattray Taylor, *The Biological Time Bomb*. Within it, it said that one should not leave the environment to its own devices but instead have an action plan in place. That was the idea behind Der Plan; the ability of man to control their own destiny.

RALF DÖRPER_It would have never crossed my mind to buy a guitar and strum along. That said, I did perform solo at a few punk festivals in Düsseldorf and Hamburg with my synth; presenting very rudimentary, weird and Germanised covers, including a tongue-in-cheek version of 'Warm Leatherette'. As I painfully switched between white and pink noises using my Korg's oscillators, I chanted along monotonously and for minutes on end with "Warm, cold – warm, cold" and when the audience was ready to drag me from stage I changed to "Cold – warm – hot – burnt", after which I ripped open the filters and delved into a cacophony of electronica. Interesting with what you could get away with back then – that was the definition of punk. And it was via punk that I came to making music.

FRANK FENSTERMACHER_The more experimental, the more interesting it was. I found the likes of Throbbing Gristle or The Normal, where it got more and more un-normal, particularly fascinating. Electronica offered a route, it was a tool, to be doing something new and unheard of. If you'd never learnt an instrument then you could still be musically active and no one would turn around and say: 'What you're doing is shit'. If you wanted a corrosive sound then you made a corrosive sound. It was that easy. Coming up with the nicer stuff proved to be difficult, particularly with the monophony of the MS-20.

GABI DELGADO_ If ever a song sounded somehow similar to anything else, if it sounded familiar or reminded us of any other band, we got rid of it. Even if we thought it was good. If it sounded a little close to Suicide, Devo or Iggy – then it had to go, regardless of whether we liked it or not. We didn't want to sound as if we were 'historically aware'; we didn't want to follow traditions.

ROBERT GÖRL_ We weren't interested in relating ourselves towards anybody else; as soon as we thought something sounded like another band, then it was off the table, thrown away. That's why we are as original today as we were back then. We wanted to make music that couldn't be categorised. And because people couldn't label us as this or that, they started saying we weren't actually making music at all.

GABI DELGADO_ We said that everything that had come before, regardless of whether we'd heard it as kids or not, was shit. You have to do it that way. You have to put your horse blinkers on and ignore everything around you. When you know what you don't want, then you'll find your way to something you do want. That's why it was so important for us to say: 'We're not following in anybody's footsteps. That's old shit. With your long hair you look bloody stupid!'

ROBERT GÖRL_ It all came from our desire, our want to push on and on. Freddie Brocksieper was right: as a drummer you need to rule the snare, to hold the sticks and feel the beat. For an endless number of weeks or months a drummer has to rehearse their eighth notes – *tak tak tak tak tak tak tak tak* – so as they run smoothly like a metronome, like Freddie. I learned a lot from both him and the conservatorium. He was able to play those nice little rolls, triplets, everything. Eighth, 16th, 32-note triplets. Try doing that sometime. Try to play 32 triplets for two minutes. That urge was only fulfilled when I stopped and said: "Now I'll make my own music." I had trained for so long that I recognised: 'Now is the time. Nobody can toll me what to do. For no more. Nobody.' I wanted to push on ahead and discover the whole world.

Noise Performances

PETER GLASER_I had no idea about Düsseldorf, let alone Ratinger Hof. For me it was simply a town where they spoke German and where a band like Padlt Noidlt was possible.

DANIEL MILLER_We kept a close eye on anything coming out of Düsseldorf as many of our earlier success stories had also come from such an industrial and noise environment, such as Fad Gadget, Boyd Rice and my The Normal stuff. One genuine crucible of performance art, who stood alongside the likes of Padlt Noidlt, was Minus Delta T; or as they wrote: -Δt. That was the formula for the difference between two negative time values.

PETER GLASER_The reason I came to Düsseldorf was actually because of a band that I'd previously seen perform three times at the Steirischer Herbst, a great avant-garde cultural festival in Graz. They went by the name of Padlt Noidlt, and to us they were like some UFO from another planet, exploring sounds and spaces that we never knew existed. As something so radically new, they were hard to comprehend at first. Those involved were: the electronic musician Mike Jansen, who had already worked with both Beuys and John Cage; the brilliant drummer Frank Köllges; and Mike Hentz, who later went on to found Minus Delta T. With Mike Hentz I had met someone for the first time in my life to whom there existed no difference between shock performance and normal life. If you travelled with Mike Hentz you had to be aware of him breaking out into performance at any given second.

CHRISLO HAAS_We were deliberately provocative. Via our Graz connection, Robert Görl and I ended up with Minus Delta T, and our first show at the Hof saw us throwing animal cadavers, cement and flour around the place. That was one hell of a spectacle and landed us in a world of trouble. We always wore camo and were often involved in fights at our gigs. In fact, that was one of our most basic principles: provoke them – until they fight back.

RALF DÖRPER_Haas was one of the founding members of Minus

Delta T, an interesting art collective who were Situationists and performed provocative actions: on one occasion, they transported blocks of granite to the Himalayas to make the highest mountain even higher; on another, they transported barrels of oil to Saudi Arabia during the times of the oil crisis. These Situationists made a performance out of everything. The music was the least harmful thing in their repertoire.

PETER GLASER_When Mike Hentz entered a packed bourgeois coffee house and announced: "Now we're going to do a screaming concert," then you had no more than five seconds to decide to either step aside as if you weren't with him, or join in. If you were part of it or not was irrelevant to Mike, just as long as you did something. On one occasion he dressed up as an SS officer for Cologne Carnival... and was immediately arrested! It was Heinrich Böll who vouched for him and got him out of prison. Everything was a performance to Mike.

DAF

PETER HEIN_Kurt was without a doubt the first to introduce the whole synth set to the original Deutsch Amerikanische Freundschaft. It was the instrumental line-up, which Gabi was yet to be a part of. This early band played the Hof a couple of times – and that's how we came to know them. They had their synthesisers and sequencers. We kinda liked what they were doing, 'cause they reminded us of Pere Ubu, Suicide and The Normal. That's why we didn't shower them in plastic cups. Back then they were basically a jazz-rock group who'd been accidentally thrown together and featured two guys in leather jackets. The electronic input came from Kurt; he obviously wasn't interested in playing classical piano or accordion any longer. When I heard DAF at the Hof, they didn't really sound electronic at all. What was actually the dominating voice was Spelmans' noise like guitar. The noise came from him. And the synthesisers somehow just went along with it.

KURT DAHLKE_Back then I was living in an industrial-style loft in Wuppertal and was trying to record my debut solo record, *Inland*. That was around the time when I first got together with Moritz and Frank from the Art Attack gallery, and started making music with them as Der Plan. The three of us then founded our Ata Tak label on Fürstenwall 64 in Düsseldorf. Chrislo replaced me in DAF and in my opinion it was he who created the DAF sound with his revolutionary sequencing.

CHRISLO HAAS_When Pyrolator, that was Kurt Dahlke, quit the band, I was persuaded by Robert Görl to buy a synthesiser and join DAF. It was only much later that he started to get into synthesisers himself, and that was thanks to me. I bought the synthesisers to use especially with DAF. We'd driven to Holland and bought some hashish, which I then resold here in Düsseldorf, and after a week I had the 3000 Deutschmarks that I needed. On our return journey we started to get a little nervous around the border but thankfully everything ran smoothly. From Düsseldorf it doesn't take long at all to get to Holland. So that was how I financed my Korg synthesiser and sequencer.

ROBERT GÖRL_We decided on 'Deutsch Amerikanische Freundschaft' as our name simply by ballot. We'd all sat around the table noting down various names on little pieces of paper. Someone had written 'Deutschland', that's all, just 'Deutschland'. The others I can't recall. Anyway, we sorted out the papers and in the end 'Deutsch Amerikanische Freundschaft' was the one left over. The name stuck because of its deeper meaningfulness. It was critical, political and unusual. We thought it sounded extremely provocative and we liked that about it. Immediately we felt that this name was something new. It wasn't the typical name for a band, certainly not back in those days, so everyone thought: 'What?' They thought they'd misheard. At some point we were contacted by a conservative American women's club who were wondering if we were somehow connected to the German-American Association. That was how absurd the name was. And in the end everybody simply referred to us as DAF. That name was a winner. For a good band you have to have a good name. There are no good bands with bad names. My advice: find a good name first.

PETER HEIN_ At first we found DAF real shite. Suddenly you had the idiot deputy from Mittagspause – the one renowned for his dancing around the mic stand – disappear, only to then reappear without any warning with DAF. At first we thought, you've got to be kidding me. Then the yellow debut album popped up, and although you'd kind of heard about it, you thought it was pretty boring. To us that was DAF.

GABI DELGADO_ Our name DAF is still as ironic today as it was back then. Back in those days if you drove through East Germany you could read all those posters: 'Long live the German-Soviet Friendship'. In contrast, we had slogans such as 'Drink Coca-Cola'. That's how it was in the East and West, we always saw the parallels. We wanted a hard and provocative name, and DAF was exactly that. It was abstract and served as political propaganda.

BOB GIDDENS_ The first time I saw DAF was in February 1979. It was in Hamburg at the Into The Future festival, which had been put together by Alfred Hilsberg, who then went on to organise a second edition, which took place in June of the same year at Hamburg's Markthalle. I was writing for *ZigZag* at the time, an English magazine which had started out as a real hippie paper but later became more about punk rock. *ZigZag* was well known and in its heyday sold up to 50,000 copies. It was basically a professionally made fanzine. So I'd been sent to write about this festival, and other than DAF, Male and Mittagspause were also on the bill. I was in my mid-20s and simply fascinated by DAF, who sounded like nothing else I'd heard before – you couldn't say that about Male, who sounded a little too Clash-like, more like a cover band. With DAF it was different, you couldn't hear their influences. They seemed to be completely original.

JÄKI ELDORADO_ The interesting part was that music wasn't just played different, it was marketed and financed differently as well. That's why Alfred Hilsberg was such an important guy. He recognised that early on and chose to bring it out on his own label ZickZack.

BOB GIDDENS_Following the festival, I met with the band in Düsseldorf. They played some of their demos for me, featuring Gabi as a singer, and I thought they were quite good. A few days later, I gave them a call again and said: "We can do this. I'll try and get the cash for Cargo Studios." The band agreed, making it their clear mandate. They wanted Cargo because they liked everything that came out of that studio, in particular the sound of Gang Of Four. So I went to Düsseldorf as a journalist and returned to England as the producer and manager of DAF.

JÄKI ELDORADO_Düsseldorf always had this elitist artistic flair; it was all about being chic and elegant and even the local punk bands looked like high school students. At least that's how it felt to me. It had a real charm and the more sophisticated bands always looked up to Düsseldorf. Hilsberg signed a lot of bands from there, not only DAF but also Minus Delta T, *Stahlwerksinfonie* and all that other intense stuff as well. In Düsseldorf you had more of a chance to come across an art performance than an honestly felt 'no future' protest. There was widespread conflict across Germany between the ambitious, avant-garde art-student crap and the 'spare change' leather jacket-wearing punks. In Düsseldorf you would always go with the former.

BOB GIDDENS_At the beginning the band was very exciting, probably because of the diverse characters within: you had Gabi and Robert, the latter studied classical drums; Chrislo, the mad synth scientist; Wolfgang Spelmans on guitar; and Michael Kemner, who ended up with Fehlfarben, on bass. On the one hand, they all held equal status and functioned as a real band; on the other, I got along best with Robert, who seemed the more musical and business-orientated of the lot and had the best overview. I also was in touch with Spelmans, but the others were pretty much hiding.

ROBERT GÖRL_That's what we call destiny; you meet the right guy at the right time: Bob Giddens. He came to Düsseldorf – many say he dug us up – and told us he had some contacts back in England. If we wanted he could organise a trip. It was Bob Giddens from Quakenbrück, the Englishman, who discovered and inspired us.

BOB GIDDENS_I immediately wanted to work with this band and so I offered to finance the first recordings for this five-man line-up. They wanted to record in Rochdale, England, at John Brierley's Cargo Studios, which was well known in the punk and new wave circles. The small studio in Kenyon Lane was surrounded by an industrial wasteland and looked like something out of a war film. It was there that Joy Division had recorded 'Atmosphere', The Fall 'Rowche Rumble', and OMD had polished up their first single. Now DAF started to work there as well.

CHRISLO HAAS_Prior to going to England, we rehearsed our songs in an old factory in Düsseldorf. I had my VW van, in which I lived – I lived out of cars for many years – and as such I was DAF's driver. Anyway, we then drove to England in my van and Bob Giddens' Golf.

ROBERT GÖRL_So there we were; off to England! I wanted to take my drums to London – I had this amazing black Gretsch kit – but everywhere we went they already had a kit set up. So we set off to London in our VW van, like a proper young band. All packed. Next stop London. One day we were in Germany, the next day on our way to England, with Bob, minus any money and no contingency plan. It was like in some weird movie.

TINA SCHNEKENBURGER_It was just cool – adventurous; no money, no idea where we were going. No accommodation. But all of that didn't matter. We were in London!

BOB GIDDENS_At the last minute Gabi decided to bring his girlfriend Tina along; she was always around. Later on, when the band was falling apart, she even appeared onstage, changing the playback tapes in a cassette machine, whilst Robbi drummed and Gabi sang.

RALF DÖRPER_We knew Tina from the Ratinger Hof times. Back then I wasn't entirely sure if she was into guys at all, but then suddenly she was with Gabi. And then upon her return to Germany, she met Jürgen Engler.

FRANK FENSTERMACHER_She was always into the dark-haired, beady-eyed, tall, good-looking gentlemen and dancers. One of the most beautiful woman of the Ratinger Hof, sweet yet cheeky, spent her time with DAF.

TINA SCHNEKENBURGER_When we went to London I'd just turned 23, which in punk-rock-years made me a grandma already.

ROBERT GÖRL_All of a sudden, we were staying with Bob's mum in northern England, near Manchester, and Bob was trying to establish first contacts. We starved at Bob's mum's or aunt's place. Yeah, so what now? What comes next? Then Bob booked our first recording session in Rochdale at the well known Cargo Studios.

BOB GIDDENS_We spent one night at my mum's place, then another at my aunt's, and then during the recording sessions we stayed at a friend's place in Manchester. I knew John Brierley, the head of the studio, and it was he who put us in contact with John Peel. Peel repeatedly placed Cargo productions on his radio show. If you produced something good at Cargo then the chances were high that John would play your stuff. Over the 10 days we were recording there I met all the bands, from Joy Division to OMD to Gang Of Four. They worked the day shift; we the nights. That was the inspiration for our song 'Nachtarbeit', working through the night... did I just say 'our' song?

FRANK FENSTERMACHER_That guy loved DAF. He took the whole band to Rochdale with him. Kurt and myself even went to visit them there once. After that they lived in London. Things there were a little too stressful, which ended up being too much for Michael Kemner, who left the group soon after. It was actually Spelmans who stayed the longest.

BOB GIDDENS_We met Manchester band The Fall at Cargo Studios, who'd come to visit. They'd previously recorded several records there. One afternoon, their manager Kay asked me if DAF wanted to support them on their next tour. So we played Swindon, Brighton, amongst other cities that would be close to London – as we always had to return after our shows. Those were DAF's first ever shows in England.

TINA SCHNEKENBURGER_That was all across England. And it meant something to be the support band for The Fall. DAF were the no-names while The Fall were already on their way becoming a household name. Supporting them certainly generated some cult status for us.

CHRISLO HAAS_To be honest, the framework behind DAF was fairly simple: I produced some backing tapes which the others played along to. At the shows I worked with two cassette decks as well as operating my sequencer. That was why the sound had this unbelievable tension. It was breathtaking.

BOB GIDDENS_When you listen to 'Kebabträume' you pick up on the sequencer slowing down and speeding up. There are fluctuations in the timing. The Korg sequencer didn't react well to the English voltage; that said, it wasn't that easy to operate it in the first place. Between songs Chrislo had to adjust several sounds by hand; the older equipment was always unstable in regards to rhythm and intonation. Today you've got your iPad that can generate all the sounds at the press of a button; back then you needed to accurately twist the exact right knobs to get the best out of the machine.

CHRISLO HAAS_Analogue machines are controlled by voltage. Oscillators can go in and out of tune because of heat, cold or humidity. Same for the sequencers. When others joined in and played to this, it could sound very alive and organic. You had to take care of the sequencing in a live situation; it provided a further level of complexity. When the drummer got faster, for example, then you had to speed the machine up, or down, depending. If I was to slow the sequence, then Robbi had to adapt to the groove; and that had the potential to create magic moments between Görl and myself.

ROBERT GÖRL_To me it's still a miracle. We'd never played here before, our record was not out, yet it was said that our live performances were something special. People were interested in us. We weren't a guitar-band in any sense of the word; we'd always had a heavy electronic tendency. Over the course of time Chrislo's Korg became so much more important than Spelmans' guitar. We developed into an electronic band that really let loose live.

CHRISLO HAAS_It's simply impossible to be in complete control of analogue equipment, but that's what's nice about it; that it lives independent from us, the owners. On the one occasion that it worked out good, when they all march in step with each other, it's like three metronomes ticking in time. For the shortest of moments everything is in time, happy, and unheard of till then. That was the best but it only happened rarely. I had to treat my synthesisers with a lot of care, like my big love. I'd completely fallen for them.

CHRISLO HAAS

++ **FEB 80** DAF support Wire at the Electric Ballroom, London ++
MAR 80 DAF single 'Kebabträume' released on Mute ++ **APR 80**
Der Plan release album *Geri Reig* on their own label Ata Tak ++
MAY 80 Abwärts' seven-inch single 'Computerstaat' released through
ZickZack ++ **JUN 80** DAF's *Die Kleinen Und Die Bösen* released as
the first Mute album with catalogue number Stumm 1 ++ **JUL 80**
Cabaret Voltaire's *The Voice Of America* released via Rough Trade
++ Ultravox release their album *Vienna*, produced by Conny
Plank ++ **SEP 80** Bowie album *Scary Monsters* released ++ OMD
hit the German singles chart with 'Enola Gay' ++ La Düsseldorf's
Individuellos and Rheingold's 'Dreiklangsdimensionen' released ++
OCT 80 OMD release *Organisation* and Fehlfarben *Monarchie Und
Alltag* ++ **NOV 80** Visage release 'Fade To Grey' ++ **DEC 80** Dörper puts
out experimental 'Eraserhead' seven-inch ++ John Lennon shot dead
++ DAF start recording *Alles Ist Gut* with Conny Plank ++

DAF.co.UK

DANIEL MILLER_I knew DAF because Ata Tak had sent me their
first album. At some point, the manager contacted me here in
London and so we met up at the Rough Trade shop. Later on we
made some recordings together. By then they'd already recorded
'Kebabträume' I think. It was around this time that I first saw them
live as well. They'd been invited by The Fall to support them on
their tour of England. I remember their first gig at London's School
of Economics; they were simply fantastic!

BOB GIDDENS_The first time Daniel Miller saw DAF was at some
charity gig at the London School of Economics, where they appeared
alongside The Pop Group and Scritti Politti. I'd invited him to come,

and he'd come along with three young guys from Basildon who now became fans of DAF. They took the opportunity to distribute some of their own material on demo tapes. The Rough Trade people also came, and there we all were, transfixed by DAF.

ROBERT GÖRL_We met the guys from Mute, as well as Depeche Mode, who already come to our earlier shows, although at that point they weren't yet called Depeche Mode. Back then they still hadn't formed their band; their first single on Mute was released in the autumn of 81 and ours had already been released in March 80. You could almost say ours was a whole generation earlier. At this time, Mute didn't even have an office; nor any releases other than Daniel's very own: 'Warm Leatherette'. And there he was: Daniel Miller, the very quiet, very grandfather-ish guy. He was still living with his mum, and it was there that he'd recorded his single, at home. He called his project 'The Normal', and that was exactly what he was: perfectly normal. This was his tag line, his image, and it fitted him perfectly. Daniel discovered us and helped us a lot during that difficult period in England. Very quickly, more and more things started happening and different people got involved: we did 'Kebabträume' with Daniel, which we recorded at Cargo; suddenly everything started moving.

BOB GIDDENS_I'd already established contacts with Mute and Rough Trade; actually that was pretty simple in the case of DAF; somehow the band was already 'happening'. DAF were of interest to the English public not only because of their support slots for The Fall or Wire. They originated from Germany, they appeared very German with their short hair and clean-cut look; and they sang in German. They arrived on the underground scene at exactly the right time and were met with much positivity.

ROBERT GÖRL_It was important that we sung in German; that such progressive music was possible in the German language was a big thing for us. Up until then the Brits and Americans had the monopoly on modern music. We broke their domination.

RALF DÖRPER_At least one of their songs had pretty provocative lyrics: "Die lustigen Stiefel marschieren über Polen", meaning 'The funny jackboots march all over Poland'. With them most of their stuff related back to Germany in some way. It was a deliberately German music movement.

BOB GIDDENS_For me, being a Brit, DAF was the only band – aside from Kraftwerk – who managed to form a unit out of German lyrics and music, reflecting German culture without any Anglo-American influences. You didn't have that before – maybe with Brecht and this staccato German speak-sing. Here we had Gabi singing in his broken German as a result of his Spanish roots.

COLIN NEWMAN_For sure we also had bands in England who integrated machines into their music-making process, so that wasn't entirely new. Take Cabaret Voltaire, for example. They'd already had releases on Rough Trade; in fact their first single came out back in 1978 and included 'Do The Mussolini (Headkick)'. Only there they used their synthesisers and rhythm machines for conceptual reasons, out of principle. DAF, on the other hand, evolved in the heyday of post-punk where you could mix everything with anything. Live they used an acoustic drum kit in combination with their machines – and you could really dance to that! In a way, this distorted dance music was a step further away from punk. I've no idea how successful that was in Germany, but here in the UK people loved it.

ROBERT GÖRL_We were simply 'The Germans'! And suddenly there we were, the Germans, hanging around the Rough Trade shop for days on end, the holy temple of indie culture. Strange that they never kicked us out.

COLIN NEWMAN_They came over with no money, slept on people's floors, begged their way through each day, and, as a result, didn't make too many friends. But, from the very beginning, you could tell they were going to become something very interesting.

BOB GIDDENS_It could be said: at first the English had no idea what to make of DAF. Nobody had seen anything like them before. Five German-speaking musicians, certainly self-assured, full of confidence, with the paramilitary look of Christos' camo and the shaven skinheads sported by Gabi, Wolla and Robert.

ROBERT GÖRL_From the outset our outfit was very basic. Jeans, normal loafers, corduroy jackets and T-shirts; and only later did we add the English-style Harrington jackets. We never copied the Sex Pistols. In England extremely short hair was 'in' at that time. We wanted to come across as very straight, yet not in the military way. We wanted to convey a strong energy.

BOB GIDDENS_At their first show in Swindon, there was absolutely no applause between the songs at all; the little punks simply stared open-mouthed, not knowing what was happening to them. I've never experienced anything like that at a concert again. For half an hour the audience simply stood there, with eyes and mouth wide open, not knowing what to do. They just couldn't decide whether to clap, shout, shut up, or leave!

COLIN NEWMAN_I met Gabi once. He wasn't at all arrogant yet his appearance was one of self-confidence. He explained to me that he was a part-time member of Düsseldorf band Mittagspause. He knew that I was aware of who they were, even though they were close to unheard of in the UK in general; I'd got to know them through friends of mine from Düsseldorf and the Ratinger Hof.

TINA SCHNEKENBURGER_What I genuinely can't remember is what it was like back in the very beginning. I think it was Bob Giddens who first got us a basement flat in Earls Court. Before that came along, though, we often didn't have a place to stay and so ended up having to squat.

DANIEL MILLER_They even stayed at my mother's house. That was simply hilarious. Originally, it was only supposed to be Wolfgang and Gabi who stayed over, but suddenly all of them came over.

BOB GIDDENS_In London I met Mike Williams, who had Zircon Records, a smaller label. It was he who organised an apartment for them in Earls Court, which was where they experimented with the sequencers and rehearsed for their shows.

ROBERT GÖRL_Deutsch Amerikanische Freundschaft – although the Brits couldn't pronounce the name properly they were interested in its meaning. They knew it meant German American Friendship of course, but to them we were always only *Dee-Aye-Aff*. Our

GABI DELGADO

association with skinheads, though, didn't come about because of our name, but rather it was the energy of our shows that attracted them more than anything else. And suddenly people were turning up who liked the power of our sound. They all had shaven heads.

CHRISLO HAAS_Back in those days in England a lot of Nazis liked DAF, and I was the only one who was okay with that. Gabi hated it, but I didn't have any real problems with the skins.

GABI DELGADO_It was mostly due to Chrislo; he was such a radical guy. He had something that most of us softies lack – to him provocation was a fashion statement, combat aesthetic was chic. Chrislo, Robert and I; the three of us together, that was really something. We had the power of an army behind us. We were real paramilitary. We were simply radical.

MICHAEL KEMNER_I didn't have any money and quickly lost interest. The only one with some cash was Bob, although he certainly wasn't rich. He had a small budget put away for us and from day one he said: "Let's go to London. I can cover the costs for the rehearsal space, accommodation and some of the food, but that's all."

ROBERT GÖRL_We always had to rely on others to pay for our breakfast and coffee. Those were the days – as young men we could do that and still be optimistic about life. Gabi and I, we had this running gag to meet people, sometimes business people, and have them pay for our meals. We pretended to be interested in whatever they had to offer just so as to secure ourselves a dinner. We always thought: "After all, the food is good, and paid for." Somehow we could get away with that. Sometimes it got weird though, but regardless, those were the days.

CHRISLO HAAS_Mike Hentz gave me a box of paperbacks of Adolf Hitler's *Mein Kampf*, which I always carried around with me. There was once this awkward situation: after one of our concerts, during our encore, some of the punters were about to rush the stage, which really stressed out Gabi – so I started to hand out these little books to calm everybody down; and everyone seemed happy in the end.

GABI DELGADO_On one occasion I was beaten up by some skinheads. It only happened once, but once was enough! It was horrible. And all over some girl.

MICHAEL KEMNER_ For a long time London wasn't good for me. I was as sick as a dog, minus any health insurance, with horrible toothache and a badly infected jaw. I had no idea what to bloody do. That was real shite. On top of that there was a lot of tension within the band with Chrislo. With Gabi it was already difficult enough, but with the both of them it got impossible. And then eventually, one day, I simply had enough and was completely done with it all – so I left. Now, when I think back, I can't actually remember how I made it back home to Germany.

CHRISLO HAAS_ On another occasion Mike Hentz gave me a shirt from some American Nazi organisation. He'd written to them and had received some of their uniforms and promotional material in return. The shirt had the SS logo on the sleeves, as well as a Death head. All in all it was a very cool shirt. To me it was just another piece of military outfit; not a fascist statement but rather a fashion statement.

ROBERT GÖRL_ It was body art, so to speak: hard, clear, pure. If it came across as military, then good for us. Some people saw it as an SS reference but we just thought it was a fantastic outfit. Strong and straight. Not weak. To us there was never anything else to it. It was just a great look.

MICHAEL KEMNER_ They just wanted to prove their point and I always had the feeling that they would not stop at nothing. They would not let anything get in their way. In the end, that's the way it was. If i didn't leave on my own, they would have had me go. I knew that. With Wolfgang and Chrislo it was the same thing.

CHRISLO HAAS_ Immediately after our first headlining show, they told me they no longer wanted me in the band. That was fine with me though. And soon enough Michael also left, he was already fed up after the studio sessions in Rochdale.

DANIEL MILLER_I thought their five-man line-up was best and I was very disappointed when Chrislo left; his talent was simply unique. Later on it was we who released his next project, Liaisons Dangereuses. He had so many good things going but then threw them all away.

GABI DELGADO_At first, it was Robert and myself as DAF, and it was all fairly conventionally thought out, and then we added some extra musicians into the mix – Chrislo, Wolla and Michael. But then it all felt too old school, and they weren't as tough as us. Then along came the sequencer and we thought: now we don't need bandmates any longer, only the machines. Machines are patient, they always play the same thing, they don't get too involved and they don't have egos. That's how we evolved into a duo, step by step.

MICHAEL KEMNER_Then Wolfgang fell ill with jaundice and hepatitis and lay in hospital for weeks on end. Nobody from DAF ever came to visit him. Nobody. There was absolutely no contact. They seemed to be happy that he was away.

DANIEL MILLER_When they started working on their second album Wolfgang came down sick. I think he had some serious health problems and, as such, missed some of the earlier recording sessions. Anyway, by the time he was well enough to return, the others had already discovered their new musical direction and he was no longer needed. From then on there were only two.

KURT DAHLKE_Wolla was a little more stubborn than Michael and actually went along to Conny's studio with them, wanting to be part of it.

MICHAEL KEMNER_Although he was no longer welcome.

GABI DELGADO_When Spelmans later came to join the production, it was already a finished block, musically speaking – it was done. We couldn't find anything for him to do. In the meantime, we started to hate guitars; we couldn't see no guitar any longer. Felt like guitars were the leftovers from the old world.

DANIEL MILLER_All at once, they came to see me and we got into endless discussions about this and that; there was a lot of trouble and ego problems within the group. By then we were already on our way to Conny Plank to start recording the first Mute album. Suddenly everybody was the spokesman or head of the band. In the end, the reason they gave up the quintet was because they all wanted to be the boss.

FRANK FENSTERMACHER_What concerned me about DAF were the cutbacks in personnel; even if it was consistent, it was still a shame.

They were cutting down, but losing their resources. I got it: as a duo you can navigate, work and split way better.

PETER HEIN_Musically, they maybe shrank for the good, but on a personal level they rather shrank it to ill. Michael got toothache and was out, whilst Chrislo was fed up and returned to Berlin. Spelmans went down with illness and was lying in a hospital in England. In that way *Die Kleinen Und Die Bösen* became 'The 10 little Wuppertalians'. They started as a football team, but only two of them made it.

BOB GIDDENS_Then they recorded *Die Kleinen Und Die Bösen* at Conny's studio. That said, it was only the first side of the album that was recorded with Conny; the B-side was a live recording taken from their Electric Ballroom show back in February, when they'd supported Wire. On the album cover it read: 'Recorded at Electric Ballroom by accident'. The session at Conny's took place in March 1980. It was the first Mute long-player and had the catalogue number Stumm 1.

DANIEL MILLER_Chrislo's departure was partly planned, partly not. He had been frustrated, not wanting to perform live any longer. There had been constant power struggles within the band, so he ended up only being on this album. We took the live tracks from the Electric Ballroom, as well as others produced in the studio. I didn't have any money. So when they told me that Conny was interested in producing their album I couldn't believe it; I have always been such a great fan of Conny Plank. So I quickly booked Conny's studio for three days. After the first two days, though, hardly anything happened and I was going crazy. My whole existence was now in jeopardy. Conny told me to stop worrying and gave me a calming feeling. And then, on the third day, the album was cut, almost recorded like a live album with no overdubs or any additional technical gimmicks. And there it was. The first album for Mute.

CHRISLO HAAS_For the studio recordings I was still involved, but after our return to England I stood down. We drove all the way over from London and then back again just to work with Conny. After getting back I jumped into my VW van, drove to Berlin, and moved in with Beate Bartel.

ROBERT GÖRL

GABI DELGADO_We went to Conny's studio with our tapes, cassette tapes to be correct, and those we played to him. "I like it," he said, which is why he agreed to record with us. Conny was a real hippie, a hippie in the best sense. And because the real hippie spirit is to share, we suddenly had three days to record *Die Kleinen Und Die Bösen*. That was our first project with Plank.

BOB GIDDENS_Looking back I wouldn't want to have missed any of that, and perhaps it will say on my tombstone that I was the manager of DAF. We had an amazing time and opened the door a little for other bands to push through. For me it was all very appealing, at least up to the point when it all fell apart. DAF's music opened a new dimension, far away from any given blues scheme. Completely different to the vibrating punk movement in London, with bands like The Clash or The Damned, who were still following the traditional chord structures of rock'n'roll; this was something completely new. As equally new as Kraftwerk, although Kraftwerk lacked the pushing, aggressive approach of DAF. Let's say you want a German band imitating the West Coast sound, that wouldn't work well – but these guys here been brave enough to sing in German and, in doing so, made a movement like Neue Deutsche Welle possible, even if that was the last thing they had in mind. I think it was all some kind of pressure relief. Suddenly you had people at the record companies who said: 'Okay, go ahead, you can sing this in German'. To get there it needed people like Gabi Delgado or Peter Hein. Even Male were seen as a cool new punk band because of their German lyrics rather than their adapted music. German lyrics were suddenly not only accepted within the schlager world, but also for serious, no-bullshit music.

TINA SCHNEKENBURGER_Somehow, one after the other got lost. We never had any money, were always living off scraps and half the time not even having the 10p for Rough Trade's Space Invaders machine.

ROBERT GÖRL_We told Daniel we wanted some money, we were starving. Yet, despite the release of our single, his reply was: "I am sorry, but we don't have any money."

RALF DÖRPER_Suddenly a three-piece DAF was making the rounds in Germany; they made an appearance at the Ratinger Hof as well. That was Lopez, Görl and Spelmans – and to be honest, the guitar actually worked really well. Spelmans' guitar style was similar to that of Andy Gill from Gang Of Four: staccato with a touch of white funk to it. That must have been back in the late summer of 80. Soon afterwards – following the Belehrung And Unterhaltung Festival in Berlin – Christina Schnekenburger replaced Spelmans onstage, operating the tape decks with the sequencer-driven backing tracks of their songs.

PETER HEIN_I didn't take any of this too seriously; not *Die Kleinen Und Die Bösen*, not anything else about DAF. Everybody was raving about it, but it wasn't for me. One day I bumped into Michael Kemner on my way from the main station to the Altstadt: "I thought you were in England?" "Nope – that didn't work." "You can play bass in my new band, Fehlfarben." And so Michael happened to be in a band again only two weeks later.

WERNER LAMBERTZ_ There I was, sat at the neighbouring table, as Wolla dealt with the two of them: Robert, who later became a good friend of mine, and Gabi. The three of them were discussing Wolla's departure. Talking about his severance payments and copyrights, and which version of which songs had to be released and in which way. I was only there on Wolla's request to witness the agreements. I then went on to record an album with Wolla and Michael Kemner at my own studio, while the others went to Conny's place. Later DAF released 'Der Rauber Und Der Prinz' without Wolfgang's guitar, and that is the better known version produced by Conny. The other version, the one with Wolla's guitar, was released as a seven-inch single with 'Tanz Mit Mir' on the flipside.

TINA SCHNEKENBURGER_I was no longer with Gabi, but I was still living in Finsbury Park. By then all the others had left, so I had the rooms to myself. I only remember some snapshots, for example me sitting in the Rough Trade back room typing the inner sleeve for *Die Kleinen Und Die Bösen* and then demanding in an emancipatory manner that I, as I have typed the notes, get a credit as well. That's why it still says 'Typed by Tina Schnekenburger' on the sleeve.

JÜRGEN ENGLER_Chrislo was with them up until *Die Kleinen Und Die Bösen*; then Robbi did all the well-known EBM sequences. EBM stands for 'electronic body music', a term which only really came into use when the Brits and Belgians stepped into the 'sequencer business' with bands like Nitzer Ebb and Front 242. There you could find that sound again, where it was catchily picked up and labelled. In our days all these terms didn't exist, not 'industrial' nor 'post-punk'. Anyway, Robbi then was in charge of the music, though playing 16-step sequences wasn't exactly rocket science.

KURT DAHLKE_My theory, although it has always been strongly denied by Robert, is that he actually copied a lot of what Chrislo was doing. If you confront him with this, of course, he will say that he was the one who came up with it all. But in my opinion it was Chrislo. It was Chrislo who introduced sequencing to the group in the first place, and he was the one with all the right equipment: the Korg MS-20 and the keyboard-less Expander MS-50, which he channelled through a guitar amp instead of playing it directly into the mixing desk. "Plug the thing into an amp and see what happens," he said. It wasn't until much later that Robert had his own MS-20.

PETER GLASER_Whether or not Chrislo Haas, Kurt Dahlke or Robert Görl invented these EBM blueprint sequences is beside the point. There was this basic pattern, a primeval feeling that this would be the sound of the times. Everybody developed this in his own style. With Chrislo it was less than with Görl about a purification, but about something dirty, about scratching off the old forms. Of course, Chrislo scratched the meat off the bones, but he wanted the dirt to stick, whilst DAF were only asking: 'What or whom can we leave out next?'

KURT DAHLKE_Bob Giddens was treated particularly poorly. He put all his savings into DAF but got nothing in return. He was the sponsor – all his cash went into the band – but it was others who cashed in.

BOB GIDDENS_It was an adventure and probably meant to either weld the band together or tear them apart. 'Make 'em or break 'em', as they say. In the beginning it was a band decision to go to London, then some members went back home and others made a concept out of that. What can you say. This mixture of synthesiser music with a regular band wasn't meant to last. Robert was able to take the musical heritage from Chrislo and did it by himself from then on. All good.

Fehlfarben

PETER HEIN_The lyrics for 'Kebabträume' came completely from Gabi. We'd already played the song with Mittagspause and Franz and Thomas Schwebel had provided the music. But as always: when we started playing it with Fehlfarben, it wasn't yet in DAF's repertoire – but I rather shouldn't discuss this here. I don't know whether Michael and Kurt had brought it with them from their DAF period or if the DAF version was musically different. I never really listened to the stuff, but I always liked the song; I thought the text was great. For me it was a Mittagspause song and so I took it with me to Fehlfarben. The title then became 'Millikturk'; so we weren't using the same title, but it was basically the same song.

MICHAEL KEMNER_'Abenteuer Und Freiheit', Fehlfarben's first single, was recorded at Klangwerkstatt studio in Düsseldorf. In total we ended up pressing a couple of hundred copies ourselves, one of which I took along with me to Cologne's Stadthalle in Muhlheim, in Cologne's east, where The Specials, The Slits and various other bands played. It was there that I met Alan Bangs, presenter of the *Rockpalast* TV show. I gave him the single and said: "Here, Fehlfarben. Play it on your show." Three days later he did. That started the ball rolling. Then John Peel picked it for his show as well, and things really took off.

FRANK FENSTERMACHER_For the first Fehlfarben album Kurt was part of the studio team. Though there were hardly any electronic elements in it, you can hear a Prophet 5 and a Minimoog on the last track, 'Paul Ist Tot'; that was about it. We may have had some sequencer lines on 'Ernstfall' as well. 'Paul Ist Tot' fitted perfectly well to the whole punk thing and became an anthem for the Ratinger Hof, mostly because of the lyrics: "Was ich haben will, das kriege ich nicht, was ich kriegen kann, das gefällt mir nicht", meaning 'What I want I don't get, and what I can get I don't like' – with these words Janie got immortalised. Everyone was quoting it. "Wir flippern zusammen, Paul ist tot, kein Freispiel drin", meaning 'Let's do the pinball now, Paul is dead, no extra ball for us'. These were all images from our life at the Hof, and so the song got bigger and bigger. It's the instant anthem of the new era – lasting a little less than eight minutes.

PETER HEIN_We had made these opening helicopter sounds with the MS-20, but somehow we were stuck, so Kurt had to help us with the sounds for 'Ernstfall'. The ticking clock click on 'Paul Ist Tot' is actually made with guitar, muted with the palm of your hand and played close to the bridge; that wasn't a synth. 'Paul Ist Tot' has a certain Joy Division feel to it, and the song structure is basically: forward, played straight through. We weren't good enough for three chords, so we just came up with these two.

FRANK FENSTERMACHER_With Fehlfarben, I was in the lowest rank. They heard that I played saxophone, although they'd never actually heard me play it. They only asked: "You play saxophone, right? Yeah, that's right. Why not come along and play with us then?" Then they got stuck with me; and it was only later, when things started to get serious, that they had a more in depth chat about things with me.

PETER HEIN_Michael's bass playing was heavily influenced by Joy Division. Beside the scratchy guitar sound all that matters was the bass; and with us it didn't play the typical eighth note backing, but the melody instead. Same what Hooky did for Joy Division. And here it was Michael Kemner.

Der Plan

FRANK FENSTERMACHER_Moritz and myself started making music after attending a concert in our very own Art Attack gallery, given by two students of Joseph Beuys. One of them, Jürgen Kramer, had an exhibition with us but was playing music as well; nowadays you'd call it a music-art performance. It inspired us to do something with music ourselves. We were both artists more than musicians. Jürgen Kramer was in contact with Cabaret Voltaire, The Residents and many others. We founded our first band: Weltende, meaning 'world's end', and then quickly moved on to be the Weltaufstandsplan, which was Moritz, me and a young bass player. When the bass player left Weltaufstandsplan became Der Plan. Then Kurt joined and it was our big chance to get our hands on the first MS-20.

ROBERT GÖRL_I was a founding member of Der Plan, but that is not widely known. Kurt hadn't joined yet, so it was only Chrislo Haas, Moritz, me and Fenstermacher. We founded Der Plan in the basement of Mary Lou Monroe's detached house in Düsseldorf-Wersten. It was where we recorded our first single, 'Das Fleisch', as well, on 15 Milrather Street; recorded straight to the Sanyo dictaphone we had. That was in the beginning, when we were testing and trying things out; it was a pretty fun time. First came the friendship, the chemistry; then we were handing out instruments.

FRANK FENSTERMACHER_We had cut up a text by Georg Wilhelm Friedrich Hegel and were bouncing this back and forth on the intercom. At the same time we looped a synthesiser in and out. Before Kurt had joined we'd released an EP called *Das Fleisch* with Robert Görl and Chrislo Haas, who had already been playing around with the MS-20 previously, but perhaps this was his MS-20 debut. Chrislo Haas and Robert Görl were members of Der Plan for a short period of time, maybe two, three or at most four hours! Quite funny really, and further evidence of how mixed up the Düsseldorf scene was back then. The recordings took place at Bielmeier's reheasal room and were quite the extreme experience. It started out as a drug-inspired session in a cellar in Wersten which I taped with my Sanyo dictaphone. The machine broke at some point during the session and started slowing down. When we played the recorded music back later it sounded like it was getting faster and faster. It was our debut, and an international breakthrough at the same time, becoming more and more widely recognised. The first pressing of 300 to 500 copies sold out almost immediately and we suddenly had contacts all over the world. We then went on with our first full length record, *Geri Reig*, which topped it all.

KURT DAHLKE_For Der Plan, 1980 kicked off with *Geri Reig* and *Normalette Surprise*. We had a shared flat split into two sections: on the left was our office and centre for distribution; on the right our living quarters.

FRANK FENSTERMACHER_Our first record was self-released; we founded our own label, Ata Tak. For Moritz and myself that meant the end of our gallery work. We then moved to Düsseldorf.

KURT DAHLKE_We founded Ata Tak and from then on released all our own stuff via that. Additionally it made some sense to release other artists through our label as well. We knew Holger Hiller from Hamburg and got his first single out. Soon after we signed Limburg-based band The Wirtschaftswunder. Then in 1981 we had Andreas Dorau. So slowly we built up our label, one block at a time, until eventually we also took charge of the distribution as well.

FRANK FENSTERMACHER_After one year we had a real surprise success with Dorau's 'Fred Vom Jupiter'. That piece fell somewhere between children's song and electronic noise. Because of its success, though, it was later looked down upon.

KURT DAHLKE_By then Germany had several distribution companies: Rip Off from Hamburg, who were responsible for the north, and Eigelstein and Zensor, who took care of the south. That was how the market was divided, so we had to position our own distributing company accordingly.

FRANK FENSTERMACHER_We were lucky because in those days we had independent music journalism, or at least that was what we thought. For example, Hamburg's *Sounds* magazine. Without having to go door knocking, there were people who were promoting what we were doing, who wrote: 'That is something completely new, what we're hearing. You have to tune in!' Diedrich Diederichsen and Alfred Hilsberg, among others, were writing about us. That's how people started paying attention. The flavour of the moment, one might say. It could have easily slipped through the cracks, though, and interested nobody.

KURT DAHLKE_All of Der Plan's material was released on Ata Tak with only one exception: the 12-inch maxi single 'Gummitwist', which was released by WEA; additionally, there was a co-production done for 'Da Vorne Steht Ne Ampel' on green vinyl, which later got bought by Teldec. Other than that we had to stand up for our crimes alone.

FRANK FENSTERMACHER_Back then the distribution and exchange of records, with our products, was our way of getting in touch with people all over the world before we had today's internet. We had our network where we sent out records and tapes, and we usually added something personal, such as a letter or something graphical.

JÜRGEN ENGLER_From very early on Der Plan was working with electronic equipment. *Geri Reig* was released as early as 1980, and I really liked it. They were one of the first to be purely electronic, even if it did sound a little bumpy and childlike at times.

FRANK Z._To me Der Plan was more of an art project. They probably saw The Residents at some point and were inspired to add some children's melodies. They were very different to Kraftwerk, and certainly not as skilful. In all honesty, it was utter crap. Frank Fenstermacher is a nice guy and we had to deal with them on the distribution level, but as for their own band I didn't know what to make of that.

MEIKEL CLAUSS_In regards to German electronic music, Kurt Dahlke will be considered as having an important role in it some day. He is extremely underrated regarding how innovative and ahead of his times he was. What he lacked, though, was the right product, the right band.

KURT DAHLKE_But then it all just fell apart: the bankruptcy of Rip Off, Eigelstein went bust, and we had a ton of records which we couldn't get out fast enough. There were some bad years to come, that's for sure.

PETER GLASER_At some point I was in the studio when Pyrolator was recording. And the way that he just jumped into his melodies had a completely different virtuosity to it than Kraftwerk. He was able to convey a human element through his synthesiser, whereas Kraftwerk tried to eliminate that from all of their material and aimed to reduce everything down to the robotic skeleton. He could show you what was left over technologically, the non-digital, non-computer-based stuff, stuff that you could never google. He was able to craft that with great elegance and ease. You needed enormous amounts of artistic craft to be able to do that. And aside from all of that Kurt always remained a wonderfully nice person.

RALF DÖRPER_I was a semi-member of S.Y.P.H. They went through a number of different phases; first more punk rock and then somewhat experimental. And just did these synthesiser performances, with some recordings taken from the radio.

MEIKEL CLAUSS_Dörper? For a time he performed using only a shortwave radio. He'd stand onstage fiddling around with the tuning knobs.

BERND CAILLOUX_In Berlin, I had this woman who took me along to see DAF and Der Plan at the Rostlaube, at the Uni, and maybe around 200 people turned up. DAF came onstage, set up a little radio at the front and from that it all kind of just started. Conversely, Der Plan were more like an accidental joke: they appeared onstage as white ghosts with their pointed hats, looking really clumsy and all. Straight away these lads did not have any chance with any of the girls.

RALF DÖRPER_That must have been at the Belehrung And Unterhaltung Festival, with DAF, Fehlfarben, Der Plan, Mania D and Vorsprung, in November 1980 at the audimax of the Berlin University. To be more precise: Saturday, November 1 at the Technical University Charlottenburg. And why do I know that? Because I was there. I probably was performing with some S.Y.P.H. spin-off – I think it was just me and one other guy. We delivered the most horrible noise performance you could have asked for. Jürgen was there as well; he'd unfortunately just changed the name of his band from Male to Vorsprung, although nobody seemed to really get that. With a new musical decade beginning they didn't really seem to have any kind of a Vorsprung, meaning 'lead', at all. Nobody liked the name change and so it got more ignored than honoured. And yeah, P.D. also played. They were a noise band from Mainz. Uh huh, that's right. That stood for Permutative Distortion.

BERNWARD MALAKA_This Belehrung festival with DAF must have been what triggered it. Jürgen and I were standing backstage, were pretty impressed and all and said to ourselves: "Let's forget these songs, we should move away from these old song structures." We also wanted to go in this more minimalistic direction and threw everything overboard. As soon as we returned back home, Jürgen only played noisy chords on his guitar with heavy feedback, and I kept concentrating on only playing the low E-string on my bass. That became a healthy basis for Die Krupps and the blueprint for *Stahlwerksinfonie*.

JÜRGEN ENGLER_Absolutely, that was the time post-Male: the revolution was over, but the battle was not yet won. We needed something new, at least that's what we told ourselves.

PETER GLASER_DAF approached their shows in a fairly sportive way. They had this fitness element where Gabi was constantly on the move. He fashioned his own particular style of dancing, and back in the Eighties everybody copied that. In Berlin, this dance style was much better received than the honorific Pyrolator sophistication.

MEIKEL CLAUSS_Der Plan was humorous and well done, or rather well thought of, one would better say. But they didn't have any sex appeal; Der Plan is the most unsexy band on this planet. The unsexiest band alive.

WERNER LAMBERTZ_The film *Die Letzte Rache* by Rainer Kirberg featured only music from Der Plan. That is Moritz, Kurt and Frank. Kirberg was always hanging around with Der Plan, contributing the strangest of things. He was involved in the first cover artworks as well. Then he directed *Die Letzte Rache* with Frank Fenstermacher playing the role of detective. All very weird. A late Der Plan album was then consequently named *Es Ist Eine Fremde Und Seltsame Welt*, meaning 'It is a strange and bizarre world'.

Experimental Performances

RALF DÖRPER_Soon after there were other electronic concepts next to DAF and Der Plan. The idea behind my double-A single 'Eraserhead'/'Assault', for example, was that of a midnight movie special. I originally thought of it as a double A-side, with Carpenter on one side, Lynch the other, and on both I worked with sound collages; that was in the pre-sampling era, with tape recordings. I adapted the 'Assault' theme with atmospheric synth sounds and underlaid it with a German news report about a poison gas cloud over the Bayer chemical factory. For 'Eraserhead', I mixed my sounds with original dialogue taken from the film. Those I'd taped secretly at some cinema with a dictaphone. Just as secretly I took some pictures of the film with a very long exposure. The results featured these surreal cross-fade effects. One ended up on the cover of the single, which was released by Rondo, and another I used for the cover of Die Lemminge.

JÜRGEN ENGLER_Die Lemminge are a little forgotten nowadays. There has only ever been this one single release on the Pure Freude label. It was an early electro thing by Ralf and myself from a time prior to the *Stahlwerksinfonie*. We recorded it at Ata Tak studio on Fürstenwall; Kurt was involved and so was Frank Fenstermacher. Kurt was 'the man with the 4-track machine', which is why he was our go-to man.

PETER GLASER_The novelty of this era was that some production goods, which were previously exclusively owned by the record industry, were now owned by musicians themselves. Not only did they now have the same 4-track tape machine but they also shared the knowledge that The Beatles had recorded the entire *Sgt. Pepper's* album on only four tracks. That both inspired and embarrassed. It lent wings but paralysed at the same time.

RALF DÖRPER_This even led to a point where our hip hairdresser Teja Schmitz thought he should start dabbling in experimental music as well. He belonged peripherally to the night owl clique and

Kraftwerk entourage. He managed to produce an obscure and very unique single, 'Säuren Ätzen Und Zersetzen', in minimal style. For me it was one of the absolute best local underground productions ever. Teja released this outstanding and surprisingly good piece of music himself; then returned to take care of the party scene of the state capital, Düsseldorf. You'd see him in the daytime riding his racing bike in Kraftwerk style or during summertime hanging at the sun terrace of the Rheinstadion, together with Wolfgang Flür and other 'women whisperers'.

KURT DAHLKE_At that time, Boyd Rice had also released some pretty strange records on Mute, mostly endless vinyl grooves with three holes punched into the record, pure noise, complete industrial stuff. We attended a show of his in Berlin where he used only a metal box with two knobs: one for white noise, the other for pink noise. Before the show commenced he threatened the sound technician, telling him if he didn't turn the volume up he was a dead man. And yeah, then he irradiated Berlin with his white noise. "Noise, noise, everybody dance. Noise!"

JÜRGEN ENGLER_DIN A Testbild played the Ratinger Hof, and it was probably meant to be an art performance more than a gig. Mark Eins, together with Gudrun Gut, performed some sort of weird, 20-minute-long mockery of Kraftwerk, singing "We are the robots" over and over again at the most annoying pitch. At the end of which they said: "You don't need to clap, we are robots." I have no idea if that was something they did in other cities as well.

RALF DÖRPER_In London it was Chris Bohn who took care of all things German. It was thanks to him that DAF became well known. His reviews were always particularly positive. He wrote for the *New Music Express*, or *NME*, one of the three weekly published music papers. In fact, that was how my homage to Carpenter/Lynch, released by Rondo, came to be *NME*'s record of the week. Wow. That was brilliant. That was a killer. Something I accomplished twice: he made Die Lemminge single of the week as well. Which led to even more joy, but mostly the scene's disappointment. Everyone begrudges you for that. The British label Cherry Red later put both singles out on one EP. Well, better be envied than pitied.

KURT DAHLKE_ Boyd Rice came and stayed with us here in Düsseldorf. He was was quite an outlandish guy to be honest; for example, one night he went to some cemetery to record the voices of the dead. He told us: "You Germans have such a rich musical tradition. Why is it all buried? It's all been hidden away by the Nazis. You have, for example, Robert Stolz!" That said, Robert Stolz was actually Austrian, but that's besides the point. "You have Paul Hindemith," he said, "and so many other great composers who have all been banned by the Nazis. Take a look at your schlager! The German schlager of the Fifties is magnificent!" He was a great fan of Cornelia Froboess and knew all her stuff from the Fifties. When he found out she was living in Solingen, only 30 kilometres away from Düsseldorf, he immediately set off with all his noise records under his arm. Yeah, he drove down there to swap records with Cornelia Froboess. True.

PETER GLASER_ In our living room, real records came to life, and all self-recorded onto four tracks: Padeluun with 'Nazis Are No Fun', flipside 'Ich Gehe Wieder Mal Durchs Düsseltal', and other obscure stuff as well. It couldn't be obscure enough, and always used the cheapest of electronics; it was anti-professional by choice, litanic repetition of programmatic phrases, and every other possible sound and noise texture.

MEIKEL CLAUSS_ In Germany, electronic music was immature, boring stuff, really boring, produced by mummy's boys who, in the best of cases, were only a little interested in science fiction or Airfix model airplanes.

RALF DÖRPER_ With 'Klammheimlich', you'll find a piece from my early performances with the band S.Y.P.H. and it's prominently featured on their first EP: *Viel Feind, Viel Ehr.* 'Klammheimlich' was a sound collage that despite the title, did not refer to the 'Göttinger Mescalero Text', an often-quoted letter which talks of the 'clandestine joy' felt about the RAF assassinations. Clandestine meaning 'klammheimlich'. Rather, the song refers to a newsreader's statement about the RAF members' suicides in Stammheim, and the fact they more or less have been 'suicided'. Harry Rag and I took the voice recordings from the TV news and mixed them with some evil sounds from my Yamaha CS-10. We shouted with an awfully vocodered voice: "Heldentum, Eigentum, Eigenheim, Stammheim", meaning 'heroism, possession, homestead, Stammheim'... complete Dada.

KURT DAHLKE_S.Y.P.H. and Der Plan have always been closely connected. Once there was this matchless situation that evolved when we played in Mainz. We were performing as Der Plan, and then after a short break S.Y.P.H. were meant to play. But somehow Harry Rag had found out that the festival was funded by a political party, the Young Liberals, so effectively the FDP party. He was so annoyed and said he never would have confirmed to play had he known this. Then he got the total fee changed at a local bank into small coins, got onstage after the break, and threw all the 10 pfennig coins into the audience screaming: "We don't want your fuckin' FDP money!" Whilst doing that he tried to smash his white Fender guitar in a way The Who would have done it. But that's a solid guitar. It took him nearly half an hour to finish it off, and it was painful to watch. What a shame. All in all.

Individuellos

KLAUS DINGER_Our *Individuellos* album was in many ways the final component of our rise and fall. The Rise and Fall of La Düsseldorf, which came about in three parts. *Individuellos* is not our most euphoric album and we did have some problems putting it together. The song material was quite substantial, but in the making we took some wrong turns. And as such it didn't really sell as well as the other two.

HANS LAMPE_*Individuellos* was our follow-up to *Viva*. Seeing as the latter had sold so well – because of 'Rheinita' – we had to come up with a worthy successor quite quickly.

KLAUS DINGER_Just In Germany our second album sold around 300,000 copies. As such, I quickly realised that with *Viva*, La Düsseldorf was becoming a household name in the bigger markets, like America, Japan and England. As well as France and Italy – in fact, let's say Europe in general.

HANS LAMPE_We were experiencing some problems and as a result, by the time we got around to the production, Thomas, having been frustrated by the constant fighting with his dominant brother, had already left. One minute he was there, the next he was on his way to the south of France with his long-term girlfriend Tina Schneider-Esleben, the younger sister of Florian.

CLAUDIA SCHNEIDER-ESLEBEN_Tina, my younger sister, was the more sensible one, the introvert, the romantic. The opposite to me. Where only two-and-a-half years separated me from Flo, she was considered the latecomer and had been the nestling. Born in 1955, she was six years younger then me, and was the baby of the family.

MÂRI PAAS_The relationship between Klaus, Thomas and Hans soured over the years and became more and more difficult and tense. On the one hand, you always had to submit to Klaus' rules, while on the other, everyone wanted some private life on their own, and that minus Klaus. You couldn't really get both though.

CLAUDIA SCHNEIDER-ESLEBEN_Thomas was Tina's greatest love. They had a shared interested in fashion, music, graphic design and photography. They had a spiritual connection and passion; he was Scorpio and she was Pisces. There are still some funny pictures floating around from some experimental sessions of the two of them dressed up, made up and posing in a transgender look. One was even used as a cover image. At one point the four of us went to France together, and when I was visiting Düdo, I always stayed with them.

HANS LAMPE_*Individuellos* included our track 'Dampfriemen', meaning 'steam belt'. The inspiration for and melody of this piece came from Thomas; that is why you can see him on the cover of the maxi single – a picture where he's dressed in women's clothes. The photo was taken by Tina Schneider-Esleben; she is credited on the cover for that. The artwork and design came from Thomas – that was all his domain, and so too this whole plexiglas thing: neon roses and plexiglas; that was Thomas. He had an eye for visuals, and also loved to dress up. He'd already been living with Tina for some time so she had a whole bunch of private photos of him. It wasn't the concept, but the look, the styling, the outfit for La Düsseldorf – all this came from Thomas.

GERHARD MICHEL_These days I find some of the songs from their last album really, really good; particularly the marching song 'Tintarella Di...*', which is truly beautiful, as well as 'Dampfriemen'. Previously I'd always thought of it as a little too carnival-like, but now I can hear something anarchic in it, although perhaps I am the only person who hears that. Nevertheless, it's just funny, that two of my favourite songs from this album are written by Thomas Dinger.

HANS LAMPE_'Dampfriemen' was released as the single from the album *Individuellos* and was considered good enough by the radio people to be played as often as 'Silver Cloud' or 'Rheinita', which always had great radio coverage.

CLAUDIA SCHNEIDER-ESLEBEN_Tina dived straight into the Dingers' middle-class world and it maybe provided her with a safety she was always looking for. Often they drove to Thomas' house in Holland, Zeeland, which she furnished lovingly with vintage furniture from the flea markets in Amsterdam. Tina would often accompany the Dinger brothers – both had houses in Zeeland, where they always holidayed. Tina witnessed closely the success, the rivalry and the collapses of both brothers. Unfortunately, there had always been too many joints, cigarettes and alcohol. Quintessentially.

KLAUS DINGER_What can I say? First album, second album, third album – and then we were history. It was 1980 and by now things were getting difficult. Quite some money was earned and we never learnt how to deal with it; my colleagues probably even less than myself. It followed the usual: quarrels.

MÂRI PAAS_There were the typical money problems which led to Thomas and Hans joining forces. It came to an eventual split and an out-of-court agreement concerned with Klaus not being allowed to use the band name La Düsseldorf solely on his own. And that was that for the next 20 years.

CLAUDIA SCHNEIDER-ESLEBEN_I always thought of Klaus as an unrefined bundle of energy with a shamanistic attitude. Because of his wild lifestyle and his exaggerated opinion of himself, he ended up burning himself out. I found him to be the manic egotist; and I don't think that he was ever interested in the relationship of Tina and Thomas. He just maintained his rivalry with Thomas and was always in search of recognition.

BODO STAIGER_He was a straightforward guy, and it was actually something I liked about him. If things were shit, then they were shit, and if he didn't like you, then he told you right to your face. Yeah, maybe he wasn't exactly the type of guy you would want to meet on some dark corner in the middle of the night. I don't know.

KLAUS DINGER_My answer to *The Man-Machine* was *Individuellos*; La Düsseldorf's third album was my response to the machines and working environment of Kraftwerk. Songs like 'Menschen 1' and 'Menschen 2' were my counter to *The Man-Machine*. To me it was the man who was playing the more important role, not the machine.

CLAUDIA SCHNEIDER-ESLEBEN_Thomas, on the other hand, was the smart one, quiet, a diplomat; at the same time sexy and sophisticated. He looked marvellous with his tall thin body, his long blond hair and his piercing blue eyes. His Bowie-Impersonation also had a wide range of androgen roles which combined with an appealing gender mix. Sadly he stood in his brother's shadow and only rarely stepped out of his role as the younger brother. This destiny Thomas and Tina shared equally with their extroverted older siblings.

BODO STAIGER_I'd already met Hans Lampe at Conny's, when he was a slim, blond youngster with long hair. And later, when these attractive young guys were hanging out in the late evenings in Einhorn with their glimmering, satin jackets and thick mirrored sunglasses – that left some impression.

MICHAEL KEMNER_DAF and some other Düsseldorf bands had their own look and style. In every way, both musically and visually, they were all completely different. La Düsseldorf always wore their white overalls and leather jackets, which sported their La Düsseldorf logos. And it was this logo that they sprayed all over the pavements. It was like their own guerrilla-style advertising campaign.

PETER HEIN_I, together with the guys from Male, always made fun of La Düsseldorf. Their lyrics were somehow cheap and always reminded us of the worst of rock theatre. With their white overalls they looked as if they'd come straight from Andy Warhol's Factory, and not at all like prog rockers or whatever else used to be fashionable. They were too old for punk, somewhere between, caught in the middle, but all in all slightly out of touch.

MEIKEL CLAUSS_ When you saw Dinger with his high-heeled shoes he looked real bizarre. Klaus, with his straggly hair, haggard expression and ankle-high Beatle-boots made from polished white leather – that was quite a sight!

PETER HEIN_ Left of the bar at the Hof was the artists' corner, for those from the Art Academy. There you always found the La Düsseldorf guys. First of all, Thomas, the younger one, with bling and chains and stupid cowboy boots. He had a mullet haircut and wore his silly scarfs which he'd certainly got from the Raphael shop on Ratinger Street, where all the hippies got their outfits. Oversized sunglasses and a leather jacket completed his look. To be fair, though, we also looked kind of stupid, with our kids' sunglasses, paperclips and passport photos attached to our lapels. But as punks it was our job to look more stupid than everybody else, we had to.

KLAUS DINGER_ It's hard to say what changed in the years after our start in 76. For me it was an ongoing thing. Surely something had changed. La Düsseldorf now started to sound fairly organised; after Neu! I took some lessons in music and harmony at the adult education centre with teachers and all that. I asked the guy: "How do melodies materialise?" But he couldn't answer my question so I left. I then took six guitar lessons but quickly noticed that this guy too couldn't teach me anything. I finally asked Bodo to give me some lessons, as I found him a first-class guitarist.

MEIKEL CLAUSS_ Rheingold owe a lot to La Düsseldorf; they sound so much like 'em. It makes me wonder if they actually know each other. Bodo Staiger is such a cool guitarist and was probably fascinated by Michael Rother as well. I can hear elements of Rother in both La Düsseldorf and Rheingold. This softer style and chords that sound so light yet exude a real funkiness. Rother could do that; Bodo too. That's so typical of Düsseldorf; it got the lifestyle, it's cool, decadent and nicely atmospheric – and suddenly you understand where it's coming from and where one is coming from. Here you had Düsseldorf, the lifestyle, cool, decadent, nicely spheric – and suddenly you understand where all that is coming from and where you belong.

BODO STAIGER_The strange thing about Düsseldorf is that nobody here can deal with the success of others. I played here in bands for years, was always well liked and had the respect of others, and not because of my nice shoes but because I was good at what I did, because I worked hard and played well.

MEIKEL CLAUSS_Here you were just ignored, as soon as you started being successful. This wouldn't have been the case in England or America. In Düsseldorf everybody feels threatened by the others' success. If they are doing that, then what am I doing? That's typically German, typically Düsseldorf – this competitiveness. It isn't envy, though, it's fear. It's truly weird.

BODO STAIGER_As soon as the whole Rheingold thing was really taking off, the Düsseldorf scene only thought: 'What a bastard; he is such an arsehole'. From one minute to the next I was labelled arrogant and snotty. This stiffness is quite big in Düsseldorf, it has a grand tradition.

MEIKEL CLAUSS_If you look at who is actually making music in Düsseldorf and what sort of interaction is happening between them, if any, you'll see that they actually have nothing to do with each other. From the outside everybody thinks Düsseldorf is the centre of the electronic music scene. But if you come from Düsseldorf then you know that in actual fact there is no real scene at all. There are just individual freaks muddling around alone, all in fear that the others will become more successful than they.

LOTHAR MANTEUFFEL_There are the personal performance indicators that have mostly little to do with how success is defined by the outside world. Everybody is crafting their individual success formulas and it is important to keep at it. To be one with one's work. To overcome shortcomings. To leave the vanity at the studio door. The support, the recognition from outside, only helps if you stick to your own rules, also when you go commercial. The work must always take priority.

BODO STAIGER_Lothar came from the Kraftwerk periphery. He was a friend of Emil Schult and was introduced to me by Karl Bartos. Lothar always wanted to be involved with Kraftwerk, for example writing some lyrics for them. He was quite some years younger than myself. I must have been 30 and he was maybe in his 20s, but it was a a great collaboration, he had a good feeling for language.

ANDY McCLUSKEY_In every interview we gave for the release of our third album, *Architecture & Morality*, we mentioned the strong influence of Kraftwerk and how much they changed our lives. And so too the whole sound from Düsseldorf. It's odd that we never name-dropped Rheingold or La Düsseldorf, as their stuff was also very inspiring for us. Of everybody, it was probably Bowie who was most impressed by the La Düsseldorf sound, and with his Berlin trilogy he was much closer to the sounds of Rheingold, Riechmann, Rother and the Dinger brothers than he was to Kraftwerk.

MÂRI PAAS_Klaus was more and more ignored by the record industry, and so when Bowie showered him with so much praise, naturally he felt a strong sense of satisfaction. In one interview Bowie dubbed the music of La Düsseldorf as the 'soundtrack of the Eighties' and that meant a lot to Klaus. He couldn't read it enough and regularly gave out copies of that interview. He'd say: "You are all so stupid, you've got no bloody idea. Do you know how many people think I'm a genius?"

BODO STAIGER_Klaus was certainly a diva; he was a real vain prick and naturally proud of the stories or references from Bowie. But why shouldn't he be? Check out the photos of him with the silk scarf and mirrored sunglasses. There is a reason for everything.

RALF DÖRPER_That was a classic moment in German TV history: David Bowie's 1997 appearance on German TV show *Wetten, Dass…?* Bowie is seen seated on the couch where he is greeted by host Thomas Gottschalk and asked to list his favourite bands. Bowie willingly answers, but nobody at the show knows what to make of it. He goes on to say that during his stay in Berlin he was listening to all sorts of amazing German music; bands like Kraftwerk, Neu!, Harmonia, and goes on to address the audience and ask if anybody present had ever heard of Neu!. Only one small, insecure hand can be seen going up. Bowie's irritation is clearly visible. He was going to chat easily with Gottschalk about something that was common to him and German people, but nobody had ever heard of his favourite German bands. And that was most incomprehensible to Bowie. It's like going through England and finding out nobody has ever heard of David Bowie!

BODO STAIGER_On 'Dreiklangsdimensionen' you can hear one of those early, self-programmable rhythm machines; one of those can also be heard on 'In The Air Tonight' by Phil Collins. In fact, that cool Roland CR-78 is still with me in the studio today. At the beginning of the Eighties, that was great fun, and even the pre-set rhythms were really good and amazingly groovy. Via a special rubber button you could play along live whilst adding snare rolls and fills. And you can hear that when you listen carefully. This sharp and defining ARP Odyssey sound, this brutal electro-snare in 'Dreiklangsdimensionen' – that's Conny!

DIRK FLADER_Bodo Staiger was a good friend of Klaus. Klaus always raved about him as a guitarist and for a short time he took guitar lessons with him. Bodo had a very old beautiful SG from the very early Sixties. It's the one that can be seen on the Rheingold sleeve; when you open the gatefold sleeve you can see him with his guitar. He'd bought it from Wölfi Riechmann.

BODO STAIGER_We worked at the first Klangwerkstatt studio, in some ground floor cellar studio in Babara Street. The second studio was then in Stockhamp Street, a crossroad to the Prinz Georg Strasse, which was partly funded with money from Rheingold licenses and royalties. The early Eighties was a very good time for the Klangwerkstatt. At that time it was a real happening, cool studio. In the beginning of the Nineties Karl Bartos took it over, after he'd finally departed Kraftwerk. There he worked with the likes of Andy McCluskey and Bernard Sumner on the first Elektric Music album, his follow-up project, together with Emil Schult and Lothar Manteuffel of Rheingold.

ANDY MCCLUSKEY_We were often in Germany, and it was always something quite special coming to Düsseldorf. That said, Berlin was equally as great a place for us to play. One of my most intense memories is of a show at Kant Kino, an old movie theatre in Berlin on December 8, 1980. Our album *Organisation* – the name of which was naturally a direct reference to Kraftwerk – had just been released and we were on tour to promote it. Ralf and Florian's predecessor to Kraftwerk was called Organisation. We played our new hit, 'Enola Gay', about the plane which dropped the atomic bomb over Hiroshima, as well as songs like 'Messages' and for sure 'Electricity'. The atmosphere was simply fantastic inside this little club, and after the encore we were forced to play songs from our set again, the crowd didn't want to see us go. It was one hell of a long night and wasn't until late when we finally made it to our hotel beds. The next morning we heard the news that John Lennon had been shot. For us Liverpudlians that was something particularly devastating. The whole world was in shock and couldn't comprehend this cold-blooded assassination. And the way in which it happened was too unfair. With it came the death of the hippie protest dreams of the Seventies. Now it was time for a new decade.

FRANK FENSTERMACHER_Bodo Staiger was less of an electronic musician and more of a guitarist. He had a great song with 'Dreiklangsdimensionen' and knew the whole Düsseldorf School of the Seventies. At the time he was our contact to this scene and we became labelmates at EMI, he with Rheingold and us with Fehlfarben on our own subsidiary label Welt-Rekord.

JÜRGEN ENGLER_We didn't really view Rheingold as an electronic band; the vibe was more that of a guitar band that used some additional synths. I really liked 'FanFanFanatisch' as a song, although it was very much in the style of DAF. As a guitarist Bodo played very softly with a lot of delay and other various effects.

BODO STAIGER_Jürgen Engler I met at some Südwestfunk TV show. Rheingold and Die Krupps were on the same show, and they had the four-piece band line-up. That was the first and last time I saw him though. Maybe again we had this stupid Düsseldorfian competitiveness, you know, in that sense people are quickly a bit uptight.

JÜRGEN ENGLER_The TV show was produced in Baden Baden by Eckhardt Schmidt, who also directed the film *Der Fan* starring Desiree Nosbusch and Bodo Staiger. She played an obsessed fan – nowadays she'd be labelled a stalker – and Bodo a successful singer. All the music was done by Rheingold; by then he was fast on his way to becoming a celebrated star of the airwaves and screens.

CHARLY TERSTAPPEN_Marius Müller-Westernhagen and Bodo knew each other from their time together playing in a band in Düsseldorf in the early Seventies, before then later joining the Lilac Angels. Lilac Angels and Wallenstein ended up on the same bill sometimes and later on Bodo took me aboard as a drummer for Rheingold's *FanFanFanatisch* album. And so the circle was complete.

BODO STAIGER_Charly Terstappen played on our second album, one of the few drummers I was happy to work with. Finding the right drummer was always the biggest problem for me; too often I met shit drummers. In fact, that was one of the main reasons why I started working with machines, rhythm machines, instead of people.

MEIKEL CLAUSS_Oh yeah, Rheingold belonged to the 'Electri_city'; Bodo's rhythmical, funky and elegant guitar passages did it. That's simply epic dance music from DUS.

++ **JAN 81** Ronald Reagan becomes the 40th president of the United States of America ++ **FEB 81** Annie Lennox and Dave Stewart start recording as Eurythmics at Conny Plank's ++ **MAR 81** Ralf Dörper and Jürgen Engler release an experimental single as Die Lemminge, and start recordings for *Stahlwerksinfonie* ++ **MAR 81** Roxy Music have their only number one single with 'Jealous Guy', a tribute to John Lennon ++ **APR 81** Release of DAF's *Alles Ist Gut* ++ **APR 81** Ultravox hit the German charts with 'Vienna', which also became single of the year in the UK ++ **MAY 81** Kraftwerk release *Computerwelt* ++ Die Krupps release *Stahlwerksinfonie* ++ **JUN 81** Kraftwerk play at Philipshalle, Düsseldorf ++ DAF join the 'Tag Der Deutschen Einheit' Philipshalle festival with Fehlfarben, Palais Schaumburg and The Wirtschaftswunder ++ **JUL 81** Die Krupps release their 12-inch 'Wahre Arbeit – Wahrer Lohn' ++ **AUG 81** DAF's TV debut with 'Der Räuber Und Der Prinz' on *Bio's Bahnhof* ++ **SEP/DEC 81** Rheingold record the soundtrack for the film *Der Fan* at Düsseldorf's Klangwerkstatt ++ **OCT 81** Liaisons Dangereuses release 'Los Niños Del Parque' 12-inch ++ **NOV 81** DAF put out their second duo album, *Gold Und Liebe*, produced by Conny Plank ++ **NOV 81** OMD release *Architecture & Morality* ++ **DEC 81** After touring England, Italy, France, Germany, Japan and Australia – a total of 96 shows – Kraftwerk play for the second time this year at the Philipshalle ++

Der Mussolini

GABI DELGADO_ In fact, it was only after this whole process of kicking everybody else out, when only Robert and I remained, that we really started to work with Conny Plank. We played him some of our new material and straight away he said. "Great, let's do it! Just the two of you – and me as producer."

ROBERT GÖRL_When we visited Conny he made us an offer we couldn't refuse and then he said: "Guys, I've heard a lot about you, and about the shows you've done as well. I know your background." He told us that he was working with a publisher, namely Walter Holzbauer at Wintrup Music Publishing. "We won't experience any difficulties in finding a label," he said. Okay, the others also did a good job in prepping us; but Conny was an explorer. He was our great discoverer.

BOB GIDDENS_At that time, it was pretty tiring for me, as the guys weren't the easiest to work with, which is why I passed them over to Walter Holzbauer, who had a large publishing company. I was glad to get out without losing any money. They were genuinely exhausting, yet real geniuses at the same time. That's the way it is sometimes with the great artists, you have to suffer so as to allow the art to come out. Only then can you hope to achieve the big results.

ROBERT GÖRL_At that time, Conny was already one of the top producers in Germany. He was well known, having been active for more than 10 years, and he had basically done all the krautrock acts of the early Seventies.

GABI DELGADO_Before punk rock came along you really only had Conny and Dieter Dierks, the latter of whom had his Dierks Studios in Cologne and produced all eight important Scorpions records. Dierks and Plank took care of all the krautrock acts of the Seventies, they were all done in Cologne. The two of them only got involved when they really liked a project; so you were lucky if they liked your stuff, because that was your only chance to get a date at Conny's. Invitation only.

ROBERT GÖRL_Walter Holzbauer and Conny Plank then figured out a three way deal with Virgin England. Again, England!

BOB GIDDENS_Holzbauer was bloody well connected. Funny thing was, though, that when he tried to sell DAF to Virgin in Germany he was turned down. Afterwards he ended up selling them to the successful mother company in England, owned by Richard Branson. The Germans were therefore compelled to release the stuff, despite having been initially unimpressed by what they'd heard; that said, they later had the big hits.

ROBERT GÖRL_ In a flash, we had a deal from Richard Branson, that is Branson himself! Hard to believe nowadays. Today he has his airlines and is building space shuttles and such. On one occasion, I held the door open for him at Virgin Records, in some courtyard near the Portobello Road. He was carrying two large boxes and asked if I could help out. It was Virgin Records who really pushed DAF in Germany, England and the USA, and always in the original versions, in German; there were no English versions.

GABI DELGADO_ We weren't salesmen, we weren't marketing buffs, and never have been. And we had fun shocking all those managers, label people, publishers and producers. We took great delight in doing exactly the opposite of what we were expected and thus driving them to despair. It must have been hard for the others, that we always got our way, how we wanted it. We learnt from an early stage that success was due firstly to the music, secondly to the image and finally to the contracts.

ROBERT GÖRL_ Daniel Miller was understandably pissed off at the time but that is now long forgotten. He was real angry though, and everybody knew it. It wasn't fair of us, as he had done the first single with us. There was never any contract, with Miller I mean, as his policy was and always has been 'no contracts necessary'. There were only ever verbal agreements. Throughout the entire Eighties all dealings with Mute were only ever done with a handshake. It's exactly as Depeche Mode sang: "The handshake seals the contract; from the contract there's no turning back". Okay, then they went on to sing: "The grabbing hands grab all they can. All for themselves. Everything counts in large amounts."

DANIEL MILLER_ Mute was quite small back then, really only two people. DAF wanted to go to a bigger label in Germany, and that was okay for me. So they went to Virgin, who signed them worldwide, and so it was that Mute lost their rights for England. I was very angry but that was at the time that I'd just started working with Depeche Mode.

GABI DELGADO_We always wanted to handle the business our way, according to our own notions; we only ever allowed licensing deals and insisted on full artistic control over our cover designs. But doing things that way meant we were quickly stepping on people's toes, and so the word got around that one couldn't work with DAF. And that was true: you couldn't work with us because we were already at work ourselves.

RALF DÖRPER_DAF anticipated the 'minimum-maximum principle' of the new economy: with minimal input you have a maximum return on capital.

GABI DELGADO_With Conny, we had a genuinely alternative deal: the studio was for free and in return he got a third of the profits, which was pretty hippie-like. Back then a day in the studio would have cost you close to 2000 Deutschmarks, and we needed a month to six weeks alone to finish an album, so doing it this way meant we were able to afford it. Otherwise it would have cost us close to 100,000 marks, and we didn't have anywhere near that. Today it's different: in a Marxist sense the result of production belongs to the worker so nowadays you can produce everything by yourself with a laptop costing you 500 euro and a music program for 30.

ROBERT GÖRL_We stayed for six weeks at Conny's, that was the deal. Six weeks in a row. At that time he worked exclusively with us. We lived with him as well. That must have cost Conny quite a bit of money, but he was a generous guy. And he got a good cut, as he had a good deal as the third party. He did the same with other bands as well – Neu!, for example. His third was only for the mastering rights, not the compositional rights. He never interfered in our compositions, but he worked us, he drove us hard.

GABI DELGADO_Conny was also important for PR reasons, especially in the UK. To have the tag 'Produced by Conny Plank' was certainly worth something. In the UK, Conny was a cult figure; at that time Ultravox were high in the charts and had just achieved single of the year in England. That guaranteed us strong sales figures.

ROBERT GÖRL_Conny had a vision for us; he saw what was possible.

He polished us. In fact Conny was our biggest patron, and he made things happen. Every musician likes to make a living out of his art, so when you get an offer like this you won't refuse it. It wasn't a betrayal of our alternative roots, as such; it was just too good an offer. And Daniel couldn't feed us. Not at that time. Suddenly we were able to pay the rent for a three-bedroom apartment on Holland Road, directly on Holland Park. Gabi and I stayed there together. We relocated to London only after we had to stay in Düsseldorf for a little less than a year.

GABI DELGADO_I would say the workload was split 50/50, whereby the first drafts came from us and Conny then transformed them into finished works in the studio. Apart from when Holger Czukay came by for a joint, we were pretty much alone: Conny, Robert and myself. Conny took care of everything himself, even the sound engineering; it was a very isolated process.

JOCHEN RAUSCH_I think Conny liked the guys because of their radicalism, and in turn they liked him for supporting them. Aside from that, he was able to capture their minimalistic approach and make it sound like a complete production.

GABI DELGADO_When it was time for us to get our own Korg MS-20, we pre-ordered one from Synthesizerstudio Bonn from Matten and Wiechers. It arrived with their next shipment and even before we actually held it in our hands we knew: that's the way to make music; from here on in we will be successful.

ROBERT GÖRL_He did let us work without him as well though. Often I spent half the day on my own, while Conny was in the kitchen cooking with his wife Christa. I had the studio mostly to myself, and I'd play around most of the day. In the larger room I had the synthesisers. I had my Korgs with me and used Conny's studio equipment as well. I worked on his ARP Odyssey; that I loved. Genius. It ran like clockwork, with those coloured slide controls looking like sherbet bonbons. What a machine that was. And that thing really had a kick to it.

GABI DELGADO_In the first place, we wanted to produce our records by ourselves, but we couldn't do that. We didn't know which knobs to turn. That's why I said to Conny: "Show me everything! I want to learn it all, know it all, know how it's done." And he said: "Great, you can do an apprenticeship here." So for half a year I learned everything there was to know from him. Everything I know about music production I learned from him – how to record a drum set, how to use the compressor and so on. If it is something I am really interested in, then I want to know everything about it and I want to know how it's done. The best way to do this is by searching for a master, somebody you respect. It's from those people that you learn the most. In Japanese you have only one word for emulating, copying and learning, it's all the same word. Because if you copy a James Brown beat then in the long run you will learn how to do it yourself.

GERHARD MICHEL_That's how I always pictured it would be, working with Klaus. One looks out for a master, and spends the whole day with him learning everything, from making coffee to setting up the microphones. But Klaus didn't really want to give anything away.

ROBERT GÖRL_DAF's working method has always been that I start with the sequencer and not the drums. Most bands first lay out the beat. I think even Kraftwerk were doing it that way. They do the rhythm first and then add the notes and harmonies. I always began with the sequencer. And Gabi would join me in the room, dancing away. And that in turn inspired me. The way Gabi moved, and how he reacted; that told me what to take and what not to. Sometimes I would potter around with only one loop for half a day, maybe even the whole day, until there was a smooth groove, with the correct notes at the correct time and then the atmosphere kicks in. Then Gabi would slowly start, like an agitator, to inject text. Piece by piece, more and more, and then… Conny came into play and we had to get it done.

GERHARD MICHEL_For Klaus, Conny Plank was always one of the good guys, he would only ever say positive things about him. For him, he was the guy who would always capture the right sounds. Aside from that, he was fully impressed by his lung capacity, which even Klaus, as a professional pothead, had to admit. There's one story that Klaus always liked to retell: whenever it was working really well in the studio and you were about to record, Conny's wife would turn up with something she'd cooked and you would immediately have to sit down to eat. That was a total horror for Klaus.

ROBERT GÖRL_With Conny we recorded the sequencer first and then the drums, then you'd have almost everything. At that point Gabi would join. That's the way it was done. It never clicked when we worked separately, that was something we'd also tried. DAF only ever functioned like this: together. Everybody was doing their thing; I made the music and Gabi was responsible for the lyrics, but put it together and it just grooved, you would turn the other on, and that worked. Another day, another song.

GABI DELGADO_*Alles Ist Gut* is my favourite DAF album, although, that said, we haven't actually done that many, but it is the one I like most. We were in a cloud of creativity back then, and for us that was exactly the way of doing things, knocking out the records really quick and never worrying about strategies. The record companies and publishers were throwing their hands up in despair. 'Already another album? We haven't even sold out the previous one.' In our contracts, though, it said we were allowed to release the next one after half a year.

CHRISLO HAAS_To me *Alles Ist Gut* was a genius record, but it pretty much went all downhill from there. They were simply too fast into the business, always wanting to cash in on the next advance. With Liaisons Dangereuses we made use of the industry as well, distribution-wise, as we had our own label. But the two DAF guys were simply too greedy, and then it was over.

GABI DELGADO_We didn't follow the traditional market laws. After we'd done our three records, all of which had been great, we said: "Let's chuck it in." The outcry was: 'No, we're now going to take you to America.' But we were never interested in that: to fulfil the market requirement, to follow a normal career path, that wasn't what we wanted at all.

ROBERT GÖRL_Those killer sequences all came out of the ARP Odyssey. We only started using the Oberheim later. The three records we did with Conny feature ARP and some Korg as well. For example, 'Der Mussolini' is ARP. The ARP rocks. Even so, I have to say my most beloved baby was my Korg MS-20. It was on the MS-20 that I prepared everything. All the ideas. I also had an MS-20 in my flat. I practised the MS-20 in the same way that I used to practise drums. Day and night. Even in the flat I shared with Gabi. We each had our own room and I would sit in mine, headphones on, all night long, just me and my Korg. I had to prepare everything. Some songs I did with the Korg and sometimes I transferred the melodic sequence ideas over to the ARP. The ARP was able to translate it much more powerfully, while the Korg is freakier and softer.

CHRIS CROSS_Nowadays I get it: Conny combined theoretical knowledge and technical understanding with practical application. And, above all, he put so much enthusiasm and love into his work, so much so that he was completely absorbed by it. He was such a heartfelt person. He knew so much and was happy to share his knowledge and everything with you – sometimes this started over the breakfast table. And because of his self-confidence and experience he was able to get the best out of our wild and obscure ideas.

ROBERT GÖRL_My advice to every musician: if you want to master your instrument to a point that it starts singing to you, that it starts talking to you, then you have to live with it day and night. Like a Buddhist Zen master, you have to play it for days and nights on end. A bit like a maniac. Until even your friends start thinking: 'What's wrong with him?' But every artists works this way. Painters paint all day and night until they collapse, until they fall asleep next to their paintings.

FRANK Z._We once checked out Conny's studio, but found it boring, all the way out in the countryside. What were we supposed to do out there? To me the whole area was a bit suspect. I didn't have any interest in hanging out in some old cowshed; I couldn't see any romance in that. After a day's work in the studio I liked to go out for a drink, and not stand around in the middle of some field, in the middle of the night, watching cows shit. To me that was all too esoteric, and not really my thing.

CHRIS CROSS_I met all the bands at Conny's: the whole arcane crowd, the cosmic crew; Can, La Düsseldorf, Annie and Dave from the Eurythmics, and all the rest. Conny and Christa burst out laughing when I innocently asked if 'King Dinger' was coming around. King Dinger was my nickname for Klaus, and they said that if I knew him I'd laugh as well. My top five from Düsseldorf have always been: *NEU! 75*, La Düsseldorf's *Viva* and *Individuellos*, Kraftwerk's *Radio-Activity*, and for some reason I also really liked Trio, but they came from somewhere else. Personally I would have loved to have been in a band like La Düsseldorf.

BODO STAIGER_ My mate Conny was one of the big chiefs. He had a good eye for things and a good ear as well. But have a listen to DAF's 'Der Rauber Und Der Prinz', for example. That is quite hairy, what they did there with the sound technology. At times a remarkable transfiguration happens. One has such a positive memory of them and you're then quite surprised at how the songs sound today. Nothing ever sounds as good as your memory of it.

RALF DÖRPER_ Following their great success and good sales, DAF no longer belonged to the scene. DAF simply disappeared, they wanted it big time. They wanted to become massive, they wanted the success. After the years of going hungry in Gevelsberg and London it was now the time of Sex, Drugs and Sequencer.

GABI DELGADO_ And then we were stinking rich. Then we only ever flew first class, bought only Armani clothing, stayed in the most expensive hotels, each day two or three thousand down the drain. Cocaine as if there was no tomorrow.

RALF DÖRPER_ Suddenly they were making six figure payments, which was going straight into champagne and cocaine. A PPL royalty cheque could easily have been half a million, which was a complete new level for them. If you were to see them at all in Düsseldorf, it was only shopping in the posh stores on the Königsallee. But that was the way things were going: past a certain point it was only the losers who were going to Ratinger Hof.

New Wave Style

PETER GLASER_Seen from the outside, Düsseldorf, with its glamour and androgynism, robo-automation, and the hardcore homo leather style of Gabi and Robbi, may have been a forerunner to women's lib, asexualism or gay pop culture; but one needs to separate the different layers. On the image level that might have been true, certainly compared to the rock standards of those days. In real life, though, all the old role clichés lived on. A paradoxical sexualisation of the asexual took place. Take an astronaut's outfit, for example, seated at a white neon-lit table listening to abstract electronic music. To some that could have been erotically stimulating. Utterly de-naturised and dehydrated. That was the horror of the hippies who couldn't understand why nobody wanted to join their knitting clubs any more. To style oneself in such a way was cool. And because we had women feeling the same way, a new sex life grew underneath the neon lights. In the same way as in every other scene. Encouraged by style, the first gay people came out, but there weren't too many within the music scene. Nor girls either.

GABI DELGADO_In those days, one favourite hang out for Kraftwerk and associates was the Milchbar 2000, in Düsseldorf-Oberkassel. For the real industrial punks, though, that was the no-go area. But there they sat, with their leather ties, sipping their non-alcoholic drinks. We hated that; and their styling was out of order.

LOTHAR MANTEUFFEL_Emil Schult and I converted to vegetarianism at the start of the Seventies. No cigarettes, no alcohol, no drugs. At that time that was fairly uncool and unsexy.

WOLFGANG FLÜR_Drugs were never a part of Kraftwerk. We enjoyed a nice glass of bubbly but that was about it. Quite boring really, but nothing else would have fitted us.

MEIKEL CLAUSS_Sign of the times. Nowadays one can't imagine how uncool – back then the word 'cool' wasn't even invented – how uncool a lot of things were received, which today are considered quite positive. Kraftwerk, judged by 'boredom factor', were located somewhere in the region of Richard Clayderman, the French easy listening pianist. I am far from being an expert on those times, but I remember the mood; and for a long while no one was listening to Kraftwerk any more.

JÄKI ELDORADO_It was easier to be elegant in Düsseldorf than in comparison to say, Berlin or Hamburg, where you had to be extra-unsexy to be authentic. A deep divide grew between reality and elegance; elegance distorted reality. In Düsseldorf, however, things were easier, it had something playful about it.

FRANK Z._In Hamburg too, after the punk rock times, there grew quite a strong fashion scene as well. People who looked so new wave-ish, they were all so very stylish. We had the likes of Andreas Dorau or Palais Schaumburg and other bimbos. And their audience looked the same. So too DAF, who went all stylish. There was a lot of attention given to clothing and it was more than okay to look a little gay.

JÄKI ELDORADO_That was the tragedy of new wave; that it initially began as something quite complex, where fashion, music and art influences came together. But by the time that it had shrunk to one complete version, which even the most simple could read, it was already over.

PETER GLASER_Towards the late Seventies Kraftwerk became relatively inaccessible, and you only ever knew them through others, for example via Claudia Schneider-Esleben, who was far more communicative than her brother. That then became their image.

WOLFGANG FLÜR_DAF, Der Plan, Die Krupps – we didn't know any of those bands. We stayed out of the scene; in fact, we barely even knew the scene existed. Sure we went along to the Ratinger Hof, but I never saw any bands there. It was on one occasion whilst there that I received a hefty kick in the backside from a foot that came out of the darkness.

MEIKEL CLAUSS_Kraftwerk weren't interested in anything else, beside making music in their stupid Kling Klang Studio. They weren't aware of anything else. Perhaps the exception was Florian, who sometimes came along to the Ratinger Hof, but the others I never saw there. Once I had the dumb idea to have a go at him, thinking of myself as the very cool punk rocker. In those days, within the punk circle, it was considered uncool to like Kraftwerk.

ROBERT GÖRL_They occasionally frequented the Ratinger Hof, although they didn't feel too comfortable there. They only ever came along to check out what was going on and what the punks were up to. They knew of DAF as a band who were not only part of the punk scene but also made use of electronic elements. That they found interesting, the weird electronica that we were making.

JÜRGEN ENGLER_If you did indeed see Kraftwerk at the Hof, then only ever at the front, left of the bar. That was a small safe haven for them. We occasionally chatted with them, especially Ralf, though seldom Florian. Rather, you'd see them more often at Bambi, a smaller art house cinema, or at Match Moore, which was a more sophisticated place than the Hof. That's where I'd go with Ralf Dörper, who was always wanting to go out. Back then we always used to go out together on weekends, and always to the Altstadt. We went out together every weekend, from 1978 till some point in the mid-Eighties. Ralf Hütter and Ralf Dörper knew each other well and they'd often chat away with me standing alongside them. Florian Schneider always seemed untouchable; he wasn't interested in small talk.

ROBERT GÖRL_Back then I often went to the Checkers nightclub. That was my world. It was at Checkers that the Kraftwerkers were hanging out. And that was where I first started to get to know them. I know the guys quite well. I often chatted with Ralf Hütter. In those days he was a very respectable, normal guy. He came across as very sober. He'd stand there in his suit, on the Checkers dance floor at three in the morning, looking so serious. But that was also part of their image. On the dance floor in their suits, very straight-looking. I found that kind of funny, it just wasn't my thing.

TINA SCHNEKENBURGER_At that time Kraftwerk were big stars in Düsseldorf and everybody wanted a piece of them. Musically they were so far ahead, but on a personal level I found them quite laughable. They'd stand around in the discotheques, completely

TINA SCHNEKENBURGER

snobby. It was quite a culture clash really, going to the disco in the first place, but somehow all of a sudden everybody was going to discotheques – Kraftwerk amongst others. They'd hang out there, pretending to be very cool, with their straight sourpuss faces.

PETER GLASER_Match Moore was their social ground. Other than a handful of chicks that big-mouthed about being fucked by Kraftwerk, it would have been extremely uncool to get close to them.

MEIKEL CLAUSS_If you'd said you like Kraftwerk, or you think they're cool, everybody else would have sacked you and thought: 'Okay, this guy is useless. He's out.'

PETER GLASER_For me the interesting thing about Kraftwerk was their disputable irony; an irony that I am afraid they may not have intended, or understood, but delivered perfectly. The further you went into detail the further you opened yourself up for amateur psychology: Are they truly that relaxed? Or do they laugh themselves to death back at the studio? Would they take off their short-hair wigs and smoke a spliff? Or in reality was it more like an office job wearing virtual oversleeves and whatever else you needed as a clerk? Was everything finished in five minutes but only released over the next two years, thereby communicating their Faustian pioneering and German engineering to the outside world? Or did they just sit in the Milchbar 2000 the whole time looking infinitely cool yet infinitely stupid? For me, within this styled stiffness hides a lot of humour, but you never know if it's intentional or not.

WOLFGANG FLÜR_I was kicked in the backside a further three times. And with full force, and sometimes with the knee. Unfortunately I never saw who it was who was doing it, but certainly it was one of the punks. They always said: 'Let's beat up the Kraftwerker'. I guess behind this aggressive attitude there was some kind of envy; they certainly seemed jealous when we turned up in our big Mercedes 600.

ROBERT GÖRL_Wolfgang I liked a lot, he is a really good guy. I often stayed over at his place. For a time we shared the same girlfriend, that was a great time. Wolfgang was the womaniser, the others not at all.

Stahlwerksinfonie

JÜRGEN ENGLER_First we only made the music, we didn't even have a band name yet, or song titles. We then came up with *Stahlwerksinfonie*. What we did, the whole noise, sounded like a massive machinery hall. As it was such a long piece of music, I came up with the title *Stahlwerksinfonie*, which we decided to stick with. We wanted to make something industrial and noisy, to replicate the sound from inside a steelworks. Bernward and I put together our first record sleeve, but we were still minus a band name. We did a lot of brainstorming, toying with all kinds of ideas. We started thinking about the local steel factories that we knew of. We jumped from Mannesmann, to Rheinmetall, to Krupp – and that's how we became Die Krupps, with all the historical significance. Krupp stood for the rebuilding of Germany after the war, but also for Hitler's war machines, and, as such, it was a good conceptual name for us. Abroad Krupps represented everything German: the good and the bad. In our eyes, the name was a deliberate criticism of the German character, which always busily and righteously dedicates itself to the production of weapons without reflecting upon the political dimension. It was opportunist to sacrifice political belief for an individual benefit.

RALF DÖRPER_What I found most fascinating about David Lynch's film *Eraserhead* was the soundtrack, which used all these hazy, industrial sounds. There were these constantly steaming, squeaking kettles and machines, as well as atmospheric industrial sounds, and in some parts it didn't sound all that far away from the anticipated sound of the *Stahlwerksinfonie*.

JÜRGEN ENGLER_With Ralf I'd already done Die Lemminge. Since we were always hanging out together I told him about this new project I was planning with Bernward and what we wanted to dub Krupps, and that totally clicked with him too. I can still remember his response: "Hmm, I think I will be part of this too." It wasn't as if I invited him, or asked him to join, he simply said he wanted to be part of it. That I'll never forget. He was the fourth to join, after Bernward and Köllges, other than Eva Goßling, who joined us for a short period.

BERNWARD MALAKA_For a short moment we had the feeling that we could break with everything. Traditions: who gives a shit! They didn't mean anything. And certainly not to us. We had no traditions to oppose; we could do whatever we wanted. We didn't have to stand against anything, unlike the 68 hippie generation who stood up against Germany's past. We were free of that. I thought that was a strong position to be in, and as such we started Die Krupps. Additionally, we had all these new electronic instruments and the possibility to capture everyday sounds and use them within your music, a little like Pierre Schaeffer. This offered great freedom, because with all other instruments you were always struggling with their historical background, defined by the great masters. You'd forever be the dwarf standing on the giants' shoulders. But we made the decision to climb down from these shoulders to do something new and different.

JÜRGEN ENGLER_As there was no label for that kind of music we christened it 'Industriemusik', not industrial or something like that, simply Industriemusik. It was experimental instrumental music – with a strong emphasis on experimental song forms, as in minus song structure, and industrial in an original sense. Sometime later in the Eighties people started referring to it as 'industrial', and nowadays that is what it is called: industrial. We were amazed the name stuck.

BERNWARD MALAKA_We didn't see ourselves as an electronic band; in fact we weren't really electronic but more an industrial band, even when that label did not yet exist. We basically made it out to be heavy metal, which is why the catalogue number on the back cover states: 'Heavy Metal 1'. We had our own definition of what we were doing. Well, to be fair, there wasn't even a name for what we were doing, it was more composed of a variety of other things. Super minimalistic structures with not so traditional instrumentation. The only real difference between Side A and B of *Stahlwerksinfonie* was that the B-side was more a dub version of the A, but with more echo.

PETER HEIN_Funnily enough, we too as Mittagspause also labelled it industrial, or more so: Industriemusik. We always said that we were making Industriemusik, which is why we then quickly covered 'Industriemädchen' by S.Y.P.H. Additionally we had our own song called 'Industrial Rabotni', or something like that, and for a quarter of an hour or so it just went *ding, dada, dong*. We loved to play that, especially in Berlin, so as to annoy the audience and give ourselves a break. In one go: 'Industrie total, zurück zum Maschinensaal'.

JÜRGEN ENGLER_In 1981 the term EBM wasn't even known yet. When 'Wahre Arbeit' or 'Der Mussolini' were released we never once thought of labelling it 'electronic body music' or EBM. To us it was sequencer music, that was what we did. Nowadays people try to squeeze themselves into certain categories that back then didn't exist. We came up with the music first, and the labels came retrospectively.

BERNWARD MALAKA_It was around that time that Ralf joined. He already had a synthesiser, a very simple machine. Ralf wasn't a trained musician but that made for some interesting contrasts. Frank Köllges was an extremely good jazz drummer who came from a dynasty of drummers and who could play 16th notes without loosing the beat. Köllges joined in on drums because we needed something to provide structure. We soon realised that with a bass and a feedbacking guitar you needed something else to provide the structure to work within. It had to be someone who was really good, the best drummer in Germany. So we started looking out for someone and everybody told us: 'Whoever he is you'll find him in the jazz scene. Don't look in the rock scene, they won't be able to do it. They won't understand it. They can only play four-to-the-floor, and that doesn't help you at all.'

JÜRGEN ENGLER_The money man behind *Stahlwerksinfonie* was Pitter, that is to say Peter Hein. He was present during the production process, he banged on the steel, he was even with us at the mixing desk, pushing the faders. It was Xaõ Seffcheque who first proposed Frank Köllges as a drummer; he knew him through Padlt Noidlt, which for him had been an on-again/off-again project. Frank didn't stay too long with us though. For the 'Wahre Arbeit – Wahrer Lohn' maxi single we instead worked with Ralph Albertini. Our drum stool was always vacant; on each production somebody else played. That's still the same today.

PETER HEIN_After my departure from Fehlfarben, I spent half a year or so doing bugger all, or just some real crap with a few mates. I then decided to produce *Stahlwerksinfonie* because I was asked to as a friend. In this case production meant providing the cash, like a film producer. Unfortunately it wasn't like John Cale, though, who'd produce from the control room where he lay on the sofa smoking. Through my studio work at EMI I had a few contacts that I was able to ring in; although disappointingly I noticed that I am no longer credited on the CD rerelease.

RALF DÖRPER_There was a demo version of *Stahlwerksinfonie* that Bernward, Jürgen and Frank Köllges had recorded together, and although it only featured bass, guitar and drums, the basic idea was there, and I thought the whole concept and name was amazing. So when I joined I brought with me my syncussion and synthesiser and soon after the five of us were on our way to the Can studio with Peter Hein as investor and producer.

PETER HEIN_We took the piss out of Jürgen Engler when he suddenly denounced guitars as old-fashioned and dead. We only said: 'What's up with him? Is he for real?'

BERNWARD MALAKA_We were still considering where to record. At that time Jürgen was friends with Eva Goßling, and she knew a studio technician in Cologne who worked for Can, René Tinner. So Eva and myself drove to Cologne to meet René and Holger Czukay at Café Central at the Cologne Hotel Chelsea.

JÜRGEN ENGLER_We explained our whole concept to them, of the interior of the steel factory, etc. He liked our ideas and offered his studio in Weilerswist.

BERNWARD MALAKA_We brought a tape with us, although it didn't yet feature saxophone or drums; it sounded quite weird, basically

JÜRGEN ENGLER

a collage of factory noises. With that tape we went to EMI and told them: 'Here, this is a completely new thing! The music world was changing dramatically and this could be your seat in the front row.' And we spoke to the typical A&R manager, who was obviously living in the past, in the late Sixties or early Seventies. Aviator shades and a mullet – he looked more like somebody out of The Sweet, and unfortunately didn't have any clue what we were on about. Instead he said: "This is not commercial at all, we won't find a single customer. Forget about it, guys." We didn't speak to any other record companies, but instead concentrated on doing proper recordings.

JÜRGEN ENGLER_We rehearsed a couple more times before heading into Can's studio. That was where we recorded. Jäki Liebezeit hung around the whole day, René Tinner worked as engineer and Czukay joined me at the mixing desk. He told us: "For my ear that has too little life in it." And we asked ourselves: "What can he possibly mean, too little life? This is not about representing life, it's a musical portrayal of the inside of a steel factory... but okay." Anyway, Czukay was there the whole time, sitting like a hippie on the floor behind the console, so most of the time you didn't even notice him. He wasn't particularly chatty but rather more reserved, hippie-style. Regardless we thrashed away on the pieces of steel we'd brought with us, giving commando-style workers shouts. Bernward played his famous one-note bassline on the low E and I played endless feedback with a screaming chord I'd borrowed from Robert Palmer's 'Looking For Clues'.

BERNWARD MALAKA_We dragged the Stahlofon into the studio, together with drills, hammers and everything else that was available to us to work on. Unfortunately all of that destroyed the wooden floor of the studio. I returned 20 years later and saw that they never had it fixed. It was still all there, as a monument to the recording times of Die Krupps. Afterwards we went with Holger Czukay to Conny Plank's studio in Wolperath. They always worked together, and Czukay told us: "It would be best to do the mixing at Conny Plank's." Ultravox had just landed a massive hit which brought in a lot of money for them, with which they used to book themselves into Conny's for a long period of time. As such, the studio gave us a good price because their costs had already been covered. They said: "So as to support upcoming bands, we'll give you a special deal." It didn't end up costing that much at all, maybe 500 Deutschmarks, and that was paid by Janie. Plus, he always drove us there in his huge and comfortable Citroen DS.

PETER HEIN_We did the final mix a week later, the following weekend, at Plank's. On the one hand, I couldn't be bothered returning, but on the other, I was kind of in awe of what they were doing. I don't really remember who really wanted to return but I ended up having to pay for it.

RALF DÖRPER_Conny Plank was The Krautrock Producer, and at first this deterred many of the punk bands. But suddenly that changed and it became trendy for younger German bands to work with him, perhaps because Devo and DAF had recorded with him.

CHRIS CROSS_Everything about Conny was extraordinary: the man, his wife Christa, the sound engineers, the whole set-up. Everybody there was so enthusiastic about their work and were open for everything. I found that totally inspiring, the way Conny and Christa kept that similar-minded, experimental, friendly bunch together. They were one with their creativity. There we worked hard, but we had a lot of fun as well; it was the perfect mix for a musical alchemy pot.

PETER HEIN_We only spent one day at Conny Plank's. I remember that Mrs Plank had cooked a lamb roast and everywhere you went it stank of lamb. All in all, I found it all to be horrible, hippie shite. In 1981 Conny Plank was a big player though. He was a real star, and even then he was still sitting behind the desk himself doing the mixing. That's right, we did it there because Conny had the most amazing echo – he had one of those Goldfolienhall echoes.

BERNWARD MALAKA_Conny Plank had these exciting echo chambers. He played the sound over a loudspeaker into those cellars, everything completely analogue. At the end of the room he had these huge aluminium foils so that he could control the reverb. The way in which the foils were arranged determined how long or short the reverb was. It worked solely by mechanics, and behind it there was a mic which recorded everything. Very spaced out.

WERNER LAMBERTZ_The studio there was a dream. He'd designed his own desk and had it custom built. You'd come into this short room and there it stood, directly behind a door with two thick glass panes in it; it looked like an airport, everything was already automatic. I went down there with Wolla Spelmans, shortly after he'd left DAF. Conny was selling off some microphones, good mics from Sennheiser, and we'd gone there to show him some of Wolla's new stuff. I still remember how we went into some side room where he had one of those cheap cassette machines. He never listened to anything on his massive studio speakers which wasn't his. He listened to the demos and then only said: "Hmm, so that's where you're going now. Mhmm." Nothing more. Nothing less. And that's how I first met him.

BERNWARD MALAKA_Conny was open to everything, including what we brought to him. He wasn't simply enthusiastic though; he was also critical and gave us his opinion and advice.

WERNER LAMBERTZ_Conny must have put an enormous amount of money into the studio. You'd open the next door and all of a sudden you'd be in this huge barn with tiled walls; this he used to get the echoey live atmosphere. For DAF they built a small drum stage where they developed the drum sound so that it sounded live. Around another corner and you'd be in another large room, six metres high, and quite unique. And the best of all: no neighbours.

BERNWARD MALAKA_I remember he told us we should work more in the reverb rooms. However, we had too little time for that, as we were only there for a weekend. Sometimes I wish we could have worked longer with him. I am sure we could have got much more out of it.

WERNER LAMBERTZ_For me Conny Plank was the Pope. You always listen to the work of others, but what he did was absolutely first class. It was technically well done and with the right equipment. As a producer he had a good ear and a knack for handling the various bands. He was God, the Pope, the Best.

Pure Freude Record Label

JÄKI ELDORADO_I went with Palais Schaumburg to the first Mute festival in London. Present-day film director Oliver Hirschbiegel drove us there. Even Daniel Miller looked like a teenager. Called 'Mute Night, Silent Night at the Lyceum', the event took place on one Sunday in April in 81. Frank Tovey, a.k.a. Fad Gadget, headlined, and I met Depeche Mode there for the first time. Boyd Rice had not received a visa for England so he instead played over the telephone. He punished the audience with his white noise and everything, and all done over the phone. It was predominantly static and bleeping sounds. Next on the bill was Depeche Mode, who looked exactly like their own fans; they'd secured a support slot with Daniel's help. Everybody was excited. The new, highly anticipated Kraftwerk album *Computerwelt* was about to be released after a three year gap, and perhaps that added to the excitement. It was through this festival that Palais Schaumburg and Holger Hiller got in contact with Daniel Miller, who had previously checked them out. Through the same connection Moritz R was asked to design the early Depeche Mode cover sleeves.

MORITZ REICHELT_ One day Daniel Miller called me from London. He was interested in DAF and wanted to do something with them; additionally, he commissioned me to design the early Depeche Mode singles 'See You' and 'Meaning Of Love'.

JÄKI ELDORADO_*Stahlwerksinfonie* was released by ZickZack and so too 'Wahre Arbeit – Wahrer Lohn', before Die Krupps moved to WEA, Warner. Alfred Hilsberg had his own plan. He had envisioned, as the company's motto suggested, 'Lieber zu viel als zu wenig' – rather too much than too little. His concept was: release everything, economical or not. He came from a left-wing socialist direction, from some hardcore Stalinistic community in Bielefeld.

His daring idea was not so much to release the artistic collection of chosen individuals but rather to release anything from anyone, no regulation but rather flooding. It resulted in a wild mix and, in the end, nothing really that serious emerged. In its first five years ZickZack had well over 100 releases. That's how Hilsberg was; he simply wanted to shit everything out.

FRANK Z._I found Die Krupps okay, although they weren't really my thing. Musically it was a bit flat, and you could hear that it was all produced fairly simply. If you wanted to be judged by your sound then you always had to follow the English, unless you were DAF, Kraftwerk or Neu!. Mute's releases, Daniel Miller's in particular, certainly had a lot more *oomph* to them. But Die Krupps always had this more independent sound. Only if you cranked everything to the max did they kind of work. You had to put all controls on 12 to make 'em sound good.

DANIEL MILLER_I was familiar with Die Krupps, I liked their industrial style and the industrial sound collage that was *Stahlwerksinfonie*. For some reason, though, they were never so well known in England. I liked their music, but I loved their name: Die Krupps. You can't be more German than that. I liked everything about them.

BERNWARD MALAKA_ When I started with Die Krupps, we were making industrial music. *Stahlwerksinfonie* was never really that electronic, and that's what people associated with Düsseldorf – electronic music and Kraftwerk. And we never had that much contact with Kraftwerk; they were too soft for us.

MORITZ REICHELT_ People didn't really know how to take Kraftwerk: 'Should I like technology? And the fancy uniforms?' For the hippies that was all too evil. And in my day I never listened to Kraftwerk, they were too German. Being German was embarrassing to begin with.

JÄKI ELDORADO_ The years 80 and 81 had such a power and such a momentum, like really good rock'n'roll; unbelievable, especially by German standards. Nobody thought of what to make out of it. This naivety, just to make the unknown, you need madmen like Alfred

Hilsberg, who drank a bottle of vodka daily to keep running, and all the other lunatics too. If you look at it, analysing and wondering why England still is such a great place for amazing bands, then you quickly realise that the people behind all this are also real maniacs. There is hardly anybody normal.

BERNWARD MALAKA_*Stahlwerksinfonie* we performed live a handful of times, including in some traditional German pub in Krefeld, the Haus Blumenthal. It was quite an arty-farty event. There were lots of Japanese people in the audience, including one artist who published an eye-catching, hand-produced art magazine. He made a flexi disc from our live show and inserted it in his magazine. Die Krupps didn't play too many shows; we played mostly in Krefeld, at Match Moore in Düsseldorf as well as a show with Siouxsie And The Banshees in Amsterdam, after which we went on tour with DAF as their support.

RALF DÖRPER_We played shows for *Stahlwerksinfonie* in Moers, Hagen and Aachen. We played around with all this steel onstage, creating a real industrial atmosphere. Funnily enough, our tour manager at the time was Marc Chung of Einstürzende Neubauten. The tour was organised via Hamburg, either through Rip Off or ZickZack, hence Chung's involvement.

JÜRGEN ENGLER_I first met Jäki when he was the tour manager for DAF. Previously I only knew his tag line: 'Jäki Eldorado, Germany's first punk rocker'. He became famous after biting Iggy Pop's leg at one of his shows. Throughout the DAF tour everyone referred to him as Herr Goldmann, I've no idea why, although perhaps it was because he dealt with all the accounts and payments. It was only ever Herr Goldmann. They were the days pre-political correctness.

RALF DÖRPER_*Sounds* magazine, for a while, had this column, GröFaz and Goldmann, which been received quite controversially. Behind the pseudonyms you had Alfred Hilsberg and Jäki Eldorado. Gröfaz stood for 'Größter Feldher aller Zeiten', the 'Greatest Warrior of All Time', an ironic reference to Mr Hitler, while Goldmann was the most common Jewish surname. Naturally that column really polarised. They wrote Dada stuff like: 'Form gangs! Destroy all record shops! Destroy all empires! Stop all record shops from selling their wares, other than Rip Off!'

JÄKI ELDORADO_Back then I was working as a tour manager for Hilsberg's company. Everything was always a big drama, but I was making money, so that was cool. Hilsberg was a servant of his own madness; he had all kinds of bands on the road in Germany, including DAF, Palais Schaumburg, Abwärts, as well as The Fall and many other unbelievable acts. I hardly spoke any English and the bands did what they wanted anyway. Unfortunately my enthusiasm sometimes slowed down, when it became too traumatic.

BERNWARD MALAKA_To support DAF was a big influence on us. I found it mind-blowing, what they were doing. I thought Robert Görl was great and so too Gabi as frontman. A short time after touring with them we came up with 'Wahre Arbeit – Wahrer Lohn', which featured a sequencer part that really worked well for us.

JÄKI ELDORADO_That was one hell of a German tour I did with DAF for Hilsberg. We went all over the place, from the big cities, to the smaller venues such as Rheinterrasse Bonn and then a lot of places in the countryside too; every dump where somebody had a discotheque with the odd punk and new wave night. You could easily tour for two to three weeks. Alfred put it all together, he knew where the interest lay, and I accompanied the band on tour as tour manager, collecting all the cash. If things worked out it was down to luck more than anything else. I was pretty impressed by DAF as they presented a certain independence and ambivalence. Naturally it was clear to everybody that they were not in any way involved in the right-wing scene, they only played with that. At least, internally everybody knew that. But the reception from the outside world was different. It wasn't always seen as an ironic or artistic statement. There were people who took everything at face value, and mistook a song like 'Mussolini' as a pro-fascist statement.

PETER GLASER_DAF often ran up against this social pedagogic rubber wall. Before they could be played on the radio, it needed a 10-minute-long explanation by some cultural scientist to decontextualise the matter. As such the actual irony of their approach was often lost, as the critics would immediately jump on the Third Reich references and neglect their post-punk musical elements.

GABI DELGADO_It's a demystification of fascism. In Germany, naming Hitler and Mussolini is taboo. But that can potentially have a dangerous impact on younger people, as we are drawn to things we can't attain. What we were doing was taking these themes and putting them into a silly disco context. We were demystifying these taboos.

FRANK FENSTERMACHER_Robert Görl was a good friend. But at first I was a little shocked and needed some time to come to terms with this disco-fetish-erotic-Nazi attitude.

ROBERT GÖRL_'Der Rauber Und Der Prinz' was a massive success. The lyrics and music went well together. It was supposed to sound like a children's song, a real fairy tale, yet it was also quite provocative. That soup was correctly salted. And the people bought it. We had some nice romantic songs as well. The sequencer is able to produce such beautiful tones. Wow, such great sounds are within it. 'Verlieb Dich In Mich' or the already named 'Rauber'; because of the video many thought that I could play the glockenspiel. But no! That was the sequencer doing that. I'd programmed it in a way to make it sound like a children's glockenspiel. I really have to emphasise that the sequencer is a real instrument, with tones and harmonies. When it is played polyphonically you can let all the sounds resonate, so that a kind of harmony evolves.

German Unity Festival

JÜRGEN ENGLER_At the festival in June 81 with DAF, Fehlfarben and Palais Schaumburg, we were completely neglected, even though as Die Krupps we were kicking off. *Stahlwerksinfonie* and the accompanying shows, they were hard to ignore, we were hard to ignore, but promoter Jochen Hulder didn't want us for some reason.

RALF DÖRPER_It was the Day of German Unity, which in those days was on June 17 in commemoration of the 1953 uprising in East Germany. And so Jochen named the festival after that and held it on the public holiday. Like me, Hulder had worked for the city magazine *Überblick*, although later he became the manger of Die Toten Hosen. He never liked us.

MICHAEL KEMNER_As Fehlfarben we had a spot at the Philipshalle festival, alongside Palais Schaumburg and DAF; how quickly you can meet up again. It was at this that the infamous mustard assassination of Uwe Jahnke took place. Two weeks prior, Janie, a.k.a. Peter Hein, had quit the band, and so Thomas Schwebel assumed singing duties and Uwe joined. For this gig he'd dressed himself from head to toe in white. A white shirt with stiff collar, very tight, white trousers; he looked like an angel. And in front of the stage there stood 500 hardcore punks, all dressed in black. Uwe's outfit was apparently quite provocative, and after the third song someone threw a paper plate at him, one of those plates you eat your sausage from, and it hit him fair and square on his white shirt, covering him in mustard. And it just splattered everywhere, dripping down on to his guitar; everything was yellow. Uwe freaked out; it was a total disaster. Highly embarrassing; we ended up looking like idiots. The audience didn't like us; with no Janie and Thomas covering vocals they didn't know what to make of us and we stood there, on the wrong side of a losing battle. And then when DAF finally appeared all hell broke loose. Ours was one of the most horrible shows I have ever experienced.

BERNWARD MALAKA_By this point DAF were already in full swing; they were much more successful than we ever were. 1981 was their time. We'd come from the same stable, had spent our time together at the Hof, but here we were on a very, very different level.

JÜRGEN ENGLER_It wasn't that we didn't have anything to do with each other, but there wasn't really a scene that you could belong to and say: 'Yeah, we are part of the Düsseldorf electro scene.' Nothing like that existed.

MICHAEL KEMNER_Janie stood in the crowd and laughed his head off. There had been a bit of aggro beforehand as we hated that he had walked out on us, something nobody really understood, and we all felt betrayed and pissed off. He was pissed off, we were pissed off, everybody was pissed off.

ROBERT GÖRL_We did two European tours. After *Alles Ist Gut*, we played a big tour, and much later, another. We played the Philipshalle festival on our first tour. Back then any tour easily had at least 20 dates. Once in a while Conny would come along, and although he wasn't able to come all that often he did join us for this festival where he monitored the stage sound. Apart from him, we had other technical personnel from the label as well as a psychological nurse.

MICHAEL KEMNER_Palais Schaumburg started the evening's events, after which Fehlfarben flopped and then DAF cashed in mercilessly.

JÄKI ELDORADO_DAF live had a real punch to it; nobody had experienced anything like that before. It was all incredibly forceful. Especially Gabi, who didn't take any prisoners. Never again have I seen anything like this. The audience couldn't actually believe what they were witnessing.

RALF DÖRPER_I followed DAF's career from their first show at the Hof to their show as a duo at Philipshalle. Gabi and Robert were the only ones from this time to consistently pursue their goal. They wanted success. The gold and the love. And in the end it was these two who shared the success and the revenues.

MICHAEL KEMNER_Robert and Gabi have always been very close, right from the very start. They must have cooked up stuff secretly. I believe it was clear from the beginning that they wanted to be just them two at some point. One was used for a while but it was always understood: in the end it will only be the two of them. I had the feeling that for Gabi it was never about the music. He just wanted fame, brutal fame. He wasn't there with his heart, nor with his feelings, always only mentally. Wanted to achieve something with this. Everything was calculated. Success counted, success above everything.

JÄKI ELDORADO_I was tour manager for DAF when the stage was invaded at Philipshalle – wow, those were the glory days for Düsseldorf. What a magical moment of anarchy.

ROBERT GÖRL_ The whole stage was invaded and Conny just stood there with his desk in the middle of all these people. Later on he told me he'd never experienced anything like that before in his life, people just surrounding him and dancing. And in the style of Gabi. He developed a whole new style of dance. A mix of jumping, dancing and twisting. They took our energy and transformed it into new movements.

RALF DÖRPER_ To replace Tina Schnekenburger, who for a while had operated the ghetto blaster, Gabi himself took charge of the backing tapes, which featured the sequences that had been produced with Conny earlier. That whole concept was genius. And now, instead of their sole ghetto blaster, they had a whole wall unit of tape decks. They'd set up 20 Sony cassette decks, four by five; it looked like some kind of art installation. Each contained one backing track, and with that Gabi was able to change the running order of their show: "What do you want to hear next?" Righto, click. Görl drumming along with his stoical beats to whatever he was told to, sometimes with fade added to the playbacks. That was made for the big screen.

FRANK Z._ They had one tape deck for each song. Samplers did not yet exist, they only came towards the late Eighties and even then they were huge containers that looked like stereo amplifiers with which you could only sample five or 10 seconds. Pretty stupid and not too useful. Instead with their tape decks they were able to do what samplers were later able to do, but on a much bigger scale.

GABI DELGADO_I actually find it good that bands have to earn their money giving shows rather than with their records; it's a very direct and party-orientated way. Our show at Düsseldorf's Philipshalle, that was great, the stage was invaded and, as such, we experienced this party aspect at close range. It shouldn't be that people just stay below and watch what happens up above; it's not about consumption and delivery. It's a communal experience, and at Philipshalle it developed into a real party.

ROBERT GÖRL_It was cool, being with a big record company. They really took good care of us. We always had a nice lady with us on tour, asking us after each concert: "Is everything okay? Is the catering good enough?" That was cool. In Germany Ariola took care of the touring, and in England it was Virgin. They'd send out a sound engineer, an assistant, a tour manager and a bunch of roadies.

GABI DELGADO_We now had the chance to present our songs on TV. Our TV debut came on *Bio's Bahnhof*, a show hosted by Alfred Biolek, where we played two songs. Robert and I stood there in our sleeveless tops made of black leather, and apart from a snare and my mic we didn't have to bring anything else with us. From memory we played 'Als Wär's Das Letzte Mal' and 'Der Räuber Und Der Prinz' and Mr Biolek seemed to be impressed. Cologne used to be the gay capital.

RALF DÖRPER_Chris Bohn was leftist to the point that he was basically a communist; he seemed to like odd stuff and absolutely hated commercialism. Strangely enough, at that time DAF weren't selling that well in England, although in Germany they were making six figures. Chris Bohn once wrote in an article how irritated he was when Görl picked him up for an interview in Düsseldorf in his fancy sports car. He didn't get it. In England you had belonged to the underground and in Germany it was pop or New German Wave. If you as a band opened yourself towards the industry, you could make a lot of money within a short period of time. At least what we thought would be a lot of money.

Wahre Arbeit – Wahrer Lohn

JÜRGEN ENGLER_I've no idea who introduced us to Werner Lambertz. But, all of a sudden, he was there. Maybe we met him through Ata Tak, perhaps Kurt had suggested him and introduced us. Even though I've said there was no real scene, we still had our contacts.

WERNER LAMBERTZ_I had this huge hall in some courtyard at 32 Linien Street; adjacent to a garage and right of the studio. There we had the studio. An industrial estate right off Krupp Street. At the time there was a massive brown gateway. It had been a small petroleum lamp factory before. Horrible dust and dirt. I went in there with a mouth mask one day and ripped the whole place to pieces. I piled what was left and thought: 'With these pieces I will now build my studio.'

JÜRGEN ENGLER_ He wasn't exactly a musician but rather a trained electrician, or to be exact a communication engineer, who had built his own studio and a monstrous 16-step sequencer. We went to see him because he was the first to have a so-called computer studio, where he could program his stuff. That meant that he could pre-program all his drum parts with this giant box and then somehow tap that into his Korg or Roland rhythm machines. Those early drum machines had amazing sounds, but unfortunately they weren't programmable, nor did you have MIDI to synchronise them, and that was the same for the Roland TR-606 and 808, which came out two years later.

WERNER LAMBERTZ_ There was no MIDI, and therefore no synchronisation. The first MIDI that I ever came across was a Hohner String Melody, quite a small unit yet not that bad a sound. I started looking into it, to find out how it worked when you pressed down a key. Then I started experimenting with relays; I came from electrical communication engineering where I'd seen these little magnetic relays which worked really quick. I soldered one relay underneath each key, to function as a contact, then switched on the 12 volts and the relays went 'ping'! Later on I had thick computer cables running from both the keyboard and synthesiser and ran them all into a patchbay, the keyboards plugged in below, the synthesiser on top. I was never actually planning on setting up a sound studio. I'd previously directed a film and wanted to synchronise music to the film. That proved almost impossible so I said to myself: "If you want it done you have to do it on your own." So I started building my own sequencer and triggered that via a pulse generator. This allowed me to create multiple sequences which I could combine either one after the other, or together. It also included some mad technical gimmicks, such as a counter which allowed me to play one sequence three times and the next five times. Depending on how you set up the sequences determined how long it took for the melody to repeat itself for the first time. Sometimes it took as long as 23 hours!

BERNWARD MALAKA_For our second production, which we started only three months after *Stahlwerksinfonie*, everything ran differently. We recorded in Düsseldorf, at Werner Lambertz's place, the Lambertz/Brahm Digital Studio. It was a stone age version of digital, but digital all the same. There Werner had his switchboard with thousands of patch cables and thick jack plugs, all of which were connected to each other. It looked a little like an old telephone switchboard, but it was completely digital. Other than our second Die Krupps album, Werner did little else. He was basically an amateur within the music industry, but he was always very interested in the engineering side of electronic music.

FRANK FENSTERMACHER_Die Krupps had already been to Werner Lambertz's studio by the time we recorded Pyrolator's album there, but the first there was Andreas Dorau with his single 'Fred Vom Jupiter' and his album *Tulpen Und Narzissen*. That was in 1981. That was Werner's world; he was a real tinkerer, a puzzle freak, the original Gyro Gearloose. It was he who built the Brontologic for Kurt, the one that is now exhibited at the Rock and Pop Museum in Gronau.

WERNER LAMBERTZ_And then I needed to synchronise the music to the pictures. What would be better than using the film projector as the device, like an emitter? Twenty-four frames per second. Nice idea, but at first it didn't fit. How to put 24 frames on a 16-step basis? Difficult. So I had to split. First I tinkered with the keys that did the split for me and adjusted them differently; afterwards I had converted 24 pictures to 16 steps of music. I was able to use each tone synchronised to the frame. That was the idea. Genius in a way.

KURT DAHLKE_Werner was a maverick; capricious, headstrong, and very, very stubborn. That's the way it is with geniuses. They need to be a little crazy. But I did do some early stuff with him, last but not least the Brontologic.

JÜRGEN ENGLER_Werner Lambertz and Ralf Dörper both had a Yamaha, which was easier to get and a little cheaper than a Moog; that's why the whole record sounded like that. 'Wahre Arbeit – Wahrer Lohn' has this typical Yamaha sound, but sent through distortion, estranged and pimped. Not pure.

BERNWARD MALAKA_The starting sequence of 'Wahre Arbeit' was fairly basic. We'd planned for the album to be more a rougher disco record, and that's exactly how it sounded. We noticed that people were even dancing to *Stahlwerksinfonie*, which is why we thought: "We need to take this sound – and make it danceable." By then Jürgen had already dispensed with his guitars; he was much more into synthesisers. He was the real musician amongst us. Ralf didn't really have a musical background. We all wrote the lyrics together; for that, there was no fixed process.

RALF DÖRPER_Once we came up with some fairly martial lyrics. On the one hand, they could be interpreted as some type of communist manifesto for the working classes, but on the other, they could be read as something faithfully German: "Meine Muskeln sind Maschinen, Sehnen stählern, Schweiß wie Öl. Schmutz und Dreck ist wahre Arbeit, Schmerz und Tadel wahrer Lohn", meaning, 'My muscles are machines, my tendons are of steel, my sweat is like oil. Dirt and grime is our work, pain and blame the plain reward'.

WERNER LAMBERTZ_Whoever it was said: "I know somebody, a musician, I gave him your number, he'll call you." And that's what he did: "Hi, Kurt here from Der Plan." And I was like: "Plan? What plan do you have in mind?" "I heard you have some kind of weird computer. Could I come by and have a look at it?" And then he swung by with Frank Fenstermacher. I, as yet, had no name for my machine, but later on it became known as the Brontologic, and it can be seen in some museum today.

FRANK Z._ At the time of 'Wahre Arbeit – Wahrer Lohn' I was working at a record shop. We had everything there. All of the stuff came from ZickZack, a Hamburg-based label run by Alfred Hilsberg. To be fair, he released a lot of shit as well. There, every idiot and his mate could do a record. I don't mean Die Krupps of course, they certainly belonged to those where you thought: 'Okay, these guys know what they are doing.' The problem most people had with Die Krupps, though, was the frontman, who, after having played in a punk group, now wanted to take the fast lane to this whole new style. As such there were people who thought Die Krupps were only one of those bands chasing the latest trends.

MEIKEL CLAUSS_ The 'Wahre Arbeit – Wahrer Lohn' maxi single – that had one hell of a sound that just banged on no end. Werner, at this time, did some weird stuff in his little eight-track studio. A sexy studio, all hand built. The guy was utterly mad and had delivered some real shite, but on occasion he came up with some timeless masterpieces.

KURT DAHLKE_ Then came my next solo abum. The question was though: 'Where do we do this?' It was no longer possible at Fürstenwall. So we then ended up at Werner's. He had just finished building his strange pluggable sequencer that was later named the Brontologic, and I liked that a lot. I told him: I'll definitely do my record with you. And the result was *Ausland*. I was so impressed with his machine that I wanted one for myself as well. So we spent months designing and building the Brontologic 2, Werner and me together. Werner did all the circuit boards and I did all the soldering and bolting. It took us three months to finish it.

WERNER LAMBERTZ_ Half a year later I read an interview and asked myself: "'Bronton'? What the fuck is he talking about a 'Bronton Logic'?" I remember he asked and I said: "'Logic'. Mine is called 'Logic'. And yours would be 'Logic 2'." And then they just named it 'Brontologic' in that interview and it further read: "With participation from Kurt Dahlke". I mean it was a commissioned work, exactly to his needs and what he wanted to have. Completely. I built it from scratch, delivered it and got paid. Most of Der Plan's music came from it. It was mainly a controller, in fact an impulse trigger. What you combine it with wasn't important. But I had built the whole thing. It was my invention. My baby.

RALF DÖRPER_On 'Wahre Arbeit – Wahrer Lohn' you can hear the original Lambertz sequencer. Pyrolator named it Brontologic, perhaps because it was as big as a brontosaurus. It was at least as big as a fridge. Doepfer went on to produce something similar, but in smaller and more stable units.

BERNWARD MALAKA_All the steel that we played in our studio we'd found on a junkyard behind the Main Station, where there now is a huge library. Back then there was a half-torn-down steel factory. Right on Eisen Street. We once did a photo session there and saw all these shiny pieces of steel lying there. We took them all home with us: these hollow square parts from which Jürgen built his original Stahlofon. They looked like massive xylophone keys. You can see the first Stahlofon on the back cover.

WERNER LAMBERTZ_Jürgen then played a solo, and that sounded amazing and I thought to myself: "Where is this guy getting the energy from to do this?" It was fairly long, the solo, but he kept just going on and on. In the end, we had to get him some muscle-healing cream and gloves for the next show.

BERNWARD MALAKA_It was a mad, screeching sound, as if someone was playing on metal bottle necks. Completely industrial and spaced out.

WERNER LAMBERTZ

++ **JAN 82** Kraftwerk top the British single charts with 'The Model'/'Computer Love' ++ **FEB 82** OMD play at the Zeche in Bochum and meet Kraftwerk ++ Second album by Rheingold: *R.* ++ **MAR 82** Kraftwerk perform 'The Model' on Thomas Gottschalk's TV show *Na Sowas!* ++ **APR 82** Liaisons Dangereuses play in the canteen at Düsseldorf university ++ **APR–JUN 82** Falklands War between Great Britain and Argentina ++ **MAY 82** Liaisons Dangereuses and Die Krupps play at the Rocktage at the Munich Alabamahalle ++ **MAY 82** DAF record the album *Für Immer* at Conny Plank's ++ **MAY 82** Nena releases the single 'Nur Geträumt' ++ **AUG 82** Yazoo release *Upstairs At Eric's* on Mute ++ **SEP 82** Die Krupps release the album *Volle Kraft Voraus!* on WEA, produced by Werner Lambertz ++ **OCT 82** Helmut Kohl is elected Chancellor following the break up of the SPD/FDP coalition ++

Computer World

RALF DÖRPER_The first direct contact that I had with Hütter and Schneider was through my job as a music writer for the city magazine *Überblick*. At that time I'd already been making experimental music for a couple of years and had released several recordings, also with Die Krupps. The boss of *Überblick*, Klaus Hang, knew the Kraftwerk guys and managed to get us an interview with them. The interview took place at our offices and all four gentlemen appeared dressed in black. Unlike nowadays they all spoke, it wasn't just Hütter, and even Bartos got a word in. All in all, the atmosphere was very relaxed; in fact we even swapped records. 'Das Model' for 'Wahre Arbeit'.

WOLFGANG FLÜR_Strangely enough, the preparations for the *Computerwelt* tour were done with the help of The Scorpions. There was this big removal and haulage firm called Schenker, they transported our equipment and provided a big hall near Hannover, where we rehearsed for the tour. That was more or less the family of Rudolf und Michael Schenker from The Scorpions. We stayed there for a week at a bed and breakfast whilst we practised. Every day we'd rig everything up and then take it all down again with the help of our stagehands.

JÜRGEN ENGLER_I hadn't bought a single Kraftwerk album, except for *Computerwelt* and I only bought *Computerwelt* because I'd worked on the cover as lithographer. That was the trade I'd learned. At that time I was working as a lithographer at Urlich's on Benzenberg Street. Ralf Hütter was always in and out of that place and they'd had their black and yellow cover with the four stylised heads done by us.

WOLFGANG FLÜR_All the racks and cases for the tour were built by me out of plywood, as it was totally stable and everything was dowelled and glued. Then, I attached stainless steel plates with contact adhesive; this high-grade V2A 0.6 mm thick stainless steel was hard for me to work with and I cut myself quite a few times. Cut, pressed, folded, all according to my plans as I am actually a trained carpenter. The metal workshop Huiskens in Schwerin Street must have loved us for all the work we gave them. I picked up the specially cut steel plates, brought them back to the studio and glued them there with Pattex contact adhesive. Then you had to hit them hard with a rubber mallet, and after that nothing could budge them. Next I bought little dark blue fluorescent tubes and tucked these and the power cables into the racks. They were double racks, standard 19-inch with a partition panel and you could slide the equipment into the racks on the guide rails. After that everything was put into flight cases and packed or sent on tour. We planned to take the whole Kling Klang on tour with us. The stands for the *Computer World* tour were made out of square section steel and were welded for us in Tönisvorst. Those you could also completely dismantle and pack in flight cases.

PETER GLASER_The Kraftwerk concert at the Philipshalle was a decisive event for me. I still remember the stage design; it was like wall bars, absolutely identically constructed ladders out of fluorescent tubes and, in front of that, four aluminium chassis on long legs, looking like bar tables. They'd made their Kling Klang Studio portable and simply put it onstage. And that was when I first realised – brilliant! Of course, the whole studio is an instrument.

WOLFGANG FLÜR_Later on I also built really simple yet elegant things for the stage and fitted out the racks purely with fluorescent tubes. I started to cover all our cases in stainless steel; and to hide all the cables on the floor, there was this stainless steel catwalk. I was extremely proud of building these things and seeing them on the stage, proud to be the Kraftwerk designer. We ourselves walked onto the stage on about 70-centimetre wide, 14-centimetre high catwalks, to our equipment that was arranged in a V-shape. These flat boxes were clad in stainless steel and all the cables ran through them so you couldn't see them on the stage. There were huge multi-core connectors inside, that in the end were as big as irons and connected up to 250 contacts with each other. The cables ran underneath to the various consoles. They came out at the back again and ran on to the next one, so we could all connect to each other double quick.

PETER GLASER_I suddenly realised that everything that would usually put me off rock concerts was missing: no dry ice, no spotlights swooping over the audience, nothing that was too flashy. Instead these four guys just came on in black trousers and red shirts and got on with the job. That was also the first tour with the robots that 'performed' the last song alone. Kraftwerk had soaked up this digital and trans-human myth like a sponge and to such an extent that they now themselves became producers of it.

WOLFGANG FLÜR_But it took a long, long time till we got everything right and working and only then could we go on the longest tour in our band's history. Because the technology was so unreliable we had Joachim Dehmann with us the whole time. Over and over again something went wrong with the cables – soldered joints came apart, some other little thing stopped working. He was kept pretty busy making sure everything was functioning.

PETER GLASER_What impressed me most about the concert and this concept was that they showed us how to handle the new technologies. These machines offered billions of tone variations and constantly invited you to lose yourself in infinity. Kraftwerk actually did quite the opposite, reducing everything to a couple of notes, sometimes one-word texts like in children's songs. By doing this they accepted that their material would become incredibly banal, aesthetically speaking, but they did it to such an extent and so consciously that in the end it was again also innovative. What this reduction to something elementary taught me was: 'You have to stay in charge! You are the authority, not the machine!' I thought this was a very human message.

GLENN GREGORY_I'm afraid I never saw them live. No idea how I managed that. Why did we miss it; we saw every other band, but never Kraftwerk. A *Computer World* show with Wolfgang and Karl, the really classic quartet – that must have been great. I could so easily have gone to the Hammersmith Odeon; they even played there three nights in a row.

MARTYN WARE_You had to have seen Kraftwerk in the Seventies, when everything was new and fresh. They were in a league of their own. I don't watch any of their shows now. Today, I'd be afraid that if I went to a concert, I might not like it. That would be awful.

WOLFGANG FLÜR_It really was a great time. Once we were in Rome and after the concert, Helmut Berger took us back to his house. We drove through Rome from the concert hall, with him in his Mini Cooper leading the way, and us in the bus behind him, through alleys so narrow that we almost couldn't follow. Then we partied at his place till six in the morning.

BERNWARD MALAKA_In America, I was at an uncle's for a couple of weeks in Washington and happened to see that Kraftwerk were playing there, so I went in August. They were on their *Computer World* tour. I was amazed to see how the Americans got off on Kraftwerk. I saw the prophets in another land on a different continent. It was a great big theatre with tiered seating. Basically like a big cinema. How many seats would there have been? Maybe 1500. It was really cool and everybody loved it. But kind of weird too. At the end the yanks were chanting: 'Kraft durch Freude', German for 'Strength through Joy', which has a strong negative Nazi connotation. But you couldn't be angry at them, because those were probably just the only German words they knew.

WOLFGANG FLÜR_It was the Warner Theatre where we played in Washington. A big old movie theatre that had shown the great films of the Fifties and Sixties – *Ben Hur*, *Doctor Zhivago* and so on – before it degenerated to a seedy cinema and was later used for concerts. It held 1800 people.

JÜRGEN ENGLER_I saw the Kraftwerk show in Düsseldorf, although despite playing their hometown once again it was still not a full house. It really was a good show though. In the background, films were being shown on separate screens, though nothing as impressive as they have today; no comparison to today's multimedia. The robots were there too and the highlight of the show was Florian playing about with his pocket calculator; he even let the people in the first row press the buttons and that made the music. It made such piercing sounds and was just like it said in the lyrics: "By pressing down a special key, it plays a little melody". That was the one and only time that I ever saw Kraftwerk live.

RALF DÖRPER_ It has to be said that in that year they came to the Philipshalle twice, because the promoters assumed they'd have a home advantage, but that worked for them as little as it did for Die Krupps. In other towns they played more the club scene like Berlin, Metropol; Munich, Zirkus Krone; Cologne, Sartory-Saal; Kiel, Ball Pompos, but definitely no big halls and huge venues. Memory can be deceiving.

WOLFGANG FLÜR_The idea with the pocket calculator was Florian's. Florian's and mine. Florian was a big kid and he'd bought a Texas Instruments pocket calculator as well as a Speak & Spell toy where you could type in words and press the button 'Voice' to learn English. So he played around with this for a bit and I thought it sounded quite interesting. He'd also bought a decent pocket calculator that played notes when you typed, so you could play a genuine melody on it. It could even do a minor key, with semi-tones and all.

MARTYN WARE_Kraftwerk never moved away from making concept albums. Only you aren't really allowed to say that any more. Our *Penthouse And Pavement* was also a concept album. We loved it. British Electric Foundation [B.E.F.] was the conceptional scaffold for Heaven 17, the name we had because of Alex, the main character in *A Clockwork Orange*. He is shown in a record store and in the background you can see a fantasy chart list. What was at number one? Correct: Heaven 17. Well, here with this album there were six or seven new, clever, innovative songs that all conceptually dealt with the blessings of the Computer World.

GLENN GREGORY_The song 'Computer Love' was chosen from the album *Computer World* to be released as a single in the UK and for some reason, a song from a different album was chosen for the B-side, the three-year-old track 'The Model'. English DJs like Rusty Egan usually played the B-side. As a result, EMI released the single again, this time with 'The Model' as the A-side and this reached number one on the UK singles charts in 1982. Suddenly, in February 82, with a song from 1978, Kraftwerk were number one in the charts.

MORITZ REICHELT_In 1982 I knew: synth-pop is the new thing. For me it was a way out of the noise productions of punk. Songs with melodies. Depeche Mode, Heaven 17, Human League were the classic bands for this style. I had a great respect for them. I really admired them.

RALF DÖRPER_On January 30, 1982, Kraftwerk were suddenly at number one in the UK charts with 'The Model' and everyone was amazed. In the same week OMD's 'Maid Of Orleans' and Human League's 'Being Boiled' were also in the Top 10. Even in Germany, 'The Model' got to number seven in the charts and became Kraftwerk's most successful single to date.

WOLFGANG FLÜR_Shortly before we recorded *Computer World*, we had an idea: We should all have such gimmicks like Florian had. Ralf remembered that the Kunze music shop at the station had such mini-organs and got one for himself. And there we also discovered the Stylophone that you could play with a little stylus; so Karl played that. So everybody had their mini-instrument, except me, I was again the only one who had to build something himself. I only had these 'hotplate' drums, I'll call them that, so I bought an aluminium lunchbox at Elektro Arlt, then I got three small stainless steel plates at Huiskens metal workshop; I had everything measured out perfectly. To stop it conducting I glued an insulating film in between. All out of metal. And underneath I clamped little cables and connected all of those to a 24-metre-long cable. I put a bass drum, snare and hi-hat on the little contact plates, so I could easily carry it and now I had my gimmick too. 'Pocket Calculator' was always the highlight for people at live performances, because they could join in and play on it.

PETER GLASER_Despite Kraftwerk's indisputable merits throughout the Eighties, time caught up with them. When *Computer World* came out maybe there was already an inkling, as regards the content in the statements, that they were not really that stunning any more, but actually a bit banal.

WOLFGANG FLÜR_We started every show with the computer voice from tape: "Meine Damen und Herren, Ladies and Gentlemen, heute Abend aus Deutschland, die Menschmaschine: KRRRAFT-WERRRK." 'Numbers' was our first piece. Even if it is just counting from one to eight in six languages, it's one of our most important songs, not least because of the rhythm track that Bambaataa stole.

PETER GLASER_The mysterious minimalistic poetry that develops from just one word, like in 'Metropolis', can't be heard on *Computer World*. The vague attempt at social criticism, as suggested by the choice of album name, was not really convincing at all.

GABI DELGADO_They had to back-pedal to make sure they weren't misunderstood; first they sang "Radio-Activity" and then later it's "*NO* Radio-Activity". I find stuff like that just incredibly pathetic, you have to stick to what you say. "Radio Activity, give it to me!" If you've said it like that once, you can't change it years later to

"NO Radio Activity", just because there's an anti-nuclear campaign. I can't suddenly start singing "Don't dance the Mussolini", just because a few neo-Nazis are jumping about, that'd be wrong.

BOB GIDDENS_DAF kind of overdid it as well later on with their hyper-German-ness: 'What can we do to shock a little bit more?' was all they were thinking of. Nevertheless I was always a fan of the German language; same with Kraftwerk, the German versions were always the best.

WOLFGANG FLÜR_Our text trio was always Emil Schult, Ralf and Florian, though Emil did the most, especially with the English lyrics. As a painter, he wasn't much of a success, he was more reproducing things with not so many ideas of his own, although he was in Beuys' class. But he was a great lyricist.

PETER GLASER_'Computer World' – that was more like the watered down version of Abwärts' 'Computerstaat' single. And we thought to ourselves: "Is this for real?"

WOLFGANG FLÜR_We made 'Computer World', but there was already a song by Abwärts called 'Computerstaat', which clearly had a similar theme. It's about exactly the same topic, that the banks collect all our data and that we're all under surveillance. Ralf thought it was great, and although we had different lyrics, it was similar. Again we wanted to present a concept album with this and the topic really fitted with computer mania, home computers and all that.

FRANK Z._'Computerstaat' dealt with the police investigation methods back then that were becoming more and more sophisticated. The IT-based concepts from the head of the Federal Criminal Investigation Office, Horst Herold, and especially his dragnet investigation programme, was a hot topic back then. It was brand new, but also somewhat threatening and was only intended to give Joe Public a feeling of security. This is all a question of perspective.

BERNWARD MALAKA_Die Krupps got off to a really good start. In the *New Musical Express* the *Stahlwerksinfonie* wasn't only reviewed, it was album of the month and 'Wahre Arbeit' was the single of the month. Both in the same issue. Not bad for a German band. It's not easy to get noticed by the British press. Kraftwerk even reached number one on the singles charts with 'The Model'. That was the time when we thought: "This could really turn into something." I guess all of us had kind of thought about having a real career in the music business. Jürgen and Ralf, most of all, really pulled it off.

ANDY MCCLUSKEY_Finally, we came to Düsseldorf and performed at the Philipshalle. I never liked the place. That was on the *Architecture & Morality* tour, it was terribly cold and I really didn't like the atmosphere. Before that, on the previous tour, we were booked at the Zeche in Bochum, where we met Kraftwerk for the first time. Paul and I were backstage, Malcolm and Martin were out there having a drink. When they came back, they said, 'do you know who's out there? Kraftwerk!' They had seen them in the stands. Paul and I were just scared stiff and felt sick right at the same moment. I don't think I was ever so nervous onstage. We were up there and saw the four guys dressed in black in the audience. I couldn't think of anything else but: "Do they like it? What are they thinking? Do they like it? What are they thinking?" We met them after the show. I didn't want to come over as just another adoring fan, but I did want to thank them for the music that had basically changed my life. So I thought, you've got to ask something intelligent and I can remember exactly that I asked Ralf which speakers he used in the studio. Oh boy, how embarrassing, as if that was important. Karl commented a bit ironically, but approvingly that I danced on the stage like a whirling dervish. I remember those two things as clear as day. It was quite an experience for us, we didn't talk for long, but this meeting was very important for us. We felt honoured and encouraged.

Full Steam Ahead!

BERNWARD MALAKA_Whilst I was in New York, the others started working on the next Die Krupps album. Tina Schnekenburger was already there, but Ralf was not often around – everything was in

BERNWARD MALAKA

upheaval. Tina was with DAF before and then she changed to Die Krupps because she was now going out with Jürgen. You can see her on the back cover of *Volle Kraft Voraus!*, which translates to 'Full Steam Ahead!' and was the name of our next record.

TINA SCHNEKENBURGER_I was going out with Jürgen and he asked me if I wanted to join Die Krupps. I always liked *Stahlwerksinfonie*. That was a cult record and so too was 'Wahre Arbeit – Wahrer Lohn'. I liked all that. Jürgen asked me and I thought it was a good idea. Bernward Malaka was there, Jürgen, of course, and Ralf was still in the band; Waldi came later.

JÜRGEN ENGLER_'Volle Kraft Voraus!' I wrote that at home on that really little thing from Casio, the Casio VL-10. I recorded it all by hand on a cassette tape, then I went to Lambertz and told him: "You've got to program that for me, stick it in your Brontologic." This sequencer was as big as a fridge, there's a photo of it in the booklet of *Volle Kraft Voraus!*. You had to plug in and out like at an old telephone switchboard. First the 16-step sequences were programmed and then you could transpose them to the synth. That was the good thing about the Brontologic, you couldn't do this with normal sequencers, just one: the Fricke. You could transpose it to the keyboard, so while the piece was playing I changed the pitch and recorded it straight away.

TINA SCHNEKENBURGER_ Die Krupps were really good in the early stages. I only began to have doubts while we were working on *Volle Kraft Voraus!*, not because of the album, that turned out pretty good, but because of all the stuff that came with this major label deal. We were, after all, now under contract to WEA, under the spell of a major.

BERNWARD MALAKA_'Goldfinger' was one of the great new songs and quite a novel track. Nowadays I still really like 'Für Einen Augenblick'. We had good tracks, but they weren't very well mixed. It was one of Werner Lambertz's first productions, maybe we should have given it to another studio for the final mix.

TINA SCHNEKENBURGER_ There were really good songs on that album. 'Für Einen Augenblick' and one slow one: 'Zwei Herzen, Ein Rhythmus'. For that, Jürgen and I wrote the lyrics together.

BERNWARD MALAKA_There was another attempt at 'Goldfinger' afterwards in a studio in Bochum. The record company had picked it. Technically, it was the most sophisticated analogue studio on offer at that time, with a 48-track recording console. But it was in a way a step backwards for us, as we'd already been to a digital studio.

TINA SCHNEKENBURGER_WEA had a stylist called Barbara and she was actually pretty nice. She was supposed to whip us into shape style-wise. She brought clothes along and I kind of thought: "Do we really have to?" Everything was geared towards success. I could criticise myself for this now, because despite my doubts I simply went along with what I was told and so too Bernward and Jürgen. We really looked quite crappy. It wasn't a bad album, it was just all the circumstances that went with it that I found were questionable.

BERNWARD MALAKA_We didn't need 48 tracks. We had everything there on our synths. So it was totally ridiculous. Well, okay... WEA had booked it, so we went with it.

TINA SCHNEKENBURGER_The photo shoot, all the stuff going on, on the one hand it was great, because you were always hoping that somehow, someday you could live from all this shit. You think: "Oh, now this is taking off." But then somebody is telling you: "Stand like this or that and maybe you should wear this or this..." You go along with it of course but I always wondered if it was right to do so.

JÜRGEN ENGLER_*Volle Kraft Voraus!* was recorded on an 8-track half-inch tape. Sadly, the way Werner Lambertz had mixed it made it sound really flat. The way he did 'Wahre Arbeit – Wahrer Lohn' was brilliant, it sounded great, but this thing was a disaster. On top of that, a band's sound had a lot to do with what equipment you use. Very few had more than one synth; you were just happy if you could even afford one.

WERNER LAMBERTZ_It was like this: we had finished the recordings, the landlord wanted the rent, the electricity was going to be cut off and I said: "Jürgen, we have to finish this."

JÜRGEN ENGLER_Krupps definitely had their sound from Yamaha. Ralf had the Yamaha CS-10, Lambertz had the Yamaha CS-20m.

Totally awesome equipment. The only problem is you can't connect the synthesiser to a sequencer so easily. In those days there weren't too many sequencers; there was an ARP sequencer, but nobody had that, then you had the Korg SQ-10 – Chrislo had one – and later there was one made by Oberheim, the Oberheim DSX; Robert got that one.

WERNER LAMBERTZ_Then the next thing was, who's going to take the tapes personally to Hamburg to the record company WEA? It was a fucking freezing cold night; at three in the morning we finished the last mix and then I got into the car with my then-girlfriend and drove in a snow storm to Hamburg to my date with the guys from WEA.

JÜRGEN ENGLER_I had got myself an ARP Odyssey, because I wanted to have a synth too, and then I played 'Zwei Herzen, Ein Rhythmus' on it in one go and recorded it. It's played by hand on *Volle Kraft Voraus!*; as we couldn't trigger it, I had to play it. That is the ARP, everything else is the Yamaha.

WERNER LAMBERTZ_Jürgen wasn't with us, he went off home to bed while we went off in the car to Hamburg. I was getting fed up waiting for my money for the production; it took more than half the time again and there was no money coming in. I was owed 10,000 Deutschmarks and I needed that urgently.

JÜRGEN ENGLER_Since there was no suitable sequencer, Werner Lambertz opened up the panel of the synth and without further ado just wired the synth in and connected it to the sequencer. It wasn't so easy as it had a strange voltage. Werner just unscrewed it and wired it in so he could trigger it directly.

WERNER LAMBERTZ_Then I met the guy from the record company – what a prick, a total wanker. Anyway: "Ah yes, Die Krupps, I see." There was a Revox there, he throws my master tape on it, threads it through and starts and I sit there and wait. "Why is there no sound? There's nothing on it!" I go over to him and say: "Listen, turn the tape over, please!" He did that on purpose, the bastard. You can be one hundred percent sure of that.

JÜRGEN ENGLER_Werner was a total psycho. He was really weird and, at some point, he noticed how lousy the record sounded, so

I was supposed to sign something that said I had produced it. He forced me to do it and he had a gun with him, I swear to it. I heard, too, that with some other band that he produced, he was shooting about with the gun. Anyway, he said: "You sign that now." Ralf was there, standing right next to me, so I just signed it. "Okay, so it was me that produced it, what the fuck. Who cares!"

WERNER LAMBERTZ_They just handed us the cheque, just before one o'clock and told us: "You can cash this in Hamburg-Eppendorf." So off I went to the bank, and the clerk just looked at the cheque and said: "Nope, sorry, but we don't have 10,000 Deutschmarks here, you'll have to go to the main branch." One minute before one, I get to the square where the main branch is, they're just about to close the door, I say: "Nope, no way, you can't do that, I've come from Düsseldorf, you just can't do that, I want this now, right away." Ten thousand marks was a lot of money and Die Krupps had been producing with me for months. With that money I bought me a nice Moog.

MEIKEL CLAUSS_Werner Lambertz was the best guy around. Werner was cool, a real pioneer; this guy was about as cool as you could get. But as it is with most stoners: in the long run you can't really get along with them. You arrange a time with them to meet at the studio but when you get there you find out they're still in bed.

Liaisons Dangereuses

BEATE BARTEL_After Chrislo left DAF and Minus Delta T and, following my stint with Mania D, we eventually came together to Düsseldorf. That was a nightmare. I'm definitely not a fan of the Rhineland joviality, and certainly not of carnival; that could make you feel really depressed.

JÄKI ELDORADO_Mania D was an all-girl Berlin underground band. Beate Bartel played bass, Gudrun Gut drums and Bettina Köster sang and played saxophone. These girls created a new image of women in Berlin: short-haired, confident, sexually ambivalent. At least that was the impression and it was modern.

BEATE BARTEL_ Our first release together was under the name of CHBB, our initials, Chrislo Haas and Beate Bartel. Altogether there were four cassette tapes that we sold to Klar! 80, the independent cassette tape label. That was all part of the rebellion, and all of a sudden new techniques were around: you could copy cassettes, there were photocopiers, Polaroids. These were quick methods and new media. And beside CHBB, Liaisons Dangereuses also quickly formed.

RALF DÖRPER_ These four cassette tapes that Beate and Chrislo had released with Rainer Rabowski's cassette label Klar! 80 were the Holy Grail of the German tape scene. They were four unspectacular audiotapes, each about 10 minutes long. Fifty copies were released and were named after the colour of the plain cover: black, red, blue and silver.

JÄKI ELDORADO_ With Mania D there was a mix of fashion, film, art and music all together; they rehearsed at their own hang out, the shop Eisengrau. Later, out of this shop, the band Malaria emerged, a follow-up to Mania D, as well as Einstürzende Neubauten. Beate was away anyway, she went to Düsseldorf with Chrislo.

MEIKEL CLAUSS_CH and BB: these initials stood for Chrislo and Beate. The two of them were together and that was a fatal relationship; correctly suggested by the name of their next project, Liaisons Dangereuses. On the one hand they were a couple, but quite often they beat each other up onstage. They were pretty explosive. On top of that, they had the loopy Krishna, more of a walking disaster than a singer.

BEATE BARTEL_ The more material we had together, the clearer it was that purely instrumental music was out of the question. So we thought about singers. Chrislo didn't want to sing and neither did I, at least not in the forefront. We did some auditioning in Düsseldorf but nothing came our way. By chance I met Krishna, who I knew from Spain. I asked him and he joined. In the end an easy decision.

PETER GLASER_ For a long time Liaisons Dangereuses were the unknown descendant of DAF, although everyone assumed that this sequencer sound originated from somewhere around Chrislo Haas.

I was close with them because he and his then-girlfriend Beate, together with the Korg MS-20 and other equipment, moved into our basement for a couple of months.

JÜRGEN ENGLER_Der Plan, Liaisons Dangereuses and DAF: I thought they were all great. To me they were all part of the same thing. And so too Die Krupps, we were also part of it. One after the other we all dug out our synths and started playing around with electro beats. We felt of the same breed. It was like in the punk times, when you saw somebody in leather jacket and skin-tight jeans, and you thought to yourself: "Hey, he's one of us. A kindred spirit."

WALDI JAEGER_DAF and Liaisons Dangereuses were incisive experiences, they were really something. The sequences were sensationally programmed and then together with that raw singing thrown in, that was something.

RALF DÖRPER_Chrislo was the electronic pioneer and together with Beate he gave the arty-conceptual-thinking dance floor group of the post-punk scene their first big club hit: 'Los Niños Del Parque'.

BEATE BARTEL_You don't have to explain and understand everything, and certainly not the analogue sequences that came about via our working techniques. If you ask me the secret behind the piece? It isn't in the sequence.

KURT DAHLKE_Chrislo was an absolute genius! He was a real superhuman. What he was able to get out of his MS-20; nobody else could ever top that. Bloody brilliant stuff.

BEATE BARTEL_Chrislo and I were always working together on the music; the girl's voice you can hear is me. It was only on the track 'Mystère Dans Le Brouillard' where you can also hear Krishna's sister Joana singing; all the other vocals are done by me.

MEIKEL CLAUSS_Chrislo was really the motor and the heart of the whole development. He was the guy who invented techno. He was a maniac who could twiddle around for hours, weeks or months on something. These sequences, the drifting rhythms, everything that was later used in techno: all of that came from Chrislo. From Chrislo alone. Everybody else just copied him.

JÜRGEN ENGLER_He was a weird kind of guy. And not at all the easy-going type. That was a kind of generation thing. He was a bit older and had already been in a band for a long time; in the beginning, as the long-haired saxophone player in jazz group You, well before DAF. Like most of them he had a former life with jazz or hippie music. Many had: Robert Görl and Wolfgang Spelmans too. In the end they were all just jazz-rockers from Wuppertal, before they cut their hair and became DAF. Most of them were ex-hippies who'd turned to punk, and now with the arrival of post-punk they became electronic.

MEIKEL CLAUSS_The way he was in Düsseldorf I couldn't really relate to. Chrislo was always checking everything out, completely hyperactive; he was on one hell of a weird mission. I can't really describe it exactly, but the guy was driven by something else. He was possessed by such a radical and progressive spirit that he couldn't be stopped.

PETER GLASER_Chrislo and Beate worked differently to the others. They always gave you this feeling that they had a set plan, like running a strict routine with different processes. Chrislo was unbelievably serious, always with a certain depth and darkness. You could tell that he didn't take any generic material from anywhere else but instead absorbed it from something inside. He tried to drag himself out of his sequencers. Beate was always very concentrated as well, and they both behaved very straight, which, at the beginning of the Eighties, wasn't particularly usual. The idea was to come across as truly effective.

FRANK FENSTERMACHER_Chrislo Haas was great. I can still picture him in his army pants and his Minus Delta T action outfit that he never took off, in the middle of two MS-20s, and speakers that were chugging and clanking away for all they were worth. He supposedly recorded everything onto cassette, things he'd conjured up and that couldn't be repeated. You've got your preferred settings but then the next day you unplug everything, then you've got to start all over again.

CHRISLO HAAS_We recorded the entire album in Karel Dudesek's flat. Up in the attic. There was a little chamber there. The album

BEATE BARTEL

was finished within a week. In some parts it was just done with a 4-track cassette recorder. Others were done with an 8-track Teac tape machine. That was only possible because the first portable things were becoming available. We could have never worked like that in a studio. I'm a night owl, I work nights. We just took the best stuff, but we didn't make any cuts. No overdubs. Nothing. This album owes its existence mainly to my dangerous liaison with Beate. Created in the strong force field of sex and machines.

PETER GLASER_I witnessed the creative process of the Liaisons Dangereuses tracks first hand; about as close as it gets. It was inevitable in a two bed apartment with no doors. In retrospect our coexistence actually went surprisingly free of conflict.

BEATE BARTEL_We did everything ourselves, but we didn't have it all; for example, we had to borrow the tape recorder. And for the mix we had to go to Conny's studio. I designed the cover for the album myself, all on my own. And Jürgen made the repros, as he was working as a lithographer. He made the film for it, that I remember.

CHRISLO HAAS_'Los Niños' was similar to 'Mussolini', we just used a different beat. Suddenly there I was minus a drummer and so I thought to myself: "What do I do now?" So our drum sounds now had to come out of the two sequencers. Basically just these two black boxes. I didn't have any real rhythm machines, because I didn't like them. They would have really pissed me off. Horrible, perverse machines.

MEIKEL CLAUSS_It took days, weeks, months on end of fiddling around on such a thing to somewhere find the right settings and then you didn't dare touch it. You could easily lose it; with the Korg MS-20 and all its little buttons, a tiny 10th of a millimetre in one direction or the other made a huge difference. Then it's all gone. I don't know how he did it. Such a set-up is never the same. It was impossible to replicate with such a set-up. You'll never find a sequence that is completely alike.

RALF DÖRPER_The Korg MS-20 and the MS-50 defined for several months the style in Düsseldorf. You could hear them with Der Plan and Chrislo also used them too. The little Korg wasn't too expensive and was absolutely post-punk: monophonic with lots of inputs, nasty filters and the like. The MS-50, its big brother, had no keys at all. And the undisputed magician of the Korg was Chrislo Haas, without a doubt.

WERNER LAMBERTZ_Chrislo Haas certainly had it. He was allowed to do productions at Conny's studio. Chrislo was the master of the loop. There was this one sequence that turned around after six-eighths; that was his speciality. And, on the machine that I'd built myself, he was able to create the greatest loops.

BEATE BARTEL_I'm a qualified sound engineer and the greatest thing was that when we were at Conny's we were free to do what we wanted. That meant that we were able to work at Conny's and we would do the mixing, he wouldn't do it for us. We did it all on our own. We mixed the album in two nights. When the studio closed for the day we were able to go in and spend the whole night there till eight the next morning. We did that for those two days. That was the deal.

RALF DÖRPER_You really have to say that depending on the approach, the same equipment could give you quite different results. The MS-20 signature sound of Chrislo Haas was quite unique to that of Der Plan, and in the same way they were quite different to DAF.

BEATE BARTEL_We only had the Korg MS-20 and our minimal touch was a raving result of the lack of sophisticated equipment. On the one hand, it was a real challenge, but, on the other, it was cool. Playing live was difficult enough, as the Korg didn't always do as it was told. So we solved that by playing back from tapes, 4-track cassette players; there was no other way around it.

RALF DÖRPER_Another thing was that it took time to find the right synth. It was that there were sometimes shortages and that your favourite synth, that you'd found down at Matten and Wiechers, was sold out and you had to be happy with something else instead. There were phases with certain machines, though, when some machines were very much in, and played a massive role.

BEATE BARTEL_It was all just for a very short period of time. We weren't really into gigs then either. Once we played at the canteen of the Düsseldorf University and then later on, on May 21, 1982, we played at the Munich Rocktage Festival at Alabamahalle together with Die Krupps and Peter Hein's Family Five. That festival went for three days. Besides that, we also played Manchester's Hacienda, run by the guys from Factory, on July 7, 1982.

TINA SCHNEKENBURGER_I had such stage fright every time we were about to go onstage. Even in those times when I was no longer drinking, I always had to knock something back. I can still remember, with Die Krupps in Munich, either the Schlachthof or Alabamahalle or wherever, I had to have a couple of beers before the show, before I dared to go onstage. Afterwards it was all like in a black tunnel.

BEATE BARTEL_So why we were so explicitly associated with Düsseldorf, that I'd like to know. Some in Berlin wrote that we were a Berlin band, but that's also not true. In actual fact we don't belong to anywhere, we were stateless. Chrislo came from Bavaria, Krishna is cosmopolitan, I'm from Berlin and our song 'Los Niños Del Parque' has a Spanish title. Over to you, Mr Esch. Your turn.

PETER GLASER_They just arrived from Berlin, and that at a time when no one would have ever dreamt of asking, 'How come? Why are you here, or why are you together now?'

BEATE BARTEL_Maybe it could have all happened somewhere else. But then again, maybe not. I was definitely homeless, that I'd emphasise. We found a kind of home in Conny's studio, and we even considered for a short while finding a place to stay around there. It got to the point where we even drove around the Bergisches Land, looked at houses we could share, but it never went further than that. I don't want to deny it, but to say 'We were a Düsseldorf band' would be a bit of an exaggeration; I wasn't even around that area for more than a year.

PETER GLASER_There was this tacit agreement that everyone was allowed to reinvent themselves at any time. It wasn't as though talking about the past was taboo, it just simply didn't happen, that's all. Instead you looked forward, onwards and upwards, always towards the future.

BEATE BARTEL_Actually, I even object to the term 'band'; we weren't really a band in the traditional sense. It was Chrislo and me doing it and we needed someone who sang; today you'd call it a project, but in those days everything was labelled 'band'. If more than two people got together you were a band, projects didn't exist yet. People had only heard of The Alan Parsons Project but nobody wanted anything to do with that at all.

MICHAEL KEMNER_Later on I'd often bump into Chrislo in Berlin, but by then he was in a bad, bad shape, as he really overdid it a little, drug-wise; I mean, I know he'd always been extreme.

BEATE BARTEL_When Chrislo was in Berlin we were often in contact. Yeah, we phoned each day, so his death came as quite a shock, as he was actually getting a little better and we were just about to start working together again.

MICHAEL KEMNER_Sometimes he really left me speechless. Once he showed up round lunchtime at the Café Madonna on Wiener Street, totally filthy as if he'd crawled out of the gutter, so totally greasy, with a dirty face and he stank so much that I had to sit elsewhere. Almost like a hobo, so desperate. The people were all staring but all he said was: "Yeah, I know I smell bad." Then he pulled out a bottle of mountain pine oil and, in the middle of the café, poured it over his head and rubbed it all over himself.

KURT DAHLKE_By the end he almost had no teeth left, and at some point Daniel Miller got a hold of him and told him: "You've got to go to the dentist, I'll pay for it," and treated him to some new teeth.

MICHAEL KEMNER_Daniel Miller really admired him a lot. He tried to finance tons of things for him, and kept telling him: "Come on, do it, go on and do it." I don't know why nothing ever came of that.

KURT DAHLKE_Walter Holzbauer, who published all of Chrislo's songs, said that he still had all the royalties. Chrislo never asked for them. And when he sent him a cheque, he simply tore it up.

MEIKEL CLAUSS_People bent over backwards to help him. Daniel Miller went there once a month and begged him to get out of bed, made him coffee and begged him to come to the studio. No chance.

BEATE BARTEL_Chrislo only ever lived through and with his machines.

Tech Stuff

RALF DÖRPER_ Same as with makes and models of cars, there were also a handful of manufacturers of electronic equipment, whose synthesisers were a class apart in sound, concept and price. And accordingly there were very different preferences.

JÜRGEN ENGLER_Later on Robert Görl bought a big Oberheim system from the money he got from Virgin. Every band, be that Der Plan, DAF or us, bought what they saw and what they could get their hands on or afford. Unlike today, you could only get what you found. If Kurt bought the MS-20 then I couldn't buy it any more, it had gone. So Robbi had to buy something else instead, and because he had more money he could.

RALF DÖRPER_At first electronic music seemed to be made only by millionaires or their sons, such as Jean Michel Jarre, Florian Schneider-Esleben or Florian Fricke of Popol Vuh. Eno also seems to have had the right kind of background – isn't his full name: Brian Peter George St John le Baptiste de la Salle Eno? Doesn't exactly sound working class, now does it?

RAINER ZICKE_Today it's easy to get your hands on production resources. In the past if you wanted to make a decent recording, there was always some wrangle to overcome. You had to get into some studio, then you needed the tools, but they weren't easily available. That meant that either you had money, which was rarely the case, or you tried through various contacts to borrow the necessary resources. Along the lines of: I'll help you with this or that, and then, when the studio is empty in the evenings, I'm allowed to practise my own stuff.

RALF DÖRPER_It wasn't until Korg and Roland were mass produced that there was equal opportunity in electronic music. Up until then there were real class differences. The equipment was terribly expensive and reserved exclusively for upper class households. And so it was that the musical renderings of a Bach fugue were more likely than the industrial noise concepts of Die Krupps. Jean Michel Jarre, son of the French soundtrack composer Maurice Jarre, had the necessary finances to experiment with electronic music in the Seventies. Bach's *Brandenburg Concertos* or *Oxygene* are certainly different concepts to, let's say, 'Los Niños Del Parque'. Walter Carlos is a different calibre to Chrislo Haas, on financial opportunities and musical education alone.

BEATE BARTEL_You could only just afford the Korg MS-20, but we always dreamt of much more, like the Oberheim system, which we did eventually buy. Just as Conny and Robert got themselves one. But I thought it sounded stupid, I just didn't like the sound. It was too clear for me and musically didn't really help us to move forward.

JÜRGEN ENGLER_Today you can have everything and you'll rarely hear a band with a clear sound of its own. Everybody can have everything, and that's the problem.

RALF DÖRPER_An Oberheim was as expensive as a used Mercedes. The Oberheim rhythm machine cost almost 6000 Deutschmarks. All together a rhythm machine, sequencer and OB-Xa would set you back almost 20,000 marks. Oberheim was always utilised by the big rock bands such as Emerson, Lake & Palmer. It also had something to do with the high dollar rate, but anyway, Oberheim was the most expensive system. When you saw that onstage you immediately knew: 'Whoops, rich kid.' All the Moog stuff, in fact everything from America was ridiculously expensive.

JÜRGEN ENGLER_At 2500 Deutschmarks the Minimoog was really expensive, so I wanted to go with the MS-20 instead. No luck though as Kurt had already bought one, so end of that then. All I could do was look for something in a different price range, and so I ended up buying an ARP Odyssey, which cost exactly 1500 and was also pretty cool.

RALF DÖRPER_I distinguished conceptually between a musician's machine and a music machine. With the musician's machine it was about the closest possible reproduction of sounds, like strings or wind. Oberheim or Yamaha, for example, are in this category. In contrast, the music machine had a life of its own, with strange and unheard sounds, with rigid rhythms and sequences, like with Korg and Roland.

KURT DAHLKE_I only had one thought in the beginning: "When can I buy my own synthesiser?" I was about 15 years old then. From my pocket money I had no chance. "How long would I have to save?" So I decided not to go on holiday with my parents in the summer and to instead stay in Düsseldorf and work the entire time. I spent the summer labelling at Woolworths and bought myself my first synth from my wages, a Davolisint. From then I knew: synthesiser is the instrument that I want to play. Even today I insist that I'm never credited as a keyboardist on the records. A keyboard player is some kind of all-round entertainer, sat at his keyboard using various pre-sets. I insist on synthesiser.

RALF DÖRPER_Once the cheap mass products started coming in from Japan, everybody was happy: the punks, other brilliant dilettantes and myself.

PAUL HUMPHREYS_In the beginning synthesisers were too exorbitant. I had studied electrical engineering and put together our first synths and rhythm machines out of separate parts. We couldn't afford anything. We were working class and had no money. Because of our bad record deal Andy was still living at his mother's and hung up the gold discs in her living room. We didn't make any real money to buy new equipment until *Dazzle Ships* came out, and to be honest I don't miss that old unreliable stuff. Every evening when we went onstage I was always hoping and praying that everything would just run smoothly.

RUSTY EGAN_I took care of the sequences on 'The Anvil', and it went like this: you take the TR-808 from Roland, that's got four, eight, 16, 32 knobs. You send a trigger to the Minimoog, so from the 808 to the Minimoog, then you only need to press one button and off you go. At first only garbled noises came out, but then when you switched off the random generator, chose a sound and made a loop, you had it.

PAUL HUMPHREYS_We used a lot of Roland instruments, as well as the Korg MS-20 and a Sequential Circuits Prophet 5. Mostly it all went through the Korg Micro-Preset that we used on the early albums; you can hear it on 'Enola Gay'. And of course Andy had his Fender Jazz Bass that he played the wrong way around, with the thin string at the top.

CHRIS CROSS_I had my Fender Fretless Precision Bass, as well as my Gibson EB-3, plus a couple of pedals for delay and phaser. Conny had an old Fender Bassman and a Fender Cabinet with two x 15 speakers; he absolutely loved that thing. Every time I turned up the volume to the max and made some terribly uncontrolled sound, Conny would jump up and scream: "Yeah, man… you got it. That is some real wild raw bass. That's beautiful."

PAUL HUMPHREYS_Most synths had very limited abilities. They only made certain sounds and so you really had to play around with them so as to sound different to others. I remember the Korg Micro-Preset very well because that was the first one we got, and we did two great albums with it. The good thing about it was that it couldn't do all that much, so the sound range was limited. For songwriting that can be a good thing, because with a synth there are billions of sounds available, you just have to sit the whole day searching for a better sound. Eventually you can lose sight of the basics. Those synths that offered limited possibilities were the best, because you only had to get a couple of sounds and then you could concentrate on the music rather than the sound. Nowadays, with the huge range of sounds available, I try to keep the palette of sounds that I use on a project as restricted as possible, otherwise you can spend weeks working through series after series of pre-sets. Most of them are boring anyway and you've heard them somewhere before on another album.

PETER GLASER_I was quickly surrounded by electronic equipment. All in all, I was happy as long as I was able to type error-free on my electronic Brother typewriter. I was always jealous of the musicians with their cool electronic equipment, which really looked impressive, no matter who was playing or what was coming out. The only thing was, though, that I realised you were at an advantage if you were able to make clear decisions. You find a note and think to yourself: "That's not bad." Then you'd turn the knob a bit more and think: "That's not bad either, maybe even a bit better!" And some time later you've got a three-day beard and you're still on the first note.

CHRIS CROSS_I played on an EMS VCS 3 Synthi AKS, to me that always sounded the best. Aside from that, for Ultravox we had a Roland CR-78, a Minimoog, an ARP Odyssey, an ELKA Rhapsody 610 and a Yamaha CS-20 and CS-40 for the string sounds. The sounds of the older machines are often glorified, sometimes rightly and sometimes wrongly. Discussions about instruments are usually boring and lead to a dead end, good or bad, modern or analogue. Basically it doesn't matter; what's actually more important is where the ideas come from, be it a pile of rustling leaves or the sound of a beehive, an ARP Odyssey Mk II or the sound of a Stradivarius. All sorts of things can be responsible for the magic.

MEIKEL CLAUSS

++ **JAN 83** Nena single '99 Red Balloons' released ++ **MAR 83** CDU/ CSU and FDP gain majority in general election, Helmut Kohl elected as Chancellor again ++ **APR 83** Belfegore release *A Dog Is Born* ++ **APR 83** Heaven 17 release *The Luxury Gap*, including their biggest hit, 'Temptation' ++ **JUN 83** Margaret Thatcher re-elected as Prime Minister ++ Kraftwerk release 'Tour De France' 12-inch ++ **JUL 83** Ralf Hütter is badly injured whilst cycling shortly after the release date ++ **OCT 83** Belfegore release 'Belfegore' 12-inch ++

Belfegore

MEIKEL CLAUSS_*A Dog Is Born* was released in April 83 on Carmen Knoebel's label Pure Freude; thus I had an album but no band to actually go with it. So I thought to myself: "Keep your eyes open for some suitable musicians." And it was then, when I went along to a Killing Joke gig, that I met Charly Terstappen. He quickly climbed aboard. Now the only thing missing was a bassist. I told Charly that I knew a guy who would fit and who seemed pretty cool. That's why I approached Waldi Jaeger, who I knew from Ratinger Hof. To be honest, Charly was never too thrilled with Waldi, but it did work quite well at first. Waldi had this formidable Memorymoog – perfect for electronic music – as well as his very cool, quasi self-made Alembic bass; very cool piece of equipment. Together with Waldi we only played three shows: at Okidoki, which Conny Plank came along to, at Ratinger Hof, and another one in Cologne. Prior to those we had recorded a maxi single with Waldi, which was produced by Jon Caffery. That is one cool record. 'Helllge Krlege'. 'Sacred war'.

WALDI JAEGER_At that time I was DJing at the Hof every weekend. At home I was tinkering with my instruments and my American cars. That was my world. Over the summer of 83 I was playing Captain Sensible's disco wonder hit 'Wot!' on heavy rotation. The Hof sound also included 'Wahre Arbeit', 'Los Niños Del Parque', 'Bela Lugosi Is Dead' by Bauhaus, 'A Forest' by The Cure. They were only maxi versions, released in 12-inch formats, as they had just started to become available. Naturally I also promoted our own stuff; firstly Belfegore and then later Die Krupps.

MEIKEL CLAUSS_The Belfegore maxi was extremely hot, as if it had been made for a horror movie. Conny saw Belfegore play live at the Oki Doki in Neuss; he came especially for us. That was one hell of a gig. Charly played like an animal and rocked pretty well together with Waldi on bass, who operated the Memorymoog during live sets as well. We had chosen menacing outfits for the show, complete with studs and leather wristbands, and all topped off with the bold mohawks Waldi and I were sporting. We blew the audience away. We produced a turbo sound with our giant stacks that were far too big for the place. It was the big bang. Conny agreed. He immediately fell in love with what Charly was doing, as he played like a berserker and is a real character.

WERNER LAMBERTZ_I recorded Meikel Clauss' and Belfegore's *Es Wird Die Nacht* at my place. That's the album with a blue cover showing a dead dog: *A Dog Is Born*. We produced it at my studio and René Tinner mixed it afterwards.

MEIKEL CLAUSS_The first Belfegore album was recorded in April 1983, and for that we needed plenty of sessions at Werner Lambertz's studio. Incidentally, he was another freak: speciality ultra-druggy, glam, electronic – an unbelievable guy. I'm unbelievably proud to say that I have experienced all these crazy people first-hand. And I include Werner Lambertz in that, Jesus!

WERNER LAMBERTZ_Meikel was still tied to CBS, who had an option on his next project. He was fed up with them though and came to me saying: "Listen, I need a really badly mixed tape, so bad CBS won't want to take it. Not in this lifetime." So I obliged and mixed some crap together for him. Then along came the A&R guy from the record company, he was a really big guy and was accompanied by some doe-eyed lapdog. Meikel wanted me to play the tape for them and I realised: "Oh My God. He really wants to go through with this! He can't seriously want to present this mix to them!" They listened to what we had to offer, looked at each other, then at Meikel and me and finally said that it wasn't a good fit with the current direction of CBS and for that they were sorry. Mission accomplished.

RALF DÖRPER_The song 'Radio' that Meikel wrote with his former band Nichts stood out because of its remarkable quality as an earworm. Although we never really trusted or liked anything seriously that emanated around Meikel. When Rolf Spinrads, director of *Bananas*, invited the band onto his TV show it became clear that the exploitation machinery had kicked in to gear. Therefore they moved from Düsseldorf-based independent label Schallmauer to major players CBS in Frankfurt at the right time. For many, though, seeing Nichts marketed by a big corporate was readily seen as an act of betrayal.

MEIKEL CLAUSS_Nah, this is how it actually happened: I was frustrated with Nichts; this German new wave thing was really starting to get on my nerves. Sure I had wanted to put out an easy trendy punk anthem; something funny, something fresh, but not this NDW, New German Wave, rubbish. The refrain "Dear God, all I wish for myself is to hear my voice on the radio" got immediate airplay and became a huge hit; therefore it quickly became indistinguishable from all the other NDW crap. Our status changed from independent artists to commercial exploiters and for that we were heavily criticised. Journos used that against us and accused us of betraying the scene.

WERNER LAMBERTZ_There may have been a few songs added by René Tinner; in any case, it was him who did the final mix. The credits on the album had some reference to my Digitalstudio Lambertz, but it was one of the last productions I did. Sometime later Micha Grund bought the studio and called it Grundfunk.

MEIKEL CLAUSS_Then I had to produce the record myself, so I went to see René Tinner. He'd worked as sound engineer for Conny Plank from time to time. A Swiss guy, bright as a spark. I said to him: "Listen, I have got some brilliantly chaotic recordings made by Werner Lambertz. He's got some mental issues at the moment but I want to release this album." I went to see him at the Inner Space Studio and was quickly convinced that he's the right man for the job. He was very good and an excellent guy. I think he really made something out of this album. If you compare it to the original tapes, it's hard to believe that it's all made from the same material.

JÜRGEN ENGLER_The crazy thing was: it was only later that I found out that Fricke had a sequencer capable of playing eight sequences simultaneously. It was a small grey box with a 64-step sequencer that allowed eight sequences to be created at the same time. All within this little box. 64 steps by eight different sequencer tracks, that was a real quantum leap. Werner had built this massive brontosaurus, but now we had this tiny thing with 100 times the power. That was sick. Such a small thing just beat him to the line. In the end, Andreas Dorau finally recorded something there, but over the course of time Michael Grund took over the studio and called it Grundfunk. Lambertz had bailed out. It wasn't happening for him any more.

MEIKEL CLAUSS_Waldi was a great musician. I really liked him, but he kept on getting sidetracked by all sorts of things. First he had to fiddle with his cars, then he had to go to the hardware store, before looking after all his many girlfriends. He is a great, great guy, but unfortunately we had to part ways because of this.

WALDI JAEGER_Meikel could be quite difficult from time to time. He was haunted by his very successful predecessor band Nichts. That got him overambitious and you couldn't argue about anything musical. I was simply trying to have a good time, a little fun, and, most of all, I just wanted to play. I wasn't too interested in his thoughts on styling, image and ideas.

CHARLY TERSTAPPEN_We quickly ended up in Conny's studio, where we were introduced to Raoul Walton, whose bass playing I preferred to that of Waldi's, most of all because he wasn't such a dizzy guy as Waldi.

BODO STAIGER_I met Raoul on his first day in Germany. He'd come straight from America to Conny's studio in Neunkirchen, with all his luggage and his bass guitar. Conny had invited Raoul over. I can't remember where he knew him from. He was still very young, in his early 20s. Previously he'd worked as a session musician in New York and had come here purely because of Gabi Delgado's solo album *Mistress*. That's how he got to know Belfegore and then later Marius Müller-Westernhagen.

WALDI JAEGER_I played my last show in August 83, during some sort of festival in an art gallery in Cologne. Finally the record, this 12-inch featuring 'Heilige Kriege' and 'Nacht In Sodom', got released after my departure. Between you and me: I preferred the Jon Caffery production of our maxi as it had much more punch to it, than the album version delivered by Conny Plank.

CHARLY TERSTAPPEN_We always divided everything five ways: Carmen Knoebel, Conny Plank, Meikel, Raoul and myself. Carmen was our manager, Conny was in charge of production, everything was equally split.

WALDI JAEGER_I met Die Krupps at Spiecker and Pulch. That was the big music shop where I worked in the guitar workshop. DAF were also customers in the shop, but I didn't know them personally. One of them seemed particularly shy, whilst the other always seemed to have a problem with his eyesight. One day Jürgen Engler came by to the shop and started talking to me. I showed him how to play slap bass. That was pretty new and modern and seemed to impress him a little. Shortly afterwards he called me and told me they needed a drummer, and that's how I ended up playing drums with them. What the hell. Pretty soon after we were playing our first gig on a ship – for a big party organised by *Überblick*, the city magazine. The *Überblick* parties were legendary. Later on we played on the *Dr Mambo Show*, a TV show from Berlin.

CHARLY TERSTAPPEN_We settled in well at Conny's place. We had met earlier when I had my rock band Wallenstein, and he enjoyed telling stories about all the other bands. When Ultravox first came to him to record the album, he wasn't too keen on their material at first and told them: "There's a nice lido close by, why not go there and have a nice time. In fact go to the pool tomorrow, and when you have a good idea, why not come back then."

JOCHEN RAUSCH_I got to know Conny as someone who didn't like compromises. When you were in his studio then you had the feeling that you were in the right place; you were standing on the right side of things. As soon as we sat in the car to leave his property again, I said to my fellow musicians: "So, now back to normal. Back to being idiots." It was like joining a sect. Not in an ideological or religious sense, but Conny gave everyone a feeling that they were creating something special; not just some cynical music but something that was self-sufficient and where commercial aspects were secondary.

CHARLY TERSTAPPEN_So Ultravox went swimming for five weeks. Eventually Midge Ure came back with the idea for 'Vienna'. That Conny liked, and immediately created the bass drum intro that everybody knows today and became kinda eternal. That was him.

WALDI JAEGER_On that day, when Jürgen told me I could join them as their drummer, I immediately ordered myself a Simmons electronic drum kit; back then nothing happened without those ultra hip then stupid Simmons sounds. It was featured on every production, and people thought that real drums were going out of fashion. No more lugging it around, setting up the kit or any microphones. It looked to be the ideal solution for everything, though unfortunately the sounds lost their appeal relatively quickly as bands like Duran Duran appeared, who'd beaten the living daylights out of the Simmons with their 'Wild Boys'. So much so that you didn't want to listen to it any more. That was at the time after our WEA album, when Bernward was no longer part of it. Tina played on my self-made Alembic bass and I played drums.

BERNWARD MALAKA_Jürgen imagined something along the lines of Human League, Heaven 17, ABC, Soft Cell and stuff like that. Something quite clearly in the direction of pop music. Later on, though, Jürgen changed direction again, but back then that was the way he was heading. It was at that time that I started to take an interest in other things. First and foremost, I am not a nostalgic person, and even with music I was always more interested in discovering new things.

WALDI JAEGER_I was surprised that it was possible to write music that way. Jürgen played the keyboard using both of his thumbs, and he only ever used the black keys. I called it 'do the flip book'. At that time his role models included ABC, Depeche Mode and even Paul Young. We were supposed to produce something poppy. Our industrial period was behind us. Jürgen was also influenced by Duran Duran for a while. I preferred listening to Seventies funk. It's for that reason that our next album, *Entering The Arena*, turned out so undecided; it sounded like a poor man's version of Duran Duran. In addition, Jürgen insisted that we change our name to 'The Krupps' in order to have a greater international focus.

BERNWARD MALAKA_Jürgen and I started to have different opinions about how the whole thing was going to continue. I was interested in the experimental approach, because it gave us lots of free room for development. Jürgen, on the other hand, was more interested in pulling the whole thing back to songs with structure. Then he started to write musically complicated songs that no one really understood. That was around 1983. The recent album that we did for WEA was not fully satisfying for me; but now we were really heading in the wrong direction. Suddenly there was a session bass player with us. I came into the studio and asked: "Who is that?" "That's Waldi, he plays the bass." "What, he plays bass?" Nice. That wasn't a proper thing to do.

CHARLY TERSTAPPEN_With Belfegore we didn't know that we were good at the time. You only appreciate that with some distance after all this time. At that time goth rock was the new trend, but slowly arguments started within our band; Raoul and I were working together whilst Meikel was doing his own thing. The Americans, who we sent our demo tapes, thought we were just crazy Germans. Only one firm showed any interest in us: Elektra. The son of the managing director saw us in London and was totally impressed. He was 22, gay and totally in awe of us. We were the biggest mistake of his life, because he thought that money was no object. So we cleaned him out and were paid a massive advance; I managed to waste my share within three months. For example, I went to Spiecker and Pulch in Ratingen to buy a mixing desk; simply asked the price: "What's it cost? Fifty grand? Okay. I'll have it then." I went home and set it up. And it's been standing there ever since. Daft.

WALDI JAEGER_Meikel was always the Godfather of Doom. Belfegore was supposed to be dark wave and industrial-like; similar to Killing Joke or the other stuff he liked. With Jürgen it was different, he was also concentrating on the fun side of things. I liked that better. What I didn't like: that we never played live. On TV it was only playback, totally fake and boring.

BERNWARD MALAKA_I haven't actually made music since 1983. At some point Jürgen and I had a pretty frank and open discussion at the Sudgrill, a local chippy, where we came to the outcome that we both felt it was best to go our separate ways. Sorry, pal.

Tour De France

WALDI JAEGER_Yeah, I span the 'Tour De France' 12-inch, but it was noticeable by then that they had reached a plateau. I never really played that much Kraftwerk anyway, but after that it was over. 'Marcia Baila' by Les Rita Mitsouko excited me. That was cool. We liked that one. Conny Plank produced it too. For me, the icing on the cake was 'Slave To The Rhythm'. That was a little later but this was the best piece, the best maxi single ever; produced by Trevor Horn. Even today I think it's sensational.

PETER GLASER_The whole concept wasn't working any more. 'Tour De Fance' was the beginning of the end. Kraftwerk's final sprint.

WOLFGANG FLÜR_We had released the 'Tour De Fance' maxi and now sat in the studio twiddling our thumbs; at least Karl and I were. In the meantime the Kling Klang Studio had become a store room for tyre tubes, spare parts for racing bikes. Nothing mattered any

WALDI JAEGER

more, apart from cycling. It was terrible. Then Ralf was knocked off his bike and we were seriously worried about his health.

RAINER ZICKE_Ralf didn't even spend a week in hospital; despite a light concussion, it was nothing serious. But in the aftermath, his condition worsened each time the story was told: first he spent a month in hospital, then a year; and in the end they had to transplant a new brain.

WOLFGANG FLÜR_Ironically, he suffered a bad cycling accident on the Rheindamm. Right in the middle of his rrrrrrrrrrracing troupe his bike collided with that of one of his sports companions and his head hit the asphalt hard. He suffered bad injuries, because foolishly he hadn't been wearing a helmet. They took him straight to hospital, where he remained unconscious for a long time. We went crazy with worry, and his recovery took weeks and weeks. Nothing was ever the same again.

Dazzledorf

RALF ZEIGERMANN_I can still remember my first day at the GGK Dazzledorf branch. Heaven 17 and Joy Division were playing blaringly loud there. I had just finished university and wasn't expecting anything like this from an advertising agency. I thought, "Hey, these people are just like me." In the evenings we went to the Ratinger Hof, the artists, the musicians, they were all one crowd. The agency was located on Immermannstraße, and after work we all went straight to the Hof.

JÜRGEN FRITSCHE_Gredinger had opened an office with the former student of literature Markus Kutter and the painter Karl Gerstner in Basel at the end of the Fifties. He wanted to assist clients with their communication. They used the initials of their surnames to form the company name: GGK. This trio quickly acquired such prestigious clients as Swissair, Volkswagen and the Oetker Group. At the end of the Sixties they opened a branch in Düsseldorf in order to be able to better serve their international clients, like office supplies manufacturer IMB or VW.

RALF ZEIGERMANN_GGK had offices in Düsseldorf, Stuttgart, Hamburg and Munich. Outside of Germany, they had offices in New York, London and who the hell knows where else. That was one of the first big agency networks. At the start of the Nineties it all came crashing down like a house of cards.

JÜRGEN FRITSCHE_ Paul Gredinger headed up the company on his own at some point, because he had paid off his former partners to become sole owner of an agency with a volume of orders of 300 million Deutschmarks. As a qualified architect Gredinger had no idea about advertising and instead hired the most creative heads by making them offers they couldn't refuse.

RALF ZEIGERMANN_GGK's bold reputation resulted mainly from Schirner's PR work. He famously discussed with Beuys about what exactly was art in relation to advertising. Beuys argued that standing in front of the Persil washing powder box could already be deemed art. Schirner argued against him. Advertising couldn't be art without intelligent adverts. It must have been an odd and embarrassing event. Embarrassing for Schirner, as well as for Beuys. Who cares, there is no such thing as bad PR.

JÜRGEN FRITSCHE_ In the summer of 83 I had already completed my first year as a graphic artist at GGK, although even before that I had freelanced for this Düsseldorf agency during my student time. At that time they were the bee's knees, although looking back on it now, it seems as if their best days were already behind them. We were listening to Heaven 17, The Cure and Cocteau Twins. The studio was on the fifth floor and there were lots of big tables where you could spread out your A2 sheets of paper. Within the studio there stood this SK4 'Schneewittchensarg', a Braun 'Snow-white coffin', a massive music trunk, which played The Velvet Underground most of the time. My colleague Dieter was renowned for reaching for the bottle at the end of a long overtime session. He also had a bottle of kerosene in his desk and he liked to rub it onto the long metal rulers we used like architects on the drawing board and then set them alight and give a Jimi Hendrix Monterey performance.

RALF ZEIGERMANN_Scholz & Friends made me an offer in Hamburg in 85, and so I moved there. They were also good, but completely different to GGK. GGK was more like art. Paul Gredinger was known for hiring Swiss artists as his art directors. Harry Rowohlt wrote copy for GGK, same as Hans Wollschläger, who previously had translated James Joyce's *Ulysses* into German.

JÜRGEN FRITSCHE_The perfect peak for GGK came in the second half of the Seventies, with clients like IBM, Pfanni and Jägermeister. In 1974 the head of the agency in Düsseldorf, Wolf Rogosky, designed the Jägermeister campaign for Günter Mast's distillery in Wolfenbüuttel. We had these unique ads in which everyday people were fooling around with Jägermeister: "I drink Jägermeister, because..." The Jägermeister campaign turned out to be one of the most successful and long-lived in the German advertising industry. The first of these colour ads, which were placed in magazines with high circulation, showed a jolly man drinking the stuff "because I prefer to look for joy in the woods or on the heath". Paul Gredinger himself posed as model. There was also an ad with Ralf Zeigermann.

RALF ZEIGERMANN_That's true, there is a motif where I'm seen with a bottle of Jägermeister in my hand. My slogan was: "I drink Jägermeister, because my computer is waiting for inspiration."

JÜRGEN FRITSCHE_Gredinger then got 33-year-old Michael Schirner to move from Hamburg to Düsseldorf, where he started out as a copywriter and then later took over as managing director of the Düsseldorf Head Office. Schirner brought new ideas with him; he rediscovered large billboards; he covered whole advertising pillars with one poster for Continental tyres. Even if it sounds obvious today to turn an advertising pillar into a stack of tyres, back then it was new and innovative. He designed a huge poster for German food manufacturer Pfanni, depicting a single potato fritter with the caption, 'The Last Supper'.

RALF ZEIGERMANN_It was Schirner who started the 'Advertising is art' line. Complete bollocks. Advertising isn't art. Especially today it isn't.

JÜRGEN FRITSCHE_Unfortunately the Jägermeister campaign was also responsible for losing us a big advertising client: the German Postal Service stopped working with GGK because of a single Jägermeister ad. The text read: "I drink Jägermeister, because the parcel I sent by post has been lost by the post." The managers at the post office didn't quite see the funny side and decided to drop GGK.

RALF ZEIGERMANN_Paul Gredinger – he was the second G in GGK – made electronic music in the Sixties. There is even a record. He was one of the first to ever make electronic music. Gredinger lived directly above the agency, quite conveniently on the third floor. He had furnished a massive office with old brown leather furniture, an antique brown writing desk and white wall units filled with secondary literature about Arno Schmidt.

JÜRGEN FRITSCHE_Prior to Schirner it was Charles Wilp who was responsible for Düsseldorf's excellent reputation within the advertising industry. Wilp always referred to it as Dazzledorf and, during the Sixties, took care of significant clients such as Stiebel Eltron, Pirelli and Volkswagen. For the VW Beetle he wrote the slogan: 'He runs… and runs… and runs'. For Wilp, advertising was part of the product, in the same way that electricity is part of a light bulb. He also advised Willy Brandt on his public image.

RALF ZEIGERMANN_Wilp already caused a stir with his most famous campaign in 68 for the soft drink Afri-Cola. He came up with the ingenious slogan 'Sexy-mini-super-flowerpop-op-cola – all that you find in Afri-Cola'. The ads depicted famous Sixties models like Marianne Faithful, Amanda Lear, Donna Summer and Marsha Hunt behind glass screens decorated with ice crystals.

JÄKI ELDORADO_Charles Wilp and advertising – this was evident very early on. What you didn't understand, though, was why all of a sudden advertising was supposed to be art. This kind of thing didn't matter in Berlin. Schirner proclaimed 'Advertising is art'. Beuys thought every person was an artist. This blend of culture and commerce was so typical for Düsseldorf. All we understood was: "Okay, Afri-Cola, that's a strange spot. I'm not sure about the advertisement, but I for sure like the models." The whole nonchalant attitude was something new and thus created a stir.

RALF ZEIGERMANN_ Then there was this connection with Milan Kunc. He was a painter from Prague who lived in Düsseldorf. He created a motif for Hertie when Schirner ran his own agency; funnily enough it was called KKG. He commissioned Milan Kunc to paint a pear. This pear was printed on Hertie plastic carrier bags.

PETER GLASER_I once wrote a story for the cinema section of *Überblick* about the 'Behaviour of Gummy Bears in Extreme Situations' and for that I got paid a fee of about 28 Deutschmarks, 31 pfennigs. A week later someone phoned and asked if he could reprint the gummy bear story. He offered me the princely sum of 200 marks for it. He said, "Well, the copywriters here have run out of copy and you write about gummy bears." To cut a long story short: he invited me to his place in Oberkassel where I first came across these people, typical Eighties ad men who were wanting to be Zen Buddhists at the same time. Men in black bathrobes who spent their evenings practising Japanese archery. That was in pre-sushi times, when they polished thin air with 100 mark notes.

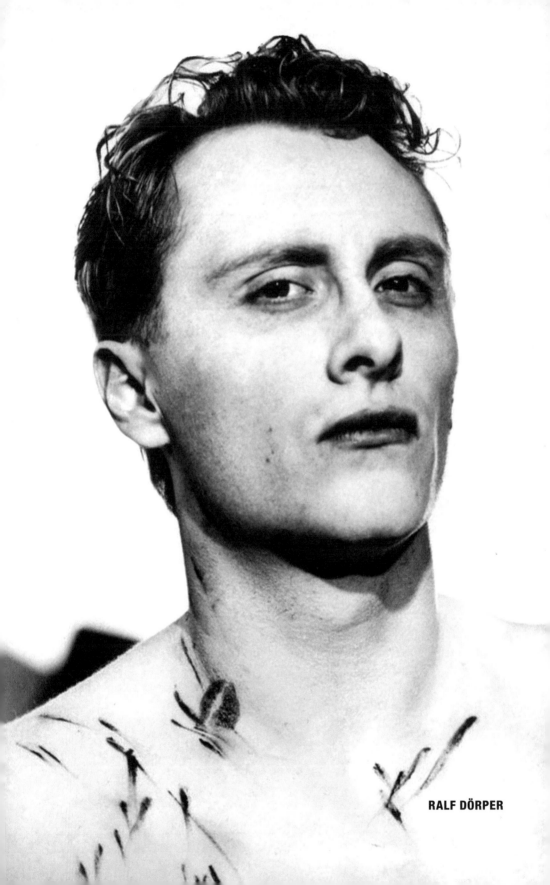

RALF DÖRPER

84

++ **JAN 84** Apple develops the Macintosh computer ++ **MAR 84** Propaganda release 'Dr Mabuse' ++ Rheingold release the album *Distanz* ++ **JUL 84** Kraftwerk postpone the *Techno Pop* album ++ **SEP 84** Belfegore release their eponymous second album, produced by Konrad Plank ++ **DEC 84** Band Aid single 'Do They Know It's Christmas?' is released, destined to become one of the most successful British singles of all time ++

Propaganda

MICHAEL MERTENS_"Open sesame!" was quite obviously demanded by Ralf Dörper and no one else. Full stop. Someone has to say it. He simply saw things that others couldn't foresee. Of course, luck played a role. The whole thing wouldn't have taken that direction without luck. But significantly Ralf saw things and implemented them accordingly.

SUSANNE FREYTAG_Yes, absolutely, the name had already been decided: Propaganda. The name was really cool. Ralf and Andreas had devised the whole concept. Both of them were very good and complemented each other well.

ANDREAS THEIN_I met Ralf at a gig at the Stadthalle in Cologne-Mülheim – Kid Creole And The Coconuts were on the bill and so was Alan Vega. We hit it off straight away. That was back in June 82, I think. We met again soon after and founded Propaganda. Naturally we had to experiment in the beginning, before we found the right direction, but we were quickly satisfied with the outcome. Our songs included 'Disziplin' and 'Sünde' and 'Doppelgänger', one of which was later released by ZTT.

RALF DÖRPER_Propaganda's music was at first inspired by the British industrial scene, Cabaret Voltaire, Throbbing Gristle and John Carpenter. And I liked Kraftwerk's work ethic and clothing style. In regard to the lyrics, especially 'Mabuse' but also 'p:Machinery', we quite clearly referenced Fritz Lang with that. I even orientated myself towards the *Man-Machine* theme of 'Metropolis', which was quite obvious.

SUSANNE FREYTAG_Andreas and Ralf were a strange duo, but their music was very interesting. That was why I agreed to sing in their new band when they asked me. Ralf had his synthesiser, and he and Andreas fiddled around with the various rudimentary basslines. That was good. It was a sound I hadn't heard before anywhere else.

RALF DÖRPER_Initially Andreas and I were able to work in Walter Dahn's studio. There, the only things available to us were a sequencer and a Roland 808. We had the idea to release something under the name Propaganda with him at some point. A name with the same meaning in all languages and internationally marketable. The idea was to strongly identify the product as German. We were working towards the first pieces: 'Disziplin', 'Sünde' and 'Mabuse'.

WERNER LAMBERTZ_When I think back to the recordings of *Volle Kraft Voraus!*, where Dörper kept on constantly missing the beat on his syncussion thingy. Then Engler interrupted and said: "You have to beat it like this. Here is the beat," but Dörper was still slightly off. When he appeared for the first time with Propaganda I thought to myself: "That can't be true, how did he manage to get there?" He just stood there. The shy guy.

RALF DÖRPER_There was one thing that Kraftwerk, Propaganda and technically also DAF had in common: all three outfits had a classically trained drummer. Michael Mertens trained together with Karl Bartos at the same conservatorium. Classical percussion includes not only timpani and triangle but also vibraphone and marimba, and those are used like sequencers. All of these classical-trained drummers appeared to have an affinity for melodic sequences.

MICHAEL MERTENS_When I was young I played accordion, and I wanted to become a jazz musician. My role models were Milt Jackson, Gary Burton and Chick Corea. Gary Burton developed the four-stick technique on the vibraphone, and he was quite the virtuoso. I wanted to go in the same direction. My first teacher in Berlin played the jazz vibraphone. I learned improvisation and harmony there, not classical, but jazz style. Popular music, but not ternary, without using triplets, and played straight, no swing music. Rhythm is the defining element of pop music. It defines the style you want to achieve.

ANDREAS THEIN_Prior to Propaganda I had released the single '1000 Gelbe Tennisbälle' with Kurt Dahlke. We pressed 1000 copies and had a few gigs and performances under our belt. I had started to fiddle with abstruse sounds on my Korg MS-20 to accompany texts by Kurt Schwitters or taken from Mickey Mouse cartoons that I read aloud. The whole thing sounded quite weird. It was through my one off performance of *Industriemusik Für Das Tote Huhn* ['Industrial Music For The Dead Chicken'] with the New York singer Julie Ashcroft that I got my nickname: 'Das Huhn', meaning 'The Chicken'.

MICHAEL MERTENS_It was because of psychedelia that I first started making music. Jimi Hendrix used a vibraphone as well, so too Pink Floyd; not a lot of people know that. Their records feature a vibraphone. I liked King Crimson, but I loved Hendrix.

SUSANNE FREYTAG_We are, in every sense, a Düsseldorf band. At that time we all lived in Düsseldorf. I knew Claudia through some mutual friends. We were both in an all-girl band called Die Topolinos. At first we had only very simple melodies on the synthesiser and played only micro gigs, such as that at Din-A-Null. I think Ralf came to spy on us there and finally said, "Okay then, maybe we can do something together."

MICHAEL MERTENS_I went to Berlin at the beginning of the Seventies. I left home at 18; I just wanted to play the vibraphone, which was totally my thing. And I thought to myself that that would be a super addition to Tangerine Dream. So I went into a

SUSANNE FREYTAG

telephone box, opened the phone book, started to look for Edgar Fröse and called him straight away, "Hello, I am Michael Mertens from Bielefeld. I would like to come over. Can we play a session together?" I asked him this with my late-pubescent naivety. But Edgar Fröse talked to me for at least five minutes. "Well, you know, it's not always that easy, Michael. We sometimes meet up to record things, but..." He didn't just hang up, he really talked to me. He noticed that here was a young musician with a dream, and he took the time to let me down very gently.

SUSANNE FREYTAG_Together we were four girls in short skirts made out of aluminium foil. Claudia was part of it by then. Ralf and Andreas Thein then asked me if I wanted to come to the studio to record a narration or to sing something. I can't really sing, but I can talk, and I was happy to give that a go. So that's what we did. Ralf then sent the recordings to Chris Bohn. He in turn gave them to Paul Morley, who worked with Trevor Horn at the time; and that's how it progressed further and further.

RALF DÖRPER_In the very early phase we were influenced by Kraftwerk's minimalism, but Trevor Horn brought the bombastic element into play. We quickly rejected the initial purism to just use electronic sound production. A real flugelhorn does sound better than any sample.

SUSANNE FREYTAG_Then Paul Morley came to Düsseldorf, and I was scared shitless. I thought, "Shit, I can't sing, I'm not a singer." I needed some support and I suggested adding a second singer: Claudia. To start with, we produced 'Doppelgänger'. It was a quite good track, but it was never released. Later on Die Krupps released a song with the same name. Ralf always seemed to be able to use his ideas over again.

MICHAEL MERTENS_I first met Ralf when I put a small ad in *Überblick* selling a drum box. Eventually the phone rang and there was Ralf at the other end of the line asking if it was still available. Thereupon I said: "Sure it's available. But tell me, how did you know it is for sale in the first place? The ad hasn't been published yet." His reply was, "Well, I work here and saw it when I was looking through the next issue." The next day he came by with 50 Deutschmarks in his hand; and whilst in my flat he noticed my Oberheim synthesiser and asked in amazement if I came from Düsseldorf. I told him that I was a member of the symphony orchestra. The fact that I owned an Oberheim simply fascinated him. He also knew where Ralf and Florian had found Karl, namely the Düsseldorf Symphony Orchestra as well. We had a long chat. He told me about his project, but he had no idea which direction to go. He also told me about his contacts in England. I didn't really have much to do with pop music then; I played classical and jazz and had no real idea who Trevor Horn was. Eventually he said that they had a problem concerning the band: they had two girls who took care of the singing, he wrote the lyrics and was working on the concept of the whole thing, another guy was responsible for the rhythm, but they were lacking a genuine musician in the group. It was his way of asking if I was interested in writing arrangements for them. It sounded very interesting. That's how I joined Propaganda.

SUSANNE FREYTAG_Tevor Horn had heard 'Disziplin', 'Radetzkymarsch' and a third piece as well. All true German stuff though, but he liked the concept. Two boys, two girls, it was somehow handy. At that point Michael hadn't joined the band yet. The song 'Disziplin' was so out there. I hadn't really noticed how controversial it must have come across. It could have been seen as far right wing, but we thought: "Nah, that's what we are going to do"; that said we never wanted to be pigeonholed in any way, we just wanted to play with the image.

MICHAEL MERTENS_Ralf Dörper wrote the lyrics for Propaganda, and was in charge of the content. We produced the songs in my living room and in the little demo recording studio I had in Düsseldorf-Derendorf.

SUSANNE FREYTAG_We underestimated just how provocative the name Propaganda was at that time.

ANDREAS THEIN_In an interview with *Formel 1* in 1983 we were compared to the Hitler Youth. Peter Illmann said, "When I look at you I see some sort of hybrid between the Hitler Youth and

MICHAEL MERTENS

the 'Good Shot' Schutzen Team." We had just delivered a furious stage performance in front of a backdrop we'd designed ourselves. The whole thing came across as quite fascist, because Susanne and Claudia were singing behind lecterns with a number of microphones mounted on them and adorned with our 'P' logo. It was supposed to conjure up the flair of old Fritz Lang movies; but it was completely misunderstood, because we also used the fanfare of the *Tönende Wochenschau*, the Nazi propaganda 'weekly news show'. The whole thing with lecterns and everyone dressed in black was altogether perhaps a bit too much. Well, sorry for that. If you try to be controversial, you get controversial responses.

SUSANNE FREYTAG_The name served its purpose: it polarised; but the English were looking for a German band that also looked as if they came from Germany without being afraid to use such a name.

ANDREAS THEIN_On English TV Propaganda was labeled as 'ABBA on acid'. It sounded very good, but didn't have anything to do with our original ideas. The English love such catchphrases, though, and they open up completely new points of view.

SUSANNE FREYTAG_When it kicked off in London, we often had to commute over, and I even lived there for a year. Back then Claudia was in a relationship with Paul Morley, who was working for the ZTT record label and was also living in London. At first there were five of us there. Andreas was an unbelievably important element of the band, as he took care of all the PR work, it wasn't just Ralf. Andreas kept pushing things forward. He was good at it, but it was also difficult to work with him in a team.

MICHAEL MERTENS_As a band Propaganda enjoyed an unbelievable luxury. We couldn't do anything wrong. They implemented even the smallest idea and served it to us on a silver tray with the question: 'Do you like it like that? Anything else?' Trevor Horn took care of that. Twenty to 25 people were involved with each recording. The arranger was incredible, the guest musicians outstanding, and the session players amazing. Trevor Horn's main characteristic is, of course, overproducing. It's okay to call Propaganda overproduced. Exactly that is a tradition with Trevor Horn, and it fitted

Propaganda. The orchestral, big, German, Fritz Lang-like – all of this fitted the bill.

SUSANNE FREYTAG_At some point Derek Forbes played bass and Brian McGee, both Simple Minds, played drums in the band, and there were Michael, Claudia and I, as well as a guitar player, Kevin Armstrong. We didn't play in Germany that much, only in Hamburg, Frankfurt and at the Alter Wartesaal in Cologne. That was pretty much it. We did have a small European tour, plus we went to New York, Boston, Chicago as well as to the East Coast. Ralf didn't join us then; he stayed at home and went to work as a clerk.

MICHAEL MERTENS_At the airport Claudia confessed that she wanted out of the band. That was the downfall, and for the management one thing was clear: Claudia was the star. Paul Morley was a genius at creating a persona, and Trevor Horn was a great producer. They didn't know failure. I thought to myself, "Shame, it was a very good time, I would have liked to have continued." There was a lot of trouble behind the scenes with Morley, Trevor and his wife Jill Sinclair. In addition, we had separate management in England, the same ones used by PiL and Heaven 17. It all got complicated and by the end we'd paralysed ourselves with the whole business.

SUSANNE FREYTAG_There was often friction within the group. Boys versus girls, I would call it. Ralf and Michael were one faction, especially when it came to money. There was also conflict between the girls, partly because one of them had a very close relationship with the record label. Add to that some petty jealousy and you can easily lose control of the whole thing pretty quickly. Today I can see that, but sadly not back then.

RALF DÖRPER_We obviously had signed one hell of a bad contract. Frankie Goes To Hollywood had the same issue. They therefore wanted to sue the record company. Our only problem was that we had a singer, Claudia, who wasn't too keen on suing her husband and was probably promised a solo career in return.

ANDREAS THEIN_In November 84 I was fed up. I left the band because I couldn't cope with the permanent arguments with Trevor any more. I didn't want to be bossed around by him like this: "Fucking artist, leave the studio!" I know that he continued to produce quite a few terrific hits, but I was sick and tired with the pompous turd.

Techno Pop

WOLFGANG FLÜR_1985 was coming fast, and we recorded a few more songs for a new album that was supposed to be called *Technicolor*. Fearing we would get into trouble with the copyright holders of the term 'Technicolor' we were constantly looking for a different name instead. We searched high and low. Then we decided on *Techno Pop*, but when we finally realised the album it was under the name *Electric Café*. In my opinion *Techno Pop* would have been the better choice.

JÜRGEN ENGLER_There is another excellent story concerning the lithography agency I worked for: Ralf Hütter arrived with a design similar to the one used on 'Tour De France', four cyclists cycling in a line, one after another. The album following *Computer World* was supposed to be called *Techno Pop*, and we were supposed to do the lithography. During the production process we were fooling around with the material and gave the cyclists massive arses. We changed the name of the album from *Techno Pop* to *Techno Popo*, meaning 'botty', and made our own lithographic films for home use. I had a massive poster myself above my work space for a long time. It looked great.

RUSTY EGAN_I wasn't crazy about the cycling shit and the whole 'Tour De France' thing, but everybody is allowed to have one failure. For me Kraftwerk were finished. There and then.

JÜRGEN ENGLER_Eventually Hütter came back and said they had changed their minds. The album was no longer called *Techno Pop* but rather *Electric Café*. How can you call an album *Electric Café*? *Techno Pop* was perfect. Especially considering techno wasn't even invented then. That would have been the perfect name. I didn't get that at all. Anyway, now the album has been rereleased under its original name.

WOLFGANG FLÜR_Ralf always found it difficult to let go of his work, and so it was that we were confronted with this stalemate. The release had already been agreed and catalogued with EMI. An official order number had been issued to the dealers, and we even had a suitable cover – and then Ralf started a complete overhaul, and the album had to be withdrawn.

ANDY McCLUSKEY_You could sense the handmade quality of Kraftwerk's music in the past, which gave it charm and humanity. With this album, though, it was gone. The more Ralf Hütter has refined his art, the less interesting it has become. No longer did he sing; the voices came only from the vocoder or he uses robot voices instead. The human element was completely lost, and for me it's not nearly as enticing and captivating as what came before. But, I know where he's at. I understand what he is doing and I can see where he is going.

JaPlan

FRANK FENSTERMACHER_On one occasion Der Plan toured Japan with a show called Evolution Striptease. It was accompanied by a record: *JaPlan*, which was released exclusively in Japan. The Japanese liked the childlike melodies of Der Plan; fundamentally they liked the electronic elements. We performed this show eight or nine times, that was well paid. We used playback and visualised the music as a stage show – Moritz was very much responsible for that. Evolution Striptease started with giant papier mâché stones that moved millimetre by millimetre across the stage. We stood behind the stones wearing masks, one above the other.

KURT DAHLKE_The idea was to depict evolution with the aid of costumes worn in layers. It started with massive papier mâché stones on the stage that were then moved aside. We were behind those, dressed up as cactuses. After a short time we then took them off to reveal a rubber foam worm costume. Underneath the worms were mutant costumes that morphed into robots and finally humans. Evolution.

FRANK FENSTERMACHER_We appeared in black suits and white shirts. And then underneath we had a skin-tight body suit sprayed to look like a skeleton. Underneath that we were naked. That was the final step.

KURT DAHLKE_That was the idea. Actually it was very exhausting, because of the layers of costumes. You had difficulty breathing and you couldn't see a thing. Onstage it wasn't possible to just adjust something that had slipped out of place. You had to fly blind for the rest of the show.

85

++ **JAN 85** Ronald Reagan is re-elected as President ++ **MAR 85** Mikhail Gorbachev becomes General Secretary of the CPSU ++ **APR 85** Propaganda release their single 'Duel' ++ **SUMMER 85** Die Krupps record *Entering The Arena* ++ **NOV 85** Klaus Dinger releases *Néondian* ++

Entering The Arena

TINA SCHNEKENBURGER_When Die Krupps recorded *Entering The Arena* in London with Zeus B. Held, I totally stuffed it. I was too nervous. But I was just happy to have both Waldi and Chris there, who not only recorded the stuff with Jürgen but also had a good idea about the technical side of things as well. I had real 'recording studio stage fright', if such a thing exists.

CHRIS LIETZ_On the one hand, I liked the sequencer stuff from the likes of DAF or Liaisons Dangereuses because it sounded so physical and sweaty; and the live drums of DAF added that authentic touch. On the other, we were to produce our album in England and wanted to compete against the likes of Duran Duran and Human League. Which was ridiculous of course. But we had switched to using the LinnDrum in reference to Human League to get off to a good start.

TINA SCHNEKENBURGER_We were working out of the Eastcote Studios in Kensal Road, which is in the area of Ladbroke Grove, London W10, the cool corner of my beloved London, from where The Clash had originated. I was the first to arrive for the production; the others came later in Waldi's American car with the extra-long tail fins on the back. We lived out of the studio for one or two weeks before all the cash was gone.

CHRIS LIETZ_The studio wasn't overly huge, but it had quite a lot of good analogue equipment, as well as a Trident mixing console and JBL monitor speakers. With this we really could record well and Zeus had made the decision of renting this studio for the time of production. He had been on the road for a long time as a member of the krautrock band Birth Control and was a good 10 years older than the rest of us. As such he had a lot of experience.

TINA SCHNEKENBURGER_I was always in a state of panic, particularly in the studio, and I was constantly worried I wouldn't get it right, the basslines that is. Waldi or Jürgen would have to take over because I was far too nervous. Some nights I still dream of Jürgen saying: "Tomorrow we have a concert here or there, come on," and I think to myself: "Oh God, I have to practise the basslines. I can't even play."

CHRIS LIETZ_Jürgen bought everything. Whatever charted in England at that time – he bought it. Sometimes he even liked the stuff. For about a week he thought Nena's '99 Red Balloons' was hip and cool, because he liked the slap bass middle part. That's how we got to know Waldi, because he could play slap bass. Back then English synth-pop was massive and we wanted to cash in on that success as well. There's nothing wrong with this, considering how the English tried to imitate German electronic music in the beginning. In any case, we didn't succeed. Our attempt at being deliberately commercial was the wrong approach.

TINA SCHNEKENBURGER_As a producer, Zeus B. Held had just mixed Dead Or Alive, and Jürgen found their hit single 'Spin Me Round' brilliant. Exactly, that was it! That was why he wanted Zeus. Although it was produced by Stock, Aitken & Waterman, it was Zeus who had mixed it. In London it was a massive hit, even when Chris and I may have actually thought: "What a load of rubbish!"

WALDI JAEGER_On the one hand, these were excellent new productions, but at the same time you could describe it as a musical diaspora. For *Entering The Arena* we used ABC, Depeche Mode, Duran Duran and even Paul Young as inspiration. We desperately wanted to make something specifically for the English market, and we so called ourselves The Krupps instead.

TINA SCHNEKENBURGER_ In London there were so many bands that were more about image than anything else. Image was the most important thing. And then came the music, hidden underneath. The music was almost irrelevant.

CHRIS LIETZ_ We had songs sounding like 'Wild Boys' up our sleeve as well, namely: 'We're Gladiators' or 'Risiko' – and as a matter of fact we had Mel Gaynor of Simple Minds to play drums on that. Things like this only ever happen in London.

TINA SCHNEKENBURGER_ Still, it was fun. It was London. It was for the sake of *Entering The Arena*. The cover was brilliant and everything, but for some reason the album never became all that popular. It never found the great success it longed for or deserved.

CHRIS LIETZ_ Had we had Ralf on board at that time, with all his connections to Trevor Horn and ZTT, those would have been really cool songs. Instead we released them with Statik, just before they went bust.

Néondian

DIRK FLADER_ Klaus had tried to build a recording studio at his place in Holland, but in the end only one session ever took place there. So he transported all the equipment back to Augusta Street in Düsseldorf, because he realised he needed a home here as well. One morning he arrived at quarter to seven with a lorry from Holland carrying the massive MCI desk on the back. He had to cut out an extra piece of the door with his hacksaw so as to get it into the flat.

KLAUS DINGER_ We had bought our own studio for *Viva* in 78, and in 84 I found myself all alone with this studio in Zeeland. The whole thing had become a one-way street. I just wanted to get back.

DIRK FLADER_ From then on, he lived in a back yard on Augusta Street and later he rented the semi on Lilienthal Street in Lohausen in 1985. That was number 54, although when the neighbour passed away he also took on number 56 next door. He then cut through the walls to connect both houses.

GERHARD MICHEL_We lived in one side of the semi-detached house. On our side we had an office and a meeting room. So as to access the studio, Klaus himself cut through the wall. He was very proud of his handiwork. He covered everything with plastic foil and for two days he had a ball. He looked strangely dapper standing there in his workman's vest. A rejuvenated version of the former architecture student. With the stones he took out of the wall he built a tower in the garden. Like a high-rise. He didn't break up the stones, instead he stacked them neatly one on top of another. The tower had a height of one-and-a-half metres and, thanks to its firm construction and architecture, it never once tumbled down.

HANS LAMPE_Frustrated and far away from home, Thomas Dinger came up with the idea to record a solo album – an album with just his own musical ideas, without anyone else interfering or patronising him. "I want to create something all on my own – created by myself for myself." That's how it got its name: *Für Mich*, meaning 'For Me'. We recorded the six tracks as early as 1981 in our La Düsseldorf studio: instrumental, melancholic, elegant, dominated by smooth synth sounds. Looking back these tracks seemed more like music by Michael Rother or Wolfgang Riechmann. In the context of La Düsseldorf, tracks such as 'Rheinita' or 'Silver Cloud' were the closest reference. We spent a great amount of time experimenting during the recording sessions, and Thomas didn't want Klaus to be in the studio at all during any recording or mixing sessions. Thomas' apartment had a balcony at the back looking out onto an overgrown back yard. There we'd often sit, listening to music and putting the world to rights. We complemented each other very well, played ping pong with our ideas, and had a lot of fun. You can hear the gravitas, as well as the playfulness of the album. We only interacted with Klaus via lawyers. The relationship had cooled well below zero.

KLAUS DINGER_In the meantime, Conny had built a massive studio; he'd even hired his own assistants and two chefs. During one visit Charly and Raoul suddenly arrived at the studio because, I believe, Conny was mixing their stuff for Belfegore. The two of them were Belfegore's drummer and bass player respectively. I liked them a lot; they were a lively duo. Then, at my request and with Conny's support, they played along with my pre-recorded tapes. My original plan had been to mix them as they were but they added a few layers that gave the whole project a totally different flair.

CHARLY TERSTAPPEN_I met Klaus Dinger through Conny. He probably said to Klaus: "Hey, why not let Charly play?" And despite being a drummer himself, Klaus agreed and said: "When you play, it really kicks off. With you it's guaranteed to rock good." He had recognised what it could sound like when I played it. He himself could be clumsy at times. His playing was okay, but he looked a little helpless; he couldn't even tune the drums properly. He was more of an artist. Crazy. A fruitcake, friendly but flaky.

KLAUS DINGER_ After Charly and Raoul added that thunderous sound to my pre-recorded tapes, I realised that I was done with the whole machine thing. All this computer technology is great for recording music, but not for making it. Take a drum machine, for example. It's super effective, cost-efficient for the producer, but for me it's always lacking something.

GERHARD MICHEL_ It was then that Klaus finished his *Néondian* album with Conny. With its white vinyl and a large poster it proved quite expensive to produce, but Teldec released it regardless of the costs. Originally it was planned as the fourth La Düsseldorf album, but because of the legal issues Klaus was forced to release it under the Néondian moniker. Unfortunately it didn't reach the heights achieved by the previous albums.

KLAUS DINGER_ Conny Plank was sensational, he was one of a kind. He was incredibly important to all of my projects: both Neu! and La Düsseldorf. Without Conny none of it would have ever been possible, not even *Néondian*. Conny seemed to have a soft spot for lunatics.

GERHARD MICHEL_ Klaus could be quite combative. He never walked away from a fight. Mâri, his significant other at the time, worked for a solicitor, where he got advice for absolutely everything. In particular, the rereleases of Neu! caused trouble with Metronome, because they didn't have the rights for CD releases, even though they owned the rights to the back catalogue. There were quite a few legal problems

KLAUS DINGER_Those were legal disputes. First of all internally between the members, alternately and successively two against one. Then, after the courts had decided, we united to sue the industry.

MÂRI PAAS_Klaus saw himself as the Lone Ranger, he always thought he was at war with something. His look by then was supposed to be an archaic outlook, but not necessarily one rooted in reality. He chose the name Néondian to give it a martial expression in harmony with nature.

BODO STAIGER_Klaus wasn't simply a diva, he was also a slave driver. Hans and Thomas must have suffered a great deal under him. It must have left its mark. I don't want to even think about how many court battles were fought between the members of the band. It sounds too terrible to contemplate. You don't sue your own brother, do you? One shouldn't really talk about this, but I saw Thomas quite a lot just before he died; he lived nearby and I'd often see him riding his bicycle, completely red-faced and inebriated. He had been a handsome kid, but this unfortunate development did not come about by accident. Even though Klaus had bestowed a lot of good on his little brother, his personality had always been too overbearing. It seems like I remain the only one that has never been sued by Klaus.

MEIKEL CLAUSS_The guy was something else, with his gaunt appearance. Crazy. I'd diagnose: mad hatter disease. The white trousers, slightly too short, always stoned or drunk, addicted to harmony, he was not! I am sure he could be a bitter arsehole at times. We probably would have got on well.

PETER HEIN_At some point I met up with the older Dinger; that must have been in the mid-Eighties and it was exactly how you imagine crazy people to be: "Hey, you there, we need to do something together." I still don't know how he got my office number. It was a chaotic afternoon in the Nordpark. I didn't really understand what he wanted from me; it was all so unclear, he wanted to cooperate but totally ignored that I was not a singer. He simply shuffled along barefoot, or rather with such simple flip-flops, talking conspiratorially and with no end. He looked a bit like Jesus.

GERHARD MICHEL_He was always using Mâri's white VW Golf or her racing bicycle, with his white trousers turned up at the bottom and his white, platformed Beatle boots. He wore home-made rings made from Coca-Cola can ring pulls on his fingers, smoked roll-ups and drank Cointreau from his bicycle flask. Cointreau was his drink of choice, but he also liked sparkling wine, Metternich and then later Freixenet, but also beer and wine. The sparkling wine was a habit from his La Düsseldorf days. Was he an alcoholic? I don't know. He used to drink all the time. He saw it as a pathway to his art. Drugs open the path to creativity; that was his belief. Also: never eat enough. It served a purpose. To increase pressure all the time. He could have eaten normally, but Klaus wanted to start the creative process by being constantly hypoglycaemic: fasting makes you hallucinate. That was his trick. Never eat enough, be high all the time in order to be constantly awake to be creative. A musician needs to be hungry.

KLAUS IMMIG_Klaus was rigorous and domineering with everything. I had to fight for my talent as well and practise loads. He was very demanding and had high expectations. Later on, after we started Die Engel Des Herrn, it became difficult to be the drummer in a band with Klaus Dinger. It wasn't an easy task.

GERHARD MICHEL_There were phases where he hardly slept at all, and then there were others, like the whole of November, where he did nothing but sleep. Klaus hated November. He started to get going again slowly in February or March: "It is only the farmer who faithfully plants seeds in the spring who reaps a harvest in the autumn," that was Klaus' motto. He was always looking forward to May, regardless how far away it seemed at the time. There were weeks and months in between where he was nowhere to be found. His belief was that November was to blame, but his depression could strike at any point, even in August.

KLAUS IMMIG_Klaus' ear was excellent. He had a very sensitive ear for sounds, tones, rhythms, and I always had to suffer because of that: "You'll have to run that again, it can't stay like that, that's not in tune, you're behind the beat." And he was right. He trained my hearing too, even though he defo wasn't a good teacher.

GERHARD MICHEL_On a rare occasion Klaus got out some of his old tapes, the ones where he was playing with Michael Rother and Florian Schneider. They were great though! They'd been recorded live with some old tape recorder, but what was captured there was even better than any of the released albums. It seemed more authentic. Only the name Kraftwerk prevented it from being the highlight at jazz festivals like the ones in Viersen or Moers. It was pure jazz, free jazz. Beautiful guitars rhythmically linked – featuring the über-drummer Klaus Dinger. He was a born drummer. And, above it all, a flute with 50 or so echo effects added to it, or whatever else Florian was experimenting with at that time. On these particular recordings the guitar was extremely loud, but that was irrelevant because it was also extremely good. Michael Rother. Nowadays you try to put down tracks like these, ones that always sound the same despite minimal variations. This guy was predating all of that. It was all about a trance. For me it felt like someone projecting a primeval forest with an electric guitar. This was the trance idea of Dinger and Rother: a constant with slight variations so you wouldn't remember where you were even a minute ago, still thinking it was the same material. Klaus could do exactly that with his drum kit, and then sometimes, after a minute he'd start adding a beat. In this world, Klaus lived forever. That was his benchmark, and that was what he expected of us as well.

EBERHARD KRANEMANN_I rated Klaus Dinger very highly as a musician, even though he wasn't a musician really. You could say both about him: he wasn't a musician, at the same time, he was a good musician. He couldn't play the drums properly either. I come from the jazz scene and there I played with several marvellous drummers. Their playing was sophisticated, and they knew what they were doing. Klaus couldn't do any of it. All he was able to do was a primitive *boom, boom, boom, boom, boom* – just his eighth notes. And no more. But he was exceedingly good at it. He was good at playing simple drums. I never really understood that before now.

MICHAEL ROTHER_Klaus Dinger wasn't really a drummer. Jäki Liebezeit was a drummer, a jazz drummer who decided at some point to cut down on everything and to forget what he had learned. Klaus was a drummer, yet at the same time he wasn't. His timing wasn't brilliant to start with, but the energy emanating from him was fascinating. This unconditional forward-striving beat, storming ahead. He was thinking further ahead than a drummer would. Playing the drums was just one element for him. He was always looking at the whole picture, otherwise we wouldn't have been able to collaborate so well.

KLAUS IMMIG_Klaus had no special name for it other than 'lange gerade', meaning long and straight. That was what he called a segment where there were few variations and where it simply floated along: constantly moving forward, but with a real inherent swing. It sounds paradoxical, but that was the art of it.

EBERHARD KRANEMANN_Klaus played very simply, and he became known for his 'motorik beat' – or as he himself referred to it: 'Apache style'. He called it this because it was in the style of Native American Indians playing their hand drums, only he used felt mallets instead. He played this Red Indian style, but on the drum kit. And he played it so perfectly clean and smooth: really good.

KLAUS IMMIG_In addition to the 'lange gerade', there was also the 'Apache' or 'Apache beat' for Klaus, where he added his floortom.

EBERHARD KRANEMANN_We were sat in his studio recording something when I noticed that his music wasn't motorik, it wasn't mechanical, but it was actually swinging. I hadn't noticed that before. He had just played it, just put up a tom stand and made *boom boom boom boom boom* like an Indian with a felt mallet and I accompanied it with my bass. And he played so beautifully, it was so soft and swung just right. I had to listen to the his old recordings, and yes, "Bugger me, that swings as well!"

GERHARD MICHEL_Klaus thought this one beat through to the end. He called this simple motorik rhythm 'Apache beat', sometimes with and sometimes without a bass drum. He perfected it and completely thought it through to the end. The trance aspect of the beat is the basis similar to the chanting of native Indians. It works like the accompaniment to Indian chanting, that is why he called it the 'Apache'.

EBERHARD KRANEMANN_I had only ever heard the harsh side of his playing. That's how we played in the early Seventies. It was only ever *bang bang bang*, mechanical. Though that's not strictly true. It's not machine-like. The rhythm feels exact even though it's not. It varies: in both the speed and the intensity. It's a very subjective rhythm. It's great. You don't have to be a drummer to play the drums. You have to have soul. You have to have energy inside. Expressiveness. And he had swathes of that. The little that you do – you have to play with great intensity. That's the secret. Play intensely.

GERHARD MICHEL_Everything was engraved in his face. The hundreds of drug-induced trips, the concerts, and everything he had achieved. It was all reflected in his personality; all of it. For everybody else he must have looked like an alien from another planet. There were days when he didn't leave the house, and others where he went out without a worry in the world. You'd always notice him in the street, and not because he was Klaus Dinger, he wasn't famous in that sense, but because of his other-worldly ethereal personality. That is why the only people we ever visited were Michael Rother, Hans Lampe and Thomas Dinger. Once we met with Karl Bartos. That was it. Going out wasn't his thing at all. It was quite unusual for Klaus to be out and about. The moon had to be in the right house. He checked the moon phase before every telephone call and every meeting. If it wasn't right he wouldn't go. All in all, perfect moments were kinda rare.

BODO STAIGER_I never saw his latest band Die Engel Des Herrn live. I was too busy and all I ever did was sit in the studio and produce stuff. Occasionally Klaus would come by and see me with his recordings to firstly ask me for my opinion, and secondly to save money on the mastering. Usually I always had to add treble. That was so typical of Klaus; always broke, always trying to save some money.

GERHARD MICHEL_Financially, Klaus couldn't afford anything any more: the golden age of silver clouds were long gone. In the past, when he released *Viva*, when 'Dampfriemen' or 'Rheinita' were in the charts, he'd earned quite a bit. Champagne was the house drink in the studio and white lines were everywhere. Later he had to rely on PPL royalties alone and not much else. He produced his stuff regardless. He needed tapes. A two-inch tape holding 18 minutes of music cost 400 Deutschmarks back in the day. This is easily forgotten in the days of hard disk recording. He was an extraordinary member of GEMA/PPL and made a little extra money by that. At the same, he had expensive private health insurance. But to put it in words: he was broke.

MÂRI PAAS_I only ever went to see two of Klaus' gigs: one at Tor 3 in 1987 and the other one at the Malkasten in 1993. To be honest, both of them were disastrous. Klaus wanted to do everything himself; he wasn't going to be told, and as such both gigs went horribly wrong. He didn't even promote the gigs properly. He was such a stubborn old goat. Only a few people came to see him. The Tor 3 gig was supposed to start at 9 p.m.; instead they started at 11 p.m., because the band wanted to watch a game of football first. Finally I sent his mother Renate to get him as we were almost on our own in the audience. Come on, you just don't do a thing like that.

KLAUS IMMIG_Towards the end of our days with Die Engel Des Herrn, rehearsals became quite awful. It felt like we were suffocating inside an enormous cheese dome. Gerhard left the band eventually. He suffered badly, because of the clumsy atmosphere. He suddenly had to finish it. Klaus was a difficult character. He was demanding and used up other people's energy. He had high expectations of everything: the world, himself, but first and foremost of all the others around him. Us. This created a downward spiral. People working with him got caught up in a sort of undertow. It got too much for Gerhard. Mâri felt it as well from time to time. To me making music is a social thing, and this social structure costs a lot of energy. If things don't work out well, it becomes difficult in the long run. I stayed for a little longer, but in the end I finally had to quit as well.

DIRK FLADER_ Klaus had always been an eccentric. He had to do everything himself, and he was socially awkward. He had problems with sharing things and information. It wasn't surprising that negotiations with labels were fraught. His expectations were high, but the social side wasn't one of his strong points.

MICHAEL ROTHER_I wouldn't call myself paranoid. In any case, I don't feel I am particularly distrusting of others. Klaus' modus operandi poisoned the atmosphere within the team. Imagine one person constantly complaining about every little thing, because he isn't satisfied with some minute detail. You have to make a stand. You cannot allow anyone to take you for a ride. It was very, very difficult in the end. Very, very difficult. I was ready for the funny farm.

DANIEL MILLER_ In the Nineties I met Klaus Dinger and Michael Rother. I was a big Neu! fan and simply could not understand why the only CDs that existed were pirated bootlegs.

MICHAEL ROTHER_ There has always been some interest from abroad: Daniel Miller of Mute Records, a true music lover and connoisseur, definitely wanted Neu! to be signed to his label.

DANIEL MILLER_I got introduced to Herbert Grönemeyer by a common friend. I told him about this fantastic music from Düsseldorf, and that Michael and Klaus had fallen out big time. There was so much great material, but no one could get at it any more. We worked for 10 years to release this material. Herbert met Klaus and Michael a couple of times in Düsseldorf and persuaded them somehow to release the stuff again on his label Grönland. I was glad someone had managed to get them to do this. I always wanted people to be able to listen to this excellent music. And that for artistic reasons alone.

MICHAEL ROTHER_ That was the time when Klaus and I were drifting further and further apart. I don't want to go too much into the details of it all; it was just a terrible time when Klaus simply refused any offer.

DANIEL MILLER_ We finally agreed on a contract and had made an appointment to meet at a café in the Nordpark. We brought a photographer and a TV crew from Japan. The signing of the contract, however, did not happen, because Rother and Dinger couldn't agree on who was going to be the first to sign the document. It was madness, commercial suicide. I was very disappointed.

WOLFGANG FLÜR_This embarrassing detail prevented the contract from being signed. You just have to imagine that. Daniel took his money with him again, because the two of them couldn't agree on who was going to be the first named signatory. It's childish. Michael said it would be very important in this context, because the first named person was always deemed more important in terms of the production. With us it was always 'Ralf and Florian', even though Florian had founded the band and had chosen the name.

MICHAEL ROTHER_Daniel tried for years. One time he travelled especially with a guy from Vancouver, but Klaus stonewalled the whole thing, because he asserted that Miller's companion was a Rother man. It was a really long and difficult battle. Now that the albums are available again, I am really thrilled. Especially because of all the positive reactions from all around the world.

KURT DAHLKE_Klaus produced some wonderful stories. Take Grönland for example. I was with Grönland at the same time, with René Renner. René called me at some point. Grönemeyer was coming to Düsseldorf. It was something about Klaus Dinger. Did I want to have breakfast at his hotel? At the Radisson he explained to me that Klaus insisted on replacing the handwritten address 'Im Grund 3b' printed on the cover with the current address in his own hand. The graphic designer should help him insert the new address. So René Renner travelled from London, Herbert Grönemeyer travelled from London, the graphic designer travelled from Berlin, but no Klaus. Klaus was the only one that didn't appear at the breakfast meeting. Herbert asked René to give him a ring. René came back from the call white as a sheet. Dinger was not coming. "Why?" "Because he is with his mother." "What do you mean he is seeing his mother?" "Well, he asked me to tell you that he wasn't feeling like it today." Herbert went berserk. 'Give me the f– phone! Hey Klaus, what are you doing? We came from London especially to meet you, and the graphic designer came from Berlin. What do you want him to do?" Klaus' voice sounded from the receiver, "He can look at the sights of Düsseldorf. It's a very nice place." That was Klaus. He killed off one thing after another.

GERHARD MICHEL_There were problems with the design of the cover. The Gesamtkunstwerk Klaus Dinger wouldn't allow a graphic designer to design the cover of an album. A tick had to be placed here and there, and everything had to be handwritten. He had to initial everything with his gold-coloured paint stick. Klaus Dinger's initials, a peculiar arch with a dot underneath, were supposed to resemble the letter K. Only Klaus, maybe Michael Rother, would have been allowed to design every little detail of a rerelease. That was the only way Klaus worked, but record companies don't understand that kind of thing. It bears no relation to the profit that can be achieved. Why would you waste your time on a guy like this?

KLAUS DINGER_I have always seen myself as a Total Artist. Right from the beginning I thought a Total Artist does everything himself. No lawyers, no accountants, nothing; I'll do everything myself. I still like to do everything myself. To look after everything. But of course that limits your possibilities. I've always believed, ultimately, it is the music that matters. It's the music that prevails. Today, however, the market mechanisms are perfectly installed and in order to get in, you have to make concessions somewhere. I never had proper management. I never found the right guy to do the job. A guy where I would say, 'Okay, he is better at management than I am'. I am perfectly footloose and fancy free at the same time. No one forces me to do anything. I wouldn't let it happen to me; but I am not totally satisfied with the situation either. I feel there is untapped potential inside me that is wasting away.

KURT DAHLKE_Another thing was: we were supposed to be taking photographs, promotional photos. So you try to get the best photographer you can get: Anton Corbijn. Anton took the photos. Then along came Klaus claiming all the photos were shit. He didn't want to see any of them anywhere. "What are we going to do now? Shall we arrange for another session?" No, he didn't want to; but he wanted to know how much money the photographer was going to get for the job. His fee was 12 grand. The last thing audible was Klaus leaving with the words, "Okay, that's settled. I'll send you the photos." Klaus departed. He went on to take a few Polaroids of himself and sent them through with an invoice for 12 grand. Sure. Only logical. That made complete sense to him.

MICHAEL ROTHER_I can laugh about it today, but those were hard times. Paranoia is infectious. Klaus was always suspicious of everyone and worried that he could miss out somehow. We had to do everything together. Neu! interviews could only be undertaken together, at the same time. It got to the point where we were totally confused and mixed up. For example, when someone requested to interview me about my work as a soloist, then he wasn't allowed to do so unless Klaus would be interviewed as well. Everything had to be balanced all the time. At the same time, I am more happy than anyone about the rerelease of Neu!. No one can be any happier. It's strange. Klaus and I agreed on this point alone. Klaus was also very keen to see a rerelease of Neu!. Our goals didn't differ that much. We only ever argued about the how, with whom and when.

KURT DAHLKE_Another good one: I did a compilation with Düsseldorf bands entitled *Citybeats*. *Citybeats* had been sponsored by the local electricity board, Stadtwerke. It was a square, large format catalogue with a a vinyl record and was released as a history book about the bands and labels. Quite a nice thing. And for this I wanted to include a piece by Neu!. After I was finished I received a call from a solicitor telling me I had destroyed Klaus Dinger's piece of art. They were asking the court for an injunction. "Excuse me, what's the matter? I just copied the CD provided and compiled the album." No, I had destroyed the piece. "What exactly has been destroyed?" I had faded out the white noise at the end of the recording one second too early. Unfortunately this formed part of the piece of art. They were referring to the white noise at the end. I thought every piece has a trail of white noise and faded it automatically, finished. Klaus reckoned it was part of his piece and called his solicitor. That was him. Typical Klaus.

++ **FEB 86** Glasnost and Perestroika at the 27th congress of the CPSU ++ **APR 86** Nuclear plant at Chernobyl explodes ++ **OCT 86** Kraftwerk release the 'Musique Non Stop' 12-inch ++ **DEC 86** Kraftwerk's last album with the classic line-up, *Electric Café*, is released ++

Electric Café

WOLFGANG FLÜR_I rarely went to the Kling Klang Studio after our work on *Electric Café* was finished. Musically, there was not much to do for me any more, and a tour following the release hadn't been planned either. None of the songs made it anywhere near the Top 10.

RALF DÖRPER_ Following the to and fro over the choice of name, the album was completely reworked and then released under the name *Electric Café* on December 16, 1986. The musical world didn't appear to be ready for it; it received very few positive reviews and was not at all successful on the charts. Unlike *Computer World*, which had already been out for five years!

RAINER ZICKE_*Electric Café* sounds different to the other albums as there was a lot of internal squabbling. There was endless production work, as they kept on fiddling around with it a lot. A situation that brought François Kevorkian into play. He was involved in the final mix of the album and it was he who gave it the final touch. Someone has to mention it. He did a lot to it.

WOLFGANG FLÜR_ They flew in the American video specialist Rebecca Allen for the bizarre music video shoot of 'Musique Non Stop'. The artist worked at the New York Institute of Technology. She had studied art and made a name for herself with producing trailers and advertising clips. Our heads had to be measured exactly, and we had to produce shots following her exact instructions. This was accomplished by shooting our heads from all sorts of angles with a video camera. Picture after picture, centimetre by centimetre. The same happened with the heads of our robots, which had been shipped to New York. They taped horizontal and vertical lines all over them, creating a grid for the computer animation.

RAINER ZICKE_Frankie knows his stuff inside out. He's French with Armenian roots, but left for New York at the age of 17 or 18. The guy's ear is excellent, and he has great instincts for things that work. François Kevorkian achieves a lot with his relaxed attitude, his ability to analyse things properly and his direct approach: "We need a more open sound here. We need more space there. And this feels too compressed." I only experienced him a couple of times, but I found him fascinating. You can hear what he did on 'Musique Non Stop'. He was the sound engineer.

RALF DÖRPER_That Kraftwerk video clip shaped the MTV era, and it became the anthem of the music channel. MTV didn't hesitate to put this on heavy rotation to identify itself massively with its message: Music Non Stop. Looking back you have to say that *Electric Café* was actually much better than its reception suggested. It wasn't that bad. It was better than its success.

WOLFGANG FLÜR_We shot one final clip for 'The Telephone Call', the only track Karl was allowed to sing with Kraftwerk. When you watch the video today you can actually see just how far we had drifted apart from each other. After six terrific albums and 13 long years, the time had come for me to turn my back on Ralf and Florian.

Ex & Pop

WOLFGANG FLÜR_To this day I have not received another penny from Kraftwerk. And that's because I wasn't involved as an author but rather credited as a participating musician. Karl receives a share because of his co-composing. He still gets money from it today. Which is perfectly justified, seeing as without Karl the last

Kraftwerk records would never have been possible. Nowadays he is often quite broody. He seems melancholic, almost depressed when he comes to visit. I feel a lot happier myself. I have made my peace with the whole affair.

EBERHARD KRANEMANN_On paper Wolfgang Flür and Karl Bartos were members of Kraftwerk. In reality they were employees. They only ever got a fixed wage to make them stay, to make it appear they were a band. In the end they got money for doing nothing. Wolfgang wasn't interested any more. He didn't have to work, but he suffered greatly with the situation. That is what he told me once anyway. They didn't do work in the studio for the final five years, no performances, nothing. All they ever did was cycle. He probably said to himself, 'I'm going to call it a day.'

WOLFGANG FLÜR_I loved all of my bands: The Beathovens, Spirits Of Sound, even The Bellos. But Kraftwerk was always just a job, and I only continued with it because I got paid.

MORITZ REICHELT_Ralf Hütter became so absolutely fixated on the whole *Man-Machine* thing. So much that even Florian Schneider got fed up with it eventually.

EBERHARD KRANEMANN_They just get rid of people that are no longer required. They are blacked out. Until only they themselves remained: Ralf and Florian. But now with Florian also packing it in, Ralf is probably going to black out his name as well. So in the end he will be the only one left behind in Kraftwerk universe. Ralf Huttler [sic].

BODO STAIGER_You get next to no insight into what really happened. You don't really know how things came about with Kraftwerk, but if there was one important person, then it's Karl. Just look at what they did musically after he left the band.

JÜRGEN ENGLER_The first album by Electric Music, the band formed by Karl Bartos and Lothar Manteuffel, is quite good; some of the tracks are even better than the ones on *Electric Café*. Karl did have and still has a few problems with his ex-colleagues, however. God knows why, but he gets sued as soon as he even attempts to mouth the Kraftwerk name. Whatever happened, he isn't allowed to use the name. He gets a legal warning letter as soon as he even uses *Ex*-Kraftwerk. It gets expensive. Any promoter likes to use great names. They can't take away his 15 years with them, can they?

RAINER ZICKE_Maybe Karl was important for Kraftwerk, but his solo stuff, unfortunately, doesn't really work. It's artisanal and very industrious. I don't know. It might sound a bit nasty, but, in my view, his own stuff still sounds too much like Kraftwerk. He can't escape it. It's a pity, but it's also the problem. You have to see it realistically: he is without a doubt part of the later stuff. He is credited as a co-composer and has every right to play those pieces live. But it just leaves a bit of an aftertaste when you see a poster with: Karl Bartos is in town and 'Ex-Kraftwerk' is printed in bigger letters than his own name. It makes me uneasy. You don't have to do it that way. I'm not too keen on his stuff anyway. No, unfortunately not.

JÜRGEN ENGLER_I don't understand why the person that was significantly responsible for the good stuff gets gagged. I also don't understand how it is possible for Mr Hütter to just appear onstage with three new stand-ins chosen at random. It's the same as if The Rolling Stones appeared with Mick Jagger, but without Keith Richards; he appears without Florian Schneider, who has also run for the hills. Or, to stay with the analogy, without Charlie Watts, because Wolfgang was always mild-mannered, same as Charlie. People underestimate that. The Stones without Watts, Kraftwerk without Wolfgang, is boring. As a musician you know that. As a fan you might put up with it. Come to think of it, Karl would be Ron Wood. He joined last, but had to play everything, because the older gentlemen had become too comfortable with things.

WOLFGANG FLÜR_The two of them definitely used Karl, but he allowed it to happen as well. He didn't get enough money or credit. His name is on every important album, but he is only referenced and not specifically credited. Remember, Konrad Plank disappeared at some point as well. My efforts didn't get credited either after everything I did for Kraftwerk on 'Boing Boom Tschak' or 'Metall Auf Metall' – it happened in my workshop by accident when we were hammering sheets of metal. The list goes on. It doesn't even get a mention like 'developed from an idea by Wolfgand Flür' or anything. They are a little dishonest with that, or like to adorn themselves with borrowed plumes. But, I guess that's just the business part of the music business.

EBERHARD KRANEMANN_ You can see it clearly now: it's not about art. It's definitely not about music. They haven't released anything new for more than 20 years now. They just dress up the old stuff over and over again. They have had no new ideas since Wolfgang and Karl left.

OUTRO

GERHARD MICHEL_I remember well, just how dejected Klaus was when he first heard of Conny's death. He drove to the funeral in Cologne on his own and didn't speak for days. He wore a dark, long coat over his normal clothing as he had no black to wear. He looked so hunched and broken, it really hit him hard. This thing affected him a great deal. Strange to think that he himself has been dead for a few years now.

CHARLY TERSTAPPEN_I was touring with Marius when Conny died in December 1987, and so I couldn't make it to the funeral. It was some time after the fact that I first found out, because no one had told me on tour; they knew how close I was with Conny and that it would have knocked me off my feet.

KURT DAHLKE_ Fehlfarben were the last to record at Conny's studio. Shortly before Christa died as well. Conny's son Stephan decided to sell up all the equipment as he wasn't interested in keeping the studio open. So he sold it away.

KLAUS DINGER_I think everything is screwed up today. Maybe I shouldn't really say too much about it; but things didn't really turn out as intended for me. Around the time of John Lennon's death, pretty much from 1980 onwards, music just seemed so banal to me. Somehow the whole thing is one big, long car crash that continues till today. Unchecked.

BODO STAIGER_ No one told me that Klaus had died. Even Michael didn't know. I went to the funeral in tears. I only found out the day before. I was completely devastated. I have never been this badly touched by someone's death before or since. Two years before his death we had met up, when things were good with Klaus. I liked him a lot, his intransigence, especially when we were battling the rest of the world.

GERHARD MICHEL It's strange that Klaus never really understood the effect he had on people all over the globe. Really strange. He didn't know about his image at all. He was certain that he would become famous after his death. He thought of himself as a high artist in eternity. That's why he sealed himself off from the world around him. It was paranoia as well. All his life he was afraid that someone could steal something from him. In the end he was afraid someone would steal his tones.

BODO STAIGER_Later Michael rang and asked if I had read the news that Klaus had died. I told him that I just had spoken with him only a week ago. He had been in Zeeland. We also talked about the last mixes, the ones we had produced in his studio. He seemed very relaxed.

KLAUS IMMIG_After the session in Zeeland, Holland, in 2005, I went to see Klaus. I brought a case of beer with me and we got drunk together. Klaus kept everything, his house was like a museum. He kept his stuff – and other people's stuff. The empty crate was still standing there when I visited his girlfriend after he had died. So I took it with me then. It made me feel sad, because it reminded me of that evening. He was a wacky guy, really different. No one keeps an empty beer crate for years.

ROBERT GÖRL_I felt like I had dropped into a great big hole. From one day to the other this big thing was finished and my whole level had dropped. I retreated to Paris for a year. I just wanted to change reels like they do in a cinema. Gabi and I had spent five years together. Day and night. I was speeding along the whole time, riding the crest of the wave. Then for the first time in my life I didn't do anything any more. Absolutely nothing. Apart from thinking.

GABI DELGADO_This is how I am. I keep on going on. When I am with a new crowd, with other people, I am no longer interested in the past. For me the people continue to exist, but they become a memory. It's the same for my personal and professional life. I'm not loyal, and I don't keep in touch. They are all wonderful human beings, but I have left them behind. Strange emotions develop. Not with me; but others could have them. They don't understand my abrupt moving-on.

CHRISLO HAAS_It was an experiment, going to Berlin, the lifestyle, the life we were living then. Everyone was using. Everyone was high on drugs. Everyone! Neubauten, Liaisons Dangereuses. We lived this life 48 hours a day. Otherwise the whole thing couldn't have been created. An endless supply of speed was important. It changed me; and I knew it. I wanted it.

TINA SCHNEKENBURGER_I got to the point, some time in 86, where I was growing fed up with the whole music scene. Music got worse and worse. People were just blowing hot air. They were all talk and talk and no action.

FRANK FENSTERMACHER_We only ever produced our own stuff. We were far too eccentric for other producers. One day I drew a picture with the words, 'Start building your own model'. Today I would say, 'Actually it was a mistake to try to do everything by yourself'. What I mean is, to record stuff without any experience of recording stuff, to design stuff without any experience in designing stuff, to market stuff without any experience in marketing stuff, without knowledge of business. We had to do everything ourselves. Suddenly the distribution company folded and we were carrying debts of 100,000 marks around our necks. We weren't able to move until the Nineties, because we had to service bank guarantees. But finally we were able to start breathing slowly again.

TINA SCHNEKENBURGER_Jürgen was in debt as well, but he had managed to borrow some money from his dad. I was the only one with a job or dole money. But then I stopped. I was 33 and thought to myself: "Shit, here I am now. Facing a 70,000 debt of my own."

FRANK FENSTERMACHER_Probably it was a mistake not to use the backup of stronger forces. Maybe we would have been able to work on a different scale. I am not about to quarrel. I am a concept artist who earns his corn with music. Someone who has been able to find a way to express himself. Someone lucky enough to be in the right place at the right time. With the right people. I always remained independent. I could choose what to do. I didn't have to bend over for anyone. So what? Even if no one remembers me tomorrow, I don't give shit about it today.

WALDI JAEGER_Herbert, who worked in the bass and keyboard department and in many of the various studios around, said: "They've bought so much of this German new wave stuff, watch out that they don't just let it rot inside some sort of drawer." Finally Nena released '99 Red Balloons' and then it was all over. Bam. All gone to pot.

GABI DELGADO_We didn't want anything to do with the German new wave shit that over the years turned into shallow schlager. We didn't want anything to do with it. We thought it would be best to just disappear. That is how we achieved cult status.

PAUL HUMPHREYS_We were always looking to the future. Electronic music was always the future, but all of a sudden we were left dumbfounded. Brit pop and other retro movements appeared out of nowhere, and electronic music was no longer futuristic. It became the music of the past. The path ahead was blocked by revivals. So we drew a line under OMD.

ANDY MCCLUSKEY_Now we are beyond even cycles. We are beyond a direct timeline. We live in this postmodern pick and mix. There is nothing about this replaced this and this replaced that, etc. There are just all these different things present at the same time: now. Architecture can be postmodern; at the same time you have great new buildings that go up and are ultra modern. Nothing said about morality, but you have pseudo classical and neoclassical, rococo and *blah blah blah*. Films, art styles, everything is becoming self-referential. It's all referencing something that has already been gone.

KLAUS DINGER

REPRISE

KLAUS DINGER_Personally, and as a matter of course, I don't believe in coincidence. Could this kind of music come from anywhere else but Düsseldorf? Well, I don't think so. Apparently not. There is nothing like it. A lot of people may have helped themselves to the stuff we developed, and then made the big bucks abroad. But nevertheless I'd go as far as saying: this was only ever possible in D-U-S, my town Düsseldorf.

EBERHARD KRANEMANN_Musically, Düsseldorf represented the centre of the world, but most people didn't even have a clue. We didn't have a clue; and we were part of it. It's only afterwards that you start to slowly realise what the likes of Eno and Bowie knew straight away. They noticed: here is the cradle of electronic music and Düsseldorf is the epicentre. It was from here that the music originated. It was us Düsseldorfers who started with this music. It wasn't in Cologne, not in New York, Detroit or in Tokyo – electronic music started here. That's why it's dubbed Electri_city.

FRANK FENSTERMACHER_For me Düsseldorf has always been the Electric City. Now, though, with the use of computers in music, the whole world has become an electric city.

KURT DAHLKE_Düsseldorf represents the departure into a new era. Especially because of the bands that made Düsseldorf one of the pillars of modern music.

JÜRGEN ENGLER_People looked at you differently when you said: "I am from Düsseldorf." It was cool then. Nowadays it doesn't matter where you come from. It was cool at the time because everyone knew that the sound of the future had been shaped there.

MEIKEL CLAUSS_Düsseldorf is an excellent place to achieve nothing. It will take you nowhere. You really can develop something in this town and lots of great guys are from Düsseldorf. But at the same time you have to leave to succeed. You stay a nobody at home. Because you are just the idiot from around the corner, and everyone knows everything of all your faults and mistakes. That really turns 'em off. Completely.

BEATE BARTEL_We never pledged allegiance to this city. For a long time people didn't know who we were. No, we are not from Düsseldorf. We are out-of-towners. We come from nowhere. The fact that we recorded our discs there had nothing to do with the city of Düsseldorf itself. We chose Düsseldorf because Chrislo had friends there and it was centrally located. We spent more time elsewhere. London. Berlin. I don't know.

JÜRGEN ENGLER_I am sure I would have made music even if I hadn't been born in Düsseldorf. My path would have been similar. But finding the right people was a massive advantage and happened here. I must have been born under a lucky star.

LOTHAR MANTEUFFEL_The original scene was quite small. And from that everyone developed into their own scenes. Musical heritage didn't matter. You could infer anything. Most people had the sheer willpower to differentiate themselves from others in Düsseldorf, or around the world. They had to be true to themselves and work for an unknown audience. They all did that exceedingly well and were in the words of Ralf Hütter:

RALF HÜTTER_We are music workers. We live in exile in Düsseldorf by the Rhine.

MARTYN WARE_Absolutely; electronic music and Düsseldorf are a great fit because of the urban and the urbane idiosyncrasies. I love cities. I was born in a town with heavy industry and, as such, I like the sound of the Ruhr area; but, first and foremost, I like inner cities. I always have to live in the centre of a town; in the country I'd fall apart. For me music from Düsseldorf represented something like a new folk music; it somehow pulled me towards this city romantically. I mean that, exactly as I say it. For me Kraftwerk and Düsseldorf were like, say, Grateful Dead and California. I stayed there for two weeks, because my wife worked for an ad agency there, and I wanted to accompany her. I would have never done this in any other town. I like it here.

LOTHAR MANTEUFFEL_It's this small stream, the Düssel, that's responsible for giving the name to this city that lies on the much grander river Rhine. That's what I call understatement. Tourists have rarely strayed here. Commerce, advertising, fashion and art are the best known compass directions. Everything seemed possible from here. In art, as well as in music.

MICHAEL ROTHER_Maybe we were something like local heroes as The Spirits Of Sound, the school band at the Rethel-gymnasium. But that we never felt with Neu!. It didn't feel as if we were doing something special for Düsseldorf or for the shape of the city. When the first Neu! album came out we were proud, no, actually we were surprised to see it in the shop windows of the Altstadt record stores. Aside from that we were ignored at best.

KLAUS DINGER_Jesus. Who did listen to Neu!? I really can't tell you. You have to be very lucky to find anyone in Düsseldorf who would just have heard the name. Actually, I don't think anyone here knows the band Neu!.

MICHAEL ROTHER_We mustn't forget Conny and his crucial creative contribution. To him we have to be truly thankful. You can't just always name the bands or the musicians. We wouldn't have been able to do any of it without Conny.

KLAUS DINGER_Düsseldorf has a certain flair. It is completely different from Berlin or Cologne or Munich. Lots of things come from Düsseldorf. It's quite impressive what has been exported all around the world from here since the Seventies; especially considering the size of the place.

EBERHARD KRANEMANN_When you start to grow older you notice that some things happen by accident. I happened to be in the right place at the right time. That I never realised at the time. For me it was reality, not history. It was my life. It was what I was doing at the time. We were friends who met up to make music. We partied together, went shopping or went for a drink. You walk along the road. You get laid. You have a piss and a shit. You have a beer. You make some music with a rich, pale boy from Düsseldorf, then you have another piss or a shit and have a shag, have a sandwich or get some chips from the chippy. It's all equally good. And it's only afterwards that you realise: 'Fuck, those four, five years were the real deal. They were happening.' But you only ever notice afterwards.

KLAUS DINGER_I couldn't think of anything better than making music. Everything else I experienced felt like shit. Everything people suggested I should do, all of the things I had to do – it was all meaningless. Well it's still the same today. I know of nothing better. Keyword self-realisation: 'Mother, how far am I allowed to travel?' That's what it has been all about during the last 20 years. Since I escaped. Long may it continue.

WOLFGANG FLÜR_To have a band was to have a philosophy. To have a lifetime goal. Other guys may have had scooters; but we had our band. What a terrible life it must be without a band; or not being a musician.

Es wird immer weitergehen.
Musik als Träger von Ideen.

Symthetic electronic sounds.
Industrial rhythms all around.

Kraftwerk, 'Techno Pop' (1983)

WOLFGANG RIECHMANN died on August 24, 1978, aged 31, after he was stabbed by two drunks in Altstadt.

CONNY PLANK died on December 18, 1987, aged 47, as a result of cancer.

THOMAS DINGER died on April 9, 2002, aged 49, as a result of his alcohol addiction.

TINA SCHNEIDER-ESLEBEN died on December 26, 2002, aged 47. She committed suicide.

MUSCHA commited suicide on July 29, 2003, aged 52.

CHRISLO HAAS died on October 23, 2004, aged 48, as a result of his alcohol addiction.

JOHN PEEL died on October 25, 2004, aged 65, from a heart attack.

CHRISTA FAST, Conny Plank's wife, died on June 1, 2006, aged 54.

KLAUS DINGER died on March 21, 2008, three days before his 62nd birthday.

ANDREAS THEIN died on March 30, 2013, aged 54, from esophageal cancer.

GÜNTER KÖRBER had a congenital cardiac insufficiency and died on September 10, 2013 in Hamburg, aged 67.

DIETER MOEBIUS died on July 20, 2015, of cancer, aged 71.

DAVID BOWIE died after an 18-month battle with liver cancer on January 10, 2016, at his New York City apartment.

DÜSSELDORF HANDWRITTEN BY KLAUS DINGER

APPENDIX

The Men

BEATE BARTEL (*1955), born in Berlin ++ Still wonders why her band Liaisons Dangereuses is primarily known as a band from Düsseldorf ++ Became experienced sound engineer after a practise year in London ++ Confident, handsome and masculine new type of woman who would become a role model for the Eighties ++ Founded the female band Mania D with three other Berlin style icons, with whom she played bass ++ Founding member of Einstürzende Neubauten ++ Co-composer and co-producer of her band's project Liaisons Dangereuses and own her dangerous liaison with Chrislo Haas in Düsseldorf ++ Provided the choral singing on the underground anthem 'Los Niños Del Parque', the most well-known song by Liaisons Dangereuses ++ Lives with Bad Seeds drummer Thomas Wydler in Berlin.

Karl Bartos (*1952), born in Berchtesgaden and studied percussion at the Robert Schumann Conservatory in Düsseldorf ++ Proficient on guitar, piano and drums, although his instrument of choice was without a doubt the vibraphone ++ Formed jazz-rock group Sinus together with Bodo Staiger ++ His teachers recommended him to Florian Schneider, who was looking for a professional percussionist to complete Kraftwerk ++ Similar to an employee, he was bound by the Kraftwerk board of directors as a second drummer prior to their US tour in 1975 ++ In addition to simply playing rhythms on Kraftwerk's songs, he was increasingly credited for his compositional contribution to their songs ++ This influence culminated in the music piece 'Tour De France' and the vocal part of 'Der Telefonanruf', which at the same time was the swansong of the classic line-up ++ Following the departure of Wolfgang Flür he remained with Kraftwerk a further three years, leaving in the spring of 1990 while they were preparing for upcoming concerts in Italy ++ Launched the studio project Elektric Music together with the lyricist of Rheingold, the Kraftwerk-trusted Lothar Manteuffel ++ In the Nineties he collaborated with the British musicians Andy McCluskey, Bernard Sumner and Johnny Marr ++ Went through a guest professorship at the University of Arts in Berlin after the turn of the millennium ++ Till this day his mood can quickly change from enormously proud to somewhat bitter when asked about his Kraftwerk past.

CHRIS BOHN (*1954), wrote under the alias Biba Kopf for the legendary *New Musical Express*, and reported about German bands like DAF and Die Krupps ++ Today he is the editor of the monthly music magazine *The Wire*.

CLAUDIA BRÜCKEN (*1963), while still at school, was a member of the all-girl band Topolinos together with Susanne Freytag, with whom she is still friends today ++ Singer of the band Propaganda and wife of the journalist and operator of ZTT label Paul Morley ++ Left Propaganda in the hope of starting a solo career and hence changed the interests of band and record company ++ Active as a singer of bands Act and Onetwo, the latter of which she founded with Paul Humphreys from OMD, with whom she lived together in London as a couple until recently.

BERND CAILLOUX (*1945), writer, came to Düsseldorf after he left the German armed forces and journalism school, establishing the psychedelic lightshow firm Leisure Society Experiments in Art and Technology with two colleagues, which broke up after rapid and commercial successes as a result of conceptual as well as personal differences and drugs ++ After spending some time in Hamburg, he moved to Berlin in 1977, where he experienced the emerging new wave underground ++ In 2005, he processed his experiences with Leisure Society in the novel *Das Geschäftsjahr 1968/69* ++ Lives and works in Berlin.

MEIKEL Michael David **CLAUSS** (*1959), born in Düsseldorf, strummed the most highly rated punk-rock guitar in town, next to Engler ++ He became guitarist of KFC during their debut *Letzte Hoffnung*, which significantly benefited from his guitar work ++ Founded the pop-pogo band Nichts and wrote their noticeable success 'Radio', which achieved radio and TV airplay in a self-fulfilling way ++ Formed the goth-rock band Belfegore and marketed his songs internationally as having been produced by Conny

Plank ++ Avid guitar collector and lovable loudmouth who has worked as a homeopathic practitioner in Düsseldorf for more than 20 years.

CHRIS CROSS Christopher Allen (*1952) studied art and psychology in London in the early Seventies ++ Sole bassist of art school band Ultravox from the beginnings of their existence ++ Also a keyboardist and partly responsible for the use of electronic equipment ++ Often worked as an instrumentalist and composer for Ultravox in Conny's studio ++ Lives in Bath and works as a psychotherapist.

KURT DAHLKE (*1958), also known as Pyrolator ++ Born near Düsseldorf ++ From an early stage he was interested in electronic music gadgets ++ Played in the jazz-rock band You together with Görl, Spelmans and Haas in Wuppertal ++ Synthesiser player in the first Deutsch Amerikanische Freundschaft (DAF) ++ Founded the Ata Tak label with Frank Fenstermacher and released the first DAF record ++ Released his solo work under the alias Pyrolator ++ Founder of Der Plan with Moritz R. and Fenstermacher ++ Provided synth on the legendary album *Monarchie Und Alltag* ++ Active as a producer and sound engineer of Ata Tak studios ++ Touring and playing with Fehlfarben and recently moved to Berlin ++ Considered the grey eminence of electronic music, being a brilliant inventor and inexhaustible lexicon.

GABI Gabriel **DELGADO** Lopez (*1958) emigrated from Spain with his parents during the Franco period and lived in Dortmund and Wuppertal ++ Began his career as a dancer for Mittagspause before he became a singer of Deutsch Amerikanische Freundschaft ++ Had a predilection for militaristic clothing like his fellow bandmates Görl and Haas of Minus Delta T ++ Style-wise he perfectly mutated into the skinhead look of London, and with his penchant for sweat, eroticism and machines, he quickly made cash in Germany ++ Played and lived his homophilic image and presented himself in Alfred Biolek's TV broadcast *Bio's Bahnhof* with 'Der Räuber Und Der Prinz' ++ Shortly thereafter he put on a provocative performance as a martial dance teacher and depicted through dancing such diverse figures and topics as Mussolini, Hitler, Jesus Christ and communism ++ With the help of Conny Plank he released three albums in 18 months and lived the fast life of sex and drugs ++ Turned his attention to solo projects and moved to Berlin, in order to live a new identity during the techno boom ++ Because of his direct, unreconstructed manner, his confused as well as ingenious verbal contributions, he is a highly appreciated interviewee ++ Reactivated DAF and lives as an artist in Cordoba, Spain with his wife.

KLAUS DINGER (1946–2008) moved to Düsseldorf with his parents at an early age ++ Went to Görres-Gymnasium and played in school bands, such as Swing Combo, The No and The Smash ++ Was part of Kraftwerk for a short period of time and played drums on their first album ++ Founded the innovative krautrock group Neu! together with Michael Rother ++ Developed the motorik beat, a stoic 4/4 rhythm presented in a confident and minimalistic manner ++ The three influential albums of the band are considered style-defining ++ In 1976 he founded the band La Düsseldorf together with his brother Thomas and Hans Lampe, presenting himself as frontman, guitarist, CEO and chief composer ++ Released three albums with this group, which in retrospect can be regarded as much a part of his legacy as his Neu! albums ++ Spent the Eighties in endless disputes with his band colleagues and record companies, as well as hopeless attempts to form a new line-up ++ In 1987 he formed the precursor to the band Die Engel Des Herrn together with Rüdiger Esch and Gerhard Michel ++ Dealt with different band projects, which related to his musical legacy and his love for Japan, until his sudden death.

THOMAS DINGER (1952–2002) was born in Düsseldorf ++ The younger brother of Klaus was taught to play drums by him in order to be able to join La Düsseldorf ++ Trained as a window dresser, he was responsible for the visual appearance and artistic refinement in terms of neon, crystals and the factory-led silver and white colour concentration ++ A renowned bon vivant, stylish Altstadt archetype and most decadent white overall of them all; always boozing excessively ++ Loved to wear make-up and to be photographed in women's clothes ++ Shared a longstanding dangerous affair with Tina Schneider-Esleben, the younger sister of Florian Schneider, which ended in death for both.

RALF DÖRPER (*1960) was born in Düsseldorf ++ Began an apprenticeship at the Westdeutsche Landesbank after having attended the Lessing-Gymnasium ++ Wrote for several punk magazines under the name Vacant and first fell into contact with the avant-garde band S.Y.P.H. during punk rock times, before drawing attention to himself with experimental solo seven-inches ++ Worked with Engler under the name Die Lemminge and formed Die Krupps together with him and Malaka ++ Was involved in the publication of the WEA album as lyricist and syncussionist and in 1983 he founded the pop project Propaganda together with Andreas Thein ++ The placement of his demo tape on Trevor Horn's new desk at ZTT was seen as a clever coup ++ With Top 20 chart successes all over Europe, Propaganda became a household name ++ After a quarrel, the band sued the record company ++ Dörper re-joined Die Krupps and preserved valuable UK networking contacts ++ The video of 'Machineries Of Joy', the 'Wahre Arbeit – Wahrer Lohn' sequel, was directed by Anton Corbijn's company, who had previously visualised 'Dr Mabuse' ++ During the Nineties Dörper worked as a senior analyst at West LB in Düsseldorf ++ He worked for Die Krupps as a lyricist, businessman and finance minister ++ This was followed by reunions with Thein as Dr Acid and Mr House and the inevitable comeback attempts of Propaganda and Die Krupps ++ As an expert on electronic music and all British topics, he was an inexhaustible and friendly advisor ++ Despite a reported stinginess and the collapse of the Westdeutsche Landesbank, Dörper looks to the future with confidence.

RUSTY EGAN (*1957) admired Klaus Dinger and always wanted to be a drummer ++ Founded the band Rich Kids with Glen Matlock after his sacking by the Sex Pistols ++ Produced the band The Skids ++ DJ at the legendary Blitz Club in London, which kick-started the New Romantic wave ++ Brought the German electronic movement to London, by only playing Kraftwerk, Rother and Wolfgang Riechmann ++ Met Ralf and Florian several times in Düsseldorf and London ++ Started the studio project Visage with Steve Strange, the doorman of the Blitz Club ++ Played on the song 'Fade To Grey', which topped the charts all over Europe, with his best friend Midge Ure ++ Still active as a DJ at the most popular clubs in London ++ Feared and loved for his raspy voice and sharp-tongued remarks.

JÄKI ELDORADO Hildisch (*1958), also known under the pseudonym and marketing slogan 'Jäki Eldorado – Erster Punk Deutschlands', a title inspired by a photograph from 1977 showing him biting Iggy Pop's leg ++ Commuting between Berlin and Hamburg, he played in bands like Ivanhoe and Aus Lauter Liebe ++ Started a hapless career in 1979 as a bass player for Nina Hagen's band project Babylon Will Fall ++ Started to focus on strategic and executive tasks behind the scenes of the music industry ++ Right-hand man for Alfred Hilsberg and his ZickZack label and Rip Off record store empire ++ Worked as a tour manager for DAF, Abwärts and Neubauten as well as for Depeche Mode on their first tour in Germany ++ Moved to Düsseldorf in order to live close to the concert agency MCT and to conduct the tours of Die Toten Hosen ++ Served as a manager of Fünf Sterne Deluxe from Hamburg and Ferris MC and has accompanied almost every national or international act on their shows over the years ++ Took over the worldwide tour management activities for Robbie Williams in 2006 ++ Has two kids and lives in Berlin and London.

JÜRGEN ENGLER (*1960), born in Düsseldorf-Bilk, founded and was guitarist and singer of the punk band Male, formed with his schoolmates Bernward Malaka and Stefan Schwaab ++ After initial successes and a concert at the SO36 – which David Bowie attended – the band were renamed Vorsprung ++ Founded the industrial band Die Krupps with Bernward Malaka ++ Led the band through its first successes ++ Worked as a lithographer in Düsseldorf at Urlich's Lithographic Printers Institute, which catered for bands like Kraftwerk and Liaisons Dangereuses ++ After failing in their attempt to jump on the British synth-pop wave with their album *Entering The Arena*, he teamed up with Tina Schnekenburger to create the metal label Atom H and signed bands like Accuser and Protector ++ After Dörper's return to Die Krupps he reactivated the band in collaboration with Rudi Esch and recorded the maxi single 'Machineries Of Joy' with the British EBM duo Nitzer Ebb ++ Followed by chart success all over Europe and first shows in Scandinavia ++ Lengthy tours on both sides of the Atlantic resulted in the break-up of the band in 1997 ++ Engler tried to carry on Krupps' successes as Dkay.com ++ Relocated his main residence to Austin, Texas ++ Reformed Die Krupps with Dörper and Esch ++ Lives with his Russian wife and his mother in Texas and works as a producer for big name acts, from Sly Stone to Iggy Pop.

FRANK FENSTERMACHER (*1955) co-founded the Art Attack gallery in Wuppertal with Moritz R., which later became the record label Ata Tak ++ Released and designed the first DAF LP ++ Founding member of Der Plan and saxophone player for Fehlfarben ++ Always connected to Kurt Dahlke through Der Plan and A Certain Frank activities, as well as with the administrative tasks of the Ata Tak empire ++ Running a bed and breakfast, he now lives with his wife and daughter at Lake Constance.

DIRK FLADER (*1960), cousin of Klaus Dinger ++ Played as a guitarist in various rock groups in Düsseldorf and supervised the equipment of Klaus as his guitar tech ++ Gained live experience with Klaus Dinger through the show at Tor 3 and with the concert tour in Japan ++ Works as a locksmith in Düsseldorf.

WOLFGANG FLÜR (*1947) came to Düsseldorf with his parents, brother and twin brother in early childhood ++ He remains loyal to his district Derendorf and Duisburgerstraße ++ Played as drummer and choir singer in the school band The Bellos as well as in the emerging beat band The Beathovens, before joining The Spirits Of Sound ++ Worked as a carpenter and interior designer after his high-school diploma and after having graduated from the Albrecht Dürer School of Design ++ In 1973, he was persuaded by Ralf Hütter and Florian Schneider to resume his career as a drummer for Kraftwerk following their visit to his architectural office ++ The first long-time companion of Ralf and Florian was instrumental in the invention of the electronic drums and built large parts of the stage and studio equipment ++ Because of his charisma and his enormous appeal to fans and females, he was internally called 'The Italian', due to his enthusiasm for *La Dolce Vita* ++ All albums of the classic quartet and the early masterpiece *Autobahn* were created with his contribution ++ The mothership Kraftwerk finally became a mental burden after production at Kling Klang ground to a halt in favour of obsessive cycling activities ++ Ever since the release of his autobiography, *I Was A Robot*, a rift has developed between him and his tight-lipped colleagues ++ Wolfgang works as a writer, DJ and music presenter in his beloved Düsseldorf on the Rhine.

SUSANNE FREYTAG (*1957), born in Düsseldorf, was selected as a singer for Propaganda by Dörper and Thein ++ Recommended Claudia Brücken as an additional singer, with whom she had already played in all-girl band Topolinos ++ After the big successes for the ZTT label she worked again as a goldsmith in London and Cologne, but always remained loyal to the one-time hit group ++ Lives in the seaside resort of Hastings on the south coast of England.

JÜRGEN FRITSCHE (*1950), the faithful and jolly prehistoric rock of Düsseldorf ++ Worked as a graphic designer and art director at well-known agencies in Düsseldorf and Amsterdam ++ In the era of Michael Schirner, he was employed at the advertising agency GGK ++ Has retired from the bustle of the advertising industry and lives as a connoisseur of fine arts and Italian cuisine in his hometown, which he feels connected to in a humble and nostalgic way.

BOB Robert **GIDDENS** (*1954), the author of the English fanzine *ZigZag* moved from the UK to Quakenbrück for love ++ Wrote the column 'Germany Calling' and reported early on DAF and Nina Hagen ++ After an interview at Ata Tak, he got the chance to take over the management of DAF and to take the band to the UK ++ Later appeared as singer and frontman of the band Cliff Barnes And The Fear Of Winning ++ Runs a small bicycle empire and the live venue Die Kantine in Quakenbrück.

PETER GLASER (*1957) says he was "born as a pencil in Graz, where high-quality writers are produced for export" ++ Came to Düsseldorf in 1978 and lived as part of the entourage of Minus Delta T and the Ratinger Hof scene ++ In 1983, he debuted together with Niklas Stiller as a novelist with *Der Große Hirnriss. Neue Mitteilungen Aus Der Wirklichkeit* ++ Internet pioneer and an early member of the Chaos Computer Club, chief editor of CCC magazine *Die Datenschleuder* ++ 2002 Ingeborg Bachmann Prize ++ Lives as a writer in Berlin-Spandau.

ROBERT GÖRL (*1955), the Munich-based drummer, began a classical music education similar to Chrislo Haas' at Leopold Mozart Conservatory in Augsburg and at the University of Graz ++ Came to Düsseldorf after completing his studies and devoted himself to jazz and the jazz-rock group You ++ Became a member of Minus Delta T and later a founding member of DAF ++ Worked as a drummer and composer for the band and accelerated the shrinking process towards a successful duo with Lopez with the words "Wir wollten lieber mit Maschinen arbeiten. We always prefered working with machines." ++ Took over responsibility for the musical compositions of DAF and combined analogue drums with electronics and 16-step sequencer patterns ++ Excelled as a master of monotony and danceable minimalism ++ Military appearance, coupled with erotic and fascist aesthetics, were the trademark of DAF ++ Next to Gabi Delgado, Robert always remained silent, leaving the artistic interpretations to the Andalusian while acting quiet and secure in the background ++ After producing three albums with Conny Plank, success came quickly in the form of cars, coke and champagne ++ After its peak phase, DAF was dissolved by mutual agreement, and Görl worked on solo stuff with Annie Lennox and Mute ++ In 1989 a serious car accident tore him out of the music business, and almost out of life ++ Görl was unable to continue playing drums and became a confessed buddhist ++ He recently resumed playing drums in the reformed classic two-man line-up of DAF ++ Lives as a vegan in Berlin.

GLENN GREGORY (*1958) had early exposure to krautrock in Sheffield's rock clubs ++ Played in the school band Musical Vomit with Martyn Ware and soon moved to London to work as a photographer ++ Founding member and singer of Heaven 17 ++ Stood out with his brilliant baritone voice on top hits like 'Come Live With Me' and 'Temptation' ++ Contributed as a singer on Band Aid's single 'Do They Know It's Christmas?' ++ Has worked with Tina Turner, Grace Jones, Propaganda and Ultravox.

CHRISLO Christian-Ludwig **HAAS** (1956–2004) came as a musician of the conservatory from Augsburg and Graz to Düsseldorf ++ A former companion of Robert Görl who studied baritone saxophone ++ A member of the art performance band Minus Delta T ++ As sequencer magician of DAF, he took over Kurt Dahlke's position and joined them in London ++ He left the band frustrated, leaving DAF's electronics to Görl ++ Back in Düsseldorf, he joined his Minus Delta T colleague Karel Dudesek in the attic and became one with his beloved MS-20 ++ Founded the band Liaisons Dangereuses with Mania D bassist Beate Bartel, the Belgian Krishna Goineau and two Korg MS-20 sequencers ++ Recorded with Beate Bartel under their own direction the classic 'Los Niños Del Parque', which was refined by Plank ++ Was considered a brilliant MS-20 strategist by Daniel Miller but refused to be encouraged or sponsored by him ++ Became addicted to drugs and had a peak as a protagonist of the Berlin techno scene before he had one final drunken stunt in 2004.

PETER HEIN (*1957), born in Düsseldorf and better known under his alias Janie J. Jones, became famous as the singer and lyricist of Charley's Girls ++ Janie and Franz Bielmeier wrote for the fanzine *The Ostrich* and founded the cult band Mittagspause ++ The ska band Fehlfarben later made him one of the most revered singers and lyricists of the new German music, though he always disliked the one-hit-wonder marketing strategies that followed their unforgettable hit single ++ Continued to work as an employee at Rank Xerox and established himself as a respected refusenik of success with his new band Family 5 ++ Lives as a writer and musician in Vienna.

ALFRED HILSBERG (*1947), editor and columnist of the music magazine *Sounds* and owner of the labels ZickZack and What's So Funny About ++ Wrote the legendary contribution 'Rodenkirchen is Burning' in *Sounds* and coined the term Neue Deutsche Welle in an article about bands from Düsseldorf ++ As head of his record label ZickZack he supported bands like Abwärts, Einstürzende Neubauten and Die Krupps, while rejecting commercially successful bands like Trio or Extrabreit ++ In the first five years ZickZack released over 100 vinyl records and cassettes ++ Suffered serious financial losses at the ebb-tide of the 'new wave' and was often under threat from bands who did not understand or approve the unconventional and autocratic label politics ++ Has lived in Hamburg ever since and is consulted as an adviser when it comes to the careers of Blumfeld or Jens Friebe.

NIGEL HOUSE (*1958) as a teenager had already worked in the legendary Rough Trade record shop on Portobello Road ++ Co-owner and manager of Rough Trade record shops in London ++ Profound music connoisseur and Mr High Fidelity ++ Still commutes between his two record stores in the East End and Ladbroke Grove.

RALF HÜTTER (*1946) was born in Krefeld, and remained loyal to his hometown all his life ++ Established Kraftwerk's precursor Organisation with Florian Schneider ++ Developed Kraftwerk's well-known recitative ++ Is the singer, keyboardist and undisputed head of the band ++ Solely responsible for interviews and pays attention to the strict alignment of the brand Kraftwerk ++ Responsible for the strategic orientation and the bare output of the band ++ Main composer and the only remaining original member of the band ++ Considered a passionate to obsessive cyclist who has not found his way back to his original form since a life-threatening fall in 1983.

PAUL HUMPHREYS (*1960), founder, keyboardist and composer for OMD ++ Interested in all kinds of electronic kits since his childhood ++ Built an electronic drum kit and his own electronic equipment modelled according to Wolfgang Flür ++ Besides his musical career, he could have imagined a life as an engineer ++ Has a symbiotic relationship with McCluskey and is considered the warm-hearted, introverted and technology-oriented part of the duo ++ Humphreys was responsible for the playful melody lines and for the sophisticated productions' sound aspects ++ Reformed OMD with the original line-up and appeared with his partner Claudia Brücken as electronic duo Onetwo ++ Lives in London, where he runs a private music studio ++ Feels familiar with and musically connected to Düsseldorf ++ Is responsible for the choral singing and is the lead singer of the chart success '(Forever) Live And Die' ++ He shares the songwriting and lead vocal credits of the debut single 'Electricity', the start of the OMD success story.

KLAUS IMMIG (*1956), from Düsseldorf-Lohausen ++ Drummer of various rock groups ++ Early Neu! fan who attended the live spectacle at Blauer See in Ratingen in 1974 ++ Solo appearance of Klaus Dinger with Klaus Immig and Dirk Flader at Tor 3 in September 1986 + + Founding member of Die Engel Des Herrn with Klaus Dinger and Gerhard Michel ++ Still sporadic friends with Klaus Dinger in the late Nineties after his exit ++ Lives in Düsseldorf and works as a street worker, helping junkies and prostitutes.

WALDI Walter **JAEGER** (*1958), multi-instrumentalist, guitar luthier and trained carpenter with a penchant for American cars, girls and guitars ++ Played by turns drums and bass for Die Krupps ++ Worked as a DJ at the legendary Ratinger Hof and in the guitar workshop of the music wholesaler Spiecker and Pulch ++ As a bassist and keyboard player, he founded the band Belfegore together with Meikel Clauss and steam hammer Charly Terstappen on drums ++ This formation attempted to emulate gothic rock and should have experienced overseas successes ++ Jaeger was replaced early on by the American bass player Raoul Walton ++ Lives quietly with his wonderful wife in a small Eifel town and plays in various Irish folk and country & western formations ++ Teaches guitar, piano and drum lessons and operates a guitar workshop in Halsdorf Rock City, located close to the Luxembourg border.

MICHAEL KEMNER (*1950) is a founding member of DAF together with Kurt Dahlke, with whom he previously played in a Wuppertal jazz-rock group ++ Played actively in bands like Fehlfarben, Mau Mau and Träneninvasion ++ Responsible for the precise and melodic basslines of *Monarchie Und Alltag* and is a member of the reformed Fehlfarben ++ Lives and works in Berlin.

CARMEN KNOEBEL (*1944) ran the Ratinger Hof from 1974 until 1979 and modelled it along the lines of New York's CBGB from a hippie meeting point to the centre of punk events ++ This mother of the punk nation hosted DAF, Mittagspause and Charley's Girls in her rehearsal room in the basement and organised legendary live performances for Wire and Pere Ubu at Ratinger Hof ++ Sole shareholder of Pure Freude label and Pure Freude record store ++ Artist management for Belfegore ++ Today she exclusively takes care of the business of her husband, the painter Imi Knoebel.

GÜNTER KÖRBER (1946–2013), A&R man of Metronome in Hamburg and responsible for Brain, the most famous German krautrock label ++ String-pulling between record company, Conny Plank and the various Brain artists ++ Founded his own Sky label and signed Rother and Riechmann ++ Independent successes with *Flammende Herzen* and *Wunderbar* ++ Experienced a nostalgic appreciation of his back catalogue and lived secluded in his hometown Hamburg up until his death.

EBERHARD KRANEMANN (*1945) studied double bass before transferring to the Art Academy of Düsseldorf, where he studied under Rupprecht Geiger, professor of painting ++ In the Sixties he immersed himself in the jazz and art of the state capital ++ Was increasingly interested in improvisation and 'No' music ++ Denied traditional musical standards and established the programmatic experimental band Piss Off ++ A young Florian Schneider joined the band on flute ++ Between 1970 and 1972 he was a member of Kraftwerk and Neu! ++ From then on his field of activity was the musical project Fritz Müller Rock, which he prepared at Plank's for Dinger's label Dingerland ++ Then primarily focused again on visual arts ++ Resides and works as an all-round artist in Boltenberg, Wuppertal.

WERNER LAMBERTZ (*1951), a trained communications engineer and brilliant inventor of electronic instruments, such as the oversized and ridiculous Brontologic computer system, one of the first universal controlling units for sequencer, as well as the diguitar, a pulse generator in guitar shape ++ In 1981, he opened quasi-digital music studio Lambertz in Düsseldorf, where he produced Die Krupps, Der Plan, Belfegore and Andreas Dorau, Pyrolator and many others ++ Sold his studio to Michael Grund, who renamed it Grundfunk-Studio and where in 1986, he also recorded among others, Belfegore and fresh music by Neu! ++ In the mid-eighties Lambertz migrated with his muse Rafaela Hucht to Mallorca, where he now works as a tourist guide, hang-glider and mountain biker out of his caravan in the port of Port Andratx.

HANS LAMPE Biermann (*1952), born and raised in Hamburg ++ Early musical exposure via the ending Beatles era on the Reeperbahn ++ Played drums and worked at the Star-Club ++ Got to know Conny Plank in Hamburg, worked as a sound engineer for him ++ Established together Conny's studio and followed his teacher to the Rhineland ++ Afterwards, he followed Klaus Dinger's invitation to replace him as a drummer in late period Neu! together with Thomas Dinger ++ After Rother's departure he founded with Klaus and Thomas Dinger the band La Düsseldorf ++ Worked as a sound engineer, one who increasingly should have replaced Conny Plank, and as a drummer for the ambitious studio project ++ After successful album productions and radio hits like 'Viva', 'Silver Cloud' and 'Rheinita' the group split up following their self-deprecatingly titled album *Individuellos* ++ Followed by legal disputes in which Hans and Thomas took legal actions against Klaus Dinger ++ Married Gudrun Biermann and took her name ++ Worked for the private broadcaster RTL from an early start in Luxembourg and is known as Hans Biermann, Head of Audio for RTL today ++ Since 2014 has toured with Michael Rother, replacing Klaus by impersonating the motorik drum machine.

CHRIS Christopher **LIETZ** (*1961), born in Düsseldorf, attended the same school as the Male musicians Jürgen Engler, Bernward Malaka and Stefan Schwaab ++ Found a musical identity on the far other side of punk hysteria, as a drummer or bass player, with excellent vocal qualities ++ In 1982 he joined Die Krupps as a drummer and established a first demo studio ++ Was involved in the UK album *Entering The Arena* as a composer and instrumentalist ++ Accompanied Die Krupps as a sound man and co-producer of several albums and established the Atom H studio in the Nineties ++ Emigrated with his wife and daughter to the Canary Island of La Palma and works as a remixer, sound engineer and producer.

BERNWARD MALAKA (*1962), born in Düsseldorf, got to know his later fellow musicians Jürgen Engler and Stefan Schwaab at high school, and founded Germany's first punk band with them, Male ++ Followed by concerts in youth clubs and dens like Ratinger Hof, Markthalle and SO36 ++ Production of the legendary first German punk LP *Zensur Und Zensur* ++ Noticeable success and ill-fated renaming of Male into Vorsprung, a name which caused confusion in the punk scene ++ Established the industrial band Die Krupps with Jürgen Engler ++ Production of heavy industry sound-collage *Stahlwerksinfonie* at the Can studio and at Conny's ++ Release of the underground disco hit 'Wahre Arbeit – Wahrer Lohn' on the ZickZack label in Hamburg ++ Production of *Volle Kraft Voraus!* at Werner Lambertz's Digital Studio ++ Internal differences with Engler about the musical direction of the band Die Krupps forced him to retire ++ Followed by business studies and a PhD ++ Years of experience as a manager for the VGS publishing house ++ Lives with his family in Cologne and works as a freelance consultant.

LOTHAR MANTEUFFEL (*1957) has a long-standing friendship with Emil Schult and belonged to the extended, sworn circle around Kraftwerk ++ Following Schult's recommendation he became a lyricist for Bodo Staiger's Rheingold, referring to the Schult/Kraftwerk collaboration ++ Collaborated with Karl Bartos under the band name Elektric Music ++ Moved to Hamburg and did live performances as a keyboard player for Peter Heppner.

ANDY George Andrew **MCCLUSKEY** (*1959) met Paul Humphreys at primary school in a suburb of Liverpool and formed the school bands Hitlerz Underpantz and The Id with him ++ The self-made man bought a left-handed bass guitar due to budgetary reasons and started playing it right-handed with an upside-down string set ++ In 1978 he founded Orchestral Manoeuvres in the Dark (OMD) as singer, bassist and main composer ++ Together with Paul, he managed to create his own sound and style out of the overpowering influence of Kraftwerk and an early orientation towards Manchester and Joy Division ++ Releases on Factory Records and Dindisc established an early cult following ++ McCluskey wrote the first chart-ready single for OMD with 'Enola Gay' and catapulted the band towards New Romantic's mainstream pop ++ At the beginning of the new decade his colleagues left him to form a new band ++ Achieved chart success with 'Sailing On The Seven Seas' under the name OMD, the band name he was allowed to keep ++ In 1997 he auditioned the girl band Atomic Kitten and wrote several hits for them as their music producer, including 'Whole Again' ++ Reformed OMD in the original line-up ++ Has a detached to self-ironic relationship with the success of the self-proclaimed anti-stars ++ He gives more interviews about Kraftwerk's influence and work in one day than Ralf Hütter in one year ++ Lives near Liverpool.

MICHAEL MERTENS (*1953), born in Bielefeld, went to the Robert Schumann Conservatory in Düsseldorf via Berlin ++ Talented orchestra percussionist with vibraphone as his main instrument and who trod a similar path to Karl Bartos, who he met at the conservatory ++ By accident, as a result of an ad in the city magazine *Überblick*, he met Ralf Dörper, who was looking for a trained musician and arranger or composer for his ambitious band project Propaganda ++ Replaced Andreas Thein as a full Propaganda member and completed the ABBA-esque line-up of the shooting stars from Düsseldorf ++ Managed the trademark of the band name and successfully composes for television, film and advertising.

GERHARD MICHEL (*1966) enjoyed a flying start with Esch in the punk band Feine Deutsche Art, a school band of the Geschwister-Scholl-Gymnasium ++ Guitar and backing vocals in the semi-professional guitar band Stranger Than Paradise, discovered at the showcase of their debut single by Klaus Dinger ++ Studio works with Klaus as a follow-up to Dinger's attempt to record with Michael Rother as Neu! in 1986 ++ Founding member of Die Engel Des Herrn ++ After the high hopes of the new band weren't satisfied, Michel refused to continue to serve as a hired hand for Mr Dinger ++ Forged a solo career with German punk chansons and then formed the band Music Cargo.

DANIEL MILLER (*1951) discovered Kraftwerk in his youth through hearing the song 'Autobahn' on British radio ++ Formed the influential band The

Normal, of which he was the only member ++ Released the harsh and genre-defining industrial hymn 'Warm Leatherette' with the historical catalogue number Mute 001 in October 1978 ++ Discovered, promoted and accommodated DAF during their time in the UK ++ Music producer and founder of Mute Records ++ Friend, manager and A&R for Depeche Mode ++ Commutes between London and Los Angeles.

PAUL MORLEY (*1957) wrote for the *New Musical Express* between 1977 and 1983 and developed a new, postmodern way of writing about pop music ++ Music journalist and producer ++ Founded the ZTT label with Trevor Horn and signed Propaganda and Frankie Goes To Hollywood ++ Founded and supported the band Art Of Noise ++ Was married to Claudia Brücken; they have one daughter ++ Published several books on the subject of music.

GIORGIO Hans-Georg **MORODER** (*1940), songwriter, guitarist and keyboard player from South Tyrol ++ Initially released easy listening bubblegum songs like 'Looky, Looky' under his first name, Giorgio ++ Worked with Michael Holm in Germany and produced and co-wrote hits like 'Ich Sprenge Alle Ketten' for Ricky Shayne ++ In early 1971 he acquired a Moog synthesiser and wrote his first hit, 'Son Of My Father' ++ Became world famous for the production of 'I Feel Love' by Donna Summer in his Munich studio, Musicland ++ Received his first Oscar for the *Midnight Express* soundtrack, followed by three Grammys and four Golden Globes ++ Lives in Los Angeles and enjoys the reputation of his electronic solo work ++ Cooperates with modern bands like Daft Punk.

MUSCHA Jürgen Muschalek (1951–2003), born in Calcutta, grew up as the best buddy of Trini Trimpop in Kierspe Sauerland ++ Came to the Art Academy in Düsseldorf in the early Seventies and due to his androgynous appearance quickly found the glam identity that also saw him through punk times relatively unscathed ++ Guitarist and founding member of Charley's Girls, named after the famous Lou Reed song; they wore make-up and chose female stage names in same manner as the New York Dolls ++ Produced experimental punk films like *Blitzkrieg Bop, Decoder* and *Humanes Töten* in collaboration with Trini, produced by their Fett Film company ++ Worked as a photographer and club owner in Düsseldorf ++ Lived the fast life and spent his last years in a relationship with Hans

Lampe's ex-wife Gudrun Biermann ++ Decided to end his life, on film, in summer 2003.

COLIN NEWMAN (*1954), guitarist and voice of post-punk legends Wire ++ Worked as a producer and songwriter ++ Celebrated a musical awakening with the show he played with Wire at the Ratinger Hof in November 1978 ++ Connected to the art and music scene of Düsseldorf ever since ++ Lives in London and runs the Pink Flag label.

MÂRI Marion **PAAS** (*1947) lived with her family in Düsseldorf and rented a converted barn on the property Im Grund 3b to Klaus Dinger ++ Was longtime partner of Klaus and lived with him during the Eighties and Nineties in Düsseldorf and Holland ++ Employee at a small law firm ++ Named as co-producer on the solo albums by Klaus ++ Co-organiser of live concert at Tor 3 in September 1987 ++ Lives quietly close to the airport and takes care of the house, garden and cats.

CONNY Konrad **PLANK** (1940–1987) worked as a music producer and sound engineer in studios in Cologne and Hamburg ++ Responsible in large part for the success of Düsseldorf bands like Kraftwerk, Neu!, La Düsseldorf, DAF, Rheingold and others ++ In 1974 he opened his eponymous studio and at the end of the Seventies was the influential producer of English-speaking bands like Devo, Ultravox and Eurythmics ++ Accommodated the national and international music scene on his farmstead near Cologne ++ Eno and others worked, lived and dined at Conny's, where his wife Christa presided over house and kitchen.

JOCHEN RAUSCH (*1956) was involved in 1982 with the LP *Wir Sind Glücklich* by Stahlnetz produced by Conny Plank ++ Currently works for Radio 1LIVE.

MORITZ R. Reichelt (*1955), all-round artist (painter, musician, illustrator, stage designer and author) who moved after his time in Düsseldorf to Hamburg and then to Berlin ++ Frontman of Der Plan ++ Designed most of their artwork and the unique stage sets ++ Designed two front covers for early Depeche Mode singles ++ Worked for many years as an illustrator for *Tempo* magazine ++ Wrote the band's biography *Der Plan. Glanz Und Elend Der Neuen Deutschen Welle* in 1993 as a remembrance of Düsseldorf and the Eighties.

HEINO Heinz **RIECHMANN** (*1948), brother of Wolfgang Riechmann, who was murdered in 1978 ++ Spirits Of Sound's close ally and an expert regarding the music scene of the early Seventies in Düsseldorf ++ Roadie and photographer of the Spirits ++ Active as a guitarist and singer in the band Bodenwelle.

WOLFGANG Wölfi **RIECHMANN** (1947–1978) joined Flür and Rother's Spirits Of Sound as a singer ++ Switched to Streetmark as a guitarist, frontman and composer ++ Intense study of his electronic equipment and recording of the pioneering solo debut *Wunderbar* ++ Supplied a perfect blueprint for Visage and Gary Numan with this one album ++ Right before its release he became a victim of a vicious knife attack in his hometown Düsseldorf.

MICHAEL ROTHER (*1950) came to Düsseldorf via Munich, Wilmslow and Karachi in 1963, two years before the death of his father ++ Graduated at Rethel-Gymnasium and was a member of the school band Spirits Of Sound ++ Played live with the band Kraftwerk, which he belonged to for a short time, when he replaced Ralf Hütter ++ Together with Klaus Dinger founded the innovative krautrock group Neu!, for which he perfected the harmonious, elegiac guitar playing ++ By the mid-Seventies he felt attracted to the music of Cluster and joined the two musicians Moebius and Roedelius ++ They founded Harmonia as a trio and shared accommodation in an old farmhouse in the Weser Uplands ++ Had great commercial success with his solo albums, which he released through Günter Körber's newly founded Sky label ++ Played *Flammende Herzen*, *Sterntaler* and *Katzenmusik* with the participation of Jäki Liebezeit on drums and Conny Plank as producer ++ His ambient guitar style influenced guitar bands across the Atlantic ++ Sonic Youth and Red Hot Chili Peppers cite him and his band Neu! as an influence.

RYUICHI SAKAMOTO (*1952), composer, pianist, actor and producer ++ Founder of the influential Japanese electro pop band Yellow Magic Orchestra ++ Worked with David Byrne, Iggy Pop and David Sylvian in the Eighties.

CLAUDIA SCHNEIDER-ESLEBEN (*1949) experienced as a 20-year-old student in the late Sixties life in an upper-class environment ++ Wild parties at a place where one can do what one likes: bubble bath in the pool, plum cake in the garden and jam sessions on stage and sofa ++ After graduation in

1971, she moved to Hamburg to study Architecture at the Academy of Fine Arts ++ Became Achim Roedelius' muse and promoter of the band Cluster ++ Established a gallery for architecture, design and art in the Hamburg Schanzenviertel ++ After losses, years of grief and depression followed ++ Happier life after becoming a yoga teacher and energetic healer ++ Lives and works in Hamburg and Ramatuelle, France.

FLORIAN SCHNEIDER-Esleben (*1947) grew up in Düsseldorf as the only son of the well-known architect Paul Schneider-Esleben ++ Two sisters, Claudia and Katharina, called Tina ++ Later abandoned the double-barrelled name ++ Flutist, appeared onstage with Eberhard Kranemann's band Piss Off and founded the precursor group Organisation with Ralf Hütter ++ Placed particular emphasis on experimental alienation effects for his flute, which he later customised into an electronic version ++ If Hütter was the mouthpiece of the band, Schneider was seen as the soul of Kraftwerk who embodied the eccentric, German engineer ++ A creative sound wizard and a grumpy concept artist ++ The innovation of speech-synthesis and the vocoder effects from *Autobahn* to *Techno Pop* can be attributed to him ++ With his departure in 2009 the great friendship with Hütter and the musical heritage of Kraftwerk seemed to be sealed.

TINA Christina **SCHNEKENBURGER** (*1956) was born in Bingen on the Rhine and came to Düsseldorf via Spain ++ Had her awakening moment with the new wave movement at the Ratinger Hof ++ Moved to London with DAF as Gabi Delgado's girlfriend ++ Had administrative tasks and was briefly the band's third member ++ Got to know Jürgen Engler, fell in love and moved from London to Düsseldorf ++ Played syncussion and wrote lyrics for Die Krupps ++ Contributed to the albums *Volle Kraft Voraus!* and *Entering The Arena* ++ Withdrew from the music business and discovered the joys of working as a painter.

EMIL SCHULT (*1946), German artist whose work is closely associated with the group Kraftwerk ++ Guitarist, lyricist and creator of the album cover of *Autobahn* ++ Longstanding friendship with Hütter always kept him close to the band.

WOLFGANG SEIDEL (*1949), born in Berlin, founding member and drummer of Ton Steine Scherben ++ Played together with Conrad Schnitzler in the avant-garde electronic primordial cell Kluster and maintained friendly relations with him ++ Played on Schnitzler's 1979 album *Auf Dem Schwarzen Kanal* and several subsequent LPs ++ 1981 EP 'Scharfer Schnitt' with the project Populäre Mechanik ++ In 2005 he published the book *Scherben. Musik, Politik Und Wirkung Der Ton Steine Scherben* ++ Lives and works in Berlin.

WOLFGANG SPELMANS (*1955), guitarist in early DAF ++ Significantly contributed to the innovative content of the Deutsch Amerikanische Freundschaft with distinctive and screaming guitar parts in the style of Gang Of Four ++ Was urged to leave the band prior the great success of the two-man line-up ++ Together with Kemner he formed Mau Mau ++ Withdrew from the music business and moved to Bremen with his wife to work as a video artist.

BODO STAIGER (*1949) was born in Düsseldorf ++ At an early age he started playing guitar with the Boy Scouts and made music with the school band Harakiri Whoom together with Marius Müller-Westernhagen ++ Founded the jazz-rock band Sinus together with Karl Bartos ++ Played on the second LP of the rock group Lilac Angels and attracted attention as a talented guitarist at their concerts ++ Achieved highest chart positions with *Dreiklangsdimensionen* and his studio project Rheingold, which consisted of his girlfriend Brigitte Kunze and lyricist Lothar Manteuffel ++ The successful NDW musician was chosen for the film *The Fan* to play a successful musician, with Desiree Nosbusch in the title role ++ Though good reviews for his film failed to materialise, his success and his elegant appearance had been envied in his hometown ++ Concentrated on works behind the mixing desk at his studio Rheinklang ++ Has been a successful producer of African and black music for a long time.

CHARLY T. TERSTAPPEN (*1953), living drum-legend from Mönchengladbach ++ After initially finding success with Wallenstein he joined Belfegore, with whom he signed an international record deal with Elektra Records ++ Can be heard on Rheingold albums and on the Neondian solo album by Klaus Dinger ++ Met his congenial partner Raoul Walton during a production at Conny's studio ++ Departed Belfegore together with Raoul in favour of a long-term commitment with Marius Müller-Westernhagen ++ Joined the legendary Düsseldorf beat band The Lords as a drummer ++

Lives right next to his own studio in Mönchengladbach, where he works as a studio musician and drum teacher.

ANDREAS THEIN (1958–2013) was born in Cologne ++ Better known under his pseudonym 'Das Huhn', meaning 'chicken', which stuck with him after a performance of industrial music he gave in praise of the dead chicken in 1982 ++ The following year he founded the pop project Propaganda together with Ralf Dörper ++ After searching for likeminded musicians they were joined by Michael Mertens ++ Made an appearance as Rififi and later together with Dörper as Dr Acid and Mr House ++ Temporarily embodied the enfant terrible of Cologne's music and art scene ++ In the summer of 2013 he died suddenly from esophageal cancer.

RAOUL WALTON (*1959) came to Germany as a trained New York bassist and earned his first money as a studio musician at Conny's studio ++ Joined Belfegore and replaced Walter Jaeger on bass ++ Can be heard on records by Gabi Delgado, Arno Steffen, Gianna Nannini and Klaus Dinger ++ Met his congenial partner Charly Terstappen and left the band Belfegore with him in favour of a long-term commitment to Marius Müller-Westernhagen ++ Lives in Munich and works for Rainbirds, Heinz-Rudolf Kunze and Jule Neigel.

MARTYN WARE (*1956) founded the band The Human League with Phil Oakey and Ian Marsh in Sheffield after hearing *Trans-Europe Express* ++ Produced their first albums and co-wrote classics like 'Being Boiled' ++ Founded Heaven 17 with Marsh and Glenn Gregory after falling out with Oakey ++ Worked as a composer and keyboard player for Heaven 17 and B.E.F. ++ Produced albums for Tina Turner, Terence Trent D'Arby, Marc Almond and Erasure ++ Lectured as a professor at the University of London and is a member of the British Academy of Film and Television Arts (BAFTA) ++ Enjoys teaching and giving lectures privately, is a fount of knowledge and great stories, and an aficionado of analogue equipment ++ Together with Vince Clarke he owns the PA company Soundscapes ++ Is married and lives with his two children in London.

FRANK Z. Ziegert (*1957), guitarist, singer and sole remaining original member of the Hamburg punk band Abwärts ++ Rose to prominence with his band with their early ZickZack single 'Computerstaat' and the classic album *Amok Koma* ++ Hard-drinking maverick always respected for his incorruptible way ++ Cynical lyricist and talented songwriter who remained committed to its possibilities ++ Was rehabilitated several times by Die Toten Hosen covering his songs at the end of the Nineties ++ Swapped Reeperbahn for Berlin-Kreuzberg and completed his first novel there.

RALF ZEIGERMANN (*1960) experienced the exciting times of punk in Düsseldorf as guitarist of the Dortmund punk band Neat and worked as a graphic designer for the cult advertising agency GGK ++ Moved to London via Hamburg and embodies the British spirit more than many natives ++ Works as an illustrator and writer and has written a book on Ratinger Hof ++ Close ally of Colin Newman and retrospective expert of the British and German punk music scenes, as well as other subjects.

RAINER ZICKE (*1961), Düsseldorf-based video editor and director ++ From the late Nineties onwards he worked as a video operator for Kraftwerk until Florian Schneider surprisingly left the band in late 2008 ++ Owns a video editing studio above the old premises of Kling Klang Studio ++ Passionate connoisseur of analogue equipment.

The Machines

MOOG MINIMOOG (1970–81) is the best-known synthesiser, the source and nucleus of electronic music ++ Designed by Robert Moog for live performances, it offered an affordable, compact alternative to the giant Moog Modular System ++ With its three oscillators, the switchable modulation possibilities and a sharp-sounding 24 dB/octave filter, the Minimoog became a synonym for powerful, fat analogue sounds ++ The filter can be set to self-oscillation; the resulting 'popping' sounds were often used as drum sounds ++ Ralf Hütter ordered a Minimoog first.

ARP ODYSSEY (1972–81) is the direct competitor to the Minimoog ++ The Odyssey was also developed by its inventor Alan R. Pearlman as a scaled-down, affordable version of the larger semi-modular ARP 2600 ++ With its two oscillators, the Odyssey does not sound quite as powerful as the Minimoog, and as such was used more so as a lead instrument, preferably in jazz-rock ++ Was affordable and proved to stay in tune during live performances ++ Florian Schneider used the ARP Odyssey from the start.

ROLAND SYSTEM 100 (1975–79) is a complete semi-modular analogue system consisting of four parts: base unit 101, expander-unit 102, four-channel mixer 103 with spring reverb, sequencer 104 based on 2 x 12 steps ++ Two additional boxes, 109, surround the System 100 and form a compact unit ++ The System 100 provides a full analogue sound range, and is extremely versatile due to its patch-capabilities and its sequencer ++ The two central units, 101 and 102, are internally wired and instantly produce sounds ++ Can be reconfigured via patch cables and is then semi-modular ++ Martyn Ware still owns the whole System 100.

ROLAND MC-4 (1979–81) is a more compact version of its precursor MC-8, which had existed since 1977 ++ Control computer and interface are no longer isolated, but housed in a simple unit with a small patch panel ++ Essentially, these hardware sequencers have more precise timing than MIDI-based systems, which transmit data using serial ports, and they stall and shut down less often ++ There is a direct cable connection between sequencer and sound generator, which means that any distribution, serial-parallel converter or anything else cannot affect timing ++ This acclaimed precision is based on a rather bulky operation that is reminiscent of old calculators: sequences become step-by-step number patterns for pitch, length and time via a numeric keypad ++ There is no quantisation function; anyone who does not play absolutely cleanly needs to re-edit numerically ++ MC-4 data had to be stored on an external tape recorder because everything was lost if the machine was switched off ++ To read or write data took a long time, and usually cassette tapes could only be read error-free by the device they were recorded with ++ Giorgio Moroder had a Roland Micro Composer from early on, and Vince Clarke is still using his Roland MC-4.

KORG MS-20 (1978–83) is by far the cheapest analogue synthesisers of its time, which the Japanese company Korg had its major breakthrough with in the late Seventies ++ MS-series included the smaller MS-10, with only one VCO, the keyboard-less expander MS-50, and the SQ-10 sequencer ++ MS stood for Monophonic Synthesiser ++ Instrument had an integrated patch panel in the chassis, and quickly became one of the most popular semi-modular devices ++ Minus predetermined wiring, allowing for numerous exotic modules for direct manipulation: integrator, inverter, limiters, divider ++ The MS-20's filters are significant for its sound, consisting of a high-pass and low-pass whose cut-off frequencies are voltage-controlled, allowing for self-oscillation ++ Due to the circuitry the filters can, in certain settings, develop a characteristic 'screeching', which creates the MS-20's 'dirty' yet highly esteemed sound ++ Some consider the sound quality to be 'Japanese plastic sound', as the Korg, unlike the major devices from ARP and Moog, never generated much pressure in the low bass tones ++ No other synth offered such extensive sound experimentation opportunities as the Korg ++ Kurt Dahlke, Robert Görl and especially Chrislo Haas were magicians and champions of the MS-20.

YAMAHA CS-10 (1977–82) is an addition to the well-known polyphonic synthesisers (CS-50, CS-60, CS-80) ++ Yamaha also built a number of monophonic synthesisers, such as the CS-10 and CS-20, which have their own characteristic tone ++ All models within this series have extremely fast envelope generators, which can produce excellent punch basses and percussion sounds ++ All bar the CS-5 have a multimode filter (12dB/octave low-pass, high-pass, band-pass), which enables such a versatile sound ++ The signal from the sound generator will not be changed with patch cables, but instead via switch functions ++ The two serially restricted filters are operated parallel, and can produce two completely different sounds which are mixed with a balance control ++ The CS-10 is a small, sometimes very clear, nearly aggressive-sounding analogue synthesiser that is often underestimated ++ Ralf Dörper consciously chose the Japanese sound generator and got himself the Yamaha CS-10 early on.

SEQUENTIAL CIRCUITS PROPHET-5 (1978–84) was the highly successful flagship of the Californian synth company (SCI) by Dave Smith, and provided the classic synth sound of the Eighties ++ The slimmed-down monophonic version was the Pro-One, which was recognisable by the upstream modulation paths ++ In addition to the sources – Env, LFO, Osc B – five modulation targets existed: Osc A pitch, Osc A pulse width, Osc B pitch, Osc B pulse width, frequency filter ++ The sources could be mixed and could be routed via the modulation wheel without patch cables ++ Complex modulation opportunities have a crucial and formative impact on the sound of analogue synthesisers which opens a full range of possibilities ++ The notes to be played had to be entered step by step, and with the lower two octaves the ongoing sequence was transposed ++ The built-in sequencer is not a real-time sequencer, but later versions were MIDI-capable, as developer Dave Smith significantly contributed to the invention of the MIDI standards ++ Even to this day, Ryuichi Sakamoto still loves his Prophet 5.

OBERHEIM OB-8 (1983–85) delivered up to eight-voice settings in proven and appreciated, warm-sounding Oberheim quality ++ OB-8 was the last of the polyphonic Oberheim instruments ++ On a high production status, the device was absolutely robust and suitable for use onstage ++ Up to 120 sounds could be stored and accessed ++ With two oscillators per voice, the OB-8 generates mighty sounds ++ Programs could be stored externally via a cassette interface ++ With its many controls and buttons, programming was easy since most of the parameters were directly accessible ++ Tom Oberheim participated in the launch of the cross-company MIDI standards and upgraded the OB-8 with corresponding ports accordingly ++ Despite its price tag it became popular ++ Beate Bartel was never convinced by the sound of her Oberheim OB-8; she thought Korg was the holy grail of analogue.

ROLAND CR-78 (1978–81) was launched in 1978, with CR standing for CompuRhythm ++ This is the classic analogue drum machine ++ There were 34 built-in preprogrammed rhythm patterns, which could all be varied ++ Alongside rock, disco, waltz and shuffle there was also swing, foxtrot and tango ++ Phil Collins and Bodo Staiger promoted the CR-78 heavily with their successful songs.

ROLAND TR-808 (1981–84) is the legendary drum machine and manifested the name Roland for rhythm machines ++ One could create complete sequences of previously generated patterns through the compose function ++ Its full name is the Roland TR-808 Rhythm Composer ++ It produced 11 sounds in purely analogue form that could be altered in terms of volume, tone pitch and decay time ++ For a particular sound processing each instrument has a single output; Roland put three trigger signals externally ++ The clear and simple operation concept and this trigger capability made the TR-808 superior ++ Chris Lietz and Jürgen Engler's Atom H Studios have had their TR-808 since the mid-Eighties.

Thanks List

It was at the turbine hall of our local power station where I had to launch an event called 'ElectriCity', whose main focus was on electronic music from my hometown. It was then that I realised how little was actually known about all our great electronic bands. I was close to finishing my 25th year of service as the bass player for Die Krupps when I was asked to curate this cultural event. The city hosted the Eurovision Song Contest and here was a chance to present alternative music to the interested international listener. One week later I found myself sat on a plane with my band colleagues on our way to Montreal to present our own electronic music at a four day festival in Canada. It was slowly becoming obvious that the further away from home we travelled, the greater the respect was towards music from the Dorf. From the outside, Düsseldorf seemed to be the melting pot of electronic music; the network's control centre and commando unit of analogue sound troopers. To us on the inside, Ralf, Jürgen and I – we somehow had a very different point of view.

This mismatch fascinated me and kept me under its spell for the next three years. It was about returning to this rich post-WW2 city with music, art and fashion; about the West German provincial metropolis of the Seventies and Eighties. Furthermore, I was introduced to many people who provided information about the glorious beginnings. I would like to thank all those who entrusted their experiences to me and shared their stories. I hope to return some of it to all of you with this book.

I would like to thank all those who helped me with the completion of this book. Thanks to the Europe Transcript Express, who turned all my recorded conversations into text: Mâri Paas, Miri Spies, Kristina Raub, Michael Schäfer, Lia Esch, Boris Rupnow and Jan Wittebrood. I received valuable advice from Krischan Lutze and innumerable photographic material from Richard ar/gee Gleim, Gunnar Tjaden, Wolf Lauenroth, George Nicolaidis, Wolfgang

Burat, Wolfgang Flür, Eberhard Kranemann, Heino Riechmann, Kris Miko, Barbara Lange, Ulli Maier, Ela Desconegut and Miki Yui. Many thanks to Markus Hoffmann from Labor Grieger and to Stefan Lubs for detailed image processing of the black and white portraits. Thanks to Dirk Rudolph for the iconic cover design that gave my book a striking appearance; and to Wolfgang Flür for the noble, well-balanced introductory words. Many thanks to Miriam Spies, who accompanied my work at the desk from day one and who quickly became a specialist for electronic conspiracy themes. Miri has edited all text under the pseudonym Miss Gonzo and has given my book a first draft. Many thanks for this. Thanks to Leon Elvis Esch for video editing and monitoring social media. Thanks to Fine Sträter and Mareike Hettler at Grönland records for the accompanying compilation that covers all important songs. I particularly wish to thank my editor Winfried Hörning at Suhrkamp and David Barraclough, managing editor at Omnibus Press, for their motivational leap of faith and the confident manner in which they had accompanied me in the process of finishing my book.

A big thank you goes out to my book agent Kevin Pocklington at Jenny Brown Associates and to Nick Jones for editing my book. The translation of the 400-page bastard was done by the great Rob Keane and yours truly, with the help of Cynthia Pilars de Pilar, Lesley Crowe, Michael Schäfer and Jäki Hildisch. Thx. I would like to thank Nigel Osborne at Jawbone Press and Will Steeds at Elephant Book Company for their supportive role in finding the right publishing house and everyone who helped me in one way or another to put my ideas into action: Klaus Schulze-Löwenberg, Dr Stephan Keller, Galerie Hans Mayer, Hans Mayer, Franz Zeithammer, Joe Brockerhoff, Wolfgang Schäfer, Conny Schnabel, Hermann Werner, Holger Esch, Karl-Heinz Borchert, Ralf Zilligen, Ralf Zeigermann, Jürgen Teipel, Nicole Herrschmann, Ela Rudolph, Emil Schult, Olaf Sprick, Richy Hecke, Jopi Boventer, Alex Miller, Anne Haffmans, Sinead McCloskey, Peter Kolb, Andy McCluskey, Georg Margaretha, Roger Lyons, Alwin Kuchler, Martyn Ware,

Axel Melzener, Till Schmerbeck, Giacomo Iozzia and Rainer Zicke, who assisted me with his expertise when I fought my way through the thicket of analogue sound generation. Many thanks to Ralf and Florian, who followed my request to not break their programmatic silence for the book. And thanks to my home team Die Krupps, whose membership allowed me to express myself so confidently about all things electronic. Thanks to my bandmates Jürgen, Chris, Ralf, Lee Altus and Darren Minter. A special thanks goes to Angela Zeithammer and Jäki Hildisch for their loyal support with the book and the patience in all formal and thematic discourses.

Thank you all for your valuable contribution. Live long and prosper.

I received continued support and cultural sponsorship for this project from the Stadtwerke Düsseldorf AG. My gratitude goes to Knut Dahlmanns, Dr Udo Brockmeier, Rainer Pennekamp and Susanne Glockmann. My thanks also goes to BASE and E-Plus Mobilfunk, who supported me during the research for this book.

The book launched a new event that takes place in Düsseldorf every October: The ELECTRI_CITY Conference. Lectures, talks, Q&As – everything about music and the music. DCSE Düsseldorf Congress Sport & Event, one of Europe's largest venue providers, is now annually hosting and co-organising this Conference. I would like to express my thanks to all those involved in preparing, supporting and promoting the ELECTRI_CITY Conference: Gudrun Hock, Hilmar Guckert, Carsten Siewert, Heiko Müller, Markus Luigs, Alexander Hacke, Isa Jaiteh and Rusty Egan. Thank you for making this the perfect spin-off to the book.

Spoken words are strong.

RUDI ESCH, 1987. AT THE STUDIO IN ZEELAND.

Exclusive Interviews

Inside View

WOLFGANG FLÜR   Kraftwerk
on 26. 2. 2012 at home in Düsseldorf-Derendorf
EBERHARD KRANEMANN   Kraftwerk, Neu!
on 17. 9. 2012 at home in Wuppertal-Boltenberg
MICHAEL ROTHER   Kraftwerk, Neu!, Harmonia
on 29. 10. 2012 via telephone from Weserbergland
ROEDELIUS   Cluster, Harmonia
on 16. 2. 2014 via e-mail from Berlin
BODO STAIGER   Rheingold
on 27. 3. 2012 at 3klang Studio, Düsseldorf-City
LOTHAR MANTEUFFEL   Rheingold
on 8. 12. 2012 at Grand Elysée Hotel, Hamburg
HANS LAMPE   La Düsseldorf, Neu!
on 9. 9. 2012 at Graceland, Düsseldorf-Wersten
GABI DELGADO   DAF , Mittagspause
on 20. 3. 2012 via telephone from Cordoba, Spain
ROBERT GÖRL   DAF , Minus Delta T
on 7. 2. 2014 at Starbucks-Café, Berlin-Mitte
JÜRGEN ENGLER   Die Krupps
on 18. 5. 2012 via telephone from Austin, TX, USA
BERNWARD MALAKA   Die Krupps
on 8. 5. 2012 at À la Tarte, Cologne-Südstadt
RALF DÖRPER   Die Krupps, Propaganda
on 14. 2. 2012 at Casita Mexicana, Düsseldorf-Bilk
TINA SCHNEKENBURGER   Die Krupps, DAF
on 9. 12. 2012 at Hansebäcker, Hamburg-Barmbek
MICHAEL MERTENS   Propaganda
on 27. 3. 2012 at Pegasus, Düsseldorf-Bilk
SUSANNE FREYTAG   Propaganda
on 19. 7. 2012 at the Bush Hall, London W12
BEATE BARTEL   Liaisons Dangereuses
on 10. 7. 2012 at Café Lenzig, Berlin-Schöneberg

KURT DAHLKE   DAF, Der Plan, Pyrolator
on 10. 7.2012 at Molinari, Berlin-Kreuzberg 61
FRANK FENSTERMACHER   Der Plan, Fehlfarben
on 29. 12. 2012 at Les Halles, Düsseldorf
MICHAEL KEMNER   DAF, Fehlfarben
on 11. 7. 2012 at Molinari, Berlin-Kreuzberg 61
MEIKEL CLAUSS   Belfegore, Nichts
on 18. 3. 2012 at home in Düsseldorf-Derendorf
CHARLY TERSTAPPEN   Belfegore, Rheingold
on 22. 3. 2012 at mbg-Studio, Mönchengladbach
WERNER LAMBERTZ   Lambertz Digitalstudio
on 11. 8. 2012 at Port Andratx, Mallorca, Spain
WALDI JAEGER   Die Krupps, Belfegore
on 28. 7. 2012 in Halsdorf Rock City, Eifel
CHRIS LIETZ   Die Krupps
on 17. 2. 2013 via telephone from La Palma, Spain

Outside View International

GIORGIO MORODER   Donna Summer
on 14. 12. 2012 via telephone, Santa Monica, CA, USA
RYUICHI SAKAMOTO   Yellow Magic Orchestra
on 4. 10. 2012 via e-mail from Tonhalle, DUS
ANDY MCCLUSKEY   OMD
on 19. 7. 2012 at The Elgin, Ladbroke Grove, London
PAUL HUMPHREYS   OMD
on 5. 4. 2012 at his Studio, Kensal Green, London
GLENN GREGORY   Heaven 17, B. E. F.
on 19. 7. 2012 at the Bush Hall, London W12
MARTYN WARE   Heaven 17, Human League
on 19. 7. 2012 at the Bush Hall, London W12
RUSTY EGAN   Visage, Blitz Club
on 22. 11. 2012 at Troubadour Cafe, Earl's Court
DANIEL MILLER   The Normal, Mute Rec.
on 15. 2. 2013 via telephone from Mute Office, London
NIGEL HOUSE   Rough Trade
on 21. 11. 2012 at Rough Trade Shop, Talbot Road

CHRIS CROSS   Ultravox
   on 30. 3. 2013 via e-mail from Bath, Somerset, UK
COLIN NEWMAN   Wire
   on 18. 8. 2012 via Skype from Wembley, London

Outside View National

PETER HEIN   Fehlfarben
   on 20. 2. 2013 via telephone from Vienna
FRANK Z.   Abwärts
   on 16. 11. 2012 at Frau Rauscher, Berlin-Kreuzberg
BOB GIDDENS   DAF
   on 18. 2. 2013 via telephone from Quakenbrück
JÄKI ELDORADO   Tour Manager
   on 27. 7. 2012 in Wood Green, London
WOLFGANG SEIDEL   Ton Steine Scherben
   on 30. 5. 2013 via e-mail from Berlin
PETER GLASER   Journalist
   on 18. 6. 2013 via e-mail from Berlin
BERND CAILLOUX   Schriftsteller
   on 29. 5. 2013 via e-mail from Berlin
GÜNTER KÖRBER   A&R Brain, Sky Rec.
   on 13. 6. 2013 via telephone from Hamburg
HEINO RIECHMANN   Wolfgang Riechmann
   on 14. 6. 2013 at home in Lank-Latum, Meerbusch
JOCHEN RAUSCH   Journalist, WDR
   on 27. 6. 2013 via e-mail from Cologne
RALF ZEIGERMANN   GGK, graphic designer
   on 20. 7. 2012 at Ship Tavern, Holborn, London
JÜRGEN FRITSCHE   GGK, graphic designer
   on 8. 6. 2013 at home in Düsseldorf-Bilk
RAINER ZICKE   Kraftwerk, video editor
   on 19. 11. 2012 at Da Noi, Düsseldorf-City
GERHARD MICHEL   Die Engel des Herrn
   on 26. 2. 2012 at home in Düsseldorf-Bilk
KLAUS IMMIG   Die Engel des Herrn
   on 17. 12. 2012 at Die Kneipe, Düsseldorf-Altstadt

DIRK FLADER Klaus Dinger
  on 17. 12. 2012 at Die Kneipe, Düsseldorf-Altstadt
MÂRI PAAS Klaus Dinger
  on 27. 9. 2012 at Da Forno, Düsseldorf-Derendorf
CLAUDIA SCHNEIDER-ESLEBEN Architecture HFBK Hamburg
  on 21. 5. 2014 via telephone from Ramatuelle, France

There was also much interesting and insightful background information that was tremendously helpful in my search for traces. Many thanks to Mike Jansen, Kris Miko, Dieter Sieckmeyer, Rolf Kauffeldt, Harald Tucht, Ann Weitz, Claudia Brücken and Karl Bartos.

Editorial Note

The author has carried out over 50 exclusive interviews within two years in which the interviewed contemporary witnesses talk about their lives. The expressed emotions and viewpoints only convey the personal views of each individual. Respondents were prepared for the conversations because they knew the concept and basic thesis of the book. The narrated stories were recorded and appropriately transferred into writing. The transcriptions were cautiously edited regarding spelling, punctuation, vocabulary, language level and scope. In some cases, there was a follow-up of what was said by the witnesses in order to clarify contradictions and to eliminate ambiguities. The interviews follow a collaged order in the chronology of events without being reproduced in full length. In a few cases the responses were delivered in writing or were part of other interviews. On June 10, 2005, Stefan Morawietz conducted a string of interviews with Klaus Dinger at Keisuke Matsuura's studio in Düsseldorf; these are provided with the kind courtesy of him and Miki Yui. Jürgen Teipel interviewed Chrislo Haas for his book *Verschwende Deine Jugend*, published in 2001 by Suhrkamp. Jürgen kindly has provided me the original transcript. Miriam Spies and Johannes Ullmaier have editorially helped to supervise written contributions by Wolfgang Seidel, Bernd Cailloux, Peter Glaser and Jochen Rausch. Thank you very much for this. My thanks to Ralf Zeigermann for recording the conversation with Colin Newman for the book via Skype. The audio recording of the panel discussion with Michael Rother at the Schauspielhaus in Düsseldorf on January 13 2013 was an additional source, which was kindly provided to me by Michael and Philipp Holstein. The direct quotes from Moritz R. originate from the interview 'The Altstadt was our Internet' from August 30 2012, which was kindly provided by Moritz and the publisher. The direct quotes from Andreas Thein originate from an interview with Karl Hirschberger from 2003, which Andreas authorised me to release with this book shortly before his death.

The great quotes from Iggy Pop originate from the BBC Four music documentary *Krautrock: The Rebirth Of Germany*. Exceptionally helpful was the access to the original first draft of Wolfgang Flür's biography, *I Was A Robot*, which was quoted at selected points with his consent.

Picture Credits

ELECTRI_CITY 2
ELEKTRONISCHE_MUSIK_AUS_DÜSSELDORF

The soundtrack to the book available on CD and VINYL including
NEU!, WOLFGANG RIECHMANN, RHEINGOLD, DIE KRUPPS, DAF,
LA DÜSSELDORF, DER PLAN, LIAISONS DANGEREUSES, TOPOLINOS,
MICHAEL ROTHER, ROBERT GÖRL [WITH ANNIE LENNOX] and many
more.

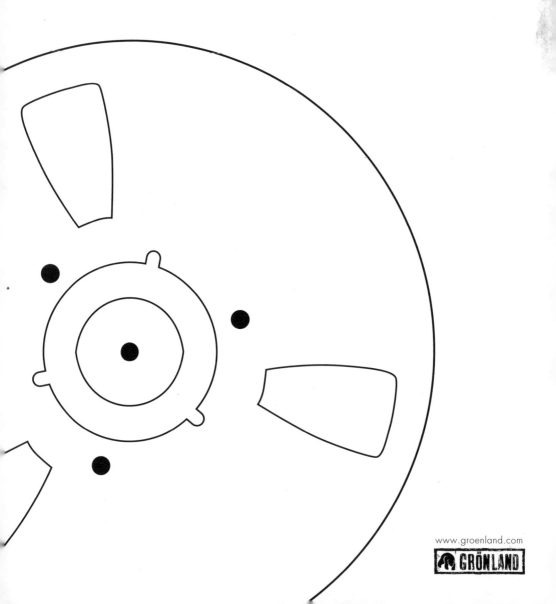

www.groenland.com

GRÖNLAND